Health Services Administration

Health Services Administration:
Policy Cases and the Case Method

edited by Roy Penchansky, D.B.A.

Harvard University Press / Cambridge, Massachusetts / 1968

Distributed in Great Britain by Oxford University Press, London
Library of Congress Catalog Card Number 68-15640
Printed in the United States of America

To my Wife and Son

Contributors

Philip D. Berlin, A.B., Ph.D. (Economics), Senior International Economist, Office of the Special Representative for Trade Negotiations, Executive Office of the President of the United States.

Marguerite Brown, A.B., professional writer.

William J. Curran, L.L.B., L.L.M., S.M. in Hygiene, Visiting Professor of Health Law, Harvard University.

Richard A. Elnicki, S.B., S.M., D.B.A. (Business Administration), Assistant Professor of Economics, Yale University.

Eugene Feingold, A.B., A.M., Ph.D. (Political Science), Associate Professor of Medical Care Organization, School of Public Health, University of Michigan.

Sagar C. Jain, A.B., A.M., S.M., Ph.D. (Organizational Behavior), Visiting Assistant Professor of Personnel and Public Health, Population Center, University of North Carolina.

Robert W. Merry, A.B., M.B.A., D.C.S. (Business Administration), Professor of Business Administration and Chairman of the Doctoral Program, Graduate School of Business Administration, Harvard University.

Roy Penchansky, S.B., M.I.L.R., D.B.A. (Business Administration), Associate Professor of Medical Care Organization, School of Public Health, University of Michigan.

A. Gerald Renthal, S.B., M.D., M.P.H., Instructor in Health Services Administration, School of Public Health, Harvard University.

Beryl Magee Safford, A.B., formerly Assistant in Public Health Practice, School of Public Health, Harvard University, professional writer.

Herbert C. Schulberg, Ph.D. (Psychology), S.M. in Hygiene, Associate in Psychology, Harvard Medical School.

Henry Simmons, M.D., M.P.H., Full-time staff member, Pratt Clinic, New England Medical Center.

Marjorie Taubenhaus, A.B., professional writer.

Preface

Traditionally, the focus of training in health services administration has been on the institutional aspects of the field with limited attention to the administrative processes, and the teaching has been largely didactic and descriptive.

This volume presents teaching material in the form of twelve cases dealing with problems and processes at the policy level within the health services environment, as well as articles about the use of this material in teaching. It has been prepared because of my conviction that training in health services administration must include development of skills in the processes of administration — the definition and analysis of problems, problem solving, decision making, planning for implementation, control, and evaluation.

It is also my belief that to develop skills in the administrative processes it is necessary to employ a teaching technique that provides the student with guided experience in such processes and, further, that the case method of teaching, as usually identified with the Harvard Business School, is one of the most useful of such teaching techniques. The articles by Sagar Jain, Robert Merry, Gerald Renthal, and myself, included in the section entitled Case Method, should serve to define the method to which I am referring. These articles make it clear that the case method, although referred to as a teaching technique, represents primarily an approach to education and that, as currently employed in teaching, it varies widely. One manner in which the case method can be applied to policy problems in the health service field is described in my article. References to most of the literature available on the case method are provided in the section on the case method.

To employ the case method — or other techniques directed to simulative exercises — generally requires the availability of teaching material that will facilitate and support this approach to teaching. Because the field of health services administration (or its sub-fields of medical care, public health and hospital administration) is relatively new and the teaching has been largely descriptive, teaching material for such exercises is in short supply. Material from other settings has limited usefulness because the administrative process must be reflective of, and in harmony with, the institutional environment—health services. This is particularly so when it is the overall administrative process at the level of policy making that is to be conveyed rather than the use of specific administrative tools. The cases in this volume are meant to fill part of the void in the availability of such teaching material.

It is hoped that these cases and the material on the case method itself will be useful to those who are now employing or planning to employ such approaches to teaching administration. It is also hoped that this volume will promote experimentation with such teaching techniques by those not now employing them. Experimentation with the use of these cases may provide some answers to two key questions: Is the case method superior to alternative teaching techniques in meeting certain of our educational objectives (assuming that we know what they are)? and Have we developed the right kinds of cases (materials) to employ the method? These questions open up a series of secondary ones: Can we evaluate the contribution of the method without judging our ability to use it? Is it so difficult to get good case method teachers that the technique is in fact of limited value? Is the case method so expensive, in case costs and student and faculty time, that we cannot afford it? My paper tries to deal with some of these questions on the basis of my experience with the case method at the Harvard School of Public Health. It also has some suggestions for alleviating the problems noted. Robert Merry's paper on Course Development will be helpful to those concerned with the general area of course planning and the selection of the teaching methods to employ.

In 1961, Dr. Robert H. Hamlin, at that time Professor of Public Health Practice at the Harvard School of Public Health, asked me to talk with a technical writer, Mrs. Marjorie Taubenhaus, about my experiences at the Harvard Business School in preparing cases. During the previous two years, much of my time had been spent in preparing cases for use in teaching industrial and labor relations, and two of the cases I had written dealt with medical care problems. The Harvard Interfaculty Program on Health and Medical Care was being developed, and Dr. Hamlin, its Chairman, was concerned about the availability of teaching material, especially cases, for it. Our discussions led to preparation of the United Mine Workers Welfare and Retirement Fund case, a revised version of which is included in this volume. After joining the faculty of the Harvard Program, I had as one of my responsibilities the development of additional cases in the field of medical care.

A further impetus to our case work came in 1965 when the U.S. Public Health Service contracted with us to develop a series of cases for them. The Division of Medical Care Administration of the Public Health Service, recognizing the need for better prepared administrators, was interested in the use of case material in training health service administrators. They requested a number of schools of public health and public administration to develop cases to make them available to training programs.

In order to begin evaluating the cases prepared for them and the use of the case method in teaching health services administration, the Division of Medical Care Administration of the Public Health Service sponsored a conference on the Case Method in Medical Care Teaching in December 1966 in Ann Arbor, Michigan. The conference, attended by teachers of medical care, public health and hospital administration, focused primarily on the use of the case method in teaching. A not unexpected conclusion of the participants was that there existed a need for case material with which to experiment in teaching — a need that it is hoped will be met with this volume.

Two of the papers included in this volume, "Course Development" and "The Case Method and the Training of Health Service Administrators," were presented at that conference.

A number of interrelated questions that recurred throughout our work in developing cases were also of concern to those attending the conference: to what extent are the cases meant to teach the substance of health services — the programs, legislation, manpower, attitudes of consumers and professionals, and so on — and to what extent are they to teach the processes of administration — problem definition, problem solving, decision making, evaluation, and so on? How do we achieve appropriate balance and interrelatedness between content and process? The balance is affected by the subject of the cases and how they are prepared as well as the manner in which the cases are employed.

In the first years of the Harvard Interfaculty Program, we usually employed as case writers graduates of the program or persons in the field with a particular interest in, or knowledge about, incidents or programs that we thought would make "good cases." Later, we used our own staff to prepare cases — a change due to our own increasing experience and our desire to prepare cases more for use in teaching administrative processes than as historical or analytical pieces for use in general discussions of medical care problems.

When outside writers not trained in case writing or case teaching were used to develop cases on areas in which they were knowledgeable, they tended to focus on the content questions and to write analytical pieces. Although they produced excellent papers on problems or incidents, this focus meant limited usefulness of the cases as a basis for students to analyze the problem themselves or for focusing on the administrative processes. An effort was made to work with the writers to insure a comprehensive description of the particular incident, program, or problem, to minimize the inclusion of the writer's opinions and conclusions, to provide an identified source for all opinions stated, and where possible, to obtain descriptions as to what happened and how it happened rather than solely why people say it happened. Many of the writers, made aware of our teaching objectives, provided the type of case desired, but the cases vary considerably in their focus and balance.

In the early days of the Harvard Interfaculty Program, cases were interspersed between lectures and seminars. With this arrangement, cases could not be used in series to develop systematic approaches to analysis and decision making, to discuss the effect of the setting on the administration process or even to contrast cases. Viewed as individual cases, the focus was on using the case as a takeoff point for general discussion of the substantive problem areas presented. Somewhat later, partly because of increased availability of cases and partly because of a changing orientation, a separate case course as part of the Interfaculty Program was established. Cases were employed for all of the fifteen or so weekly sessions of the course. Able for the first time to program a series of case classes, I was forced, and at the same time better able, to specify how the cases should be used, the levels at which they can be best used, and the change desired in the students.

The cases vary considerably in regard to the type and breadth of topic, the inclusion of reference material, the organization of the material, the inclusion of opinion, and so on. Those employing these cases might attempt to relate their own teaching techniques to these variations and to test relationships between these variations and the suitability of the cases. In retrospect it seems to me that the early cases were too broad in scope relying, as they did, on general descriptive information and did not provide an adequate basis for teaching administrative processes. In choosing topics of narrower scope, the discussion can be structured to allow for development of process skills, and the interrelationship of problems, process, and environment can be stressed, without sacrificing a basis for discussing substantive problems. Based on my experience to date in teaching, if I were to draw one conclusion about the cases, it is that the case itself is far less important to the success of the case method than the performance of the instructor in class.

Because the instructor's role and the environment he creates are, I believe, central to the successful use of the case method, it is important to consider these further. Yet, there seems to be no one successful pattern which can be described or followed. Just as in developing the student's skills in the processes of administration, there would seem to be only limited usefulness in "being told" how to teach by the case method. Let me suggest, however, that those who will be experimenting with it might find useful the literature cited in the references to the papers, my paper, and particularly Dr. Renthal's short paper on the in-class use of the method. His paper, "Considerations on the Use and Nature of Case Studies in Teaching Medical Care Administration," is included in the section on the case method.

Since 1961, I have been involved in the preparation of about twenty-five cases in health services administration. Given the page limit on this book, fewer than half of them could be included. None of the cases we developed for the U.S. Public Health Service have been included because they will be made available in separate publications by the Public Health Service. These cases are listed at the back of the book so that their availability will be known. Certain other cases have been excluded either because of their technical nature, outdated subject matter, or the sensitivity of their content. This book therefore represents a very small sample of currently available cases. Even with those to be published by the Public Health Service they are hardly sufficient for a case course. They should, however, provide an adequate basis for experimentation and evaluation.

Unlike most case books, this one is indexed. Because of the breadth of subject matter of some of the cases and the focus on "big" issues in our early efforts, many of the cases provide detailed historical data not readily available elsewhere. Moreover, every effort was made to insure the accuracy of the data included in these cases. For these reasons, we have provided an index so that the cases included will be a useful source of information in the medical care field.

The cases included in this volume involve the work and cooperation of many individuals and agencies, and I owe and gratefully acknowledge multiple debts. All who worked with us in the preparation of cases are included in the list of contributors except Leon Gold, whose case "Medical Care for the Aged: Conflicting Legislative Proposals" was not included.

I wish also to thank my colleagues on the Committee for the Harvard Interfaculty Program — Professor John T. Dunlop of the Department of Economics, Dr. Robert H. Hamlin, Dr. Osler Peterson of the Medical School, and Professor Gerald Rosenthal of the Department of Economics — for their help and support. I also owe a considerable debt to Professor E. Robert Livernash of the Harvard Business School, a member of the Committee in its first year and under whose direction I developed cases at the Harvard Business School. Dr. Sidney Lee, now Associate Dean of the Harvard Medical School, took an active part in our case course and through our discussions, contributed significantly to the development of my approach for employing the cases. Dr. S. J. Axelrod, Chairman of the Department of Medical Care Organization of the School of Public Health, University of Michigan, has been helpful in acting as a sounding board for the testing of ideas on the teaching of health services administration and in providing a historical perspective to my knowledge of the teaching in the field.

Dr. Hamlin deserves considerable credit for the contents of this book. Not only did he initiate the casework in medical care at Harvard, but in the early stages of our work he was active in selecting topics for cases, recruiting case writers, obtaining financial support, and reviewing the manuscripts. He and Beryl Magee Safford, our editor, were major architects of our first cases.

All who worked on the Public Health Service Case Contract and the Case Conference, found it both stimulating and pleasant to work with the project officer, Beverlee Myers, of the Division of Medical Care Administration, and her staff, Ilze Vaivods and Larry Cohen. Miss Vaivods, while a graduate student at the University of Michigan, assisted in the final preparation of the manuscript.

Over the period of years in which the cases were developed, while at Harvard and the University of Michigan, I was fortunate in having had secretaries outstanding in both skills and temperament. My thanks to Lorna Nickerson Kaufman, Jane Collier, Jackie Felix Thomas, Ellen Weiner and Fran Wright.

It is clear from a perusal of the table of contents, that three people were central to this effort: Gerald Renthal, Beryl Magee Safford, and Marjorie Taubenhaus. These three were the core group who developed most of the cases at the Harvard School of Public Health. Mrs. Safford, who was on the staff of the Interfaculty Program from its inception, also spent considerable time working with our other writers on development of the cases. I thank them not only for their specific contributions, but for the friendships we developed during the years of our efforts.

Roy Penchansky

Ann Arbor, Michigan
May 1, 1967

Contents

2. Case Method

Part One
Cases

Cooperative Planning for a New School of Nursing 1

April 1966

A. Gerald Renthal / Marguerite Brown

The Harvard Medical School (HMS) is the focus of a complex of medical facilities in the Boston area, including among others the Beth Israel Hospital (BIH), Peter Bent Brigham Hospital (PBBH), Children's Hospital Medical Center (CHMC), Boston Lying-In Hospital (BLIH), the Free Hospital for Women (FHW), Massachusetts General Hospital (MGH), and the Massachusetts Eye and Ear Infirmary (MEEI). Although administratively independent, each of these voluntary hospitals provides clinical training exclusively for HMS students and shares with HMS the salary costs of hospital staff members having Medical School faculty appointments. Five of the hospitals — BIH, PBBH, CHMC, BLIH, and FHW — are located in the same neighborhood as the School, and with other hospitals nearby they participate in some common planning and facilities. A number of formal arrangements exist among the institutions for various purposes. For example, in 1956 seven voluntary teaching hospitals and the School formed the Harvard Medical Center corporation primarily for the purpose of fund raising.

Four of the hospitals have operated their own nursing schools. These schools were founded at MGH in 1873, at CHMC in 1889, at PBBH in 1912, and at BIH in 1918. All are hospital-based schools, with a program leading to a diploma, and none provides a baccalaureate degree. Each of the schools has arrangements with the Harvard teaching hospitals and other institutions by means of which they obtain and provide special clinical training for students. Because of its specialized nature CHMC has the largest number of affiliations, receiving students from 16 schools and sending its students out to three hospitals. Beth Israel, on the other hand, has had affiliations with only two other schools.

Over the years there have been sporadic attempts to consolidate the four schools into a single central school. In the 1930's the first Director of Nursing at PBBH envisioned the establishment of such a combined school under the administration of Harvard University and helped raise a large sum of money for this purpose, which has since been held in trust by the Alumnae Association of the PBBH School of Nursing. A more recent, abortive movement was stimulated in the late 1950's by Dr. Cecil Sheps, then Director of BIH. Representatives of BIH, PBBH, BLIH, and CHMC met together and drafted a report in 1958 recommending establishment of such a school. They noted that each of the schools operated independently under its own governing board, although they were located within three city blocks of one another and cooperated with one another to some degree. The schools were not self-sufficient individually or as a group, each relying to a significant extent on outside educational institutions for basic science instruction. PBBH sent its students to Boston University and CHMC sent theirs to Simmons College for the basic science portion of the curriculum. In addition, Dr. Mussells, Director of PBBH, pointed out that the schools competed with one another for applicants and that there were operational inefficiencies in the duplication of faculty required to run the several schools. In justification of the proposal to consolidate the schools the 1958 report stated:

> The four hospitals feel that they are performing a noteworthy nursing education function, and that their graduates compare favorably, academically and otherwise, with those of any other school. The hospitals are not, however, complacent in this respect. They feel very definitely that there is much room for improvement in the curricula which they are offering their students. In fact they feel it might be well to develop an entirely new concept of nursing education — one that would afford the student greater depth and perception, and better prepare them for their life's work, whether it be nursing per se, or marriage and subsequently motherhood. It is logical for the hospitals to investigate this possibility together, rather than each one endeavoring to do it separately.
>
> Although it is unlikely that there would be a tremendous saving of funds by combining the nursing education facilities of the four hospitals, undoubtedly a much greater return would evolve from the present level of expenditures in the form of better education and, in turn, better nurses to render better patient care.
>
> The four hospitals are jointly appealing for the sum of twenty-five thousand dollars in order that they can retain experts in the field of nursing education to make a complete and detailed study of the possibility of developing a joint school of nursing at the Harvard Medical Center. This new school would not simply be a combination of the existing ones. It would encompass a whole new and dynamic concept of nursing education — one involving a multidisciplinary approach to the problem rather than the traditional, somewhat narrow concept.

Although the Director of the CHMC was in favor of the proposal, one or two key members of the professional staff at the hospital were quite opposed. According to Dr. Mussells of PBBH, who conferred with them, the CHMC physicians felt that their school attracted nurses of particularly high quality, and they were concerned, moreover, about staffing problems and loss of the graduates' loyalty to the hospital if the school were not located in the hospital. The representatives of the other hospitals thought that any consolidation which did not include CHMC would defeat the objectives of the merger because there would still be competition for applicants and a major source of training for pediatric nursing would be lost. In addition, the fragmentation of nursing education among Harvard teaching hospitals would not be eliminated. Thus, despite the enthusiasm of the drafters of the report, the proposal for a combined school was pursued no further.

In 1959, under the leadership of Dean George P. Berry of the HMS, representatives of six hospitals in the vicinity of the school convened an informal group in order to explore the feasibility of consolidating some of their physical facilities into a new complex. The hospitals included five of the seven making up the Harvard Medical Center (CHMC, PBBH, BLIH, MEEI, and FHW) plus the Robert Breck Brigham Hospital (RBBH). Originally known informally as The Complex, this group eventually created a separate corporation called the Affiliated Hospitals, Inc. The group's major objectives, as stated in a subsequent report, were:

> . . . greater understanding of the means whereby the advances of medicine could be applied at minimal cost to the patient, and the design of a medical care setting more closely related to the present structure and needs of the community. How best to organize facilities for patient care will be the central question. From decisions made in this area will flow the design of the basic medical and financial relationships among the collaborating institutions and the community. Should the analysis of these matters indicate that the construction of new hospital facilities would be desirable, detailed questions of organization, financing, location and the like must be studied further and a detailed plan developed to exploit to best advantage the many resources and strengths of the existing situation. New ideas must be sought without undue concern for tradition, special interest or prerogative.
>
> The services that can best be used jointly should be centralized, and the accessibility of all parts of the complex should be such as to promote the closest intellectual association and the greatest convenience for patients and staff alike.

The Steering Committee of the Complex, composed of the President of the board of trustees, one additional trustee, and one or more members of the professional staff of each hospital involved, invited the President of BIH to send a representative to the committee, even though the members realized that "in all probability it would not be practical for the Beth Israel Hospital to combine its facilities with the other hospitals." The BIH president at that time thought, however, that BIH, although having common aim and purpose with the neighboring Complex, should act independently and not become a member of the group, and no representative was sent to the committee.

To facilitate its work the Steering Committee formed a Hospital Planning Committee within which a working group known as the Professional Subcommittee was appointed. At its initial meeting in March 1961, the members of the Subcommittee noted the necessity of investigating relevant aspects of nursing and nursing education, and plans were made to establish a nursing committee. By July 1961, a committee known as the Nursing Group of the Professional Subcommittee had been formed to "evaluate nursing and its future development and organization in the hospital complex . . . both nursing service and nursing education." Officials of the Affiliated Hospitals, Inc., appointed Dr. Mussells, Director of PBBH, as chairman. He had been involved in the 1958 proposal and had maintained a strong interest in the possibility of a combined nursing school under the auspices of Harvard University.

Late in July 1961, Dr. Lee, the new Director of BIH, wrote Dean Berry that he had seen notice of the formation of the Nursing Group in a progress report of the Affiliated Hospitals, and he requested that BIH be included in the discussion and planning:

> We have had some preliminary discussion in our own Nursing School Advisory Committee of this possibility. It seems to me that the sentiments here would lean fairly heavily in the direction of giving this serious consideration for participation by the Beth Israel Hospital. This is an activity which several of the hospitals engage in, none of them as well as we might do with a single central school which would afford us the opportunity of having a shared faculty, perhaps of higher caliber than any one school can attract. In addition, especially for the Beth Israel Hospital, the possibility of reclaiming existing space devoted to a school of nursing is very attractive.

The dean, in support of Dr. Lee's request, communicated with Dr. Mussells and BIH was invited to send a representative to the Nursing Group. An invitation was also extended to New England Deaconess Hospital (NEDH) which runs its own nursing school and is adjacent to the HMS medical complex.

The initial meeting of the Nursing Group, which was composed of the administrators of PBBH, FHW, MEEI, NEDH, and BIH, the Directors of Nursing of CHMC and MGH, medical representatives from BLIH, RBBH, and CHMC, and the Associate Dean of HMS, was held on August 30, 1961, in the office of the Director of BIH. Representatives of three other committees of the Affiliated Hospitals, Inc. were present as ex-officio members (one of these representatives was the President of PBBH). At the meeting, which was primarily organizational, the chairman of the Hospital Planning Committee stated that the purpose of the Nursing Group was "to explore fully and make recommendations with respect to nursing education and nursing service." The history of proposals to consolidate the schools of nursing was related, and the question was raised as to how many hospitals would be willing to give up their individual schools of nursing. The President and Director of PBBH believed that their hospital would be willing to give up its school. The Director of BIH reported that he thought the board of trustees of his hospital would be prepared to consolidate "if they were convinced that better education of nurses would result." Because of the large size of the MGH school of nursing, the advisability of its consolidating with the others was questioned. The Nursing Group decided at this meeting to invite the New England Baptist Hospital (NEBH), which operated a nursing school in the area, to participate in the Group's deliberations.

In recalling this initial meeting, the Director of Nursing at MGH said that the suggestion that the hospitals give up their individual schools of nursing had come as a surprise to her. She had come to the meeting under the impression that she was to be a consultant to an exploratory activity and considered that the proposal indicated more of a sense of determination and a commitment to find a workable solution to the question of consolidating the schools of nursing than she had expected. Dr. Lee's impression at the time was that the idea of giving up the schools of nursing was not attractive to several of the group's members, and the possibility was not mentioned formally at subsequent meetings although some of the members discussed it informally from time to time.

The role Harvard University might play in the eventual solution of the nursing school problem was of considerable concern to members of the Nursing Group, and the possibility of a Harvard nursing school was raised at this first meeting. The representatives of PBBH had long been convinced of the need for a school run by Harvard. They believed that the most natural affiliation for any university-based nursing education program located adjacent to a medical school was with the institution responsible for the medical education. In support of this position they cited other institutions such as Columbia and Michigan Universities, which administer programs of both medical and nursing education. Moreover, the fact that PBBH was a Harvard teaching hospital entailed some financial sacrifice on its part, and its officials felt that Harvard therefore had some responsibility to meet the hospital's educational needs. The PBBH group further thought that Harvard sponsorship would maintain what they considered to be the high caliber of their existing nursing school. Dr. Mussells considered, too, that Harvard affiliation would overcome the objections of the CHMC medical staff to the combination of their school with the others.

However, Mr. Meadow, Associate Dean of HMS, made it clear that a Harvard nursing school was not a viable possibility. The university was not interested in committing itself to para-professional education. In recalling his position later, Mr. Meadow expained that the lack of any clear definition of the nurse's role was the major obstacle to Harvard involvement. "Everyone, the hospital administrator, the physician, the nurse, even the patient, has a different concept of what the nurse is, and there is no real consensus on the issue." The role of the nurse would have to be clearly defined as a "professional responsibility" before Harvard would be interested in assuming an educational function in this area. During the subsequent deliberations of the Nursing Group, according to Mr. Meadow, the issue of the professional role of the nurse was not seriously explored, the group concentrating instead more narrowly on problems centering on the hospital staff nurse and primarily on the establishment of an educational framework.

The Nursing Group decided that their initial step should be to hear the views of various experts in the field and, accordingly, various members suggested the names of possible consultants. Letters were sent to potential consultants in which the background of the nursing situation at the Harvard complex and the general objectives of the Nursing Group were outlined. "The major goals . . . are in essence to define a nurse and then to identify what her role should be to meet our concepts of patient care in the future." The consultants were asked to present alternative solutions to the problem as they saw it and to make general remarks regarding the directions which nursing service and education should take.

Between August 30, 1961, and January 26, 1962, the Nursing Group held a series of 15 meetings during which nine consultants made presentations. Each meeting at which one or more consultants appeared was followed by a meeting during which the group reviewed the consultants' presentations and attempted to summarize the issues that had been discussed. For example, following the first consultant's visit the group discussed the need "to clearly outline the shortcomings of the present and the goals of the future so that the ideal in nursing education and patient care could be visualized and sought." The following basic elements of the problem were outlined:

1. There are three levels of nursing service and education to be considered.

a. The level of the nurse in charge of a unit or service who "coordinates" with the physician for overall patient care. This nurse must have the background, education, and qualities that develop exquisite judgment and that foster the ultimate in leadership.

b. The level of the clinical nurse who carries out the physician's orders, performs bedside nursing care, and has the insight and ability to excel at the most vital of nursing functions — patient care. This nurse would require less formal education but would need the breadth of understanding brought about by a broad education.

c. The level of the "non-nursing" nurse or "unit manager," who would undertake or supervise those aspects of service not involving patient care but requiring an understanding of medical and patient needs — for example, scheduling patients for studies, ordering supplies, possibly charting, and so on. This person would require the least nursing education but would have to be fully cognizant of the goals of nursing service and patient care. She would be responsible to the nurse in charge and would perhaps have a direct responsibility to the hospital administration.

2. The educational program of the future must be flexible enough to promote all levels of nursing education — junior college, hospital nursing program, collegiate, and postgraduate education — and to foster free interchange between these levels. A composite program offering these levels of education with interchange possible among them seemed to be an approachable ideal.

3. The trend in the recent generation has apparently been to-

ward "higher education," and consequently there is some concern that young women possessing the qualities important to the future of nursing are being attracted away from hospital nursing schools. On the other hand, there is also apparently some selection between collegiate nursing programs and hospital schools of nursing arising from the lower cost to the student of the latter. Scholarships and "work as you go" plans in collegiate nursing education, as in engineering, were mentioned as arrangements that might offset these lower costs.

4. The present structuring of nursing education and service will not lead to the ultimate goal of good patient care.

5. The "colleague-ship" between nurse and physician which is essential to good overall patient care does not now exist.

During the subsequent meetings of the group the consultants discussed a variety of issues and alternatives in nursing education. The following excerpts from minutes of the meetings give the salient points of each speaker's presentation:

Miss A, director of a hospital school of nursing: "The ideal of 'more nurses oriented to nursing service' must be approached realistically. The future need for nurses requires that we build up and improve present schools rather than abolish existing ones. A sound diploma program must rely heavily on the faculty to both develop the curriculum and teach . . . A sound diploma program must attract young women of high caliber and must not only develop good nurses but good teachers. The graduate nurse must be taught to teach as part of her training . . . As the number of services involved in nursing care multiply with increasing specialization, it becomes especially important to develop the nurse who is capable of coordinating bedside care. This function is separate from that of a ward manager, which could be performed by an intelligent person who coordinates non-nursing activities, in that it requires the background and mature judgment of a nurse who understands medicine and has an insight into patient care . . . Nursing students in hospital programs are disturbed by being out of an educational environment. Hospitals should look to designating themselves as 'junior colleges' and provide a broad educational program."

Miss B, dean of a university-based school of nursing: "Able young women are being attracted increasingly to colleges at a time when the future of nursing is particularly dependent upon them. Nursing service has lost its collaboration with the physician in a clinical setting. For example, a recent study in Michigan demonstrated that patient care occupied 12 minutes of a 24-hour nursing day . . . The education of the nurse could well include a Master's degree, and must combine clinical experience and instruction in how to teach . . . The technically competent nurse may be developed by a lower level of educational program which is designed to develop nursing skills. This level of nursing training is not as dependent on 'collegiate' education."

Miss *C*, dean of a nursing school based in a medical college: "The breadth of education needed to produce a nurse who is to meet the challenges of the future requires a baccalaureate degree. Education in the Arts and Humanities provides a perspective which enables the nurse to perceive the 'nature of the problem' confronting her and provides a potential which makes her more capable in the service and practice of nursing. Specific education in nursing and basic science toward an R.N. should follow the four years toward a baccalaureate degree rather than be a part of it, and might be accomplished within a year. For those individuals having the special qualities of leadership an additional year could be added to these five which would provide a master's degree in Nursing Sciences and which should be primarily a clinical year."

Dr. *D*, director of a hospital department of patient care research: "The nurse should be the link between the administrative and medical hierarchies of a hospital. Hospital organization in the present day does not permit the close coordination required for good patient care. The nurse is ladened too heavily with administrative duties; the role of the hospital administrator has evolved into one of mediation between services rather than the leadership required for good patient care. Good patient care further requires a collaboration between the physician and nurse who must see each other as colleagues. Hospital organization must be altered to make this possible." Dr. *D* outlined a patient care unit having two lines of responsibility; one through a unit administrator directly to the hospital administration, the other through nursing service which at every level had lateral responsibility to the administration. At the patient care level the nurse had responsibility to the physician. This structuring would provide the nurse with appropriate patient care responsibilities and the administration with more directing potential.

Miss *E*, dean of a university-based nursing school: "In general there are three components to nursing: first, the nurse helps the the patient to carry out the physician's orders with the objective of overcoming illness. Secondly, the nurse partakes in health care practices as they change. Finally, the nurse is responsible for nursing care as it involves patient comfort, alleviating anxiety and meeting the needs of nurturing and weening as they arise during an illness . . . A good nurse is the product of a sound and broad education. A good program should be guided by an educational institution rather than a hospital, and its objectives should be to provide scope and perception. A degree, although not important in itself, has become symbolic of achievement in the present era. The three-year hospital program appears economically unsound, if not educationally unwise, and would seem to have limited survival. A program in nursing education should also undertake the development of the nurse's aide, but not the practical nurse who should have a separate program tailored to their goals." Miss *E* described a program which had been under way at her university for three years and which involved, first, a unit manager, who is responsible for the administrative functions of a hospital ward and is responsible to the hospital administration through assistant administrators; second, the resident, a physician who is medically in charge of the unit; third, the Nurse II, a nursing supervisor in charge of the unit, whose functions are to develop the potentials of nursing care; and fourth, the Nurse I who is responsible for patient care and for staffing the nursing service of the unit. According to Miss *E* the nurse is able to spend from 70 to 100 per cent of her time in patient care and the number of nurses required to provide good care is far below that of other hospitals.

Miss *F*, director of a hospital school of nursing, described a nursing education program which was developed when two voluntary hospitals merged and placed their nursing schools under one administration. "The program consists of two years of nursing education during which there is clinical experience but no responsibility to nursing service, and one year of 'internship' during which the student is on duty with the nursing service on all shift rotations and is salaried. The graduates are in general better prepared to assume the clinical responsibility of head nurse or team leader than other graduates. From 41 to 65 per cent of the graduates remain in the hospital's nursing service but only half of this number remain for more than one year. Colleges in general give no credit to graduates of the program . . . The school has considered becoming a junior college but decided against it because of the limitations the required curricula would impose on their program."

Mrs. G, dean of a university-based school of nursing, described a program previously hospital-centered which had been taken over by her University in 1958. Currently the school had 700 students (430 in basic nursing, 80 for the baccalaureate degree, 109 for the master's degree, and approximately 80 affiliated for special courses). There had been a 45 percent increase in applicants above the increase in regular college applicants since the new program began. Judging from general aptitude testing, the caliber of applicants has risen. The hospital provided space and facilities for the program but no financial support. "The responsibilities of the nurse in patient care must be increased to attract the highest caliber of nurse. The nurse as a clinical expert, requires education beyond the graduate level, and should assume responsibility with the physician for the grade of patient care rather than be assigned specific tasks."

Miss H, consultant on public health nursing, spoke about the British nurse who, she said, "assumes more responsibility, has more authority and is entrusted with more than her American counterpart. The generally higher caliber of British nurses appears related to the more attractive challenge offered. The American hospital nurse has assumed a role of lesser responsibility, which is probably not particularly attractive to the promising young woman . . . The opportunity for nursing education should be given to college graduates. Experience has shown that diploma programs, when incorporated into a university school of nursing have increased the number of applicants manyfold."

Miss I, dean of a university-based nursing school, described an experiment in a two-year program which had been under way for five years at her university. It appeared to be very successful in developing bedside nurses. "A two-year program would be most valuable and is of adequate duration to provide excellent bedside nurses, but it should be part of a junior college program. The leader or clinical specialist, on the other hand, should have the breadth provided by a college education. Hospitals should not be in the 'educational business,' but should provide only the clinical experience. A three-year program is too long to attract many potential bedside nurses and too short to provide good nursing leadership; it appears to have little place in the future of nursing education."

At the initial meeting of the Nursing Group the directors of nursing of the hospitals having nursing schools (MGH, PBBH, CHMC, BIH, NEDH, and NEBH) had been organized into a separate subcommittee to act as a task force which could investigate and answer technical questions the group might pose. According to Mr. Meadow, the group relied fairly heavily on the nursing directors, especially on Miss Sleeper of MGH and Miss Vesey of CHMC, for knowledge of what was taking place in the field of nursing. Both are nationally known figures in the nursing field and hold official positions in the National League for Nursing (NLN). Concurrently with the visits of the consultants, the nursing directors gathered statistics on their six schools. Data relating to student enrollment, the cost of running the schools, the value of service provided by students, and school curricula were obtained through a questionnaire sent to each hospital. These data are presented in Appendices A and B. Some of the figures — estimated cost of replacement of student services and indirect expenses, for instance — represent only the best possible estimates. According to one of the hospital directors, the lack of a standardized method for calculating indirect costs made it difficult to determine which expenses should be legitimately included, and these figures "are probably all underestimated."

These data were eventually summarized for the six schools as a whole in the final report of the Nursing Group. "These six had a total enrollment on October 1, 1961, of 1171 students and had admitted during each of the previous 5 years an average of 434 students. In 1961, there were 351 graduates of these schools and the average withdrawal rate for the class of 1961 was estimated to be 17 per cent which compares favorably with 33 per cent, the national average for all schools of nursing between 1950 and 1960." Approximately 50 to 60 percent of the recent graduates of its own school were employed at each sponsoring hospital.

Approximately 1,500 applications had been received by the schools in each of the years 1960 and 1961. "Of these it must be assumed that a sizable number applied to more than one of the schools, but no exact figures are available as to the extent of duplication. By far the majority of applicants were from Massachusetts, many fewer from the other New England States and less than 10 percent from outside New England."

"The nurse faculties combined included 143 persons for whom annual salary cost was close to $700,000 in 1960–1." School costs for the year ending September 30, 1960, were compiled but did not include data from BIH whose accounting department was unable to complete the analysis in time. Total costs for the other five schools were estimated at $2,698,048. Of that sum direct expenses, which included salaries, supplies, and equipment, in the five schools accounted for almost $900,000. "Though every effort was made to provide figures for indirect cost on a uniform basis, the group recognized that such figures are at best an approximation and that much expense attributed by this method to the school of nursing, would not be saved by the elimination of the school. However, in the method used the cost of providing maintenance is included in indirect costs; certainly this is a very large sum and one which would be saved if a school were closed."

The average gross cost per student per year was $2,590 and the average net cost per student per year (gross cost minus estimated value of service by the student) came to $1,590. The average cost to students at the five hospital nursing schools for the three-year course was approximately $1,360.

On December 18, 1961, the nursing directors of all the hospitals having schools of nursing, except NEDH, met to discuss their statistical findings and draw up a set of recommendations from their perspective as nursing directors. As factors which favored the combination or centralization of the existing educational programs, they listed the following:

Increasing cost of nursing education.
Growing need for space in which to conduct a progressing program.
Continuing lack of prepared faculty or the availability of able nurses interested in preparing for teaching.
Duplication of instruction offered to small classes in the 6 schools.

They believed that several factors had to be taken into account in any plan for combining the existing schools. These included: (1) the "level" of nurse needed in the medical center hospitals of the future; (2) the availability of nurses for direct patient care; (3) the future locus of programs for nursing education ("Although the diploma program has served the needs of people well in the past, and will continue to do so for many years to come . . . , new plans developed for the future education of nurses should be geared to and be a part of the country's educational system."); and (4) the community obligations of participating schools to schools of nursing outside the scope of the planning committee.

The nursing directors' report concluded with a set of ten recommendations. These included the following, which were later incorporated into the final report of the Nursing Group: a recommendation that "some form of program should be considered for the preparation of nurses for leadership positions. This program should be within a university, should accept only college graduates and should lead to the Master's degree. To supply this group it is recommended that support be given to the establishment of a professional nurse program within Harvard University . . . Since the trend in nursing education at the more technical level is toward the two year college, and since the two year program seems to offer the most promising source of large numbers of nurses for direct patient care," it was recommended that the hospitals and schools of nursing consider the establishment of a two year school of nursing designed "to permit maximum opportunity for progression to studies at the baccalaureate level" and with a one-year required internship added to give graduates a reasonable degree of skill for practice in the complex medical environment of the medical center.

The report of the nursing directors also contained additional suggestions: that since there were already three baccalaureate programs for nurses in Boston "no four year baccalaureate program which would further compete for applicants and facilities be considered"; that as an alternative to the internship consideration be given a work-study program after the first academic year; that "consideration be given to the possibility of finding a college or university which could absorb the size of student body required (approximately 1,500) and that such a possibility be weighed in the light of the advantages and disadvantages of the establishment of an independent single-purpose junior college." Further studies were recommended in order "to determine the obligation to schools outside the scope of the plan, which now use facilities in 5 of the hospitals."

By January 31, 1962, the Nursing Group having completed its series of fifteen exploratory meetings, a Drafting Committee composed of Dr. Walker of PBBH, Secretary of the Nursing Group, Dr. Lee, Director of BIH, Miss Sleeper, MGH Director of Nursing, Miss Vesey, CHMC Director of Nursing, Mr. Meadow, Associate Dean of HMS, and Mr. Hall of the RBBH produced a final report which included (1) a summary of the data relating to the participating schools of nursing, (2) the current status of nursing education, (3) the concept of a central or combined school of nursing, (4) the needs of the nursing service, and (5) a proposal regarding nursing education.

The report summarized the programs then available for educating students to become registered nurses:

Associate Degree Programs — Usually a two year course established in a community or junior college, which offers other programs. The nursing program is entirely under the control of the college; hospitals and health agencies accept students for experience by agreement with the college. The associate in science degree is usually awarded at the conclusion of the program.

These schools numbered 42 in 1960 [1] and they graduated in 1959–60 2.6% of all the students:[2] while these numbers are small it is significant that enrollment tripled in these schools between 1955 and 1960; the percent increase in enrollment 1958–59 to 1959–60 was 38% in these programs as compared to 2.1% increase for Diploma Schools over this period.[3] Increase in this type of school is most rapid where the public school system provides 14 years of education, as in California. It has been slow in New England where publicly supported community or junior colleges are few.

Diploma Schools — These, almost invariably conducted by hospitals, are three years in length.

In 1959–60, 83% of all students graduated from basic professional programs came from hospital schools but there was no increase in enrollment, in fact a slight decrease in these schools between 1955 and 1960.[4] There was on the other hand a significant increase in enrollment in both associate and baccalaureate degree programs over this 1955–60 period.

Baccalaureate Degree Program — This is a program in nursing leading to a baccalaureate degree and conducted by a college or university. These combine general and professional education and all clinical experiences are under the direction of the school faculty.

Contractual arrangements are made with agencies (usually hospitals) to accept students for clinical experience. Courses in nursing are largely or wholly in the upper two years . . .

There has been a steady, if slow, increase in the number of students enrolled in these schools. In 1959–60, 13.7% of the graduates of professional nursing schools were from college programs. These programs had an increase in enrollment between 1955 and 1960 of approximately 13.4%[5]

Three "significant" factors relating to nursing education seen by the nursing group were: "the gradual trend away from hospital schools"; "the serious shortage of fully qualified teachers of nursing for all schools"; and "the distinct decline in the amount of service rendered by nursing students as part of the educational process. This is true not only of college students but of hospital school students as well. That this trend will accelerate seems almost certain so that a loss of student service will come about in hospitals whatever the kind of educational program."

1. *Facts About Nursing*, 1961 ed. (New York: American Nurses' Association), p. 100, Table 5.
2. *Facts About Nursing*, p. 80.
3. *Facts About Nursing*, p. 81, Table 1.
4. *Facts About Nursing*, p. 81, Table 1.
5. *Facts About Nursing*, p. 81, Table 1.

Certain weaknesses in the present patterns of nursing education were cited in the report. "There is no education for nursing, as there is for many other professions, based on a liberal arts degree . . . Collegiate programs, as presently set up, tend to be limited in general education or nursing education or both. Community college programs seem too short to give a good educational experience in both nursing and general subjects. Present hospital school graduates, many of them excellent nurses with real intellectual ability meet serious obstacles in proceeding with college education; this is one of the major factors restricting the flow of nurses into teaching and administrative positions."

The report then discussed the concept of a central or combined school:

> The committee reached agreement about certain fundamental questions in regard to nursing education and the goals which should be set in a new endeavor: . . .
>
> In order to achieve the quality of nursing care desired and to provide a suitable setting for student experiences, quite radical changes in the organizational structure of hospital nursing services and their relation to hospital administration are deemed necessary.
>
> A combined school comprising existing hospital schools is feasible and practical.
>
> Nursing education should be conducted under the auspices of an educational institution rather than a hospital.
>
> To attain the best in patient care for the future, a nursing educational program must consider two general categories of nurse: the bedside nurse, who is gifted in direct patient care and secondly, the nurse who is a clinical expert and leader who can take an active part with the physician in patient care and who can teach. The former, needed in the greatest numbers, requires a more brief education, the latter requires the perspective and scope of the highest education.
>
> The success of nursing education rests heavily on a flexibility that will facilitate the transfer from one kind of educational program to the other, . . .
>
> Advantages of a Combined School . . .
>
> Reduced expenses to the hospitals . . .
> Stronger recruitment appeal . . .
> More effective use of faculties . . .
> Hospital space would become available . . .
> Improved library facilities . . .
>
> Disadvantages . . .
>
> Loss of service to hospitals. Though the schools of nursing are costly they provide considerable nursing service; though this service might be provided more economically by employees it is not certain that a sufficient number of employees can be found.
>
> Loss of "home school" graduate. The graduates of a new school

may not have the specific hospital loyalties that hospital graduates now have, and it cannot be assured that the participating hospitals will be able to recruit a sufficient number of graduates from this school to meet their needs . . .

Expense. Although the proposal which follows will be an immensely more effective investment in nursing education than presently exists, and the expense in large part may be offset by the savings incurred by each hospital now operating a school, there will probably be an overall increase in cost. It will be necessary to consider sources other than tuition for these expenses if the recruitment potential, particularly at the high school level, is to remain high.

Finally, as the culmination of its deliberations, the Nursing Group made the following "Proposal Regarding Nursing Education":

The Nursing Group believes that there should be exploration of the possibility of establishing in an existing educational institution(s) of recognized academic standing and within a reasonable distance from the Harvard Medical School teaching hospitals, an educational structure in which two programs of nursing education might be offered, one leading to an associate, the second to a baccalaureate degree. Further it recommends that a program in nursing education for college graduates be established in a graduate school at Harvard University.

All candidates for the first program would meet college entrance requirements and those with the requisite interest and ability might proceed to the baccalaureate program if they wished.

While the two undergraduate schools of nursing and the graduate program might all be separate with each under the control of a different educational institution, it would be essential to provide a coordinating structure that would facilitate interchange among the programs.

All programs would utilize the clinical facilities in some or all of the hospitals which have participated in these discussions; suitable facilities for other clinical experience would be required.

The three programs may be described briefly as follows:

A. *Associate Degree.* A three year program, the first two years combining general education and nursing education, the third year to be an internship. As far as possible courses would be of sufficient breadth and depth to prepare the student to proceed to upper division courses without repetition.

B. *Baccalaureate Degree.* A program of study leading to the baccalaureate degree to which a student may be admitted in the freshman year or to which she may transfer from the associate degree program. This course would need to be considerably more comprehensive in general education than most such programs now offered if existing deficiencies are to be remedied and to enable the graduate of this program to proceed on to post graduate study.

C. *Master's Degree.* A university graduate school to which graduates of liberal arts colleges would be admitted. It would offer a program leading to the M.A. in Nursing, or a similar graduate degree which would qualify her for beginning practice in nursing. By appropriate use of appraisal examinations, evaluation of nursing abilities and individual program design, graduates of schools of nursing with the B.S. degree might also be admitted to a graduate program (of this type) . . .

Such a plan meets many of the criteria which the Nursing Group has emphasized; nurses will be prepared for different degrees of responsibility in nursing with the group having the shortest educational experience being the greatest in number; each program is complete in itself and qualifies the graduate for state registration; each program prepares the student to proceed to another of a higher academic level with a minimum loss of time and without repetition of courses; it provides opportunity for high school graduates and college graduates alike to become nurses in an academic setting appropriate to the individual's educational background; it offers courses in nursing all of which lead to an academic degree.

It would appear wise in the undertaking of these programs to phase their beginning separately and in such order as to minimize a disruption of hospital nursing services. This would require considered pre-planning, and a coordination with the plans for a hospital complex. It might best be initiated in the program for college graduates utilizing existing resources to provide the necessary clinical and educational background.

Within a week after its publication copies of the report of the Nursing Group were sent to the presidents of each of the participating hospitals. In a covering letter the secretary of the Professional Subcommittee wrote:

The recommendations appear significant and far-sighted in their proposals for a joint educational program and for the reorientation of the future of nursing services. The recommendations have been heartily approved and endorsed by the Professional Subcommittee.

The Professional Subcommittee has suggested that these recommendations be sent to the presidents of each represented hospital for review so that the urgently needed further planning can begin as soon as possible.

For the next year or so the Nursing Group continued to meet in order to develop a proposal for implementation of its report. The Subcommittee of Nursing Directors also continued to act in a technical advisory capacity. President Bunting of Radcliffe and Dean Keppel of the Harvard Faculty of Education were invited to participate in the group's meetings as guests but were able to attend only a small number of the meetings. The group hoped that the participation of President Bunting and Dean Keppel might be a way of involving Harvard University in the solution, and they valued, moreover, the insight and experience of the two educators.

There was general agreement that the new school of nursing should be under the aegis of an educational institution rather than a hospital. The question was: which university? Although Associate Dean Meadow had made clear to the Nursing Group earlier that Harvard would not be interested in the undergraduate training of nurses, President Bunting, Dean Keppel, Mr. Meadow, and Dr. Walker met several times and discussed the possibility of establishing a Master's degree program under Harvard auspices:[6] Nothing concrete emerged from these talks, however. For various reasons, such as inconvenient location, specific religious affiliation, inability to handle student classes of the size envisaged, and so on, all of the other educational institutions within a reasonable distance of the medical complex were eliminated except Boston University (BU) and Northeastern University (NU). During May Mr. Meadow transmitted a copy of the Nursing Group Report to the acting dean of BU medical school, inviting a discussion with the Nursing Group of BU participation in the proposal. On June 4, the acting dean of the BU medical school replied that BU would like "further joint examinations" with the Nursing Group. Although there were many negative aspects to the proposal, its "successful implementation could well in ten years move nursing education ahead by as much as twenty-five years would otherwise represent."

Accordingly, on July 25, the acting dean of BU medical school together with the dean and three senior faculty members of the BU School of Nursing met with the drafting committee of the Nursing Group. The medical school dean "expressed enthusiasm and the interest of BU" in implementation of the report and "remarked on the administrative challenge" implicit in the "close coordination" of the hospitals, the Harvard Medical School, and the nursing program.

During the next two months BU officials prepared a twelve-page analysis of their School of Nursing in relation to various aspects of the joint school proposed in the report. BU, for instance, could "expand enrollment" in its basic program and move forward to 1964–65 its existing plans for a new nursing program designed for

6. For several years Radcliffe, in affiliation with MGH, had been running a very small program for five or six post-baccalaureate students leading to a certificate in nursing.

graduates of liberal arts colleges. To add 1,200 or so additional nursing students would require the construction of additional laboratory and classroom space as well as office and dormitory facilities. Recruitment of qualified faculty might also be a problem, although "potentially able candidates" were "seeking out" BU because of its reputation. The BU medical school dean forwarded this analysis to Dr. Walker, secretary of the Nursing Group, on October 5. In a covering letter he reaffirmed BU's wish to "explore very seriously" the proposal under discussion.

November 20 was the date set for the second appearance of BU representatives before the Nursing Group. On November 8 the BU medical school dean wrote Dr. Walker to inquire whether the Professional Subcommittee had formulated "(1) the nature of the resources (knowledge and abilities and general outlook) it hopes the graduates will possess, and (2) what types of courses and related experiences are best calculated to develop these resources?" The dean asked for a "personal comment" on these points from Dr. Walker before the November 20th meeting, noting that the material he had seen did not seem to furnish this information.

Minutes of the November 20 meeting indicate that there was lengthy discussion between the group and the BU delegation (the medical school dean, the nursing school dean, and the chairman of the staff Executive Committee of the Massachusetts Memorial Hospitals) on the education of the bedside nurse. The Nursing Group emphasized the need for a flexible yet academically sound program of "sufficiently short duration that it attracts the young woman who has her eye both on nursing care and on the other pursuits of happiness."

The medical school dean cited some difficulties in such a program from the standpoint of BU, such as "the awarding of an associate degree and the limitation of facilities." He wished, however, to review the problem further before indicating whether BU cared to go ahead with the plan. One member of the Nursing Group said later that it was their general impression at the time that "BU did not understand" what they were trying to accomplish and "would not go along" with them.

In the meantime discussions between the group and officials of NU had also been taking place. Minutes of the Nursing Group record that a first meeting between the Drafting Committee and Dr. William White, Provost of Northeastern University, occurred on July 20, 1962, when Dr. White "most ably presented a program for consideration . . . which was received with great interest by the Group."

The original version of the NU plan called for the establishment of a College of Nursing in collaboration with the six Harvard teaching hospitals. The hospitals would assist in recruitment of students and fund-raising, and would provide clinical facilities and employ student nurses who were following the university's "co-operative plan." This unique feature of NU's program allowed upperclassmen in most of its colleges to alternate terms of course work with periods of employment in their chosen fields at going wages for such jobs. Northeastern would assume "full responsibility" for the program and members of its nursing faculty would give all clinical instruction in collaborating hospitals.

The five-year nursing program was to be structured on the so-called ladder system, which was then being tried on an experimental basis at the Rutgers University School of Nursing. Under the ladder system courses were planned in a continuum. Students who completed the first two years qualified for an associate degree and a Registered Nurse's certificate. They could then become full-time registered nurses, or continue without interruption to study for the degree of Bachelor of Science in Nursing which, under the Northeastern Cooperative Plan, would be conferred after another three years of alternate work and study.

NU officials assumed that there might be an enrollment of about 100 freshmen, 80 sophomores, 48 "middlers," 42 juniors, and 40 seniors. Each collaborating hospital would sponsor 16 or 17 freshmen and might expect to fill 10 or 11 nursing posts with cooperative students from the three upper years. Total teaching requirements, both nursing and other, would cost $363,000, and there would be an estimated income of $308,900 from tuition fees.

Although the NU plan "presented some problems," as Dr. Lee recalled it, it "looked good from the beginning." The flexible, cooperative attitude of the NU officials was an "enormous contrast" to that of the BU officials, who seemed to be trying to fit the Nursing Group's new program into "their mold." Dr. White, therefore, was invited to develop his plan further for presentation to the entire Nursing Group.

Reservations were expressed about the NU proposal, however. On October 8, for example, the nursing director of PBBH wrote Dr. Walker:

1. I am not satisfied in my own mind that the two year program with its emphasis on undergraduate subjects is preparing the student

with sufficient nursing knowledge to be the kind of bedside nurse we need.

2. I am quite certain that there is insufficient clinical practice in the two year program and that an internship to provide adequate clinical practice is *mandatory.*

I feel in many respects we (nursing) are hiding our head in the sand as far as preparation of nurses goes. We want to prepare them educationally so they are truly professional, yet at the same time lose sight of the fact that the care of the patient is becoming more complex. Advanced medical and surgical techniques require higher levels of nursing skills. Many of these nursing skills must be taught during their early preparation. Why?

1. Because right now we (all of nursing) are turning over the care of the very ill patient to non-professional workers.

2. We know the greatest loss among young graduates occurs 1–3 years after training. This is the group which provides 80% of the nursing care to patients. It is neither fair to them nor to the patient to prepare them inadequately. I doubt very much if the percentage will change radically in the future, but we must change our program to meet *nursing* needs of 1965–1970 rather than nursing needs of 1950–1960.

3. Hospitals can neither afford the time nor money to provide extensive in-service and orientation programs for associate degree or baccalaureate graduates which is exactly what we are doing now. (We need skilled nurses short of 4–5 years and we need them in numbers.)

4. Nurses from a university not allied with the complex are not going to have the same loyalty or allegiance to the hospitals within the complex, and recruitment instead of improving will become an increasing problem.

In the months following the presentation of the NU plan the group of nursing directors worked with NU officials to tailor the original plan to the requirements of the Nursing Group. The nursing directors were concerned primarily with working out the details of curriculum content. The major revision was a reduction of the semester hours devoted to general education from 40 to 26 in each of the last three years, with a corresponding increase in nursing instruction — an almost exact reversal of the proportion in the first proposed curriculum:

	First proposed curriculum		Revised curriculum	
	General education	Nursing education	General education	Nursing education
First two years	40	35	40	35
Three cooperative years	40	25	26	40
Total for the five-year course	80	60	66	75

The new version also called for a heavier teaching load per instructor (21 hours per week compared with 18 in the earlier version) and for larger enrollments.

On October 18, the revised version was presented to the full Nursing Group by President Asa Knowles and Provost White. The NU officials suggested that the Harvard teaching hospitals might offer scholarships to prospective students who needed financial aid and hire registered nurses who had completed the first two years and were working toward the bachelor's degree under the Cooperative Plan. The equivalent of approximately 125 full-time nurses could be supplied to the six hospitals in June of each year, Dr. White estimated. NU was willing to increase this number if necessary. Student expenses would probably amount to about $1,140 for tuition during each of the first two years, $850 during each of the third and fourth years, and $680 for the last year. Room and board would amount to $1,100 for a 40-week year.

In a discussion session immediately following the departure of the NU delegation some members of the Nursing Group expressed concern about the "accreditation status" and "educational standards" of NU, and also about the adequacy of the first two years of the proposed program. One member, expressing the belief that NU was geared more to vocational than professional programs, questioned whether it was the proper locus for the program that the Nursing Group envisioned.

Miss Sleeper wrote Dr. Walker two weeks after the meeting that she was "very much disturbed" by this discussion of NU's educational qualifications. It seemed to her "late to question their status" after they had been asked to spend the time necessary to develop their original proposal. In her opinion it was a "rapidly growing institution" which could fill the needs of the collaborating hospitals for qualified nurses. Independently of the Nursing Group's activities, Miss Sleeper had been representing MGH for some time in efforts to work out with NU a joint project for an "alternate program" of nursing education which had started in the fall of 1962.[7] In this connection, Dr. White had written Miss

7. Under it, students recruited by MGH studied academic subjects at NU and concurrently learned nursing techniques at MGH. At the end of three years they earned an associate degree.

In 1960 NU had started a cooperative program for medical technicians under which the student would obtain a baccalaureate degree after a five-year course. An equivalent of two years of this was spent as cooperative work experience in one of the two participating hospitals, NEDH or NEBH, which had negotiated formal agreements with NU for this program. The size of the program has been small, averaging about ten students a class.

Sleeper on October 23, 1962, listing the several educational and professional agencies which had accorded accreditation to NU. The university as a whole had been accredited by the New England Association of Colleges and Secondary Schools, he wrote, and most of its colleges by an appropriate professional group. Ten national honor societies had chapters at NU. Dr. White went on to state that "we are prepared to cooperate with you in this program so that it fully meets the Hospital School accrediting requirements of the National League of Nursing Education."

At a December 13 meeting of the Nursing Directors Subcommittee there was, the minutes report, "consensus . . . that NU offered the greatest promise because of its future potentials of academic and physical growth, its flexibility, and its opportunity to meet the goals of the Group through past experience with somewhat similar programs." The subcommittee favored an initial program of limited size. "For the present it would be wise for the existing hospital schools to maintain their programs because of the magnitude of their present responsibility in nursing education."

On March 14, Associate Dean Meadow of HMS wrote Dr. Walker that he had received a telephone call from Dr. Lee suggesting that the time had come for a decision on the NU plan and asking that a meeting of the Nursing Group be called for this purpose. By this time the Nursing Group's discussions of the plan had become focused on a pilot project under which the several hospitals would accept 30 students each year from the new school, but would continue their own hospital training programs to meet their own needs. In his letter Mr. Meadow noted that both Dr. Lee and Dr. Knowles of MGH had agreed to cooperate in the joint project and that this alone might make it possible to begin operations. However, the other interested hospitals should also be given an opportunity to participate, Mr. Meadow added.

On April 2, 1963, a meeting of the "six" was convened. CHMC, BIH, PBBH, and NEDH were represented by both their Directors and their Nursing Directors; MGH and NEBH by only their Directors of Nursing. Mr. Meadow represented the Harvard Medical School.

The members were asked directly for the first time to indicate whether or not they would affiliate with NU in the new program, and only BIH voted in the affirmative. Recalling this meeting two years later, Dr. Lee used the word "traumatic." He had been "amazed" to find that after years of discussion he was the only person ready to make a commitment.

Miss Sleeper later recalled her "deep embarrassment" at the unexpected lack of support for the NU project at the meeting in view of the "hard work" its officials had put into the plan. As soon as she returned to her office she telephoned Dr. Lee and invited him and Miss Zolotin, BIH Nursing Director, to meet next day with her and Dr. Knowles. This was arranged and at this meeting the MGH officials agreed to "take some students" from the new college. However, they regarded the NU plan as a pilot project, and never intended to close the MGH nursing school. MGH regularly employed 450 bedside nurses and needed more, and the 70 nurses graduated each year by its school were the hospital's main source of supply. MGH was associated as much with Simmons and BU, from both of which it accepted students, as it had been with Northeastern in the associate degree program since 1962. On some days as many as 500 students were accommodated at MGH. Although the Simmons relationship had existed since 1919, graduates of that program "rarely" came back to work at MGH and only two or three a year came from BU.

The position of CHMC with regard to the closing of its school was "no different" from that of MGH, Miss Vesey recalled in a subsequent interview. CHMC, the only children's hospital in the United States with its own nursing school, provided a specialized type of nursing training. Not only did it rely heavily on its own specially trained graduates to staff the hospital, but it also had particular requirements for faculty who knew pediatrics. Moreover, a number of other schools relied on CHMC to provide clinical pediatric nursing training for their students. An additional consideration for CHMC, as well as the other hospitals, was the limitation imposed by the clinical facilities available on the number of students that could conveniently be accommodated at any time.

Nevertheless, CHMC intended to support the pilot project at NU. Miss Vesey personally believed that the flexible ladder plan, combined with the novel cooperative feature of education at NU, offered many advantages. The cooperative program especially was "very natural" for nursing associate degree students because it would afford more experience with patients. The failure of CHMC to enter immediately into the NU project was occasioned by administrative delay rather than by any real opposition to the plan, Miss Vesey believed. Approval by the medical staff and trustees was needed before a commitment could be made, and the former, in particular, "had great influence on the Board of Trustees" and strongly opposed the closing of the CHMC school. Indeed, the Director of CHMC said at the decision meeting that his Board had instructed him to strengthen the existing nursing school, particularly the program for first-year students, "to provide a stronger academic base and to make the school more independent." He felt that "hospital-based nursing schools, if made more academically sound, could meet the needs of the future."

PBBH had held back in the Nursing Group and was reluctant to go into the NU venture, according to Dr. Mussells, because of the strong and continuing conviction that Harvard University should take some responsibility. Hospital officials believed that the door was not yet completely closed on the possibility of a Harvard-sponsored school developing sometime in the future.

Moreover, Dr. Mussells had reservations about the NU program. Northeastern had in recent years "gone quite far" in attempts to establish its own medical school, and he was concerned that the existence there of the new nursing school would encourage NU to make renewed, and possibly successful, efforts to found its own medical school which would attract many of the graduate nurses trained there and leave PBBH "high and dry."

The PBBH group believed that their major responsibility was to "attract the nursing staff requisite for good patient care." Recruitment of students for their school was excellent, and more than half of the PBBH nursing school graduates remained to work at the hospital, which depended heavily on them to staff its large ward service. Commenting on the difference between the PBBH and BIH positions, Dr. Mussells expressed the view that BIH had a "far more acute problem staffing- and accreditation-wise."

The representatives of NEDH and NEBH agreed with the position of PBBH that their main concern was with the staffing of their own hospitals, that they had so far been successful in recruiting a substantial number of their own graduates, and that it was questionable whether they could develop the same degree of loyalty to their hospitals among the students in the NU school.

Appendix A

Selected statistical data (figures for the year 1960–61).

Category	BIH	CHMC	MGH	NEBH	NEDH	PBBH
Enrollment, 1961	163	115	354	190	166	145
Applicants, 1961	136	181	440	299	267	153
Number appointed, 1961	84	71	169	77	91	65
Number admitted, 1961	68	46	128	70	62	46
Number graduated, 1961	43	34	118	66	47	43
Tuition and fees, 1960–61	$900	$630	$1447.75	$600	$700	$1150
Affiliations (annually)						
Outgoing — students	83	153–165	200–224	260–280	223	*All juniors*
— institutions	2	4	2	5	5	2
Incoming — students	33	635	89	–	38	40
— institutions	1	6	2	–	1	2
Nurses employed						
Full-time, 1961	117	79	223	168	58	64
Part-time (expressed in full-time equivalent)	5	7.3	46.25	39	11	–
Number of staff nurses budgeted	143	139	350	–	105	95
Estimated number of staff nurses required to replace students	13	41	75	42	31	16
Estimated annual cost of replacement (staff nurses)	$54,600	$173,200	$316,000	$177,400	$132,200	$70,200
Estimated cost of additional auxiliary employees	0	$123,200	0	$94,500	$15,750	$88,200
Nurse faculty released if no school	20	22	46	21	18	16
Cost of faculty, 1 year	$99,761	$103,882	$189,400	$117,000	$104,000	$79,730
Graduates of own school on payroll						
Less than 6 months	19	18	62	–	29	–
1–2 years	17	17	24	–	6	13
2–3 years	1	15	10	–	2	6
3 years and over	21	30	63	–	20	16
Percent of graduating class remaining at hospital	44	67.6	62	47	63	60

Appendix B

Cost of Schools of Nursing[a] (year ending September 30, 1960).

Hospitals[b]	Number of students	Direct expense	Indirect expense	Total expense	Estimated value of student service[d]	Estimated net cost	Gross cost per student per year	Net cost per student per year
Mass. General	355	$322,228	$ 517,002	$ 839,230	$355,000	$ 484,230	$2,364	$1,364
Peter Bent Brigham	156	136,475	352,669	489,144	156,000	333,144	3,136	2,136
N.E. Baptist	196	112,854	287,945	400,799	196,000	204,799	2,045	1,045
Children's	200[c]	182,665	399,400	582,065	200,000	382,065	2,910	1,910
N.E. Deaconess	155	131,248	255,562	386,810	155,000	231,810	2,495	1,495
Totals		$885,470	$1,812,578	$2,698,048		$1,636,048		

Average gross cost per student per year (five hospitals) $2,590

[a] Basis for distribution of expense:

Administration in general: average number of employees
Repairs, maintenance of buildings, equipment, and grounds: floor area
Operation of plant: floor area
Motor service: percentage of use
Laundry department: pounds of laundry processed
Linen service: pounds of laundry processed
Depreciation: overall square footage
Housekeeping department: actual hours of service
Dietary: number of meals served
Maintenance of personnel: average number living in
Medical and surgical service: hours of service and cost of school supplies

[b] Beth Israel Hospital had not reported at 3:00 p.m. on November 8th.
[c] Includes affiliating students.
[d] Derived from a composite of National League for Nursing studies.

Cooperative Planning for a New School of Nursing 2

April 1966

A. Gerald Renthal / Marguerite Brown

In August 1961, a series of meetings began between representatives of the Harvard Medical School (HMS) and a group of its affiliated hospitals concerning the possibility of establishing a joint school of nursing. The hospitals represented were Beth Israel Hospital (BIH), Peter Bent Brigham Hospital (PBBH), Childrens' Hospital Medical Center (CHMC), Massachusetts General Hospital (MGH), New England Deaconess Hospital (NEDH) and New England Baptist Hospital (NEBH)—all of which had their own schools of nursing—and Free Hospital for Women (FHW), Boston Lying-In Hospital (BLI), Massachusetts Eye and Ear Infirmary (MEEI), and Robert Breck Brigham Hospital (RBBH). These deliberations culminated, in April 1963, with a plan to establish a new school of nursing by Northeastern University (NU). Special features of the plan were a "ladder system," whereby students who wished could progress smoothly up the three levels of nursing education from Associate to Baccalaureate to Master's degree and a cooperative education feature whereby academic training would be alternated with actual work experience in a hospital at going wages. Both MGH and BIH had agreed to join the NU plan as a pilot project in which each hospital would receive 30 students from the school for their clinical training.

Early in May 1963, President Knowles of NU wrote Dr. Lee, Director of BIH and Miss Sleeper, Director of Nursing at MGH, enclosing a formal statement of the proposal for a Cooperative College of Nursing to be established "with the active collaboration of the Beth Israel and Massachusetts General Hospital" and requesting endorsement by the two hospitals' Governing Boards. The Executive Committee of the NU Board had approved the plan "in principle," subject to endorsement by the two hospitals and to preparation of a more detailed statement of the commitments involved.

The May 1963 version of the plan differed from earlier drafts in that the first phase leading to the associate degree and to the RN certificate was to cover three years rather than two. In the second and third years students would be on the cooperative plan, alternating ten-week periods of academic instruction (both classroom and clinical) with ten-week work periods at one of the two participating hospitals. NU would provide the classroom facilities and dormitory rooms (second- and third-year students would have a choice among university dormitories, hospital dormitories, or their own homes), and the hospitals in return would employ second and third year cooperative students at wages of $50 to $60 per week. The university planned to initiate only this portion of the program immediately but would "ultimately" develop an additional bachelor's degree program requiring two years for full-time students or three years for cooperative students.

Scholarship funds needed for the first class to be admitted in the fall of 1965 would amount to $60,000. NU would provide $20,000, the two hospitals $10,000 each, and the additional $20,000 would be sought jointly by President Knowles and the hospital representatives from foundations.

NU would select dean and faculty for the new college with the assistance of the two hospitals and of an Advisory Committee composed of representatives of the trustees of all three institutions, the Public Health Service, nursing educators, educators from outside the nursing field, and the new director of the Harvard Teaching Hospitals Complex (Affiliated Hospitals, Inc.).

This formal proposal was examined and discussed at a meeting on May 13 of the Executive Committee of the Board of Beth Israel, which voted to "recommend to the trustees that the President and Director of this hospital . . . negotiate an agreement with NU" along the lines indicated. The Beth Israel trustees approved the plan unanimously at a regular meeting on June 10, and at the same time voted to contribute the $10,000 requested toward scholarship aid.

On June 26, Dr. Lee addressed a memorandum to the eight members of his Nursing School Advisory Committee, which included the President of the Nurses' Alumnae Association, informing them of the Board's action and enclosing a copy of the NU plan. Copies of this memorandum went to Mr. Slotnik, President of the trustees, to Miss Zolotin, Director of Nursing, and to the Associate Director in charge of the Nursing School. A separate copy with a note "Please be sure to include this in the 1963–64 budget" was addressed to the Comptroller.

Although CHMC had not joined when the plan was presented to representatives of the Harvard-affiliated hospitals in April, within a few weeks, after the plan had cleared the proper administrative channels, CHMC also joined the NU program and agreed to accept 30 students from the new school. In 1964, quite independently of developments at NU, a relationship of 60 years standing between CHMC and Simmons College under which Simmons provided basic science training for the CHMC students was terminated. CHMC had wanted Simmons to extend the basic science instruction from one to two semesters and to give students course credit, but the college was unable to meet these requests. NU was willing to fulfill the CHMC requests and, starting in the fall of 1964, began to provide all basic science training for the CHMC students.

The opening of the new school was orginally planned for September 1965, but it was moved forward to September 1964, following the recruitment of an initial faculty of six or seven "nurse educators" and a dean, Charlotte Voss, formerly Director of the School of Nursing, Cleveland Metropolitan General Hospital and Assistant Clinical Professor of Nursing at Western Reserve University.

As the venture got under way at NU, the "ladder system" was abandoned. This experiment had been given up in 1963 at Rutgers after a trial for four years ostensibly because of the difficulties involved in dealing with a heterogeneous student body and providing separate bodies of knowledge in a single program. An underlying factor of major importance, however, was "general disapproval" of the plan in nursing circles. The National League for Nursing (NLN), in particular, had been opposed to the plan from the start. Dr. White of NU said that the director of the Columbia University School of Nursing, a leader in her field, had also expressed strong opposition to NU officials who consulted her. Miss Sleeper said that she had tried to convince the Nursing Group that the plan would be unsatisfactory. "You can't superimpose a B.A. program on a diploma program." The abandonment of the Rutgers experiment had finally changed NU's attitude, even though President Bunting and Dean Keppel of Harvard had favored the ladder system.

The initial nursing program at NU would award an associate degree after three years of study. An entirely separate five-year program leading to the baccalaureate was to be started sometime in the future, but Dr. White emphasized that it would be very difficult if not impossible to transfer from one program to the other. NU had found it necessary to offer separate curricula for girls who would become bedside nurses and those who wished to go on for the bachelor's or advanced degrees. Both types of program were "equally necessary"; their relationship might be "compared with that of graduate and undergraduate schools of a university."

NU had been "successful in finding qualified faculty for the new school in the face of a national shortage," Dean Voss said, and she attributed this to the "appeal of the new cooperative plan which was unique in the country." Details of the arrangements for cooperative nursing students were worked out by the directors of nursing for each hospital involved and by President Knowles, Dr. White, Dean Wooldridge (Dean of Cooperative Education), and Dean Voss for NU. The faculty first listed jobs which students were qualified to fill, and then a written agreement was negotiated between NU and each hospital. The basic idea was to achieve a "progressive experience" — to use each student to her maximum capacity but to guard against giving her either excessively difficult work or drudgery jobs. At the end of each ten-week work period, the hospital would report exactly which jobs had been done by each student and for what professional responsibilities she was qualified as a result. Her competence in each level would be judged by the nursing faculty on the basis of academic performance.

This cooperative feature of the NU plan provided the greatest assurance to the hospital of the student's loyalty, Dean Voss believed. It had been NU's experience that about half the cooperative students in other fields stayed in the organizations with which they had worked during college. It was logical that a nurse trained at a given hospital would be considered more valuable by it and would therefore be offered more salary and more responsibility.

One of the new college's major problems was the unwillingness of the NLN to grant it accreditation, which was a prerequisite for eligibility for federal funds. The NLN refused to accredit the school on two separate occasions, giving as reasons that the school had not hired enough faculty members for the number of students "expected" the following year and that the school was giving "too much credit" for its courses. NU officials believed these reasons to be merely excuses, and thought that the NLN really was objecting to the cooperative feature of the school's program under the "mistaken idea that hospitals like to exploit student nurses." There was no question of "exploitation" in the case of

NU cooperative students, who were paid fair wages and expected to give an "honest week's work" in return, Dr. White said. He found it "mystifying" that the NLN, in a time of acute and increasing shortages of nurses, was hampering the establishment of a school planned with the advice and assistance of national leaders in the field and potentially able to enroll up to 1,000 students.

BIH had also been having accreditation problems with the NLN. Since the early 1950's the NLN had repeatedly granted it accreditation for only three-year periods instead of the usual six years. The reasons given were "high faculty turnover" and "lack of well defined direction." Faculty turnover was a widespread problem among hospital schools, largely because of their low prestige. At BIH in 1962–63 there were 23.5 faculty positions budgeted of which 19.5 were filled and there was a turnover of 55.8 percent. Corresponding figures for 1963–64 were 21.5, 19 and 25 percent, respectively. The educational background of the 1963–64 faculty was as follows: three had nursing diplomas, seven had B.S. degrees in addition to a nursing diploma, three had B.S. degrees from university-based nursing schools, and five had Master's degrees in addition to a B.S. in nursing. Faculty problems were compounded at BIH by strained relations between the faculty and the Associate Director in charge of Nursing Education. A number of people believed that the latter, although very capable, was excessively demanding of her staff and somewhat insensitive in her personal relationships with them. In addition, there had been "great faculty unrest" about the commitment to NU, Miss Zolotin recalled. The faculty had not been involved in the decision but it had been aware that the new school was being discussed. She added that the degree of collaboration envisaged — BIH's taking 30 students annually from NU — had not required faculty consultation.

During a routine accreditation visit in March 1964, the Hospital Director, in a slip of the tongue, referred to the "phasing out of the school in 1967" in the presence of the NLN visitor. The visitor went immediately to the faculty to ask what they knew about the closing. This "bombshell" changed discontent into a high pitch of resentment. The "less productive faculty members who were always complaining now had something to talk about," said Miss Zolotin.

Once again, the BIH school was accorded three-year accreditation until September 1967. The reasons given on this occasion for the limited term of accreditation were "repeated changes in the direction of the school, high faculty turnover, and many operational problems."

BIH was having other problems as well, some of which, such as the steadily decreasing supply of qualified bedside nurses, it shared with other hospitals in the country. Because of growing affluence and the widespread social pressure for academic degrees, many girls who might formerly have entered diploma schools chose instead to go to college or junior college, with the result that they became "too highly educated" to be content with careers as bedside nurses. In addition to this general problem, BIH had the further disadvantage of being in a poor competitive position to bid for potential applicants. Applicants from outside the Boston area were not generally aware that BIH is a nondenominational institution, and consequently those who did come were for the most part Jewish. And, since Jewish girls are not generally attracted to nursing, they were relatively few in number. For applicants from the Boston area, few of whom were Jewish, BIH had to compete with other hospital nursing schools which were more attractive to non-Jewish girls who anticipated that they would have a limited social life at a hospital staffed chiefly by Jewish physicians. According to Miss Zolotin, the caliber of the applicants to BIH had declined rapidly in recent years.

Moreover, the cost of running a hospital school was rising as a result of the steady shift away from the old concept of the student nurse as "slave labor." The national estimate was that it cost $2,000 per year to provide education for one student nurse, and that $700 to $1,000 of this amount was returned in service. As Dr. Lee explained, however, only the third-year students furnished a significant amount of service, first and second year students being "too inexperienced to pay their own way."

At the end of 1964, the Associate Director of Nursing Education at BIH submitted her resignation, effective in June 1965, giving as the reason a change in her husband's work which required their departure from the area. She later told Miss Zolotin that rumors of the school's closing had also been a factor.

From the time he had first become aware of the problems of nursing education at BIH, Dr. Lee had considered the possibility of eventually closing the BIH school. He had gone so far as to encourage consideration and discussion of nursing education problems in general by such potentially powerful groups as his nursing school alumnae. In 1961–62, for example, this group had devoted one or two meetings to the subject at Dr. Lee's suggestion, although without making any specific reference to BIH. Now, at the end of 1964, he was faced with a decision. Both BIH and NU were in the process of accepting students for the academic year 1965–66. If BIH retained its school, recruitment for a new associate director must begin immediately. If the BIH school were to begin a phasing out, an interim appointment to the same position should be made as soon as possible. This decision was complicated by the need for complete secrecy in order to guard against "unsettling the existing faculty, applicants to the class for next year, and the existing student body."

Because BIH seemed to be on a "shrinking platform," Dr. Lee decided to approach NU about the possibility of enlarging BIH participation in the new school in September 1965 as a prelude to the closing of the BIH school two years later. He did not expect a positive response when, with Miss Zolotin, he talked to Dean Charlotte Voss of the new college. Her encouraging response, however, led to a second meeting, this time between President Knowles, Dr. White, and Dean Voss for NU, and Mr. Slosberg, new President of the BIH trustees, Mr. Michelson, new Chairman of the BIH Nursing School Advisory Committee, Miss Zolotin, and Dr. Lee. At this meeting President Knowles indicated his willingness to enlarge the class entering the new school in September 1965, to between 140 and 150 students. By this time, Dr. Lee learned PBBH had indicated to NU that it would like to join the plan but NU would not be able both to accommodate a larger quota of BIH students and to admit another hospital into the program at that time.

On January 28, 1965, President Knowles put his offer in writing in a letter to Mr. Slosberg. NU could admit 140 students to its College of Nursing in the fall of 1965 and thereby increase the BIH quota from 30 to 80. Concurrently, BIH would increase its annual scholarship fund contribution to $25,000.

Dr. Lee established a task force composed of himself, the hospital comptroller, his administrative assistant, and Miss Zolotin whose purpose it was to determine the relative costs of continuing the hospital's school of nursing and of closing it and expanding the affiliation with NU. On the basis of a three-year phase-out period to allow the current freshman class in the BIH school to graduate, the task force compiled relative cost figures for each year, examining such items as changes in revenue from tuition fees; the size and cost of faculty needed in each year; the cost of replacing nursing service given by students; the cost of salaries for cooperative students; savings on housing, food, and laundry costs for students; additional revenue that could be expected if student housing space were freed for other uses; and the scholarship contribution to NU. Working over a weekend, the task force developed the following estimates: If the BIH school were closed, direct net operating costs would decrease from $209,000 in 1965–66 to $39,000 in 1967–68, a reduction of $170,000 over a three-year period. Offsetting this gain would be the cost of salaries and fringe benefits for the cooperative students — an estimated $194,000. This was a maximal figure which did not take into account the fact that many of the cooperative students would fill existing positions and some would fill budgeted but currently unfilled positions as nurses' aides and licensed practical nurses.

As soon as the estimates were ready, Dr. Lee held preliminary discussions with the President of BIH and the Chairman of the Nursing School Advisory Committee. Within a few days a meeting of the Executive Committee of the Board of Trustees was scheduled at which Dr. Lee was to make recommendations concerning the future of the BIH Nursing School.

Appendix A

Operating Statistics, Beth Israel Hospital School of Nursing

Category of data	1961	1960	1959	1958	1957
Student enrollment, 1961	163				
Number of applicants	136	149			
Number appointed	84	78	64		
Number admitted	68	63	56	46	61
Number graduated	43	40	47		
Distribution					
From Greater Boston	39				
Other Massachusetts	16				
Other New England	10				
New York	2				
Ohio	1				
Financial aid to all students, 1961					
Loans	0				
Scholarships	$7,265				
Income from students	*1960–61*	*1959–60*			
Tuition	$681	$350			
Fees	219	233			
Total	900	583			
Affiliations					
Outgoing					
to CHMC (for twelve weeks)	44				
to Bedford Veterans Administration Hospital (for twelve weeks)	39				
Incoming					
from BU (on Obstetrics Service for eight weeks)	33				
from NEDH (in Outpatient Department for four weeks)	55				
Graduating class remaining in 1961—44% percent					
Number of graduates of school on payroll in 1961					
Less than 6 months	19				
6 months to 1 year	–				
1–2 years	17				
2–3 years	1				
3–4 years	5				
4–5 years	3				
5 years and over	13				

(continued on next page)

Appendix A (continued)

Category of data	1961
Graduates of other schools on payroll in 1961	
PBBH	2
MGH	2
Boston City Hospital	1
Other Massachusetts schools	47
Schools outside Massachusetts	76
Nursing staff, as of November 1961	
Registered nurses	
Associate Director	1
Supervisors and assistants	20
Head nurses and assistants	32
Staff nurses — inpatient	100
Staff nurses — outpatient	6
Staff nurses — operating room and recovery room	19
Staff nurses — other	5
Staff education	2
Faculty	
Associates, assistants	2
Instructors and assistants	18
Total — Registered nurses	205
Auxiliary Staff	
L.P.N.	20
Aides, orderlies, etc.	97
Secretarial, clerical	34
School staff	
Counselors, librarians, housemothers, secretarial	10
Total — non-registered nurses	161

Salary cost for one year of R.N. faculty — $99,761
Estimated additional R.N. staff required to replace students — 13
Estimated annual cost of replacement of students — $54,600

Appendix B

Nursing Organization

There are two major professional nursing organizations, the American Nurses' Association, Inc. (ANA) and the National League for Nursing (NLN).

American Nurses' Association[1]

The national membership organization of professional registered nurses. Organized in 1896, its membership has grown to 170,911 as of December 31, 1960.

The ANA's policies and programs are established by the membership through representation in the House of Delegates, the highest authority in the association.

In order to meet the needs nurses share as members of occupational groups they are members of sections which are composed of nurses who belong to the same occupational group (e.g., general duty nurses; private duty nurses; educational administrators; consultants and teachers; etc.) . . . The sections were established in line with the basic philosophy of the ANA that the practitioners of each occupational group shall independently determine their own functions, standards, and qualification for practice as well as develop and work for desirable employment standards and conditions.

The sections continue to engage in study, evaluation and interpretation of functions, standards and qualifications. Through the ongoing activity their statements reflect the current and emerging trends in nursing practice, the competence and professional growth of individual practitioners are promoted, and the standards of nursing practice are constantly raised. Section activities include the study of general welfare and economic needs of their members and development and implementation of desirable standards and conditions of employment.

National League for Nursing

The National League for Nursing was formed in 1952 as an amalgamation of seven organizations. Largest and oldest of these was the National League of Nursing Education, founded in 1893. Next oldest was the National Organization for Public Health Nursing (1912) whose membership included lay persons as well as physicians and members of other allied groups. A third component of the NLN was the Association of Collegiate Schools of Nursing, formed in 1932,

1. Condensed from *Facts About Nursing*, 1961 ed. (New York: American Nurses' Association), pp. 237–241.

and composed of a small but "very influential" [2] group of one or more representatives of each of the accredited nursing schools in the country. The Joint Committee on Practical Nurses and Auxiliary Workers in Nursing Services and a Joint Committee on Careers in Nursing were the fourth and fifth components of the NLN; the National Committee for the Improvement of Nursing Services and the National Nursing Accrediting Service completed the seven founders. Miss Ruth Sleeper of MGH was the NLN's first president.

In July 1965, there were 47 state leagues and 88 local leagues in 24 states. Although constituents of the NLN, these groups have limited functions. Individual members numbered more than 24,688 in 1964. There were over 1,342 agency participants.[3]

A "common objective" of both the ANA and the NLN is "to provide the best possible nursing care for the American people." However, in contrast to the larger organization which places emphasis on the individual nurse, the NLN is concerned with the importance of nursing to the community as a whole, and specifically with assuring "good nursing education" at all levels.

NLN functions have been defined as follows:

1. to define standards for organized nursing services and education;
2. to stimulate . . . educational instruction to achieve these standards;
3. to promote continual study and adjustments in nursing services and educational curricula to meet changing needs;
4. to assist community surveys;
5. to provide consultation, data, etc.;
6. to conduct student recruitment programs in cooperation with the American Nurses' Association, the American Hospital Association, and the American Medical Association;
7. to carry out and promote research in connection with organized nursing services and educational programs;
8. to represent nursing services and education with allied professional and other groups and with the public;
9. to evaluate educational programs with a view to accreditation;
10. to offer comprehensive testing and guidance services to schools of nursing at all levels;
11. to prepare examinations for licensure.

The administrative framework of the NLN reflects its two primary concerns. There are two major divisions. Under the Division of Nursing Services are Departments of Hospital Nursing and of Public Health Nursing. The other major division, Nursing Education, includes the Department of Diploma and Associate Degree Programs, the Department of Baccalaureate and Higher Degree Programs, and the Department of Practical Nursing Programs. A steering committee

2. C. W. Kelly, *Dimensions of Professional Nursing* (New York: The Macmillan Co., 1962), p. 253.

3. *Facts About Nursing*, p. 75.

elected by members of each department administers the organization between the biennial membership meetings.

What has been described as "one of the most influential"[4] NLN programs deals with national accreditation of schools of nursing. To operate legally, all schools must have official approval of their programs by the state in which they are located. Although not required, NLN accreditation is "highly desirable." NLN standards concerning laboratory and classroom facilities and other requirements are in general higher than those of most states. Each year a list of accredited schools is published in *Nursing Outlook,* and later in booklet form. State-approved schools are also listed.

This phase of the League's work includes consultation services to any school seeking help with its educational program. Assistance may be given during personal visits to the school or in regional workshops.

Kelly has observed that the accreditation program "needs almost continual interpretation"[5] to hospital administrators, members of the medical profession and the public.

The history of organized accreditation of nursing schools, according to Jensen,[6] began in 1925 when some professionals decided to sponsor a "Committee on the Grading of Nursing Schools." This idea came from a similar action by physicians a few years before which had resulted in marked improvement in American medical schools. The Committee on Grading included representatives of the ANA, the National League of Nursing Education, and the National Organization for Public Health Nursing.

The eight "essential conditions" worked out by this group as basic to the adequate functioning of a school of nursing aimed at raising standards of instruction and grading to college levels.

Some work in accreditation was also done during the 1920's by the National Organization for Public Health Nursing and other groups, but there was little or no coordination until the Joint Accrediting Service brought them together in the late 1940's. By January 1, 1965, 708 out of a total of 1,158 nursing educational programs in the U.S. were NLN-accredited.

Criteria for accreditation were worked out between 1954 and 1958 by an NLN Committee to Develop More Definite Criteria for the Evaluation of Educational Programs in Nursing. Planned to provide guidance for self-improvement for schools, the criteria were to be "evolutionary" in character and were subject to change. After 1960 they would be "a guide for use by the NLN in its accrediting activities."[7]

The "Criteria" filled more than 20 single-spaced pages. They were summarized under their major headings:

4. Kelly, p. 256.
5. Kelly, p. 256.
6. Deborah Jensen, *History and Trends of Professional Nursing,* 4th ed., (St. Louis: C. V. Mosby, 1959), pp. 273–276.
7. *Criteria for the Evaluation of Educational Programs in Nursing Leading to a Diploma* (New York: National League of Nursing, 1958).

1. *Philosophy and Objectives*

Faculty should formulate clearly and completely their beliefs about "what nursing is," "what education is," and so on. They should also identify clearly general objectives, that is, "general changes in behavior which the school endeavors to help its students bring about in themselves." The total program should be "evaluated in terms of the stated philosophy and objectives."

2. *Organization and Administration*

Authority rests with a board of control which delegates executive function and authority to a director. There should be clear charts of organization; the faculty should be organized. Although the director controls the administration, the faculty must be involved "as broadly as possible" in all decisions which effect conduct of the school. The director's responsibilities are defined in sixteen points.

3. *Faculty*

The core of the faculty must be full-time with sufficient part-time personnel to implement the program in relation to the stated objectives. There should be a "reasonable teaching load" so that faculty members can participate in student guidance, attend faculty organization meetings and meetings of professional groups, etc. In selecting faculty, consideration should be given to basic and special preparation, personal qualifications (interest in people, etc.) and "professional and civic interests" which are "evidenced by membership in local, state and national nursing organizations; active participation in nursing organization activities."

4. *Selection of Students and Provision for Student Welfare*

The latter covers health, relaxation, counseling, clinical laboratory practice (learning needs take precedence over service needs of the teaching hospital).

5. *Curriculum*

Should be designed to promote best nursing care and to develop desirable personal characteristics.

6. *Evaluation of Students and Program*

Should be systematic, periodic, and thorough.

7. *Facilities*

Physical plant — classrooms, laboratories, residence, offices — should be adequate in space and aesthetically pleasing. The library should be run by a qualified librarian and contain adequate holdings. Only accredited hospitals should be used as clinical resources. Written agreements between the school and cooperating hospitals should be renewed periodically and should state the responsibilities and privileges of both groups.

8. *Records and Reports*

Detailed descriptions of adequate records and reports.

Of several resolutions adopted at the membership meeting in May, 1965, only one was not passed unanimously. This dealt with nursing education. The adopted version "strongly supported" the trend toward college-based programs and at the same time urged planning at all levels "to ensure desirable balance of nursing personnel with various kinds of preparation to meet the nursing needs of the nation."

Writing in the October 1965 issue of *Nursing Outlook*, Lulu W. Hassenplug, M.P.H., Professor and Dean of the School of Nursing, U.C.L.A., referred to "our recent decision to prepare in the future two different kinds of nurse-practitioners." She went on to note that "we have not yet adjusted our nursing services to accommodate two kinds of nurse practitioners." The "scarcity of good teachers" and the lack of acceptance by others of the fact that the "two programs differ markedly in purpose, content, and scope of learning experience," were factors retarding educational efforts. "Once nursing teachers accept the fact that they cannot in the same program prepare both the leaders of tomorrow's program and the practitioners to work under these leaders, they can then embark on the thoroughgoing curriculum revision needed."

Appendix C

Excerpts from H.R. 12, 88th Congress — "Health Professions Educational Assistance Act of 1963."

Approval of Applications

(b) (1) To be eligible to apply for a grant to assist in the construction of any facility under this part, the applicant must be (A) a public or other nonprofit school of dentistry, osteopathy, pharmacy, optometry, podiatry, nursing or public health and (B) accredited by a recognized body or bodies approved for such purpose by the Commissioner of Education, except that a new school which (by reason of no, or an insufficient, period of operation) is not, at the time of application for a grant to construct a facility under this part, eligible for accreditation by such a recognized body or bodies, shall be deemed accredited for purposes of this part if the Commissioner of Education finds, after consultation with the appropriate accreditation body or bodies, that there is reasonable assurance that the school will, upon completion of such facility, meet the accreditation standards of such body or bodies.

(5) The term 'school of nursing' means a department, school, division, or other administrative unit, in a college or university, which provides, primarily or exclusively, a program of education in professional nursing and allied subjects leading to the degree of bachelor of arts, bachelor of science, bachelor of nursing, or other baccalaureate degree of equivalent rank; or to a graduate degree in nursing.

Physician Response to a Governmental Health Plan: The Saskatchewan Experience

September 1966

Eugene Feingold / Marjorie Taubenhaus

Formerly part of the Northwest Territories, Saskatchewan was made a province of Canada in 1905. Located directly north of the wheat belt of the United States, southern Saskatchewan (where most of the population is located) is a vast plain, similar in topography to the Dakotas and Montana. And like the neighboring North Dakota, the life of the province still depends largely on the frontier crop, wheat.

Predominantly rural with a scattered population (density 4.1 per square mile in 1959 for the entire province, and 7.3 per square mile for the southern, settled part of the province), Saskatchewan has not participated proportionately in the industrial and population growth of the rest of Canada. In 1921 Saskatchewan accounted for 8.2 percent of the total population of Canada; by 1959 this proportion had fallen to 5.2 percent, although the province itself had grown from 757,000 to 902,000 people during this period. Two thirds of the population still lived in rural areas in 1959 (for all of Canada one third of the population lived in rural areas) and there are only four major cities in the province; Regina, the provincial capital (1961 population 112,141), Saskatoon (1961 population 95,526), Moose Jaw (1961 population 33,206), and Prince Albert (1961 population 24,168).

As in frontier days, almost every person is in agriculture or in an occupation servicing farmers. In 1959 only 12,539 persons were employed in manufacturing industries. The almost total dependence on farming a single crop has meant that the population has historically been at the mercy of both natural disasters, such as the severe drought of the 1930's, and man-made depressions affecting the wheat market and the price of wheat. "More than any other rural group, the wheat farmer is economically naked, completely exposed to the vagaries of the price system." [1] The repeated challenges of their precarious lives forced these western farmers to create many community institutions such as cooperatives and economic pressure groups, and the fact that all wheat farmers had

1. S. M. Lipset, *Agrarian Socialism* (Berkeley: University of California Press, 1950), p. 28

common problems meant that "solutions" to problems in one area were rapidly accepted in others.

The cooperative approach became a way of life for most Saskatchewan farmers who were forced by circumstance to unite in order to obtain telephone service, local roads, and medical and hospital facilities. On the average, each farmer belongs to four or five cooperatives and through cooperative and political action grain growers have attempted to resist the coercions of the fluctuating market economy. Thus, it is no surprise that the first electorally successful socialist party in Canada, the C.C.F., should have developed in Saskatchewan.

Formally titled the Cooperative Commonwealth Federation in 1935, the party was an outgrowth of previous Farmer-Labor Groups in the province. During the 1930's it was the official opposition to the governing Liberals, and in 1944 the C.C.F. carried 53 percent of the voters of Saskatchewan to take power as the first "socialist" government in the United States or Canada. From 1944 to 1960 the C.C.F. won five straight elections and remained in power for twenty years.

Because of the large distances between communities and the low density of population it has always been difficult for the farmers of Saskatchewan to get adequate medical care at reasonable cost. The municipal doctor plan began in the early 1900's as a modest municipal subsidy to attract doctors. It developed into the formal hiring of a doctor by a rural municipality and his payment from municipal taxes subsidized by a provincial grant. (There are 296 rural municipalities, the local governing unit, in Saskatchewan, each typically eighteen miles square with a population of 2,000.) In 1921 the rural municipality of Sarnia hired a doctor on salary to take care of the local population, mainly farmers and their families, and the system grew until at its height in 1947 it covered more than half the province and served a quarter of the population (210,000 people). Hired physicians, usually underpaid and overworked, brought medical services to thousands of people who would otherwise have received no medical attention. In 1959, some 129 rural municipalities, mainly in the northeast and some thinly populated areas in the northwest of the province, had plans in operation serving about 115,000 members. These plans now vary considerably in the range of medical services provided, the arrangements made with local physicians, and the methods of financing their operations. Their greatest expansion was in a period marked by isolation and lack of transportation; as the needs of the people of the province have changed, the municipal doctor schemes have been modified.

Saskatchewan physicians, along with members of the lay public, organized the Saskatchewan Anti-Tuberculosis League in 1911. In 1929 the provincial government began granting funds to be administered by the League for case-finding and treatment of tuberculosis patients. This arrangement has persisted, apparently to the mutual satisfaction of the government and the League.

In the early 1930's a Cancer Commission Act was passed and the first cancer clinics opened. The cancer program is available to all residents of the province and medical care is provided through a partnership of full-time salaried physicians under the Cancer Commission and physicians in private practice who provide surgical treatment and preliminary diagnosis. Since 1944 much of this service is without charge to the patient.

Some hospitalization insurance was supplied in conjunction with the municipal doctor schemes. As early as 1919 at least 10 rural municipalities had introduced compulsory hospital care plans; by 1940 there were 118 of these plans covering more than half the rural residents of the province.

The C.C.F. and Medical Care

One of the C.C.F. campaign pledges in the election of 1944 was "a complete system of socialized health services" and immediately after the election a Health Services Survey Commission was set up to recommend means to implement this pledge. Dr. Henry E. Sigerist, Professor of the History of Medicine at the Johns Hopkins University and outspoken proponent of socialized medicine, served as commissioner. His report was presented to the Minister of Public Health in October 1944 [2] and has since been referred to as the baseline of constructive or wild-eyed health planning in Saskatchewan, depending upon who was doing the referring.

Dr. Sigerist noted that any plans for the extension of medical services must take into account the geography of the province, as the population in the northern Saskatchewan was so scattered it would be impossible to do more than provide medical outposts there. The shortage of physicians was discussed: in 1943 only 408 active physicians, including those not actually engaged in prac-

2. Henry E. Sigerist, "Saskatchewan Health Services Survey Commission," in Milton I. Roemer, ed., *Sociology of Medicine* (New York: MD Publications, 1960).

tice, were available to serve a population of 896,000, and there was a concentration of physicians in the cities. The whole range of health services, preventive, diagnostic, and therapeutic, was covered in the report, which also gave attention to personnel and facilities and made recommendations for immediate action. Along with proposals for the extension of the two-year medical school at Saskatoon, the establishment of dental clinics, and the creation of a Saskatchewan Health Services Planning Commission, were suggestions for a system of complete free hospitalization and for study of a scheme of compulsory health insurance for the population of the cities. Dr. Sigerist commented that "The history of the last two decades already reveals a marked trend towards the socialization of essential medical services" and that "There can be no doubt that in the future more and more medical personnel will be employed on a salaried basis."

Shortly afterwards, the legislature passed a Health Services Act, establishing the Sigerist-recommended Health Services Planning Commission and empowering the Department of Public Health to pay all or part of the cost of providing health services for any group in the population. In February 1945, the Health Services Planning Commission proposed that the Department of Public Health establish a series of rural health centers, which would employ physicians on a salaried basis. This plan was opposed by the organized medical profession. After further discussions, the College of Physicians and Surgeons and the government seemed, by the end of the year, to be close to agreement on a health insurance scheme to be administered by an independent commission. The Saskatchewan government, however, was unable to reach an agreement with the Canadian government on the sharing of costs for such a health insurance program. Without federal funds, the provincial government did not go ahead with its broad health insurance scheme but rather enacted the Saskatchewan Hospitalization Act in 1946.[3]

The medical profession had no serious objection to the Saskatchewan Hospitalization Act, for this measure, while it satisfied the public demand for increased state provision of medical care, did not affect the position of the physician. The Act, which became effective in 1947, created a compulsory hospital insurance program. Initially the program was financed by a sales tax and by an annual premium charge. With few exceptions, all residents in

3. E. A. Tollefson, *Bitter Medicine* (Saskatoon: Modern Press, 1964), pp. 35–40.

the province are required to participate, and the benefits include public ward care and a virtually complete range of inpatient diagnostic and therapeutic services in general hospitals and maternity homes. There is no limit, other than medical necessity, to the number of days of care, no dollar limit to inpatient diagnostic services, and no waiting period for maternity and other benefits. Outpatient diagnostic and treatment services are not provided, except for accidents, and personal services of physicians are not ordinarily included.

The hospitalization scheme was quite successful in that it seemed to satisfy all those involved, and it served as a model for the Hospital Insurance and Diagnostic Services Act which was passed by the Canadian Parliament in 1957. This act makes possible federal participation in provincial hospital plans. It requires the provinces to make hospital services available to all residents, and the federal government pays between 40 and 65 percent of the costs, depending upon tax-sharing agreements. For Saskatchewan the federal share has amounted to about 44 percent of the total cost of their program. Federal participation in the provincial hospitalization program actually began late in 1958 and shortly thereafter the C.C.F. decided to take another step to fulfill its campaign pledge of 1944, "to set up a complete system of socialized health services with special emphasis on preventive medicine, so that everybody in the province will receive adequate medical, surgical, dental, nursing and hospital care without charge."

Experiments in prepaid care had taken place in the province during the C.C.F. years in power. One of the thirteen public health regions, Swift Current Health Region No. 1, had inaugurated a prepaid medical-dental program in 1946. This plan, assented to by a majority of the voters affected and financed by a property tax, premiums, and supplemental provincial grants, encompasses a population of some 53,000 persons in 12,000 square miles. Through annual contracts with 44 physicians in private practice, it offers basic medical services, including home, office, and hospital calls; limited dental care for children; major and minor surgery; and certain diagnostic outpatient services. Deterrent or "utilization" fees have been charged to patients since 1953, but the plan has no maximum dollar limits. Doctors have been reimbursed by different formulae over the years, but since 1957 the plan has utilized fee-for-service, paying varying percentages, usually ranging between 60 and 80, of the current Schedule of Fees of the Saskatchewan College of Physicians and Surgeons.

Broadening of Governmental Program

On December 16, 1959, Premier T. C. "Tommy" Douglas, popular long-time leader of the C.C.F., announced in a radio speech, "The Government of Saskatchewan is convinced that the time has arrived when we can establish a prepaid medical care plan as the next logical step in our march toward a comprehensive health insurance program." At this time 67 percent of the population was covered for some form of medical care benefits under private (40 percent) and public (27 percent) medical care plans and programs.

Mr. Douglas went on to say that the program would be based on five principles: (1) prepayment; (2) universal coverage; (3) high quality of service; (4) a government-sponsored program administered by a public body responsible to the legislature and through it to the entire population; and (5) the plan must be in a form that is acceptable both to those providing the service and those receiving it. He informed the audience that in a few weeks an Advisory Planning Committee on Medical Care would be appointed to recommend to the Government the best methods of developing a medical care program. He concluded by saying, "I would like to hazard a prophecy that before 1970 almost every province in Canada will have followed the lead of Saskatchewan and we shall have a national health insurance program from the Atlantic to the Pacific. Once more Saskatchewan has an opportunity to lead the way. Let us, therefore, have the vision and the courage to take this forward step, believing that it is another advance toward a more just and humane society."

Before the Advisory Planning Committee was created, the government engaged in protracted negotiations with the College of Physicians and Surgeons about the membership of the Committee and the scope of its studies. Agreement was finally reached on a Committee to be composed of three persons named by the College of Physicians and Surgeons, three representatives of the Government, three representatives of the general public, and one appointee each from the University of Saskatchewan College of Medicine, the Saskatchewan Chamber of Commerce, and the Saskatchewan Federation of Labor. The Committee was to study "a medical care program for the residents of Saskatchewan, and to determine the best methods of achieving and maintaining the highest possible state of health and well-being for all residents."

The College Registrar wrote Premier Douglas on March 29,

1960, naming three physicians as College appointees to the Advisory Committee. He also reminded Douglas of the resolution, passed unanimously at the annual meeting of the College in October 1959, which said: "We, the members of the College of Physicians and Surgeons of Saskatchewan, oppose the introduction of a compulsory government controlled province-wide medical care plan and declare our support of the extension of health and accident benefits through indemnity and insurance plans."

The College at this time reserved the right for its appointees to bring in a minority report at the conclusion of the Advisory Committee's deliberations. An Order in Council creating the Advisory Planning Committee was issued on April 26, 1960, and the Committee began its deliberations on May 9.

A provincial election was set for June 8, 1960, and the C.C.F. ran on the major platform plank of a compulsory insurance program to provide complete medical care for everyone in the province. The opposition Liberals challenged the practicality of the plan. The College of Physicians and Surgeons did even more: five weeks before the election the 900 members of the College were assessed $100 each to provide a war chest for a political campaign against the plan.[4] A "key man" organization was set up, with members of the College organized into groups of approximately 10 members each under the direction of a key man whose job it was to alert his group when action was desired on a medical-political issue. The Canadian Medical Association helped by sending two public relations men from Toronto to publicize the doctors' position on the election.

According to Dr. W. P. Thompson, Chairman of the Advisory Planning Committee, who was President Emeritus of the University of Saskatchewan and a highly regarded natural scientist, "The government's proposal was made the dominant issue by the medical profession who opposed it violently in a campaign which alienated the sympathies of many citizens. In fact those who are knowledgeable in such matters are of the opinion that the government owed many votes to reaction against the nature of the doctors' campaign."[5]

Although the C.C.F. received only some 40 percent of the total votes cast that June, the remaining votes were widely split among

4. Mark Gayne, "Doctors vs. The People," *The Nation* 195:25 (July 28, 1962).
5. W. P. Thompson, *Medical Care: Programs and Issues* (Toronto: Clarke, Irwin, & Company, Ltd., 1964), p. 63.

three other parties. As a result, the C.C.F. retained the same number of seats (36) it had previously held in the 53-seat legislature, the opposition retaining the other 17 seats. The government interpreted the vote as indicating popular support of the medical care program, and others agreed with this interpretation. The day following the election, Dr. A. D. Kelly, General Secretary of the Canadian Medical Association, said that there could be no doubt that the election result constituted endorsement of the government medical care plan and that the C.M.A. was therefore dropping its opposition. He said, "This is democracy. The C.M.A. accepts the decision in this light. Our efforts will be bent on avoiding the defects we see in government plans elsewhere." [6] This statement was repudiated in the *Regina Leader*, June 10, 1960, by the President of the Saskatchewan College of Physicians and Surgeons, who said the C.P.S. was "unalterably opposed."

The Advisory Planning Committee on Medical Care was requested to submit a report to the Minister of Public Health (J. Walter Erb) as soon as possible, and in September 1961 an interim report was presented.[7] After testimony from six individuals and 43 organizations, including the Saskatchewan College of Physicians and Surgeons, which submitted a brief, the Committee recommended "that a medical care insurance program be established." The following seven basic elements were to be included:

Universal coverage.

Comprehensive medical service benefits.

Eligibility based on residence, registration, and payment of premium.

Personal premium (set at a level which can be met by all self-supporting persons).

Limited "utilization" fees.

Fee-for-service method of payment.

Administration by a public commission. (It was recommended that this Commission negotiate with the Swift Current Regional Board the degree of administrative responsibility which could be assumed by that region).

Dr. Thompson, committee chairman, commented in a later interview that, had the committee not tried to placate the representatives from the College of Physicians and Surgeons, the report

6. *The Toronto Globe and Mail,* June 10, 1960, quoted in Tollefson, p. 55.

7. *Interim Report of the Advisory Planning Committee on Medical Care to the Government of Saskatchewan,* September 1961, 123 pp.

would have certainly recommended administration of the program by the Department of Public Health and a method of payment other than fee-for-service. In spite of these compromises a minority report was submitted by the representatives of the College and the Chamber of Commerce.

A dissenting opinion was presented by the representative of the Saskatchewan Federation of Labour, who endorsed the committee report with reservations. He objected to the recommendation for administration by commission. He also felt that fee-for-service remuneration would be detrimental to the quality of care and encourage emphasis on quantity of service. He suggested that doctors be put on salary, or at least that the law be so written that they would have the option of being paid on a salary basis. In his opinion "utilization" fees were related to the fee-for-service method of payment and could only lead to underutilization and the abandonment of preventive principles. Finally, he objected to the personal premium as placing undue hardship on those least able to afford it and proposed corporate and personal income taxes as a more equitable source of revenue.

The three physicians and the one businessman writing the minority report were unable to subscribe to the interim report and proposed an alternative whereby self-supporting persons would obtain insurance from private insurance companies and public funds would be "available on application in the form of subsidy of approved carriers" for persons of limited means and for all persons over the age of 65. This proposal had been made in the brief submitted by the College to the committee.

The writers of the minority report also objected to what they felt were the compulsory aspects of the scheme proposed. They wrote:

> It is misleading to suggest that the payers of substantial taxes would continue to finance their medical services privately, or that doctors would be in a position to withhold their services from insured persons. As realists we recognize that economic pressures on both patients and doctors would shortly result in the "State" plan being the only device available for the financing of personal health services.
>
> It is further to our view that the quality of medical services rendered under state monopolies tend to achieve a mediocrity which in the long term would not be in the best interest of the health of our people.

The points raised in the minority report were elaborated and reiterated in many other official statements by the medical profession during the next few years. Compulsory, universal participation was decried as a restriction of the rights of individual citizens, and the administrative commission with powers that supersede those of the voluntary agencies was seen as eliminating the benefits of competition. The profession was particularly worried about government control of doctors and of medicine. The most obvious method of control relates to payment, but the physicians were also concerned with the possibility that the commission could bring doctors into an area and supplant present practitioners who did not want to work under the plan. In addition, "Whenever government undertakes to pay the complete cost of any service it assumes the right to determine how much money will be spent on that service and what standards of services will pertain. . . . Insurance may adversely affect the provision of public funds for other essential health purposes." [8]

A special session of the Saskatchewan legislature was scheduled for October 1961 to deal with income tax legislation. The government had requested the interim report for September so that necessary medical care legislation could be passed at this same session. It was a busy and perhaps confusing time politically for Saskatchewan. Premier Douglas had resigned a few months previously to head the New Democratic Party on the national scene. He had been replaced by Woodrow S. Lloyd, Minister of Education from 1944 to 1960 and Provincial Treasurer from 1960 until he became Premier in 1961. The provincial legislature passed the Saskatchewan Medical Care Insurance Act on November 17, 1961. Shortly afterwards, in a cabinet shake-up, Walter Erb was made Minister of Public Works and replaced as Minister of Public Health by Walter E. Davies.

The 1961 annual meeting of the Saskatchewan College of Physicians and Surgeons was held while the Legislature was in session. Two relevant resolutions were passed at that meeting concerning the plan proposed in the Medical Care Insurance Act: one, directed to members, advised that no member of the College accept appointment to any commission or committee proposed by the Act without first consulting the Council of the College; the other resolution reiterated the College's refusal to accept such a plan or cooperate with it.

8. "Views on the Economics of Medicine," prepared by the Department of Economics, Canadian Medical Association #36, October 13, 1962.

The Saskatchewan Plan

An Act to provide for Payment for Services rendered to Certain Persons by Physicians and Certain other Persons.

The Act applies to all residents of Saskatchewan who are required to register and pay premiums unless specifically exempted by the provisions of the Act. All who have paid the premium, or have had the premium paid for them, are beneficiaries. The range of services covers:

a. Medical services, the diagnosis and treatment of all medical disabilities and conditions (except those covered by other acts, such as cancer, tuberculosis, and venereal disease).

b. Surgical services.

c. Maternity services, prenatal, postnatal, and attendance at confinement.

d. New-born care.

e. Specialist services.

f. Anesthesia, surgical, obstetric, and dental anesthesia in the hospital or where rendered by a physician-anesthetist.

g. X-ray, laboratory, and other diagnostic services, including interpretations.

h. Preventive medical services, inoculations and vaccinations not provided by other government or municipal agency; routine physical examination.

Additional authorized services include physiotherapy, dental services in conjunction with maxillo-facial surgery, and other services as may be specified in regulations made by the Lieutenant Governor in Council. ("Lieutenant Governor in Council" is the Cabinet, that is, the administration in power.) The act excludes services available through other provincial agencies, as well as ambulance or transportation costs, special duty nursing, and any service not rendered by or at the request of a physician.

Each city, town, or other governmental unit is designated as a collection district for the collection of premiums, which may be recovered in the same manner as municipal taxes. Although the term premium is used throughout the Act, Section 36 (1) states that for 1963 and after "the tax levied under *The Saskatchewan Hospitalization Act* and the premium levied under this Act shall be collected jointly, and if such provision is made the tax and the premium shall be known as the joint tax." In addition to the premiums, the plan derives financial support from a 6 percent increase in personal income taxes and a 1 percent increase in corporate income taxes. The retail sales tax was raised from 3 percent to 5 percent with 1.5 percent earmarked for the new Act, and 0.5 percent to meet increasing hospital costs.

According to a release from the office of the Premier of Saskatchewan on July 4, 1962, the various taxes employed and the base of these taxes were chosen so that the Medical Care taxation structure would be related to ability to pay. Every family pays the same premium, but families differ in the amount they pay through sales and income taxes. Only about one family in five in Saskatchewan earns more than $5,000 per year. Thus the governmen calculated that, given the then-current average medical care cost per year per family of about $84, 80 percent of Saskatchewan families would pay less for medical care under the Act than they would have for private medical coverage.

Section 29 of the Act is concerned with choice of physician and acceptance of patients, and states:

> 29. Nothing in this Act or in the regulations made by the Lieutenant Governor in Council or by the Commission:
>
> (a) interferes with or restricts the right of a beneficiary to select the physician, or other person providing services, from whom he will receive insured services;
>
> (b) interferes with or restricts the right of a physician, or other person providing services, to the free acceptance of a patient who is a beneficiary;
>
> (c) interferes with or restricts the right of a physician, or other person providing services, to make charges for insured services provided to a patient who is not a beneficiary.

The Act also sets up a Medical Care Insurance Commission to administer the Act. The commission is empowered to make regulations concerning method of payment, manner and form of accounts to be rendered, the appointment of committees, and similar items. The commission is also empowered to make certain regulations directly related to physicians' services. Section 49 describes the commission as able to make regulations "prescribing the rates of payments to be made under this Act to physicians and other persons and the method of assessing accounts submitted by physicians and other persons . . . prescribing the terms and conditions on which physicians and other persons may provide insured services to beneficiaries . . . respecting the maintenance and improvement of the quality of the services provided under this Act, to the end that the highest possible standards of service will be achieved."

Repercussions

Immediately after the Act was passed, the government approached the College of Physicians and Surgeons and asked for a joint exploratory meeting to discuss implementation of the Medical Care Plan and the creation of the Medical Care Insurance Commission. Dr. H. D. Dalgleish, President of the College, replied in late December that the Council of the College had voted not to confer on the plan but only on suggestions of their own for expanding certain medical services in the province. In January 1962, and again in March, Mr. Davies, Minister of Public Health, renewed his request for an early meeting between representatives of the government and of the College. However, Mr. Davies wrote on March 2: "I wish to make clear that we are not prepared to entertain any proposal, as you have suggested to the press, to repeal the Act. Nevertheless, the government is willing to discuss the Act and to consider specific changes if it can be demonstrated that they are required to protect the medical profession's legitimate interests."

Dr. Dalgleish replied that "We are not willing to provide our services through a compulsory government controlled medical care plan as set forth in the Saskatchewan Medical Care Insurance Act." He went on to complain about the recent announcement by the government that negotiations were under way for radiologists' and pathologists' services to be covered under the hospitalization plan and said that "Your intended changes would disturb profoundly the pattern of the practice of medicine for both patient and physician."

The government decided to begin preliminary steps towards implementing the plan, while leaving the door open for further negotiations. Many members of the College were asked to serve on the Medical Care Insurance Commission, but of the practicing physicians approached all but one declined.

Although it had been originally intended to put the plan into effect on April 1, 1962, the date of inception was postponed to July 1, 1962. However, the Medical Care Insurance Commission did proceed and automatically registered everyone in the province for the plan.

Unproductive meetings were held between members of the Cabinet and representatives of the College in March and early April. In April, Premier Lloyd wrote to Dr. Dalgleish, "The Government presented to you several possible clarifications and some alterations in its proposed plan as well as our reasons for being convinced of the basic validity of this program . . . We declared our willingness to amend and clarify the Act if by so doing the profession would find a satisfactory basis for acceptance of the provisional medical care plan."

The College replied in a memorandum dated April 11, 1962:

> The Cabinet's proposals for amendments to this Act were set out in Mr. Lloyd's recent letter to the College. These minor amendments do not fundamentally change the legislation which still undertakes to control all medical services in Saskatchewan. Even if the legislation were so amended, the Act would remain completely unacceptable to the profession as government would be the monopoly buyer and seller of all medical services.

Although the government was unable to reach agreement with the College on amendments to the Act which would satisfy the physicians, several administrative amendments to the Act were passed by the provincial legislature on April 14, 1962. One amendment stated, "With respect to a beneficiary or a dependent of a beneficiary the commission is the agent of the beneficiary for all purposes." This and the other amendments only served to alienate the doctors further, even though the government maintained that it was a standard insurance clause. Some observers[9] felt that the amendments were passed by the legislature in a spirit of revenge against the recalcitrant College; whether or no, they did nothing to improve the prospect of an early and amicable settlement.

On April 24, the Regina and District Medical Society sent notice to all physicians that a special meeting of the College had been called for May 3–4 in Regina, and the district society had voted that all medical offices in Regina would be closed those two days and no elective surgery done at either local hospital, so that all physicians could attend the meeting. Extensive publicity had been given to physician threats to cease practice in Saskatchewan if the government plan was instituted, and this meeting provided an implied foretaste of what the withdrawal of services would be like. Of the approximately 900 physicians in the province, 605 met at that time to discuss, behind closed doors, the position they should hold in relation to the Medical Care Insurance Act.

The government had requested an opportunity to answer questions concerning the Act and Premier Lloyd was invited to address the meeting. Before he spoke, one of the three doctors who had

9. Donald Tansley, personal communication.

submitted the minority report to the Advisory Committee, Dr. E. W. Barootes of Regina made a rousing speech which, in the opinion of one physician present, created the atmosphere of a "Nazi rally." Lloyd followed Barootes with an appeal to give the plan a "fair trial." He was hissed three times during his speech.

The atmosphere of the meeting was further heightened by an announcement from the chairman that the erstwhile Minister of Public Health, Walter Erb, had just resigned from the cabinet, giving as one reason the government's handling of the medical care dispute. The doctors reacted with thunderous applause, interpreting the resignation as a sign that the government was on the edge of a political precipice and with a little assistance might fall.

Although reporters were barred from the meeting, a press conference was held at which Dr. Dalgleish announced that if the plan prevented doctors from continuing private, independent practice, the College's members had voted almost unanimously to restrict medical care to the treatment of emergency cases. Local medical societies were asked to immediately undertake arrangements for these emergency services. Another resolution called on the government to repeal the Act.

A report by the Department of Medical Economics of the Canadian Medical Association, written about this time but not published until June 9, summarizes the physicians' point of view: "It is easy to state in broad terms what makes the Act unacceptable but it is very difficult to propose specific amendments which would so alter it that the result would be acceptable."

This report criticizes the Commission for possessing too much power, and especially for its right to make regulations prescribing terms and conditions of practice and respecting the maintenance and improvement of quality. At the same time, it indicates that the Commission has too little power, as it has no fiscal authority and cannot guarantee payment. The report concludes: "Saskatchewan doctors do not feel that they can, with confidence, place their professional future in the hands of this government or this commission. The basic issue is professional freedom." (See Appendix B for a discussion of the legal validity of their fears.)

Impasse

According to Donald Tansley, Chairman of the Medical Care Insurance Commission, who was a high-level civil servant, formerly involved in provincial budgetary affairs, until May the Commission did not believe that the doctors would withhold their services. In spite of this, in late April, the Commission turned its attention to the recruitment of replacement physicians. Recruiting activities were thought of as one way to forestall a strike, although many members of the government were unhappy about this activity as they did not want to antagonize the doctors.

During May the government was anxious to reach some form of agreement, but official spokesmen for the College were unavailable. In mid-May the Saskatchewan Hospital Association offered to act as an interested go-between, but found it difficult to assemble the Council of the College for a meeting. This was finally done on June 10, but nothing was accomplished. The physicians seemed determined to reply to the inauguration of the plan by restricting their services to emergency care, and on June 1, Dr. G. W. Peacock, Registrar of the College, wrote to Tansley, "We must tell you that the stand, in general, of the Doctors in Saskatchewan is that we are not to negotiate in any way with your Commission."

Meanwhile, the public became involved in the controversy and petitions on both sides were presented to the government, public meetings were held, and several pressure groups were organized. The largest of the anti-government groups was the Keep Our Doctors (KOD) committee, which sent a delegation on June 3 to visit Premier Lloyd, bearing petitions which carried 46,000 names and appealed for delay in activation of the medical plan. Lloyd reiterated to the citizens both his willingness to discuss changes with the doctors and his determination to go ahead with the plan on July 1.

Other citizens, protesting the position of organized medicine, banded together to seek ways of "ensuring themselves and their families of the best kind of medical care possible." [10] Local meetings were held during the spring and a meeting to consider the organization of a provincial body to develop community health services was held in Saskatoon on June 27. Their efforts were directed to the establishment of group practice medical clinics in which salaried doctors would practice and care for members of the association and their families, under the Medical Care Insurance Act.

An early casualty in the battle between the government and the

10. *Report of the Executive to the First Provincial Convention,* Community Health Services (Saskatchewan) Association, Limited, November 3 and 4, 1962.

doctors was Tommy Douglas. On June 18 a federal election was held and Douglas was badly defeated in Regina in his bid for election to a seat in the Canadian legislature. In fact, not one member of the New Democratic Party was elected from Saskatchewan.

The government went ahead, however, hopefully making arrangements for the administration of the plan. On June 20 Tansley sent out the first of a series of newsletters to all physicians in the province. He announced the inauguration of the series for the purpose of explaining various technical aspects of the plan, asked for comments and suggestions from the doctors, and enclosed a sample claim card.

Through the Hospital Association, a meeting was arranged between the government and the College for June 22; it lasted for three days. Spokesmen for the College for the first time presented a list of the specific provisions of the Medical Care Insurance Act to which they objected, and called for a special legislative session to amend the Act. The government was unwilling to call a special session or to make basic changes in the Act. However, it did offer to change many of the provisions to which the physicians objected. On June 21, Premier Lloyd had made a statement to the press in which he publicly offered to delete Sections 28 (a) and 49 (1) g and to discuss any other sections of the Act that the doctors found unacceptable. Section 28 (a) enabled the commission to act as agent of the beneficiary and "in the name of the commission or of the beneficiary take, at the expense of the commission, any action in a court of competent jurisdiction or defend or counterclaim in any action brought against the beneficiary." Section 49 (1) g empowered the commission to prescribe "the terms and conditions on which physicians and other persons may provide insurance services to beneficiaries."

The government also offered to issue regulations authorizing payment directly to beneficiaries where the physician providing the service did not wish to be paid directly by the Commission, thus permitting physicians to practice without coming directly into contact with the Commission. The government promised to administer the Act in this fashion until the next regular session of the legislature, at which time appropriate amendments to the Act would be passed. The offer was turned down on the grounds that the College did not consider regulations binding as they might be invalidated in the courts as contrary to the intent of the initial legislation. The government's comment on this point was,

"It is not uncommon for transactions involving many millions of dollars to be proceeded with on a written undertaking of the Government to introduce legislation and it is our belief that such an undertaking should be sufficient basis for agreement between the Government and the College, particularly in this case where a major purpose of the amendments would be simply to spell out more clearly certain legal powers presently inherent in the Act." [11]

The second newsletter was sent out on June 22 and enclosed a complete set of the regulations 904/62, 1032/62, and 1033/62, made by the Lieutenant Governor in Council in consultation with the Commission. These regulations were published in *The Saskatchewan Gazette* of Friday, June 22. They concerned various matters, such as rates of payment, form of accounts, mediation procedures and additions and exclusions from insured services. Regulation 6 (1033/62) specified the following services as not being insured services for the purpose of the Act:

a. Plastic and other surgery for cosmetic purposes.

b. Refractions and other services for the purpose of fitting eye glasses.

c. Dental services.

d. Drugs and appliances.

e. Advice by telephone.

f. Examination or certificate where required only for information of third party or for judicial purposes.

g. Treatment outside Saskatchewan for psychiatric disorder unless required as emergency measure.

h. Radiological and laboratory procedures, including interpretations, except

1. blood sedimentation rate
2. electrocardiogram
3. hemoglobin estimation
4. urinalysis
5. white blood count

This communication was followed on June 25 by the proposal concerning the reimbursement of physicians under the Act submitted to the College by the government. Copies were sent to every physician in Saskatchewan.

The proposal began by stating, "The Government has always acknowledged the right of a patient to get services from a physi-

11. *Commentary on the Document Entitled "Criticism of the Saskatchewan Medical Care Insurance Act" and Delivered to the government on June 25th., 1962,* June 26, 1962.

cian and to personally pay for those services and the right of the physician to render those services and accept that payment without reference to the Medical Care Insurance Act or its administration."

To supplement this relationship the government suggested that the patient could send the doctor's bill to the Commission and be reimbursed if the doctor did not wish to bill the Commission directly. Either way, the Commission would remit 85 percent of the minimum fee schedule. But if the patient paid the bill then the patient assumed liability for any additional cost if the doctor's fee was higher than the schedule. The government hoped that doctors would not charge more than the agreed fee, and asked for some definite understanding or written agreement to reduce to a minimum the possibility of their billing for amounts greater than those paid by the Commission.

> This dual system of billing and receiving payments would remove any shadow of doubt as to the right of a physician to continue to practice without any contact with the Medical Care Insurance Commission . . . The implementation of these two systems of billing and receiving payments will not require any delay in the commencement of the Plan on July 1st.

A letter dated June 26 and signed by Premier Lloyd which accompanied the proposal concluded with the statement that the government was "firmly and publicly committed to have this procedure effective on July 1st."

Newsletter no. 3, dated June 28, included new regulations stating that only physicians who requested in writing that their names be placed on a list would be expected to bill the Commission for services to patients. "A physician who does *not* place his name on the list *is free to practice without reference to the Medical Care Insurance Commission.*"

The following day newsletter no. 4, which gave further instructions about billing and fee schedules, repeated this point:

> Before proceeding with the main purpose of this letter, I should like to state that the Saskatchewan Medical Care Insurance Act, 1961, and regulations do not require you to participate in the Medical Care Plan commencing July 1, 1962 . . . Fees charged directly to the patient by the doctor will be of concern only to the doctor and the patient. However, the Commission will reimburse the beneficiary in the same amount of 85 percent as in the case of payment to the doctor. Under this procedure you will have no obligation to the Commission nor will the Commission have any obligation to you.

On June 30, Premier Lloyd and Dr. Dalgleish met in a last-minute effort by the government to come to some agreement, but the attempt failed. The government considered that the new regulations were tantamount to suspending the Act for all doctors who did not wish to practice under it; the College continued to demand that the whole Act be repealed.

"Withdrawal of Services"

On July 1, 1962, the Medical Care Insurance Act was formally inaugurated and most of the practicing physicians in Saskatchewan closed their offices and went on open-ended vacations. First rumors stated that about 90 Saskatchewan doctors had joined the government plan; later figures showed that 34 doctors had signed the agreement to work under the plan and that 55 doctors were practicing as usual. Whatever the true number, there was no doubt that the large majority of Saskatchewan doctors were on strike to protest the government plan.

By July 1, four doctors arrived from Britain in response to the government's recruiting efforts. But the major source of medical care for the province became the Emergency Service set up by the Saskatchewan Division of the Canadian Medical Association. (The Saskatchewan Division of the C.M.A. and the Saskatchewan College of Physicians and Surgeons are essentially the same organization, with the same officers.) Among the rules of procedure adopted were the following:

> 3(c) Patients needing emergency services would be seen at those hospitals staffed for such purposes.
>
> 4(a) There should be enough physicians available to provide a *safe* emergency service. In this connection it was recognized that not every hospital would be staffed.
>
> (b) The *personnel appointed* would be of such calibre as to provide a safe service.
>
> (c) The *location* of *hospitals to be staffed* is so as to provide adequate emergency service in each district in the province.[12]

About 240 doctors, or approximately one third of the practicing physicians in the province, volunteered to provide emergency service round-the-clock at 34 hospitals (of the province's 148 hospitals) strategically located throughout Saskatchewan, and many patients were transferred to these hospitals. At one time or another approximately 350 doctors took part in the emergency service which both

12. Minutes of General Committee for Emergency Services, June 3, 1962.

government and physicians considered to have worked very well. Dr. Dalgleish stated later, "In fact, some citizens felt that they received more prompt service in the Emergency Department than they had in doctors' offices. Mortality and morbidity statistics appeared to be better during this period than they had at any other time in our Province." [13]

Public reaction to the strike was immediate. Dramatic newspaper headlines announced the story all over North America and as far away as Burma and Thailand. By July 3, the first fatality "due to the strike" was turned into the favorite story of the day, as reporters wrote of a nine-month-old baby with meningitis whose parents had raced 75 miles through the night vainly seeking a doctor. There were reports of additional deaths, allegedly linked to the strike, from heart disease and other causes. None of these reports were substantiated, and later evaluation showed the hospital based emergency service to have provided efficient medical care.

The local newspapers in Saskatchewan supported the doctors, both editorially and by the weight they gave to various stories in their news columns. Papers outside the province sympathized more with the government and were criticized by the Saskatchewan press as having "a serious lack of knowledge of all the background and all the factors which have brought about the present distressing situation." [14] Rumors flew, and it was reported that over half the doctors who had closed their offices were refugees from Britain's National Health Service.

Unofficial responses to the strike came thick and fast. Fifteen doctors at one hospital in Toronto offered their services to their striking colleagues to help maintain the emergency service. The President of the Saskatchewan Pharmaceutical Association urged the doctors to resume talks with the government and said "Surely the health and indeed in many cases the lives of the people in this province are of greater concern to all of us than any preconceived idea of what a medical care insurance act should be." The Canadian Labour Congress accused the doctors of a brazen defiance of constitutional authority, and the President of the Quebec Medical Association denounced the medical care plan.

13. H. D. Dalgleish, "The Saskatchewan Experience," speech to the Montreal Medico-Chirurgical Society, March 14, 1963.

14. *Regina Leader-Post*, July 10, 1962, quoted by A. E. Blakeney in a presentation to the Canadian Managing Editors' Conference, February 20, 1963.

For a few days almost everybody seemed to be making pronouncements except the government and the College. On July 2, newsletter no. 5 had been sent to all physicians. It consisted of three questions and answers, two pertaining to the mechanisms of beneficiary reimbursement, and a third which read:

> *Q. How does a physician signify his intention to practice outside the Medical Care Plan?*
>
> A. Simply by continuing in normal private practice. No physician can receive payment from the Commission *unless he directs in writing* that his name be placed on the eligible list. In the absence of such direction, the physician has no obligation to the Commission and the Commission has none to him; he need have no contact whatsoever with the Commission.

In a radio broadcast on July 2, Lloyd appealed to the people to remain calm, but made no mention of attempts at negotiation or reconciliation. Police in Swift Current were called in to protect doctors and their families following threats made by the Citizen's Safety Committee, which had sent letters directing the doctors to get down from their chosen pedestal and return to practice OR ELSE. Emergency services throughout the province were said to be swamped and there were reports of weary physicians working 20 hours a day to safeguard the health of Saskatchewan residents.

The first move on either side came from the government on July 6. Premier Lloyd suggested mediation. Although the offer was turned down by the College, the President of the Saskatchewan Hospital Association discussed with the heads of some Canadian churches the possibility of church leaders acting as mediators in the strike. A "hint of a softening" in the doctors' attitude was seen in a statement made by Dr. Kelly of the Canadian Medical Association which called for "suspension" rather than "repeal" of the Act before doctors would resume practice.

On July 10, it was announced that Lord Taylor, a British neuropsychiatrist who had been involved in the evaluation and administration of the British health plan, had been invited to "advise" the government of Saskatchewan. Dr. Dalgleish held a press conference at which he stated that the key to resumption of negotiations was suspension of the Act. The government refused to negotiate further until the doctors returned to work, and an impasse seemed firmly established.

Meanwhile, the government continued to recruit physicians from Great Britain and the United States. All told, over 100 doctors were brought into Saskatchewan, but many of them never actually practiced. Saskatchewan physicians were not pleased with these arrivals, and one doctor commented, "This is disappointing of course and lessens the impact of our restricted services on the community." The government in turn was displeased with the reception given to the imported physicians, and on July 13 a Royal Commission was set up to investigate claims of harassment of foreign physicians. The government claimed the College was using its power of licensure as an offensive weapon against doctors who did not support the walkout. One physician who had come from Florida to offer his services left Saskatchewan rather than face threatened charges of practicing without a license.

Attempts were made by opposition political leaders to capitalize on the government's uncomfortable position. The Liberals called for an immediate special session of the Legislature and announced they would take their seats in the empty building to dramatize the need for the session. A KOD rally to protest the Act was announced for July 11 and was expected to attract 40,000 to 50,000 KOD supporters. The Liberals timed their demonstration to coincide with this rally. When the time came, only about 4,000 persons gathered in front of the Legislative Buildings, and the Liberals found the doors to the legislative chamber locked, so that both the protest march and the symbolic legislative session fizzled and received little attention.

The C.C.F. Convention

On July 17, the C.C.F. opened its party convention in Regina. The government and the College still had not met with each other since the strike had begun. Lord Taylor had arrived in Canada the previous day. He continued to refer to himself as a government advisor "because a mediator is appointed by both sides, while I was appointed by one side," but there was some hope that he would be able to bring about negotiations for a settlement.

The first move, however, came from the College. The day the convention opened, a spokesman for the College requested that one of its members be permitted to address the C.C.F. Permission was readily granted, the convention schedule was rearranged, and on July 18 Dr. Dalgleish and Premier Lloyd both appeared on the convention platform.

Dr. Dalgleish said that if the government would make certain changes in the bill he was authorized by the College to urge its members to go back to work. Dr. Dalgleish still maintained that the basic issue was one of freedom.

Premier Lloyd was given an enthusiastic welcome by the members of the C.C.F. He did not agree with Dalgleish and said that the basic issue was the ability of a power bloc to use a monopoly of skills to frustrate the will of the majority. However, he did promise that a special session of the legislature would be held to amend the Act, if the doctors went back to their practices.

The government was quick to accept the medical profession's overtures for negotiations. Dr. Dalgleish presented a proposal which the Minister of Health studied. Although some of the items objected to by the doctors had already been deleted by an Order in Council, the doctors wanted legislative amendments as they felt that anything taken out by order could be put back in by order. In addition, the College's proposal contained some new conditions concerning private medical insurance companies.

The same day that newspapers carried hopeful stories about possibilities for accord in the strike, *The New York Times* reported, "It was estimated today by Dr. A. D. Kelly, general secretary of the Canadian Medical Association, that the doctors had lost $600,000 since July 1. He estimated that the daily loss to the 700 practicing physicians was about $50 each. The average income of doctors in the province was about $17,000 a year, or about $350 a week."

Negotiations were carried on for several days, with hopeful and pessimistic rumors circulating in equal strength. The papers said Lord Taylor was giving up and returning to England; the papers said that an accord was near. In fact, both statements were true. Lord Taylor habitually threatened to walk out of negotiations when he felt it would force conciliation from whichever side was proving recalcitrant at the moment. He found, "Every citizen as far as I can see in Saskatchewan is a politician . . ." and negotiations were especially complicated because the College didn't have a single spokesman. "All week they were a sort of true democracy in the sense that they didn't have a majority decision. They tried always to get unanimous decisions and even if everybody else agreed, one objector could down the lot. This made it frightfully hard for poor Mr. Robertson (solicitor for the College) to get his instructions clear because he'd get them clear with one of them and another one would have another look." [15]

15. Transcript of tape recording of Lord Taylor's reminiscence of his visit (produced for deposit in the Archives of Saskatchewan).

In spite of these complications, on July 23, 1962, Premier Lloyd and Dr. Dalgleish signed a Memorandum of Agreement between the Government of the Province of Saskatchewan and the College of Physicians and Surgeons of Saskatchewan and the strike was officially over.

The Memorandum of Agreement

The memorandum stated that, upon signing the agreement, the College would undertake to ask its members to resume the practice of medicine, and the government would introduce amending legislation at a special session of the legislature. The College agreed that in a matter of legislative responsibility the legislature and not solely the C.C.F. government was responsible, and further that any program financed partially or wholly by tax funds must be accountable to the Legislature.

The agreement went on to state, however, "The doctors fear that if the government becomes their only source of income they are in danger of becoming servants of the state and not servants of their patients." Therefore, because there were many voluntary health insurance agencies already in the province, "It is the wish of the College that they should continue to play a part when the Medical Care Scheme comes into full operation." This would protect doctors against the risks of having a single source of income and could be developed to provide patients with additional fringe benefits. The government accepted this principle but specified that the voluntary health insurance agency must be genuinely nonprofit; extra billing is to be strictly controlled, normal enrollment fees are to be limited to the actual administrative costs, and the agency is to distinguish clearly between enrollment fees and premium charges for fringe benefits. Also, the carrier must publish full accounts and be recognized and approved by the government.

For their part, doctors agreed to work together with their colleagues, whether or not these were in the medical care plan, and not to discriminate between citizens who did or did not belong to voluntary health insurance schemes. Each doctor, however, had the right to elect to see only one type of patient. The College undertook to judge physicians solely on their professional merits when advising on hospital appointments, and both the College and the government decried discrimination against doctors by any hospital.

The agreement summarizes the four choices available to a patient or a doctor. The patient may: (a) choose a doctor enrolled in the medical care plan who bills the Commission or is otherwise paid by it and makes no further charge to the patient; (b) enroll with a voluntary health insurance agency, and pay a fee and a possible premium. He may then choose a doctor who has a service contract with the agency, bills the agency, and makes no further charge; (c) choose a doctor who bills him directly, and then be reimbursed by the Commission; (d) choose a doctor who practices only for private fees, in which case he has no claim on the Medical Care Insurance Commission.

Similarly, the doctor has four ways in which he may receive his income. He may: (a) enroll with the Medical Care Insurance Commission for a minimum set period of time, and receive remuneration as agreed upon either as fee-for-service, a retainer plus a smaller fee, or fixed remuneration only; (b) practice partly or wholly with one or more voluntary health insurance agencies to whom he submits bills for patients at the agreed figure ("The agency will collect from the Medical Care Insurance Commission a reimbursement on the general 85 percent basis and pay to the doctor the amount of that reimbursement in full payment of the doctor's bill."); (c) practice privately, but give the patient an itemized bill so that the patient can be reimbursed by the Commission, in which case the doctor will come into contact with the Medical Care Insurance Commission only if it becomes necessary to clear up some detail of the patient's reimbursement; (d) practice entirely for private fees if his patients also agree to make no use of the medical care plan.

The government and College thought that these methods of payment were complicated but workable and were unable to predict how many doctors would choose to practice each way. The government and the College agreed that doctors on a fixed remuneration should not be underemployed, and if they are the Commission can terminate the contract or offer another type of contract. "Furthermore, to reassure the doctors of the Government's good faith, the legislation will specify that the Government has no intention of establishing a full-time general salaried medical service."

The Agreement also stated that it is the intent of the government that the Medical Care Insurance Commission will administer only bills and fees, not a provincial medical service. Certain parts of the main Act will be repealed to remove fears of the College that the Commission may assume functions other than those intended. "Both the Government and the College want to see a steady improvement in the standards of medical care throughout the Province. But, in the last analysis, doctors are not made better doctors by legislation. The Government looks to the College, to the University and to the profession as a whole to maintain and raise standards of medical care."

The Agreement went on to state that, as the government wishes the College to have full confidence in the Medical Care Insurance Commission, three more medical members — a general practitioner, a specialist, and a representative of university medicine — would be added to the Commission. The doctors to be appointed will be mutually agreed between the government and the College. The original Act called for a Commission of not less than six nor more than eight members, of whom one was to be the Deputy Minister of Public Health (through whom the Commission reports to the Minister of Health) and at least two other physicians. The Agreement states, however:

> While the Government has no inherent objection to having five medical members on the Commission, they feel they must reserve the right to appoint health administrators and other citizens with wide or specialized knowledge or experience to these two places if this seems to be necessary. The Act will be adjusted appropriately. It is the wish and the hope of the Government and the College that the Commission shall function as a servant of the public and the doctors and shall not become a forum for politico-medical disputes. Good will between all members of the Commission must prevail if what we all desire is to be achieved.

Other sections of the Agreement covered permission for the Swift Current Health Region to continue its plan for the present, the problem of dealing with the physicians already recruited from abroad, and a promise by the government and the College to deal with future problems by frank and friendly discussion.

During the next two weeks over 200 doctors indicated that they would practice in association with the nonprofit voluntary health insurance agencies. One of the major agencies announced that its annual enrollment fees would be $3.00 per person, with a $5.00 family maximum; a second agency set its fees at $4.00 and $7.00.

On Thursday, August 2, 1962, at a special session of the legislature, the Medical Care Insurance Act was amended by unanimous vote to conform to the terms of the Agreement. The Saskatchewan doctors reopened their practices.

Impact

Although the signing of the Saskatoon Agreement signalled the end of the dramatic dispute, it by no means ended all conflict over medical care in Saskatchewan. Certain issues were created during the time of the strike, others merely heightened; ill will has remained close to the surface of events ever since.

The Medical Care Insurance Act had officially begun, despite the strike, on July 1, 1962. On June 30, 1963, over 93 percent of Saskatchewan's population was eligible for M.C.I.C. benefits (of the remainder, 3 percent were covered by provincial welfare, 3 percent by Federal programs, and 1 percent were uninsured). Payments of over ten million dollars were made to provide services for 58 percent of the covered population during the first half of 1963. Slightly more than half of the services were received by females (54 percent) with the largest share going to women in the child-bearing years. The most highly serviced age groups were infants under one year of age and persons over the age of 65. Infants, comprising 2.5 percent of the population, received over 5 percent of the services, and persons over 65, who make up 10 percent of the population, received 20 percent of the services.[16]

During the year ending December 31, 1963, 666,000 residents, approximately 75 percent of those eligible, received benefits costing approximately $19.5 million. The per capita payment for insured services, excluding administrative costs, was $22.05. (The Advisory Planning Committee had, in 1961, estimated first year per capita costs, excluding administration, at between $22.39 and $23.06.) Administrative costs were $1.47 per person. Excluding the Swift Current Health Region, of the families covered, 85 percent received one or more services and for these families the average payment was $67. Somewhat over 50 percent of the eligible population received benefits of under $50, while 11.9 percent received benefits of between $100 and $200 and 6.0 percent received benefits of between $200 and $500. Less than one half of 1 percent received benefits of over $500 while 15 percent received no benefits.[17]

Total payments under the Act increased by approximately 10 percent during 1964, decreased slightly in 1965, and increased by another 10 percent in 1966. During this period, however, there

16. Saskatchewan Medical Care Insurance Commission, *Six Months Report*, January–June, 1963.

17. Saskatchewan Medical Care Insurance Commission, *Annual Report* December 31, 1963.

was a change in both the population and the services covered under the Act. Appendix A presents selected data for 1963, 1964, and 1965. The per capita payment, adjusted so that it covers services offered in all years, increased by about 5 percent from 1963 to 1964, 2 percent from 1964 to 1965, and 5 percent from 1965 to 1966. Administrative costs remained approximately the same in all four years. The average payment per family receiving services (excluding the Swift Current Health Region) increased from $67 in 1963 to $75 in 1964, $76 in 1965, and $78 in 1966. The distribution of families by the size of payment they received remained similar in all four years.[18]

Various estimates have been made of how many doctors practice directly under the Act, how many through the voluntary agencies, and how many supply information so that their patients can be reimbursed. The M.C.I.C. at one time estimated a hundred odd doctors working directly through the plan. In December 1962 the College estimated 60, but the minutes of an Executive Committee meeting of the C.M.A., Saskatchewan Division, show that on February 15, 1963, an estimate of 130 was considered accurate by the medical profession. All estimates represent a small proportion of the 750–800 active practicing physicians in Saskatchewan.

Another view is gained by examining the claims submitted through the M.C.I.C. by each of the three payment methods during the first twelve months of operation of the plan: approved health agencies — 66 percent; physicians (direct) — 20 percent; patients — 14 percent. The proportion received from health agencies declined slightly thereafter, reaching 62 percent in 1966. The proportion received from patients dropped to 5 percent in 1966, while that received directly from physicians increased to 33 percent. Disputes arose almost immediately between the Commission and the doctors, who complained that there was undue delay in the payment of bills. The Commission explained that there was "an average of 14½ days extra delay involved in M.S.I. (Medical Services Incorporated, the major health agency) payments as compared with accounts handled directly by the Commission." The total average time for a claim to be processed was two weeks where the doctor practiced directly with the plan and three weeks where payment was made directly to patients.

The doctors were unwilling to accept explanations which placed

18. Saskatchewan Medical Care Insurance Commission, *Annual Reports* December 31, 1964, December 31, 1965, and December 31, 1966.

the blame on the health agencies, and suspected the Commission of discriminating against those who did not deal directly with the Commission. Tempers often ran high and the following excerpt from a letter by Dr. Barootes to the Registrar of the College demonstrates the lack of trust on the part of many physicians. The letter complains about the activities of employees of the M.C.I.C., and of one in particular: "He has tried over and over again to direct patients away from their doctors to doctors practicing directly under the Medical Care Insurance Commission. This can be documented by many patients of Dr. Barrie P. Duncan and many others who we have sent up there as shills to make inquiries."

Many doctors were said to be leaving the province in protest against the workings of the Act. In March 1963 Dr. Dalgleish reported to the Montreal Medico-Chirurgical Society, "In 1959 there were 935 doctors in the Province, with an increase of 25 doctors annually for some 8 years. We now have 880. Last year some 145 doctors left the Province, including 25 specialists. We regret that although new registrants have arrived there have been only 5 or 6 specialists. Further, the calibre of general practitioners arriving from Europe does not appear to be of the high standard prior to 1960." [19]

The Medical Care Insurance Commission, however, offered a more optimistic view:

> At present, the only comprehensive listing of doctors in the province, including medical administrators and research personnel as well as private practitioners, is that maintained as the register of the College of Physicians and Surgeons. The count of names on that register, as supplied to the Commission in April, 1962, and four months of 1963 was as follows:

1962	April	899
1963	April	897
	May	908
	June	913
	July	925

> With respect to specialists, the College supplied a list of 218 approved specialists to the Commission in August, 1962. Although this number has been subject to minor fluctuations over the intervening months, the July, 1963, list also named 218 resident specialists.
>
> With respect to physicians in active private practice, the Commission can determine for a given period the number whose bills are represented in claims for insured services. With minor adjustments, this provides an accurate count of *practicing* resident physicians.

19. Dalgleish, "The Saskatchewan Experience."

No. of resident physicians whose bills were included in Commission payments (April–June, 1963)	757
No. of resident physicians known to be in private practice whose bills were not represented	31
Total no. of resident physicians in active private practice	788

As a point of comparison, the Thompson Committee estimated that there were 755 physicians in private practice in June, 1961.[20]

The number of physicians on the College register continued to increase, reaching 1,009 in 1966, not all of whom were engaged in private practice. Nine hundred seventy-seven of these had at least one account represented in Commission payments.

Another point at issue between the doctors and the government concerned payment to radiologists and pathologists. The provincial government was anxious for X-ray and pathology services to be covered under the Hospitalization Act, in which case costs would be shared by the federal government. The College maintained that the Saskatoon Agreement guaranteed that all doctors could choose their method of payment; pathologists and radiologists are doctors, and if the government dictated their reimbursement under the Hospitalization Act it would be a breach of the Agreement.

On June 24, 1963, new regulations were issued which, in effect, were a government concession to the College. Diagnostic X-ray and laboratory services were to be covered under the Medical Care Insurance Act, even where no part of the service was provided in the hospital. These new M.C.I.C. benefits included all X-ray and laboratory procedures provided by either a radiologist or a pathologist, plus an extended list of laboratory procedures provided by a general practitioner or a specialist other than a pathologist.

The College was particularly bitter about the existence and operation of the community health clinics. A province-wide association of local clinics, the Community Health Services Association, had been formed immediately prior to the onset of the strike, and remained active after the strike was settled. By March 1963 almost 15,000 families, representing 50,000 people, had joined the community clinic movement by paying $5.00 for a life membership. Active associations had been formed in thirty-four areas; nineteen of these had secured office space for a doctor, and twenty-four doctors were working in nine operating clinics.

Although the M.C.I.C. had encouraged the formation of the clinics before the strike, with the signing of the Saskatoon Agree-

20. Saskatchewan Medical Care Insurance Commission, *Six Months Report*, January–June, 1963.

ment plans to have someone from the Commission work with the community clinics were dropped. As a result, the clinic people had some feeling of betrayal by the government, and stated in their newsletter of August 13, 1962, "The government had made no contribution, either financial or in personnel to the community health center associations, provincial or local, although Premier Lloyd in a TV address made it clear that the government will uphold the right of citizens to seek a choice."

The College considered the clinics an attempt by the government to provide a salaried service and criticized the decision of the M.C.I.C. that 350 families represented a sufficient practice to allocate a salaried doctor. This opposition may have been one reason why the Commission did not, in fact, follow through on the decision, to the great discomfort of the community clinics. The College also complained that the assignment of a salaried doctor could disrupt the normal practice of medicine in an area and accused the lay leaders of the clinics of indulging in advertising and other unethical practices. It was said that doctors with inferior education and training were being used to staff the clinics, and in smaller communities these doctors were alleged to have harassed and intimidated local practitioners. Further, the Association was charged with using highly paid organizers to stimulate the establishment of clinics for the purpose of bringing in physicians who would support the government politically.

Various methods were employed to discourage doctors from working in the clinics. On the advice of Dr. Peacock, Registrar of the College, the Canadian Medical Association Journal refused to run ads for doctors to work in the community clinics.[21] The College and the Saskatchewan branch of the Canadian Medical Association also approached prospective clinic staff members in Canada and the United Kingdom to urge them not to come to Saskatchewan.[22]

Doctors already practicing in clinics had difficulty in securing cooperation from other doctors in the area, even in emergency cases. In one instance, a clinic doctor was unable to find assistance with the anesthetic for a patient with acute appendicitis because the man he approached was opposed to the concept of community clinics. When the physician complained to the College he was

21. Position paper prepared by Community Health Services Association on March 21, 1963, for meeting with the cabinet. This paper was withdrawn on legal advice.

22. Position paper prepared by Community Health Services Association.

told that physicians who could not comfortably work together should not be forced to do so. The College recommended that he make arrangements to refer his surgery.

By far the largest cause of controversy was the inability of many clinic physicians to gain hospital privileges. One section of the Saskatoon Agreement pledged that doctors were to be considered only on their professional merits when applying for hospital privileges, but complaint after complaint was made that some members of the College were violating this pledge. On April 27, 1963, the government appointed a Royal Commission on Hospital Privileges to inquire into instances of doctors not being appointed to hospital staffs within thirty days of application, or of doctors being suspended, dismissed, or refused staff membership, or otherwise discriminated against. The Commission held hearings in the form of adversary proceedings, and released a report in December which stated: "Seven complaints by five community clinic doctors were heard. None had been granted hospital privileges. This Commission is satisfied that the problem in each case is attributable to the marked division of opinion among Saskatchewan physicians as to how medicine should be practiced. This difference led to a lack of communication which in effect prevented the parties from appreciating clearly the problems to be solved." [23]

In at least one instance, two clinic doctors were granted hospital privileges shortly after the Commission's hearings which had disclosed that the practice of the hospital in question had previously been to grant privileges before doctors were licensed in Saskatchewan, without references, or with references only from nonmedical people. An earlier appeal by the two doctors to the College had only resulted in a finding by the College that cleared the hospital of any charge of discrimination against the clinic doctors.

In 1964 another provincial election was held in Saskatchewan. The C.C.F. lost its majority of seats in the legislature and its twenty year incumbency was ended. The incoming Liberal government, however, made no effort to repeal the Medical Care Insurance Act.

23. M. Woods, *Report on Hospital Staff Appointments*, Regina, December 11, 1963.

Appendix A

Saskatchewan Medical Care Insurance Fund, selected data (000 omitted in dollar accounts).

Category	1965	1964	1963
Income			
Premium	5,573	3,416	5,272
Government grants	14,221	17,486	24,663
Interest	394	410	249
Total income	20,211[a]	21,351[a]	31,153[a]
Cash on hand	7	11	2
Investments on hand	7,900	9,700	–
Total available funds	28,117	31,062	31,155
Payments	21,444	23,155	22,579
Covered population			
Provincial plan	832,937	825,157	810,257
Swift Current Region	54,538	59,067	53,271
	887,475	884,224	863,508
Premiums			
Single person	12	6	12
Family	24	12	24

[a] Includes advances recovered

Appendix B

Excerpt from *Bitter Medicine** by E. A. Tollefson

It was objected, however, that the Act implicitly gave power to the Medical Care Commission to interfere with the practice of medicine to such an extent that the plan would not adhere to the three principles under discussion.** It was said that the commission had this power by virtue of section 9:

9. The commission may, pursuant to this Act and the regulations made by the Lieutenant Governor in Council and by the commission, take such action as it considers necessary for the establishment and administration of a plan of medical care insurance for the residents of Saskatchewan *and the improvement of the quality of the insured services provided under such a plan.* [Italics added.]

Only the most sanguine supporter of state medicine would believe that the words preceding the italicized portion of section 9 empowered the commission to determine the competence and ability of a doctor (principle No. 3), whether a doctor had the right to practice in a hospital (principle No. 4), what type of practice he might do, or where he could practice (principle No. 5). The question is whether the italicized portion of the sentence gave the commission powers inconsistent with these three principles. It is submitted that it did not. The important word in section 9 is "pursuant" [which means "following upon, consequent on and conformable to; in accordance with"] for the section only empowered the commission to take action which was "*pursuant* to this Act and the regulations made by the Lieutenant Governor in Council and by the commission." An examination of the Act fails to reveal any section or regulatory power of any kind which would authorize the commission to take action which would offend against these three principles. As this is important, let us examine the provisions of the Act with some care.

Nothing in the Act suggested that the *status quo* in this regard had been changed. The draftsman was scrupulous to avoid inserting any

* Modern Press, Saskatoon, Saskatchewan, pp. 70–73. Copyrighted in Canada, 1964. Reproduced by permission of the author.

** The statement of policy on health insurance of the Canadian Medical Association enumerated a series of principles which the College of Physicians and Surgeons of Saskatchewan "completely endorsed." The principles under discussion are:

3. That the competence and ability of any doctor is determined only by professional self-government.

4. That within his competence, each physician has the privilege to treat his patients in and out of hospital.

5. That each individual physician is free to select the type and location of his practice.

provision which *directly* authorized action by the commission contrary to these three principles. Did the draftsman allow such interference *indirectly*, by or pursuant to the delegated power to make regulations? Certainly there was nothing in the Act which empowered the Lieutenant Governor in Council to make regulations in connection with the principles in question; therefore there was no possibility of infringement thereof by the commission acting "pursuant to the regulations of the Lieutenant Governor in Council." This leaves only the question whether the commission could have passed regulations itself in this connection and acted pursuant to them. The only provision in the Act which could possibly have had this effect was the much discussed section 49 (1), especially clauses (g) and (l):

49. — (1) Subject to the approval of the Lieutenant Governor in Council, the commission may make regulations for the purpose of establishing and administering a plan of medical care insurance for the residents of Saskatchewan and, without restricting the generality of the foregoing, may make regulations:

(g) prescribing the terms and conditions on which physicians and other persons may provide insured services to beneficiaries;

(l) respecting the maintenance and improvement of the quality of the services provided under this Act, to the end that the highest possible standards of service will be achieved.

In order to operate any insurance scheme (government or otherwise) in a businesslike manner it is necessary to lay down certain minimum procedures that must be followed in submitting claims. Insofar as the quality of insured services is concerned any insurance scheme may provide facilities whereby those providing the services *may* improve the services they give. So long as those providing the services are not compelled to improve the services they give it cannot be said that the scheme is interfering with professional standards. The fear was expressed, however, that clauses (g) and (l) of subsection (1) of section 49 were so broad that the commission could not only pass regulations establishing an efficient claims procedure and offering positive inducements to improve the quality of insured services, but could exercise economic control over physicians by prescribing stringent terms and conditions on which insured services could be provided and could sit in judgment on their professional ability. Such a fear may not have been justified in view of the medical profession's many years of satisfactory experience with the Cancer Commission which has wide discretionary powers of a similar nature. But justified or not the fear was there.

These clauses were not nearly so sweeping in effect as at first sight they appear to be. It should be noted that any regulation made by the commission under section 49 (1) had to meet two requirements: it had to receive the approval of the Lieutenant Governor in Council, and it had to be made "for the purpose of establishing and administering a plan of medical care insurance for the residents of Saskatchewan". Those familiar with constitutional and administrative law will readily appreciate the limitation placed on the commission's regulatory power by the latter phrase. The commission could only make regulations relating to medical care insurance; that is, regulations relating to the insurer's (commission's) obligation to pay the cost of certain types of financial loss (medical expenses) which the insured patients might from time to time incur. Any regulation made for any purpose other than "establishing and administering a plan of medical care insurance" would be beyond the commission's power. If the commission were to make a regulation which purported to determine a physician's competence, or to tell him where or how he might practice, the courts would have little difficulty in finding the regulation to be *ultra vires* [beyond the powers] of the commission. In pith and substance such a regulation would be in relation to the "practice of medicine" rather than a regulation in relation to the "establishing and administering a plan of medical care insurance." Since any such regulation would be a nullity, the commission could take no valid action "pursuant" to such regulation. This important limitation on the commission's power was overlooked by the opponents of the Act, who alleged that the regulatory power of the commission under section 49 (1) was not for the purpose of medical insurance at all but for the purpose of controlling the whole field of medicine. From a legal point of view, such an allegation contains its own denial, for if a regulation by the commission constituted an attempt to control the practice of medicine, rather than to provide insurance, the regulation would be invalid.

Because language is at best an imprecise method for conveying thoughts and intentions, statutes are often difficult to understand. When compared with hosts of other statutory provisions in Canada, section 49 of The Saskatchewan Medical Care Insurance Act appears to be neither badly drafted nor exceptionally indefinite. But this is not to say that it was perfectly drafted. Whenever possible the meaning of a statute should be sufficiently clear that no unnecessary sense of doubt or uneasiness is created. This is especially so where the legislation is likely to be controversial. There is no doubt that certain clauses, particularly clauses (g) and (l), of subsection (1) of section 49 did arouse feelings of suspicion and hostility on the part of many doctors. This was not only unfortunate but also unnecessary, because these clauses could have been modified or deleted without any material legal effect, inasmuch as they neither increased nor decreased the commission's limited regulatory power but were only illustrations of this limited power.

Unionization of the Hospitals in New York City

August 1961

Roy Penchansky

In early 1958, only one of New York City's 85 voluntary hospitals[1] dealt with a union representing its employees. By the close of 1960, 12 voluntary hospitals recognized a union as the representative of their employees, another handful were in the process of being organized by a union, and 37 were signatories to an agreement which required them to abide by the recommendations, in regard to employee relations, of a board on which there was labor representation.

Voluntary hospitals operated without profit, with revenue derived from patients (15 percent),[2] Blue Cross (50 percent), city patients (15 percent), gifts and endowments (10 percent), and other sources (10 percent). They were generally managed by professional administrators and directed by a board of trustees whose members were of considerable stature and financial means. These hospitals were tax exempt and were excluded from the jurisdiction of minimum wage laws and other measures designed to provide employee benefits such as disability and unemployment insurance. Voluntary nonprofit hospitals were not covered by the Taft-Hartley Act; however, states could include nonprofit hospitals in their labor-management legislation if they so chose. Some states, such as Wisconsin, Minnesota, and Colorado had done so, but these were exceptions. In 1958, wage rates for unskilled workers in voluntary hospitals in New York City were between $30 and $40 per week for a 44-hour week.

The municipal hospitals, which were part of the city government and financed through taxation, followed the city's policy of recognizing their employees' right to organize into unions and bargained with these unions. The minimum hiring rate in these

1. New York City's 157 hospitals were divided into three groups: 85 voluntary hospitals having 24,000 beds, 27 municipal hospitals having 19,000 beds, and 45 proprietary hospitals having 5,000 beds.

2. Approximate figures for 1957.

hospitals was $53 per week. The two unions representing the municipal hospital employees were the International Brotherhood of Teamsters and the American Federation of State, County, Municipal Employees.

Proprietary hospitals were privately owned and operated for profit, frequently by doctors. As such, they were subject to the same tax legislation, protective labor legislation, and labor-management relations legislation as any other business. In 1960, the employees of a large number of the proprietary hospitals were represented by the Hotel & Allied Service Employees Union. Most of these contracts had been negotiated initially during the two previous years.

During the depression and World War II numerous attempts had been made to organize the workers in voluntary hospitals in New York City. The unions attempting organization were generally weak and had little ability to oppose management or support the workers in a strike; many of these unions have since ceased to exist. Therefore, although the nonprofessional hospital workers were not reluctant to join unions, the organizing attempts had been largely unsuccessful. Since 1945, there had been little in the way of union activity in the hospitals.

In the mid-1950's, the one voluntary hospital under contract with a union was Maimonides in Brooklyn. This was a small hospital supported by the Federation of Jewish Philanthropies. The union at Maimonides had changed its affiliation as different unions representing government and nonprofit institution employees were established, merged with other organizations, or died. In 1957, the employees at Maimonides were represented by Local 237 of the Teamsters, which represented workers in the New York City municipal hospitals and which later attempted to organize the New York City Police Force and the hospitals in Miami, Florida.

The key person in the Maimonides situation was Eliot Godoff, a pharmacist, who had been involved in the original attempts to organize the voluntary hospitals. When the Maimonides local, which had about 200 members, affiliated with the Teamsters, Godoff became a Teamster organizer.

In about 1957 it became obvious to Godoff that little could be done for the Maimonides workers as long as no other voluntary hospitals were organized; also he was not particularly happy with his role within the Teamsters Union. For these reasons, Godoff visited Leon Davis, President of Local 1199, Drug Employees Union, with whom he was familiar, to seek assistance in finding work as a pharmacist.

Local 1199, Drug Employees Union, was affiliated with the Retail, Wholesale & Department Store Union, AFL–CIO. This local represented 2,100 registered pharmacists, who were mainly Jewish, and 4,900 drugstore employees, which included a substantial number of Negroes and Puerto Ricans, in 1,800 retail drugstores in metropolitan New York and Long Island. This membership represented the workers of over 85 percent of New York City's drugstores. The local was an extremely democratic one, with a high level of member participation in the local's operations as well as its educational, social, and cultural activities.

The Retail, Wholesale & Department Store Union represented mainly unskilled workers drawn from poorly educated, minority groups. The International's largest unit was District 65 in New York City, with over 30,000 members. Local 1199 and District 65 operated in a similar manner and had a history of cooperation and mutual assistance.

Leon Davis, as well as the other officers of Local 1199 and similar unions such as the Building Service Employees and the RWDSU, had long been interested in the workers in the voluntary hospitals and the possibility of organizing the hospitals, though no real effort had been made to do so. These individuals were interested in the hospital workers because of the extremely low wages and poor working conditions and felt it the responsibility of the trade union movement, as well as the general populace, to attempt to alleviate such situations. Also, the hospital work forces were composed largely of members of minority groups, as were the memberships of these other unions, and their leaders felt a responsibility toward these groups. There was also the factor that large numbers of low-paid hospital workers, who were frequently changing employment or were unemployed, made it more difficult for other unions representing unskilled workers to bargain for their memberships and raise their employment standards.

Davis told Godoff that he would be interested in seeing if his union could do something to organize the hospitals. He suggested that if Godoff could get permission to bring the Maimonides workers into 1199, then they would use this group as a core, and Godoff could work at organizing other voluntary hospitals.

The Teamsters were willing to release the Maimonides workers, and they were transferred to 1199. The Teamsters union had not been equipped to do much for these workers and the workers were pleased to become part of a union that could better handle their problem.

Godoff and an organizer from the drugstore staff were assigned to the job of surveying the hospital situation, the employment conditions, and the approaches to organizing, as well as the best place to start organizing.

Early in 1958 it was decided that Montefiore in the Bronx would be the first voluntary hospital Local 1199 would attempt to organize. Montefiore, a large institution with about 850 nonprofessional employees, was chosen because the organizers had contacts with a number of employees who were interested in having the union come into the hospital.

A number of earlier attempts had been made to organize Montefiore only to fail at the first sign of management opposition. The organizers were of the opinion that most of the employees felt that there was no sense in joining a union as it would only fold and because little could be done to improve their position. This attitude was generated by the previous unsuccessful organizing attempts and the complete demoralization of the workers due to their overwhelming economic and social problems. For these same reasons, some unionists felt that these workers could not be organized because they would not band together or be willing to fight to improve their position.

In April of 1958, Local 1199 began its organizing attempts. The union people felt that their most important job was to instill a feeling in the workers that there was some chance of victory. The union's first task was to develop a corps of 60 workers who would form the organizing committee and be the center of operations within the hospital. According to union sources, a tremendous amount of field work over many weeks was necessary to form a group of people who showed leadership abilities and were accepted by their fellow workers; this group had to have the feeling that "we can break through."

As soon as the organizing committee of 60 was established, these individuals began a person-to-person campaign within the hospital. By early June, 500 to 600 workers, comprising a majority of the employees, had joined the union.

Local 1199 then attempted to devise tactics to show management the feeling of the workers and to indicate that, unless recognition was to come from management, the workers, in desperation, would be willing to strike. They also wanted to show that for once there was a union willing to put money and manpower behind the workers.

To show their strength as well as to give the workers a feeling of unity, the union began to call demonstrations before and after work; the workers would come in early, march up and down for an hour or so and then march into work. The same was done after work. Somewhat later the workers refused to eat lunches in the hospital dining rooms and ate at the union headquarters which had been established near the hospital. According to union sources, nurses, doctors, and internes joined in the union boycott of the dining rooms, and they estimated that the boycott was 95 percent effective. As a third approach to show their power, the union had the workers picket in mass formation from six to ten o'clock A.M., a period during which the workers were supposed to be at work, and then the workers would file en masse into work. The demonstrations during working hours were 95 percent effective, a union leader stated. These activities continued throughout the summer and fall.

The union's position among the workers improved, according to union sources, because management in this hospital was quite liberal. Management did not attempt any direct interference with the activities of the union, such as discharge or other forms of discrimination, which might have increased workers' fear of supporting the unions.

After various pressure tactics and a strike vote by the employees, union and hospital leaders in conjunction with the city's labor commissioner, held a series of meetings. They decided to hold an election to see if the union actually represented the majority of the employees. In December, with 95 percent of the nonprofessional employees voting, 628 voted to support the union and 31 were opposed. The hospital signed a contract recognizing Local 1199 as the bargaining agent for the hospital's 850 nonprofessional, technical, and office employees. The contract included, among other items, a maintenance of membership clause, a $30 per month raise over the two-year period of the contract, and an increment system with raises of up to $30 over the two years, this figure varying with the labor grade, a full grievance procedure with arbitration as the final step, seniority provisions, and a 40-hour work week with time and a half for all hours over 40. Under this contract the minimum hiring rate was $40 per week with a $5 per week increase after the first month and another $5 at the end of the sixth month.

The signing of an agreement between Montefiore Hospital and the union had an electrifying effect on the hospital workers in New York City. No longer was there a strong negative feeling or fear among the workers which a union would have to dispel.

The union immediately enlarged its hospital staff. Assisting in the campaign were some 500 drugstore members of 1199 who appeared at hospital gates early in the morning to distribute leaflets and talk union with the hospital workers. The response to the union was overwhelming, not unlike the organizing campaigns which took place in the mass production industries in the 1930's. As one union leader stated, "We did a mail-order business in organizing and received 6,000 to 7,000 membership cards in the mail." All of the organizing material was published in both English and Spanish.

Excerpts from an article by Dan Wakefield entitled, "Victims of Charity," which appeared in *The Nation* on March 14, 1959, provides some feeling for the movement that took place among the hospital workers as well as additional material on the hospital campaign:

> Local 1199 . . . was distributing cards and leaflets at forty-one of the city's eighty-one voluntary hospitals. Meetings were scheduled nearly every night . . . for workers from hospitals all over the city. Requests for information grew — especially from Puerto Rican workers — as *El Diario de Neuva York,* the largest Spanish language daily in the city, published more stories and editorials on what it called "La Cruzada de Local 1199."
>
> "La Cruzada" in many ways is the only union-organizing drive of the fifties that the word "crusade," in any language, seems appropriate to attach to without provoking a tongue in the cheeks of the organizers, or a flush in the cheeks of the reporters looking on. To walk into one of these organizing meetings is to walk back into a time of the five-and-a-half and six-day week, the wages under a dollar an hour, the fears of firing from the boss for "talking union," and the almost revival-meeting enthusiasm of workers suddenly awakened to a way out of their plight.
>
> . . . An organizer . . . was telling them . . . "It is no secret that till recently workers in this city felt a hospital job was one you come into, save a little, and go on. Everyone felt there was no future in hospitals. Now, for the first time, they know that if they organize well enough they can get decent wages and conditions until they can look on hospital work as a job where they can be treated as respectable human beings."

Before the questioning was over, there arose the problem that comes up in all these sessions — the balking of the white-collar and "professional" workers. Clerks and lab technicians don't fare much better than the other workers, but in the grand old tradition, attempt to supplement their income with pride through distinction from the masses. College-trained lab technicians usually make less than $50 a week in these hospitals, but along with the office workers, they are the last to accept the union. It was the constant task of the organizers to remind the other workers that the white-collar brothers and sisters usually didn't make enough to keep their collars white.

The Lenox Hill meeting was about to break up . . . when a lady hesitantly raised her voice to ask what seemed to be a possibly embarrassing question: "Some of the ladies heard they have to pay dues and a big fee to get in the union, and I don't know what to answer 'em." It was the organizer's pleasure to assure the assemblage that "We're not asking hospital workers to give us one penny for dues or anything else — until the day we get a contract for them with better wages and conditions. Then, our dues are $3 a month; but the rest of the union has decided that the hospital workers are getting so little to begin with that they won't have to pay an initiation fee at all."

. . . There to express the shame of neglect and promise of fulfillment from the city's organized labor movement was Morris Iushewitz, secretary of the Central Labor Union Council of New York, who admitted that the 30,000 unorganized toilers in the voluntary hospitals are the "shame of the labor movement" of this city.

Davis told the hall that they were finally making their way out of the wilderness: "I don't know of any organizing drive that took on the kind of crusading spirit that you have — it's taken exactly three weeks and two days to get the majority signed up at Mount Sinai . . . This is the beginning of a new day — a new day of dignity and self-respect. The hospitals will never be the same and the workers will never be the same."

After their long sleep, the hospital workers have awakened with impatience and outrage. There is still a long way to go before the traditional nonunion front of the voluntary hospitals is broken, but the first break has come and thousands of workers are knocking at the white-painted walls. Already a major step toward better conditions has been brought about by the union drive through a $12,000,000 increase in the city's payment to voluntary hospitals, announced last month by the mayor. The city contributes $16 a day for each ward patient in the voluntary hospitals, but the cost of maintaining these patients is $24 a day. The new grant will mean an increase to $20 a day for each ward patient, effective July 1; and in three more years the grant will rise to $24 a day. It has been the argument of the nonprofit voluntary institutions that they already operate at a deficit, and can't afford to increase workers' wages. The union can now point to the increase as a source to be used for this purpose.

The union's organizing drive was accompanied by an extensive publicity campaign aimed at impressing the public with the plight of the hospital workers. The *New York Times* editorial for March 7, 1959, part of which follows, is representative of the position taken by the press and the public in general:

> Obviously the nonprofit hospitals face an acute problem in granting wage increases — with all their costs rising ever closer to the limits of income from charitable giving and from charges to their patients. Also, the thought of a strike, even by the nonprofessional employees, is naturally upsetting to the nerves.
>
> But why should workers performing the same kind of jobs as in private employment be asked to be philanthropists by accepting much lower wages and the human sufferings that follow? And why should collective bargaining be denied them when that is a policy overwhelmingly approved by the American public? As for a hospital strike, the likelihood is exceedingly remote. Surely, if one did occur, an outraged public opinion, not to mention action by the courts, would quickly put a stop to it — and hamper further unionization as well.
>
> Those wise in the ways of labor-management relations know that, given widespread employee dissatisfaction and a truly representative organization, it is far better to deal with a union than to resist it. Formal grievance procedures and two-way communications alone can often do a great deal to increase morale and effective job performance. To slam the door shut on such advantages may well have precisely the opposite effect in the voluntary hospitals.

The tremendous reaction of the hospital workers and the wide public attention given to the hospital problems had one serious negative effect on the union; it instigated a unification of the hospitals within their association, the Greater New York Hospital Association, in opposition to the efforts of the union. The hospitals had not unified in support of Montefiore as, according to one hospital official, they felt that unionization would not become a general problem. When the hospitals saw the Montefiore situation turn into a larger movement, they consolidated their opposition to 1199.

The union leaders had considered a hospital-by-hospital organizing campaign and this might not have consolidated the opposition. However, they later concluded that the mass movement and widespread organizing was to their benefit because it focused the public's attention on the situation, and the hospital drive became a crusade and not solely "a union's attempt to organize some hospital workers." Also, during the campaign, 1199 received extensive support from other unions; this support might not have been forthcoming if the campaign had not been so widely publicized or so massive.

Although the union had a large staff to use in organizing and was willing to expend considerable sums of money, it could not carry on a campaign in 30 or 40 hospitals at once. Also, having large numbers of signed membership cards did not mean that the union had a strong operating unit in the hospitals. The union therefore, after the first burst of activity, decided to retrench and consolidate its position.

The union established four subheadquarters near hospitals in which it had strong worker support. Operating through these centers, the union staff developed its local leadership and established an organizing committee for each hospital. Demonstrations, similar to those used at Montefiore, were carried out to show the strength and unity of the workers to the hospital administrators as well as to the workers themselves.

The union concentrated its efforts on about 15 hospitals. As a majority was reached in each of these institutions, Leon Davis sent a letter to the administrators stating that Local 1199 represented a majority of their employees and requesting that they meet with the union to discuss recognition and a contract. The hospital administrators refused to meet with the union. On innumerable occasions the union also attempted personal contacts with various people affiliated with the hospitals to establish conferences with management, but these too were unsuccessful. As one union leader stated, the issue became "Will they talk to us? The hospital answer was, no, that they would not meet the union and that they would not recognize the union." By April 1, 1959, the union claimed a majority of 15 hospitals and the memberships at five had already voted to strike if union recognition was not forthcoming.

The Greater New York Hospital Association advised its member hospitals to refrain from dealing with the union. According to law the hospitals were not required to recognize the union. A *Wall Street Journal* article on April 2, 1959, reported on the hospitals' position.

"We don't deny that we pay a low wage," says Joseph Terenzio, the tense, dark-haired young executive director of Knickerbocker Hospital. "We want to pay higher wages but we are paying as much as we can right now." He points to a chart sketching in red ink more than five years of ascending deficits. "What do these union people expect us to do, open up a trap door in the floor and pull out a big bag of money?"

Dr. I. Magelaner, executive director of Jewish Hospital of Brooklyn, says flatly, "Wage increases cannot be given when the money does not exist."

. . . So far, most of the hospitals have taken the position that they will not deal with the unions in any way. This stand apparently is based on hospital administrators' contentions that the unions, if recognized, would interfere with the care of patients.

"Everyone in a hospital, from the janitor to the head nurse, has one purpose, the care of patients," argues New York Hospital's Dr. Pratt in a calm, patient voice. "We do not want a third party — a union or anyone else without responsibility — to stand between the patient and the people who are charged with his care."

Unions, some other hospital officials speculate, might want to set up hiring halls where union officials could determine who goes to work in a hospital — or unions might want to have a firm say about whether an employee should or should not be fired.

However, the main ground for opposition to the union drive undoubtedly is financial. Hospital leaders in New York like to point to Minneapolis as an example of what might happen if union demands are granted.

Costs per patient per day, at hospitals where Local 113 of the Building Service Employees Union has obtained a contract, are estimated at $38 to $40, compared with the $27 to $35 in New York City. In Minneapolis, orderlies earn $250 a month to start and $266 after two years. Unskilled workers such as dishwashers earn $235 monthly and $251 after two years. A hospital official in Minneapolis figures this is $60 to $80 a month more than in nonunion hospitals in "comparable cities."

The impact is equally pronounced in Blue Cross rates in Minneapolis. An official of Swedish Hospital there reports, "Our Blue Cross full family group contract is around $10 a month, probably the highest for comparable coverage in the nation." In New York, it is $5.34 and roughly comparable plans cost $9 monthly in Denver, $5.75 in Durham, N.C., and $9.55 in Fargo, N.D., according to other hospital officials. (Blue Cross health coverage is handled by 25 different regional member associations; benefits offered by these associations often vary slightly so premium comparisons are not completely indicative of the respective costs of coverage.)

Similarly, in the San Francisco–Oakland area about 23 hospitals with a work force of 2,900 employees are unionized. The average in-patient cost is slightly over $40 a day per patient, according to W. J. Kramer, executive secretary of the San Francisco Hospital Conference. He says costs have been rising 4% to 5% a year and he expects them to go up another 4% by 1960. However, Mr. Kramer believes the steady wage increases there are not due so much to unionization as to San Francisco's "generally high wage levels." Hospital wages there start at $58.90 a week for the lowest-scaled employees.

Wage levels comparable to these would have an immediate effect on New York's already deficit-ridden hospitals. Last year, for example, New York Hospital had an operating deficit of more than $1 million. Knickerbocker Hospital, with operating costs of $2 million a year, went into the red by $156,000.

To get cash to cover the deficits, New York hospitals are having to borrow from the principal of their endowment funds, which generally have no restrictions on their use, in addition to using interest on their endowment funds and soliciting contributions from the public.

They also are pushing hard to get a 20% boost in the amount the local Blue Cross plan pays the New York hospitals. This figure now amounts to $26 a day for a patient with Blue Cross coverage.

Blue Cross itself is running into serious money troubles. Last year, New York's plan, known officially as the Associated Hospital Service of New York, asked state authorities for a 40% increase in premiums to cover mounting losses. The state, after hearing strong complaints from consumer groups and some labor unions, trimmed the allowable increase to 22%. The result, according to Blue Cross officials, was a deficit of more than $20 million in the Association's operations. The Association has indicated it will appeal again to the state for a higher premium very shortly.

Because of the swift spread of Blue Cross in recent years, hospitals have become increasingly dependent upon its payments. "About 40% of our in-patient income is from Blue Cross," says Dr. Pratt of New York hospital.

Most nonprofit hospitals also are charity institutions, with indigent patients taking up a large share of the beds. In New York, the city pays $16 a day to the hospitals to handle these public-charge patients. But this falls far short of actual costs, says the administrators. New York City has promised to boost these payments to $20 a day in July and to make additional $1 and $2 yearly increases in the future.

With so much of their income controlled by the city governments and Blue Cross, hospitals say that a mere increase in their charges to private patients who are able to pay hospital bills will not be enough to solve their problems. "We raised our rates an average of 10% last year, and got only an additional $10,000 of income," says an official of Knickerbocker hospital.

According to union sources the hospitals attempted to negate their organizing campaign by the following tactics:

(1) publicly making promises to improve wages and working conditions;

(2) attacking the union as being racketeers whose sole interest was taking money from the workers through dues;

(3) firing workers who were active in organizing for the union; and

(4) threatening injunctions because of their claim of the illegality of striking hospitals.

Soon after basic organization was established among the hospital workers, 1199 established a steward's body, parallel to the steward's body for drug employees, which became the chief policy and operating group within the hospital division. On April 8, after a meeting of this body, Davis announced a strike deadline of April 22 in six voluntary hospitals unless management recognized and bargained with the union. The hospitals involved were Mount Sinai, Jewish Hospital of Brooklyn, Bronx Hospital, Beth David, Beth Israel and Lenox Hill. The union claimed to represent 3,450 of the 4,500 nonprofessional, technical and office workers in these hospitals. The strike vote, according to the union, was 2,630 for, 111 against.

The union also claimed majorities at Knickerbocker, Flower-Fifth Avenue, Beth-El, Polyclinic, University, and Long Island Jewish Hospital.

The strike deadline announcement heightened interest in the hospital situation. The press, in general, called upon the hospitals to negotiate with the union. Mayor Wagner became increasingly involved and began a series of conferences with the parties. Since the hospital administrators would not meet with 1199's officers, Harry Van Arsdale, Jr., and Morris Iushewitz, President and Secretary, respectively, of the City Central Labor Council, and William Michelson of District 65, represented 1199 in these conferences.

A number of proposals were presented for settlement of the strike issues, including one from the *New York Times*; but the hospital administrators rejected any compromise plan that would in any way mean recognition of the union. The position of the hospitals was that they rejected any third party — such as a labor union — which might intervene between hospitals and their patients. Davis stated that he was willing to submit to a representation election and, if the union won, to write a no-strike clause into contracts and submit all contract and contract renewal disputes to arbitration.

On April 21 the mayor held an all-day conference with the parties. At this conference he proposed a three-man fact finding board which would investigate the issues and make recommendations. The union agreed to a two-week postponement of the strike, and the hospital administrators agreed to present the plan to their boards of trustees for a decision.

During the two-week interval numerous individuals and organizations called upon the hospitals to accept the mayor's fact finding proposal. Among the individuals were Mrs. Franklin D. Roosevelt, former Senator Herbert A. Lehman, Senator Jacob K. Javits, and representatives of the NAACP and various religious groups.

During this same period the New York Blue Cross added three leading labor officials to its board of directors. At that time the New York City Central Labor Council, which was supporting the demands of the hospital workers, was opposing Blue Cross attempts to increase its rates.

Another interesting issue was the threat by the Amalgamated Clothing Workers to cut off their normal "substantial" support of the Federation of Jewish Philanthropies if the federation-affiliated hospitals continued to refuse to engage in collective bargaining with the union. All but two of the six strike-threatened hospitals were federation-affiliated.

On May 5, three days before the strike deadline, the hospitals, in rejecting Mayor Wagner's plan, stated: (1) that they were not required to bargain; (2) that having a union meant possible strikes which would interfere with the operations of the hospitals; (3) that the hospitals should not and could not bargain because of their financial plight since the union would not take cognizance of this and other hospital problems; and (4) that they would carry out a program to improve the wages and working conditions of their employees.

The program was:

1. *Wages.* The increase of $4 in the payments made by the city to voluntary hospitals would be devoted to increasing wages and hiring rates of hospital employees.

2. *Minimum rates.* No employee would be hired or paid less than $1 an hour.

3. *Hours.* No employee's regular work week would exceed 40 hours.

4. *Overtime.* Overtime rates would be established for any work in excess of 40 hours per week.

5. *Rate ranges.* Job grades would be established with suitable rate ranges and with equitable progressions within the ranges.

6. *Fringes.* Practices in regard to holidays, vacations, sick leave, insurance, etc., vary from hospital to hospital . . . each hospital will review such practices and, in consultation with an advisory committee representing all the voluntary hospitals, will endeavor to improve these practices wherever equitable and feasible.

7. *Discrimination.* The hospitals will make known to their employees their recognition of the right of any employee to join

or remain a member of a union without fear of discrimination.

8. *Seniority*. At each hospital a list of employees in accordance with their seniority will be prepared. Seniority is defined as the amount of continuous employment within a job classification.

9. *Grievance procedure*. The hospitals will provide for their employees appropriate grievance and appeal procedures for processing personal grievances regarding working conditions or individual wage adjustments.

10. *Permanent administrative committee*. [With the committee composed of people chosen by the hospitals] to supervise the proper and fair effectuation of the above program; and

To engage annually . . . in a review of the wage levels and personnel policies; to engage such professional assistance and advice as it may deem necessary, and to recommend improvements or modifications in light of the various economic developments of the last year and the economic circumstances of the individual hospitals.

Davis answered the hospitals:

> Local 1199 has made it abundantly clear that if the hospitals would submit to arbitration by an impartial board and agree to abide by its recommendations, there need not now or ever be a strike in any hospital . . . if a strike proves necessary as appears likely now, the fault will lie exclusively with the callous and stubborn men whose opposition to unions leads them to endanger the entire community.

The immediate public and press reaction, although there was strong support for the hospital workers, was that there should not be a strike against the hospitals. The *New York Times* editorialized:

> These terms [the improvements proposed by the hospitals] still fall short of what the union has asked — namely, union recognition and collective bargaining. No issue, however, is important enough, or provocation great enough, to justify a strike that would hamper the recovery of helpless invalids.

Upon notifying the mayor of their answer, the hospitals applied for and received court orders staying a walkout at the six hospitals. The order called on the union to show why the stay as well as a temporary injunction should not be issued. The orders were not served, however, as "Davis' whereabouts were unknown."

The mayor continued in his attempts to find a basis of settlement which would avert the threatened strike.

In viewing the question of striking, the leaders of 1199 were not concerned with the possibility of personal imprisonment but were reluctant to call a strike as it might involve serious consequences, such as loss of jobs and imprisonment, for some workers. For this reason, the leaders stated, they told the membership of their sentiments and left the final decision on striking to a vote of the stewards' body. On the evening preceding the strike deadline the stewards voted to strike.

On May 8, 1959, the six hospitals were struck. Two weeks later picketing began at Flower-Fifth Avenue Hospital. Union sources stated that this hospital was not struck with the original group because its management was meeting with the union and they felt that an agreement would be reached. The union sources stated further that it was pressure from the hospital association on Flower-Fifth Avenue which thwarted the settlement efforts.

Every major newspaper in New York City, except one, condemned the strike. The *New York Times* called for a law prohibiting strikes by hospital employees and noted that "the union's contemptuous disregard of court injunctions has made an already ugly situation worse. Whatever public sympathy the union may have developed has now been largely wiped out."

Contempt proceedings were started against Davis and other union officials. Davis was still not to be found and there was a series of postponements in the court actions. Since the court orders had not been personally served on union officials, there was disagreement as to whether the strike was illegal. The hospitals claimed "substituted service" of the court orders.

Although there was some feeling that the hospital workers had lost public support by striking, they did receive assistance from many sources; other unionists joined their picket lines, unions lent manpower and gave money, food and money were donated by the public, the building trades unions stopped work on hospital construction, and other unionists such as the laundry workers refused to cross the picket lines. Over the course of the strike, labor contributions amounted to $100,000 with an additional $25,000 from other sources. District 65 lent twelve organizers; Local 3, International Brotherhood of Electrical Workers, lent three organizers; and the regional office of the AFL–CIO, two organizers. No attempt was made to have the Teamsters Union honor the picket lines.

The union claimed that its strike was 90 percent effective, while the hospitals claimed that their service was not affected. It is doubtful that the strike remained 90 percent effective over its entire life. Similarly, hospital service must have been affected, and increasingly so over time, since the hospital staffs were reduced, frozen dinners were served, paper plates were used, little cleaning was done, and deliveries and admissions were reduced. The hospitals did receive a great deal of volunteer assistance to replace the strikers, though union sources claim (and they say that this information was acquired from management) that on the important tasks this assistance was more a hindrance than help.

The union attempted to guard against the consequences of being charged with a calamity that could be traced to the strike by volunteering to have members perform emergency services at the request of any doctor. This offer was accepted in several instances.

The mayor continued in his efforts to promote a settlement. Most of the settlement plans presented excluded any direct union recognition but included grievance procedures in which the union could represent the employees. During the first weeks of the strike the hospitals rejected every proposition which in any way meant the involvement of the union in hospital activities. At one of the mayor's conferences a charge was leveled against management which was to become a recurring theme throughout the strike: that the hospitals were abusing minority groups.

Since five of the struck hospitals were in Manhattan, while one was in Brooklyn, the legal action was taking place in two courts. By May 15, the Manhattan Court still had not issued the injunction which was requested by the hospitals. The judge had issued a series of temporary orders and there had been a number of postponements. In Brooklyn, however, an injunction was issued and the judge began hearings on why the officers of the union and strikers should not be held in contempt of court. These hearings were later postponed.

On May 20, the strikers voted on a hospital plan to settle the dispute. This plan included a proposal to arbitrate grievances with the union recognized in the arbitration step and only in that step. The plan also included the economic and fringe benefits which the hospitals had proposed earlier. The strikers vetoed this proposal because it did not include union recognition.

With the rejection of their offer by the strikers, the hospitals attempted to end the strike through legal action. After Davis' attendance at the strikers' meeting, he was served with a legal order from the Brooklyn court to show cause why he should not be cited for contempt of court. The Manhattan judge ordered an immediate trial for a permanent injunction.

The union began a campaign of secondary boycotts at the sites of businesses owned by trustees of the struck hospitals. Such establishments as Macy's, Blumstein's Department Store, and the offices of Webb & Knapp were picketed.

A series of services aside from strike benefits and food packages were arranged for the strikers by the union. The daily strike bulletins, which included news and union announcements, also noted the availability of free medical care through the Health Insurance Plan of Greater New York, reimbursement of bus fare, emergency dental care, and the extension of credit from credit bureaus and landlords for strikers.

In the Brooklyn court action Davis was found guilty of contempt of court, and a fifteen-day prison sentence was ordered. However, the punishment was never executed. In Manhattan an injunction was issued but was never enforced. It became obvious that no one would act on the court orders. To jail the union leaders would probably only serve to increase the already increasing public support for the strikers, and also there were too many strikers to jail. Similarly, with the strikers composed largely of Negroes and Puerto Ricans and the growing charges of "abuse of minorities" and "economic segregation," no one wanted to take responsibility for any action against these groups.

At the beginning of June the mayor established a special committee to study the strike situation. On June 9 this committee made a series of recommendations for settlement of the strike. The report accepted the hospitals' previous economic proposals, which they had already instituted, as well as the plan for a permanent administrative committee, but added,

> Any interested person, including representatives of any union, will have the right to appear before the permanent administrative committee during its annual review to present his views.

In regard to grievances the committee stated:

> There shall be established in each hospital a clearly stated grievance procedure proceeding from the first step in which the aggrieved employee presents his grievance to the appropriate supervisor to a second step in which the aggrieved employee presents his grievance to the personnel manager or administrator or other designated official of the hospital.
>
> The third step shall be to transfer the grievance to mediation by

two adjusters, one chosen by the hospital management and the other chosen by the employees in the hospital. The adjusters shall meet outside of the hospital unless they mutually agree otherwise.

If the two adjusters are unable to mediate the grievance they may by mutual agreement add a third adjuster chosen from a panel of responsible and experienced persons established by the parties. The function of the adjusters shall be wholly mediatory.

If the dispute is not settled by mediation it shall go on to arbitration and the aggrieved employee shall be entitled to representation before the arbitrator or arbitrators by anyone he may designate. The arbitrator's decision shall be final.

This proposal was accepted by the union but rejected by the hospitals.

In Manhattan the withdrawal of the judge from the strike case meant the presiding of a new judge over the hospitals' attempts to acquire contempt citations against the union. On June 13, in a somewhat surprising turn of events, Justice Henry Epstein upheld the right of voluntary hospital workers to organize, engage in collective bargaining, and strike when management refused to resolve their problems. Appendix I is the full text of the decision.

On June 22, 1959, an agreement was reached in settlement of the 46-day-old hospital strike. The important clauses are reproduced below:

1. *Wage Increases and Minimum Rates*

No employee will be hired or paid less than $1.00 per hour and a wage increase of at least $2.00 per week shall be given to each employee whose wage rate has not been increased by $2.00 or more per week by lifting minimum hourly rate to $1.00. All employees will continue to receive the advances in wages already put into effect by the hospitals. Commitments made by individual hospitals prior to and during the strike relative to wages, working conditions and fringe benefits will be fully honored and enforced.

2. *Regular Work Week and Overtime*

On and after July 1, 1959, no employee's regular work week will exceed 40 hours. As of July 1, 1959, overtime rates of time and one-half will be established for any work in excess of 40 hours per week.

3. *Permanent Administrative Committee*

A Permanent Administrative Committee of 12 members to be composed of six Hospital Trustees to be named by the Greater New York Hospital Association and six representatives of the public not associated with the Hospitals or Labor to be designated by the Chief Judge of the New York Court of Appeals will be established for the following purposes:

(a) to supervise the proper and fair effectuation of the above program;

(b) to engage annually, 60 days prior to July 1, 1960, and July 1 of each year thereafter, in a review of the wage levels, job grades, rate ranges, fringe benefits, seniority rules and personnel policies then prevailing in each of the voluntary hospitals; to engage such professional assistance and advice as it may deem necessary in the furtherance of its task; and to recommend to each of the hospitals on July 1st of each year improvements or modifications in existing wage levels and personnel practices in the light of the various economic developments of the past year and the economic circumstances of the individual hospitals. Any interested person, including representatives of any union, will have the right to appear before the Permanent Administrative Committee during its annual review to present his views.

4. *Grievances*

There shall be established in each hospital a clearly stated grievance procedure proceeding from the first step, in which the aggrieved employee presents his grievance to his appropriate supervisor, to a final step in which he presents his grievance to the Personnel Manager or administrator, or other designated official of the hospital. If unresolved at the final step of the hospital's grievance procedure, a grievance may be submitted to mediation and arbitration outside the hospital before a person, who shall act as mediator and arbitrator, to be appointed as hereinafter provided. In such mediation and arbitration the aggrieved employee may be represented by anyone he may designate. Upon such submission outside the hospital the representative of the aggrieved employee and the designee of the hospital may first jointly attempt to resolve the grievance without the participation of the mediator and arbitrator. The arbitrator's decision shall be final.

The person who acts as mediator and arbitrator shall be selected in accordance with the Voluntary Labor Arbitration Rules of the American Arbitration Association. The arbitrator shall have jurisdiction only over disputes arising over grievances as hereinafter defined and shall not have the power to alter, amend or vary any rules, regulations or provisions established by the hospital.

Grievances, including those subject to arbitration, are defined as individual grievances arising out of the interpretation, application or claimed breach of the rules and regulations in the hospital, including the provisions that are a part of this Statement of Policy, provided, however, that dismissals based upon lack of professional competence or incompetence, including all matters involving relations with or conduct of any employee towards patients, shall not be subject to the grievance procedure or to arbitration except when the employee claims that the dismissal has been made for reasons other than professional competence or incompetence, in which case that issue, as distinguished from the question of professional competence or incompetence, may be submitted to the grievance procedure, with the burden of proof upon the employee.

5. *Wage Structures*

Not later than October 1, 1959, each hospital shall establish job grades with suitable rate ranges and with equitable progression within the ranges, shall review practices in regard to holidays, vacations, sick leave, insurance, etc., endeavoring to improve these practices wherever equitable and feasible, and shall establish seniority rules. Interested persons, including the representatives of any union, may present their views to the Permanent Administrative Committee and the Committee may make recommendations to each hospital on these matters.

Aside from the 7 struck hospitals, 20 some other hospitals, making a total of over 30 hospitals, signed the Statement of Policy. Of this group about 20 were Catholic hospitals in which Local 1199 had no organization. During the following 18 months a number of additional hospitals became signatories to the Statement of Policy.

The union stated that it was very unhappy with the way the hospitals carried out the Statement of Policy and the way the Permanent Administrative Committee, which had no union members, operated.

In regard to the grievance procedure, which each hospital established in its own way, a union spokesman stated, "The hospitals established an obstacle course." Some of the hospitals had as many as seven steps in the grievance procedure. All of the grievances had to be filed in writing, yet many of the workers in the hospitals were not able to write. Similarly, whenever a worker was dissatisfied with the answer at one step, he had to file a written request to take the grievance to the next step. The hospitals, the union stated, also used special grievance forms which frequently were not available to the workers. There were limits on the time in which the workers could bring and move the grievance through the procedure while the hospital itself had no time limits. Additionally, in the early steps of the procedure no attempts were made to sit down and settle grievances with the union; and further, when the union became involved in the grievance procedure before the arbitration step there was still no attempt at settlement. The union also charged that whenever a grievance was brought to the arbitration step the hospital would claim that it was not arbitrable.

In regard to the policy statement which required the hospitals to establish rate ranges by October 1, 1959, the union stated that the hospitals had done nothing by that date. The PAC stated, in February 1960, that the hospitals had done everything that was required. The union claimed that only Mount Sinai and one other hospital had in any way attempted to establish rate ranges.

In the hospitals that were signatories to the Statement of Policy, the union had no union security and payment of union dues was at the discretion of the individual worker. A union spokesman stated that the hospitals paid a toll for their opposition tactics and the union's lack of security. If the union was to continue to prove its worth to the workers and keep the membership active and interested, it had to show that the union was needed and useful. To accomplish this the union leaders and stewards continuously looked for problems and stimulated dissension between the workers and hospitals. Exhibit 1 shows one technique in such activity.

The body of stewards which the union had established, though having no formal status in the signatory hospitals, became a key union force. The stewards advised the employees on grievances and were the stimulus to the employees in pushing grievances; they were the reporters to the union on work problems as well as the organizers within the hospitals and the dues collectors. They also helped to carry out the union's social, educational, and legislative campaigns.

The amount of turnover among unskilled hospital employees had been extremely high, frequently reaching 200 or 300 percent per year. With the improvement in wages and working conditions and the other effects which accompanied 1199's organizing activities, turnover was significantly reduced. However, it was still of such magnitude that the union stewards had to work continually at organizing to sustain the union in the signatory hospitals.

According to union sources, it could be stated generally that the signatory hospitals were attempting to fight the union through the Statement of Policy and the PAC; they made no attempt whatsoever to deal with the workers and live up to the policies that had been established. The hospitals, they stated, told the workers that there was no union, that there never would be one, and that the union was not aiding them. In the spring of 1960 the union decided that they could not survive under this kind of relationship, as it was impossible for the union to protect its membership and the members would, therefore, in a matter of time, quit the union.

The union decided it would have to have direct recognition and after a meeting of its steward body notified the hospitals to this effect. The hospitals answered that they were signatories to the Statement of Policy and that they would have nothing beyond that to do with the union.

In April 1960 the union held a strike vote at ten hospitals. In these institutions the union had from 35 to 70 percent of the work force as members. In the balloting a majority of the workers in the ten hospitals voted to strike, and the union claims the vote was, on the average, eight to one for striking.

At that time Dave Livingston, who was the head of District 65, represented Local 1199 in a series of conferences with the hospitals and the mayor. Livingston stated that the union wanted PAC to be an impartial body, and a sensible grievance procedure should be established to protect the workers. Similarly, the union desired a situation in which the hospitals were not going to attempt to destroy their organization but would allow a live-and-let-live atmosphere. Following these conferences and a union threat to strike, there was a basic change in the Statement of Policy. The major changes were:

The PAC became a six-man public body. This group was to consult with three-man committees from labor and management in making its annual reports and recommendations. The PAC's purposes were:

(1) To supervise the proper and fair effectuation of the program outlined in this Statement of Policy.

(2) To engage annually, at least sixty days prior to July 1 of each year, in a review of job grades, rate ranges, fringe benefits, seniority rules, and personnel policies then prevailing in all the subscribing voluntary hospitals; to issue a General Report on its general findings applicable to all the subscribing hospitals; to recommend to each of the hospitals during the month of July of each year improvements or modifications in existing wage levels and personnel practices in light of the various economic developments of the past year and the economic circumstances of the individual Hospital. In the event the Permanent Administrative Committee determines to conduct public hearings during its annual review, it shall, by suitable notice, provide any interested person the opportunity to present his views. On or about July 1 of each year, the Permanent Administrative Committee shall issue its Reports resulting from the annual review to the subscribing hospitals. Information submitted by each hospital shall be considered confidential at the request of such hospital. Each hospital shall formally advise the Permanent Administrative Committee of its acceptance or rejection of the recommendations not later than thirty days after receipt thereof. Upon receiving such formal acceptance or rejection from all the hospitals, but in no event later than thirty days after issuance to such hospitals, the Permanent Administrative Committee shall make such Reports available to all interested persons.

(3) To act, through one or more of its members or other designees as the Arbitrator for unresolved grievances as outlined and limited below.

The establishment of a simplified and uniform grievance procedure which included:

If unresolved at the final step of the Hospital's grievance procedure, a grievance may be submitted for resolution outside the Hospital in accordance with the following procedure: The aggrieved employee may be represented by anyone he may designate. Before mediation and/or arbitration on any such grievance as hereinafter provided, the representative of the aggrieved employee and the designee of the Hospital may first, jointly attempt to resolve such grievance.

With the formal changes in the Statement of Policy the union reported that the attitude of the administrators of many of the hospitals changed. The administrators were more willing to sit down directly with the union in an attempt to settle problems, and in early 1961 more and more hospitals were exhibiting this change in attitude in their relations with the union.

The Statement of Policy was revised during the period in which the original PAC was carrying out its first annual review. Its final report, a product of the original committee, took into account the changes in the Statement of Policy which were agreed to, such as the uniform and simplified grievance procedure. The committee's report made the following recommendations with the procedures for accomplishing the same spelled out in detail:

(1) Sounder and more equitable wage rates at improved levels.

(2) Clearer and more definite provisions concerning hours and overtime.

(3) Simpler and more workable grievance machinery.

(4) Clearer and more definite provisions regarding seniority and related subjects.

(5) Improved and regularized benefits.

(6) Clearer, simpler statements of all your policies and practices.

A number of voluntary hospitals that signed the Statement of Policy were homes for the aged, which were a somewhat different type of economic and operating unit from the general class of voluntary hospitals. The homes were small, had large numbers of indigent patients, and received no income from Blue Cross, but received most of their income through the City Welfare Department. Instead of receiving a fixed daily rate from the city, as did the regular voluntary hospitals, the homes were reimbursed on the basis of operating costs for the previous year. According to a union source, these homes operated as a group within the hospital association and had somewhat different problems than the other hospitals.

In one of the homes, Daughters of Jacob, the union had a very large majority. In May 1960 the union notified the hospital they would strike if direct recognition was not forthcoming. One of the reasons that pressure was applied at this specific hospital was because the trustees, or at least one trustee, was considered to be favorable toward the unions, and 1199 felt, therefore, that the hospital would capitulate. After the strike threat the union was recognized as the representative of the employees and as part of the contract received a union shop clause.

Pressure was then applied to another home, Beth Abraham, which was a signatory to the Statement of Policy. The union used pressure tactics, and during one of these demonstrations, in which the employees remained off their jobs, the hospital fired all the participants. A picket line was established by the union and continued for six days. The strike was terminated with the agreement that all employees would be returned to their jobs and the hospital would meet with the union on worker grievances. Since the hospital was, in fact, dealing with the union and because pressure was applied to pro-union directors, the board of trustees decided to recognize the union as the representative of the workers, and a contract was signed which included a union shop clause.

With the recognition of the union by these two homes the stage was set for other hospitals of this type to do the same. In 1961, Local 1199 represented the employees in six homes throughout the city.

Local 1199, during its original campaign, organized the workers at University Hospital, which was one of New York's largest voluntary institutions and part of New York University. This hospital was not struck with the original group, but the union, toward the middle of the strike, did decide to extend the strike to this institution. At that time, however, private meetings began between the union and the hospital trustees, and the strike was forestalled. After extended negotiations the hospital agreed to recognize the union as the representative of the employees. A contract was not signed until April 1960 and it did not include any form of union security.

In the spring of 1960, the union began to organize the workers in Trafalgar Hospital. This hospital was not a member of the Greater New York Hospital Association, and while it had not signed the Statement of Policy it had established wages and conditions similar to those required under that agreement. The union did not carry out the usual demonstrations that were used in other hospitals; they went directly to the hospital and requested recognition. Since the administrators were aware that 75 to 80 percent of the workers were members of the union and that the union would strike them, they began to negotiate. Although it took a number of months, a three-year agreement was reached. This was the first agreement which had an "almost permanent no-strike clause," the intent of which was clearly to have no strikes during the life of the agreement or in negotiating new contract terms. The union agreed that if negotiations failed arbitration would be the settlement procedure. The first contract included a union shop provision and called for a $45 minimum for a 40-hour week or a $5 general increase for the individual, whichever was greater. Because of the permanent no-strike clause, this contract received a great deal of attention and acclaim from the New York newspapers.

By April 1961, Local 1199 had contracts with 12 hospitals and was negotiating with a number of hospitals in which it had functioning units. There was little doubt that recognition would be forthcoming from the latter institutions.

In the spring of 1961, after reviewing the organizing activities of Local 1199 during the two previous years, the head of the hospital division stated, "We have made more economic progress than organizational progress." At that time the union had 3,700 members whose dues were not more than three months in arrears. Of the group whose dues were from three to six months in arrears, the union leader felt that 1,500 or 1,600 could be considered active members. In the hospitals which were not signatories to the Statement of Policy or which did not recognize the union no attempt was made to collect dues from the employees who were union members. At the end of the strike in 1959 the union had 2,700 members; the potential membership was estimated at 35,000.

The union's organizational progress was hampered, one leader stated, by the opposition of the hospitals during the first year under the Statement of Policy and the high rate of turnover among the employees.

District 65 continued to support Local 1199's organizing activities with manpower and money after the 1959 strike was settled. It was agreed that in 1960 and 1961, District 65 would share in the deficit Local 1199 incurred in its hospital division. This deficit was about $50,000 in 1960 and would be a similar amount in 1961. As noted earlier, the head of District 65 represented Local 1199 in the meetings which led to the revision of the Statement of Policy in 1960.

In 1959 the New York State Legislature enacted bills extending the State Disability Benefits Law and a dollar-an-hour minimum wage to the employees of nonprofit institutions. This legislation could be accounted for by union activity and public concern with the problems of workers in institutions such as the voluntary hospitals.

In the spring of 1961 Leon Davis was asked how his union was going to get direct recognition and bargaining in the signatory hospitals. He answered in the following way: first, the union could promote changes in the law to require the hospitals to bargain; then all that would be needed was a majority of the employees, and that would not be difficult to obtain. He noted that the union had already been successful in some of its legislative activities. Second, the union could convince the hospitals that they were no worse off in dealing directly than they were through the PAC. He noted that although PAC would always move very slowly and never place any severe burdens on the hospitals, in the long run the hospitals would be no better off financially with PAC than with the union. Third, as long as the union was not secure and not recognized, the hospitals would never have the worker morale and discipline that the contract hospitals had attained. He noted that the hospitals were not in a financial position to buy off the workers through high wages, good conditions, and fringe benefits. Because of this the union would always be in a position where they could criticize the hospitals and promote problems. Last, the experience in the direct negotiation hospitals was very good. Turnover in these hospitals was way down and the administrators were finding that they received certain benefits from having the union. He noted, of the union's relations with the contract hospitals, that the contract with Montefiore had just been reviewed and renewed. This took place six months before the contract deadline with no problems or antagonism. The union had been able to get something for the workers, yet it was well aware of the differences, financial and otherwise, between hospitals and industrial institutions. He added that signatory hospitals could not help but note this type of relationship.

Appendix A

Decision of Judge H. Epstein

Supreme Court, New York County.

Epstein, J.:

Five petitions have been addressed to this court seeking to punish defendants for contempt of court. The contempt charged is willful disobedience to an order of the court. Injunctive relief is also sought against the picketing by defendants and the union. On the argument of these motions this court gave counsel for both sides the following comment of the court with questions to be answered.

REMARKS TO LITIGATING COUNSEL

There have been few issues before the court in recent times as fraught with the public interest, and as likely to have lasting effect on the public welfare as the one now before this court. It is vital therefore that the issue be determined so that, within the applicable laws, the public welfare may best be protected.

The interests involved in the instant case are several, though partially overlapping — namely: The Public, The Patients, and The Employees. Obviously, the public embraces the other two categories, which are sections of the public.

The hospitals' Boards of Governors are representatives of the contributors to the voluntary nonprofit hospitals, though they are neither selected by the contributors nor are their acts in any way directed or controlled by the contributors. The members of these boards are, in most instances, public spirited persons who have volunteered to serve.

It is not necessarily a fact that either these Boards or the employees acting jointly are best able to determine the public welfare. But we should be able to assume that the employees acting jointly can determine what is best for their own interests, while the Boards should be able to determine what is best for hospital management.

Those two interests may well be in conflict, and when they are, then the public welfare must be the over-riding consideration. It is of course true that in a democracy the rights and welfare of the minority are as important and require as much protection as do the rights and welfare of the majority.

These answers are before the court and have been given consideration in arriving at the determination hereinafter set forth. This court has been most careful in its deliberation and has given the deep respect due the views of colleagues as expressed in granting the relief out of which these contempt proceedings arose.

The Constitution of New York State was amended by the people on November 8, 1938, effective January 1, 1939, by adding section 17 to article I, said article bearing the title "Bill of Rights." Two sentences of that section 17 bear directly upon the issue herein and the impact of that language cannot be mistaken:

> S. 17. *Labor of human beings is not a commodity nor an article of commerce and shall never be so considered or construed.*
>
> *Employees shall have the right to organize and to bargain collectively through representatives of their own choosing.*

This amendment was voted by the people in the days of a great economic depression and at a time when labor exploitation was a critical issue. It grants a right to "employees" — a right which is in the present proceedings questioned by petitioners. *No legslative enactment; no regulation of statutory bodies or private institutions; no court action can stand in violation of that command of the State Constitution.* Nor should a court permit such explicit language to be rendered meaningless by its action.

This significant amendment was not enacted before, but *after* the Legislature had acted — with what to this court is an equally clear impact — on the subject of labor disputes and the rights of employees. Section 876-a of the Civil Practice Act was adopted in 1935 and was clearly designed to limit the courts in granting injunctions in controversies between management and labor. Subdivision 10, as provided by chapter 359 of the Laws of 1939 (*immediately after the effective date of the Constitutional provision referred to*) reads:

10. When used in this section, and for the purpose of this section: (a) A case shall be held to involve or to grow out of a labor dispute when the case involves persons who are engaged in the same industry, trade, craft or occupation or who are employees of one employer; or who are members of the same or an affiliated organization of employers of employees; whether such dispute is between one or more employers or associations of employers and one or more employees or associations of employees; between one or more employers or associations of employers; or between one or more employees or associations of employees; or when the case involves any conflicting or competing interests in a "labor dispute" (as hereinafter defined) of "persons participating or interested" (as hereinafter defined).

(b) A person or association shall be held to be a person participating or interested in a labor dispute if relief is sought against him or it and if he or it is engaged in the industry, trade, craft or occupation in which such dispute occurs, or is a member, officer or agent of any association of employer or employees engaged in such industry, trade, craft or occupation.

(c) The term "labor dispute" includes any controversy concerning terms or conditions of employment, or concerning the association or representation of persons in negotiating, fixing, maintaining, changing or seeking to arrange terms or conditions of employment, or concerning employment relations, or any other controversy arising out of the respective interests of employer and employees, regardless of whether or not the disputants stand in the relation of employer and employee.

Can there be any doubt that we here are dealing with a bona fide "labor dispute" under the statute and the Constitution? If so, we seek in vain for any express or implied exemption of voluntary hospitals or other like employers. In fact the Court of Appeals has said in unmistakable language:

Jurisdiction to issue any such injunction is, in so many words, denied to the Courts. It makes no difference who is the plaintiff (Schivera v. Long Island Lighting Co., 296 N.Y. 26, 31).

Neither in the Constitution's "Bill of Rights" for labor nor in the statutory enactment of section 876-a of the Civil Practice Act do we find any concept of nonprofit institutions exemption. Nor is there any such exemption to institutional employers who care for indigent sick. Jewish Hospital of Brooklyn v. Doe, 252 App. Div. 581 does not truly reflect the operation of the Constitutional provision and that of section 876-a of the Civil Practice Act. Nor can the provisions of section 715 of the Labor Relations Act of the State of New York be read into section 876-a of the Civil Practice Act. The exclusion of charitable hospitals from the coverage of section 751 of the Labor Relations Law (enacted by ch. 443, Laws of 1937, amd. by ch. 764, L. 1955) in no manner calls for a cross-reference and exclusion from the clear inclusive language of section 876-a of the Civil Practice Act. All these provisions must be read in the light of employees' unqualified constitutional rights of collective bargaining (Trustees of Columbia University v. Herzog, 181 Misc. 903, reversed on other grounds, 269 App. Div. 24; Re New York State Labor Relations Board, 175 Misc. 95).

The City of New York for its own institutions (City hospitals), in a more isolated and protected area, has recognized the value of the collective recognition of employee spokesmen. And the ghost of threatened strikes, raised by petitioners, is laid to rest in the record of the relations of respondent union through contracts with Montefiore Hospital and Maimonides Hospital. These latter have not suffered any impairment in services by virtue of the contractual relations with defendant union on behalf of the member employees.

Nor is the case of Society of New York Hospital v. Hanson, 185 Misc. 943, affd. 272 App. Div. 998, controlling, because there the employee representatives' counsel conceded in that case section 876-a was not applicable. If, as this court in conscience is driven to hold, a real labor dispute exists, then no injunction may be granted without the conditions provided in section 876-a being met. Here the complaint concededly fails so to comply.

There is another, and while possibly regarded as "technical," yet a valid and clear basis for refusing to grant the contempt orders sought. In all but one of the cases here presented, amended complaints were served after the decisions in the injunctive proceedings were rendered. The injunctions ordered on May 25, 1959 were based on the original complaints. On May 21, 1959 amended complaints were served, adding a vital allegation that the defendant-union ratified or authorized the acts complained of. This was essential to jurisdiction for the orders sought (McCabe v. Goodfellow, 133 N.Y. 89; Martin v. Curran, 303 N.Y. 276; Carmody-Wait New York Practice, Vol. 10, p. 532; Wood v. Cook, 132 App. Div. 318). Also in the papers before this court now defendants Joe Brown (Bronx Hospital), Edward Ayash (Secretary-Treasurer of defendant Union 1199), William J. Taylor (Vice President of defendant Union 1199); George Goodman (Division Director of defendant Union 1199) swear they were never served with the petitions calling for their being held in contempt. Further the editor of "1199 Drug News," Moe Foner, offers an affidavit pointing out his only duties have no connection with the acts complained of.

Article 19 of the Judiciary Law, section 753, provides that:

"3. A party to the action * * * or other person * * * for any disobedience to a lawful mandate of the Court" may be punished for contempt. If, therefore, defendants were within constitutional and statutory recognized conduct in striking and picketing the instant contempt proceeding must be deemed a nullity. The question is not one of fact, but one of law. The courts must obey the Constitutional mandate of article I, section 17 of the State of New York's Consitution and directions of section 876-a of the Civil Practice Act.

On the argument of these motions to punish for criminal contempt, counsel for petitioners, speaking for all of them, frankly and courageously admitted that the employees had the full right to organize and to become members of a union of their choice. To make that admission and then to refuse to discuss grievances with such collective representatives of the member-employees' choice, is to render the recognition meaningless. It is in effect telling employees they may freely organize and join a union, pay their dues, but can never have their union speak for them.

There are other vital considerations wholly overlooked by the hospital managements. The State Labor Relations Act expressly preserves to all employees the right to strike (S. 706, subd. 5). The Legislature in enacting section 876-a of the Civil Practice Act gave not the slightest indication of an intent to exempt nonprofit or charitable associations or corporations. Such an exemption could so simply have been written. But with the full impact of the Constitutional restriction of 1938 before it, when the statute was amended in 1939, no such limitation was indicated. The courts can neither legislate — nor amend — statutes when by decision such judicial amendment would contravene the Constitutional Bill of Rights to Labor. This court will not indulge in such action, and its conscience forbids it to do so in the instant proceedings for criminal contempt.

Employees of voluntary hospitals do not have the protection of Civil Service Laws or procedures. Nor do they have the benefits derived from State or City public service. They must work out their own grievances and redress machinery. That must be done through dealings with the directorial and management staffs of the employer hospitals, none of which is subject to governmental control. Yet the City itself and at least two of the private institutions have and do maintain collective bargaining relations with the employees' union.

For the management of the hospitals — plaintiffs — to take the course herein which they so forcefully pursue is more an echo of the 19th century than the last half of the 20th century.

Since the court feels impelled to hold that a "labor dispute" is here in issue within the meaning of section 876-a of the Civil Practice Act the complaints are fatally defective and no injunction or contempt orders may properly be issued thereon. (Boro Park Sanitary Live Poultry Market, Inc. v. Heller, 280 N.Y. 481, 485–486; Bessert v. Dhuy, 221 N.Y. 342; 365; Exchange Bakery, etc. v. Rifkin, 240 N.Y. 260). Picketing is a form of freedom of speech by labor and may not be restricted by injunction absent other compelling factors not here present. (Senn v. Tile Layers Union, 301 U.S. 468, 478.) Petitioners herein refuse to accept the good faith of defendant-union in its stated willingness to waive any and all right to the strike weapon, if collective representation be accepted by the hospitals. The court cannot so indulge itself. Should such waiver be embodied in an agreement and then be violated — appropriate action can be had from this and other courts. Considerations favorable to this conclusion are found in Young Women's Christian Association v. Jay Rubin, etc., decided December 24, 1956 by Justice McGivern and Railway Mail Association v. Corsi, 293 N.Y. 315, 322-323. Lest there be any doubts on the question of the employees' wishes anent their union affiliation, the strike vote was by secret ballot in each hospital separately, and the vote was overwhelming on the strike itself. In Mount Sinai the vote was 956 to 59; in Beth Israel, 349 to 8; in Lenox Hill, 372 to 16; in Bronx Hospital 247 to 6 and in Beth David, 180 to 4.

It is the considered view of this court that the motions to punish for criminal contempt must be denied as a matter of law. Were the determination to be reached as an exercise of discretion the same result would follow

Orders signed.
Dated, June 1959

J. S. C.

Appendix B

Mt. Sinai Management Is Sick, Sick, Sick, Sick in the Head!

Here is one example: Recently the Mt. Sinai Bosses issued a list of rules. Rule number 7 reads like this: Employees are forbidden to act in "a disrespectful manner toward any supervisor, *at any time, whether on or off hospital premises.*"

How insane can they get! Of course this rule number 7 presents some problems: How far off hospital premises should the worker take off his hat to Management? Does the rule apply to the sea and air as well as land? What shall we do about the moon? "No disrespect at any time?" Can't we even dream bad dreams about them?

That isn't all. Mt. Sinai not only tells you how to behave on your own time. It also regulates your outside income.

Night or week-end work outside of Mt. Sinai is strictly forbidden. How could we think of another job? Aren't we all getting rich on the Mt. Sinai salary?

MAYBE IT'S ABOUT TIME FOR A NEW SET OF RULES AT MT. SINAI. Local 1199 has the following recommendations:

1. Every worker on the job should carry out the directions of supervisors, providing they do not directly menace the worker's health or safety.
2. In the case of unfair orders, the workers should obey, under protest, and then immediately notify the Union. We have a good supply of grievance forms for this purpose.
3. The worker's normal conversation inside the Hospital is not subject to Mt. Sinai censorship. He may talk about the weather, or the baseball scores or the union with equal freedom. The U.S. Constitution, guaranteeing free speech is an even greater authority than the Mt. Sinai rule book.
4. Within the hospital, supervisors are entitled to normal courtesy and no more. No worker is compelled to smile at them, or kiss them, or polish their apples.
5. What a worker says, does, thinks, or earns one second after working hours and one fraction of an inch outside of hospital property is 100 per cent his own business. SUPERVISORS WHO THEN INTERFERE DO SO AT THEIR OWN RISK.

oeiu/344
11/13/59

Local 1199, Hospital Division
300 West 45th Street

Inpatient Psychiatric Services in a General Hospital / The Grace–New Haven Experience

March 1964

Herbert C. Schulberg

The Mental Health Study Act passed by the United States Congress in 1955 created the Joint Commission on Mental Illness and Health to analyze and evaluate the needs of the mentally ill people of America and the resources available for their care and to make recommendations for a national mental health program. After an intensive study of nationwide scope, the Joint Commission concluded [1] that the outstanding characteristics of mental illness as a public health problem are its staggering size, the present limitations in methods of treatment, and the peculiar nature of mental illness, which differentiates its victims from those with other diseases or disabilities.

Among its various findings, the Joint Commission indicated that no community general hospital could be considered to render complete service unless it accepted mental patients for short-term hospitalization. It said that every community general hospital of 100 or more beds should make provision for a psychiatric unit or for psychiatric beds. A hospital with such facilities should be regarded as constituting an integral part of the total system of services for mental patients in its region.

The efforts of medical and lay leaders in New Haven, Connecticut, to establish additional mental health facilities in their community culminated in action at the Grace–New Haven Hospital that was announced in December 1959:

> The Grace–New Haven Community Hospital will open a 24-bed psychiatric unit in January, 1960. It is intended to meet a long recognized community need for a satisfactory place to treat patients with emotional disturbances in a general hospital and to provide psychiatric diagnostic services using the Hospital's technical facilities and its personnel trained in all branches of medicine.
>
> . . . Accommodations for 24 patients cannot fully meet the community's needs, and in order to serve the greatest number of patients possible, admissions will ordinarily be restricted to patients who would benefit from short-term hospitalization or who require diagnostic studies.
>
> . . . While it is believed that the new Psychiatric Unit will meet a pressing need, members of the community, professional and non-

1. Joint Commission on Mental Illness and Health, *Action for Mental Health* (New York: Basic Books, 1961).

professional, should recognize the limitations of the service which constitutes but one more step towards providing adequate community care for patients with psychiatric illness.

Historical Background

Although confinement in prisons, insane asylums, and isolated mental hospitals was for years regarded as the standard solution for mental illness, today the provision of psychiatric care for acute conditions in the general hospital has become one of the most widely accepted forms of treatment. Statistics on the recent growth of these units illustrate the geometric increase which is occurring. The total number of hospitals with such units rose from 32 in 1920 to 176 in 1945 to 548 in 1956.[2] Nevertheless, in that year, only 11 percent of the general hospitals in the Uniited States had facilities for psychiatric care. Fourteen percent of these were housed in separate buildings, 49 percent on separate wards, and 37 percent had no separate facilities. The scope of therapy ranged from little in the way of specific psychiatric treatment to intensive, highly specialized psychiatric programs.

The trend toward increased local facilities was slow to develop in the state of Connecticut even though the Commissioner of Mental Health in the mid-1950's repeatedly stressed that there was a pressing need for additional inpatient psychiatric beds. In an effort to assess the situation in the state and to collect detailed information on existing services, needs, and proposed plans for additional resources, the Connecticut Association for Mental Health conducted a survey in 1957.[3] Of the state's 36 voluntary general hospitals, only three (all in Hartford) were found to provide inpatient psychiatric care. The Association recommended that general hospitals in communities with a population of over 50,000 develop psychiatric units and suggested that a rate of 0.45 community hospital psychiatric beds per 1,000 population would be a desirable goal for planning.

The metropolitan New Haven area, with a population of close to 400,000 persons, had three general hospitals — the Hospital of St. Raphael with 370 beds, Grace-New Haven Community Hospital with 660 beds, and the West Haven Veterans Administra-

2. C. K. Bush, "Growth of General Hospital Care Psychiatric Patients," *American Journal of Psychiatry* 113:1060 (June 1957).

3. Committee on Hospital Services for the Mentally Ill, *A Survey of Psychiatric Services in General Hospitals in the State of Connecticut* (New Haven: Connecticut Association for Mental Health, 1958).

tion Hospital. When interviewed during the 1957 survey, Sister Louise Anthony, Administrator of St. Raphael, said that her hospital was very concerned about the need for specific inpatient psychiatric services but that space limitations made the development of a program impossible at the time.[4] The West Haven Veterans Administration Hospital had had a 150-bed psychiatric inpatient program for many years. But because the hospital serves much of southwestern Connecticut and must by law provide treatment only to armed forces veterans, it plays a limited role in the New Haven community.

A part of the Yale Medical Center, Grace-New Haven Hospital provides service to the community, internship and residency training programs for physicians, and research facilities for a variety of endeavors. Professional training is also offered for student nurses, medical and X-ray technicians, and dietitians. The hospital cares for medical, surgical, pediatric, and obstetrical patients and has approximately 23,000 admissions annually. In addition to the inpatient service, the hospital operates outpatient clinics in every major specialty of medical practice. Each year there are about 100,000 visits to the 67 clinics, and another 45,000 to the hospital's emergency room.

The medical staff of the hospital has two major components: the University Division which consists of the full-time faculty of the Yale Medical School, and the Community Division composed of the area's private physicians. The two divisions are combined into a single operating service in each of the specialties.

Of the mental health facilities available to the New Haven community in 1957, two were affiliated with the Yale Medical Center — the Hospital's Outpatient Psychiatric Clinic and the Yale Psychiatric Institute. The Outpatient Clinic was operated by the Yale Department of Psychiatry for the training of medical students, interns, and residents. It had approximately 6,000 patient visits per year and accepted 600 patients annually. The Yale Psychiatric Institute was a highly specialized private residential treatment center primarily for young schizophrenics. Only 20 to 30 patients were admitted annually to the 44-bed Institute. The median length of stay was one and one half years, and fees ranged from $10,000 to $12,000 per year. The Institute could not be expected to play any significant part in helping to meet the community's needs.

When interviewed during the Connecticut Mental Health

4. Ibid.

Survey in 1957, Dr. Albert W. Snoke, the Director of Grace-New Haven Hospital, said that an inpatient psychiatric unit in association with a general hospital was a most desirable facility, but that no definite opinion had crystallized in the Yale Department of Psychiatry as to the type of facility that would be most appropriate, considering both the needs of the community and the requirements of the psychiatric training programs of the Yale Medical Center. He indicated that neither the Board of Trustees nor the administration of the hospital had a clear idea what the hospital's responsibility to the mentally ill was, and that if a program were proposed they would then be in a better position to make a decision concerning it.

One of the reasons for Dr. Snoke's caution was the financial deficit being incurred by the existing Outpatient Psychiatric Clinic. The operating cost per visit in the Psychiatric Clinic was $10 rather than the $5 cost per visit for the other clinics of the Yale Medical Center.

The higher expenses of the psychiatric clinic for nonphysician personnel and overhead were defrayed by general hospital funds, which came in part from fees collected for inpatient medical services. The Connecticut Department of Mental Health met a relatively small proportion of the total operating cost of the Psychiatric Clinic, and there was some fear among the administrators of Grace-New Haven that the state's Department would attempt to terminate even this financial support. The possibility that the hospital administration could secure financial assistance from the Department of Mental Health for an inpatient unit at Grace-New Haven was uncertain because the Department had been considering for several years the construction of its own mental hospital in the New Haven area.

Establishment of a Planning Committee

In spite of misgivings regarding financial feasibility, the administration of Grace-New Haven Hospital and the Chairman of the Yale Department of Psychiatry, Dr. Frederick C. Redlich, called a dinner meeting on January 30, 1958, to discuss what should be done at Grace-New Haven to provide inpatient psychiatric services. The meeting was attended by 12 persons representing the hospital administration, the Yale Department of Psychiatry, and community physicians.

Even prior to the 1957 survey by the Connecticut Mental

Health Association, New Haven psychiatrists and general practitioners had been expressing considerable dissatisfaction over the lack of an acute inpatient treatment service for patients with psychiatric illnesses. Only two types of facilities were then available — expensive, private psychiatric hospitals, and the remote state hospitals. No facility was available in New Haven for patients who wished to be treated locally but who could not afford to pay the rates of private psychiatric hospitals.

An equally significant circumstance in the calling together of the group was Dr. Redlich's desire to provide Yale psychiatric residents and medical students with experience on an acute treatment service. Although the psychiatric unit at the West Haven Veterans Administration Hospital was being used for this purpose, Yale was not entirely satisfied with the arrangement because, first, virtually all of the hospital's patients were men and, second, their illnesses were generally chronic.

The participants at the initial gathering had before them a variety of knotty problems which would have to be dealt with before a psychiatric unit could be developed — the extent of the need for an inpatient service; the treatment philosophy of the program; the extent to which community physicians would participate in patient treatment and management; the relative degree of emphasis that would be placed upon the provision of community service and the teaching and research needs of the university; criteria for patient admission; the availability of professional staff; relationships with the New Haven community; and the cost and financing of the facility.

In spite of the complexity of many of these issues, there was considerable professional and lay interest in the project and a Planning Committee was established. On it were represented the administration of Grace-New Haven Hospital, the Yale Department of Psychiatry, and psychiatrists and other physicians in private practice in New Haven.

The Planning Committee spent the next several months gathering information on the types of psychiatric units operating in other general hospitals, and visiting such programs in Hartford and New York City. The Committee members concluded that the majority of the other units they inspected, which were for the most part like small, isolated, self-contained psychiatric hospitals, did not suit the needs of Grace-New Haven as the general teaching hospital of the Yale Medical Center. Over the next year and a half, therefore, they held a series of meetings at which they attempted to resolve the problems attendant on the development of a psychiatric unit geared both to community need and to the Yale medical program.

Extent of the Need

Although there was general consensus in the community that an inpatient psychiatric unit was needed, the Planning Committee had little data about the extent of the need upon which it could base its plans. About 60 patients per year were brought into the emergency service in "acute emotional storms," and the hospital received about 150 telephone inquiries annually requesting referral to an inpatient psychiatric facility. Little was known about the number of patients on other hospital services who required psychiatric treatment. The University of Cleveland had found that about 10 percent of its surgical patients had emotional problems. When the hospital administration asked the Planning Committee whether a psychiatric unit would relieve the patient load on surgical and medical floors, the Committee replied that it was impossible to answer the question. It was known that in 1955 state hospitals had admitted 710 persons from the New Haven area, but how many of these patients could have been treated in a community facility was also a matter of conjecture.

The American Psychiatric Association Committee on Standards had considered the size of psychiatric units in general hospitals and found that experience indicated that the number of psychiatric beds would vary from 3 percent to 15 percent, the most usual figure being between 8 percent and 10 percent of the total beds. For Grace-New Haven Hospital, which has 660 beds, the number of psychiatric beds would then be approximately 65. Using a different rate derived from the 1947 master plan of the Hospital Council of Greater New York and the Connecticut Department of Public Health's 1949 Survey of Hospitals and Public Health Centers, the 1957 Connecticut Mental Health Survey had recommended that there should be 0.45 psychiatric beds in general community hospitals for every 1,000 population.[5] According to this rate, the metropolitan New Haven area would require 177 psychiatric beds for its population of 394,000.

In the absence of any definitive data regarding either the optimum number of psychiatric beds or the specific needs of New Haven, the Planning Committee indicated in January 1958 that

5. Ibid.

the experience of other general hospitals suggested that "there would probably be a need for about sixty acute psychiatric beds in the community." Because St. Raphael's, the other general hospital in New Haven, had no plans for establishing an inpatient psychiatric service, whatever actual demand existed for inpatient psychiatric services would be directed solely to Grace-New Haven Hospital.

Location and Size of the Unit

Early in its deliberations the Planning Committee explored possible locations for a psychiatric unit, considering both the conversion of existing wards and the construction of a new one. One of the existing 28-bed surgical wards, Tompkins I, was running a consistently low census and appeared to be a logical choice for conversion to psychiatric needs. The Surgical Service offered no active opposition. Although its own needs for space have increased since Tompkins I was converted for psychiatric patients, no animosity over the loss appears to be directed at the psychiatric unit.

Even though the Planning Committee had estimated that over 60 beds would be necessary to meet community needs, the size of the proposed unit was now limited by the area available in Tompkins I. The Committee concluded that about 20 beds would be an initial minimum, because a unit with fewer than 15 occupied beds would not support itself. Probably a 30-bed unit could be even more economically run. Because space was needed for all the basic facilities of an acute psychiatric division, such as group therapy and occupational therapy rooms, it was decided that 24 beds would be the most feasible capacity for the unit. The decision of the Planning Committee was consistent with the view of the Committee on Standards of the American Psychiatric Association that "a capacity of twenty to twenty-four beds in one unit seems to be nearly ideal."

A construction firm was engaged to remodel Tompkins I, and the final cost of the project was $103,000. Of this sum, $73,000 was contributed by New Haveners through the Grace-New Haven Progress Fund, and the remaining $30,000 was made available from a Hill-Burton grant. Tompkins I differs in appearance from other hospital wards because modern day beds and dresser-desks have been used instead of regular nursing beds and cabinets, and the rooms are reminiscent of those in a college dormitory. The kitchen facilities of the unit are open to patients at any time of the day or night.

Type of Patients to Be Admitted

Because a great demand was expected, it was necessary to decide how the limited facilities available could best be used. At the initial planning meeting in January 1958 the Committee had agreed that "certain appropriate psychiatric conditions" should be cared for in the general hospital. These included "postpartum, post-surgical, and acute toxic psychoses, certain acute depressions, . . . neurotic conditions, . . . severe psychosomatic conditions, etc." The most significant category omitted was the schizophrenic disorders. Within these limits, the Planning Committee indicated that "urgency should be the only criterion for admission," and proposed that a minimum age limit of 16 for inpatients be set.

Several months later, however, after study of other programs, a member of the Committee, Dr. Theodore Lidz of the Yale Psychiatric Institute, indicated that "for several reasons (education of psychiatric house staff, the community needs of alcoholics and others, and evaluation of patients such as young schizophrenics) it would be desirable to accept all types of cases." It became the policy of the Planning Committee to do so, and diagnosis per se was no longer of any concern. Instead, the expectation that the patient would benefit from short-term hospitalization or diagnostic study became the primary criterion for admission to Tompkins I. This policy is much like those followed in other general hospitals, which "with increasing frequency . . . appear to be displaying a willingness to accept psychotic patients as an integral part of their caseload and not to refuse admission because of the severity of a symptom." [6]

At the same time, however, the Committee felt strongly that it should "indicate from the start that each admission will be screened as to whether the patient is an appropriate one for the unit or not. It should be stated as frequently as possible that the unit will not be able to accommodate every noisy or belligerent or drunk or otherwise undesirable person that is now a problem for the police, other hospitals, relatives, etc."

The Planning Committee made no explicit public statement concerning the sources of referral that would be given priority

6. H. C. Schulberg, "Psychiatric Units in General Hospitals: Boon or Bane?" *American Journal of Psychiatry* 120:32 (July 1963).

in admissions to the unit. Dr. Lidz indicated on November 9, 1959, that patients might be referred by a variety of sources, including the Emergency Room, other medical services in the hospital, private practitioners, social welfare agencies, and so on. The general goal of the Committee seemed to be to meet community need whatever its source.

The Treatment Philosophy

In a psychiatric unit, the treatment program has many implications for the planning and operation of the unit, affecting the type and size of staff, the number of seclusion rooms, open or closed doors, family and community involvement, and so on. The orientation may vary from the primarily psychological to the strictly organic; it may focus attention on the selected problems of the individual or it may involve the entire family. It is often a far more crucial issue in psychiatric than in medical practice because of the wide theoretical divergencies that exist.

The Yale Department of Psychiatry had done much pioneering research at the Yale Psychiatric Institute on the ways in which the members of the family of an emotionally disturbed person relate to him and to one another. Because two Yale psychiatrists active in this research, Dr. Stephen Fleck and Dr. Lidz, were members of the Planning Committee, the treatment philosophy developed for Tompkins I placed major emphasis on group and family treatment.

The director selected for Tompkins I, Dr. Thomas Detre, was also an ardent advocate of family treatment. Dr. Detre was Chief Resident at the Yale Psychiatric Institute at the time and a junior faculty member of the Yale Department of Psychiatry. He was born in Hungary in 1924 and received the M.D. degree from the University of Rome (Italy) in 1952. His interest and experience in Italian and American short-term treatment facilities were important considerations in his selection. His proficiency in clinical psychopharmacology was also important because of the extensive use of drugs expected in the treatment program. Although physical plans for the unit had been developed by the time he joined the Planning Committee in April 1959, Dr. Detre was influential in determining the treatment program.

A group of classical psychoanalysts of the Freudian school in the community, who felt that treatment should consist strictly of therapy with the patient, disapproved of the planned intensive involvement of the patient's family in the therapy. There is no record, however, that their point of view influenced the deliberations of the Planning Committee.

The Planning Committee was concerned mainly with deciding whether to have an open or a closed ward and the necessary number of seclusion rooms. These considerations are significant because of the fear many people feel of mental illness and of the bizarre behavior exhibited by some mentally ill persons. Traditionally, the mentally ill patient has been isolated from the community. The prospect of hospitalizing him in the center of the local general hospital aroused varied concerns among the Board of Trustees and the administration. A major goal of the Planning Committee was therefore to maintain a "quiet" ward.

Since the Planning Committee had decided that all types of patients, regardless of diagnosis or severity of symptoms, should be admitted, Tompkins I was developed as a compromise between an open and a closed ward. Dr. Lidz and Dr. Fleck, who were experienced in administering the residential treatment program of the Yale Psychiatric Institute, indicated that four seclusion rooms in a 24-bed general hospital unit would be necessary to maintain control over disturbed patients. A ratio of one seclusion room to every 20 beds has been suggested as a general rule-of-thumb.[7] The higher proportion proposed for Tompkins I appeared to reflect some doubt on the part of the psychiatrists whether the "ideal psychiatry" of the Yale Psychiatric Institute, where only a minimal use is made of restraints, could be transferred to the general hospital. The ambivalence felt by the Planning Committee on this point was also reflected in concern as to how much shock treatment might be necessary. Although very little shock treatment was being administered at the Yale Psychiatric Institute, where there was little pressure for space or time, some members of the Committee thought that on a busy and pressured Tompkins I shock treatment might well be administered as often as in other psychiatric units in general hospitals — to approximately 50 percent of the patients. If so, of course, the Anesthesia Department would be vitally concerned and should be involved in the planning.

Unlike the treatment programs of medical and surgical services, which are geared primarily to the individual, that planned for Tompkins I involved ward-wide programs, the establishment of a "therapeutic milieu," intensive interaction between patients and staff, and control of behavior problems. It was recognized, there-

7. Schulberg, p. 34.

fore, that medical responsibility for patient management would have to be given to a full-time university psychiatrist who would determine overall policy and procedure. This administrative policy would require that community psychiatrists relinquish primary responsibility to the hospital psychiatrist while patients were hospitalized. Upon discharge, patients would be referred back to their own psychiatrists. In many other general hospitals, such as Mt. Sinai in New York, attending community psychiatrists are used extensively in the psychiatric units, and the units' programs are not as clearly controlled by hospital staff as was planned for Tompkins I.

The psychiatrists in private practice on the Planning Committee raised no objection to the policy of hospital control over inpatients since they agreed with the proposed treatment program and in any case were reluctant to spend their own valuable time traveling back and forth to the hospital for therapy sessions with patients. The internists on the Planning Committee expressed opposition, however. They considered the proposed policy a step in the wrong direction since it might ultimately lead to the hospital staff's assuming full control of all inpatient care, not just psychiatric care.

The role of private practitioners in the treatment of inpatients on the psychiatric unit continued to be discussed, and by September 1959 the recommended policy of the Planning Committee was, "Responsibility for the psychiatric management of the patient in the Psychiatric Inpatient Unit will be delegated to the full-time (University) staff. Orders will be written or countersigned by the full-time staff. Exceptions can be made to this general policy if the best interests of the patient will be served, based upon agreement of the attending psychiatrist and the Director of the Unit."

Personnel

Because the program was located within a university teaching hospital, the availability of adequate personnel, both professional and nonprofessional, was not regarded as a problem. The staffing pattern was decided in November 1959 and called for one full-time psychiatrist (Dr. Detre), two residents in psychiatry, one psychologist, two social workers, one occupational therapist, one secretary-receptionist, approximately 13 graduate nurses, licensed practical nurses, and aides exclusive of a head nurse or supervisor or both, and two full-time porters and one part-time porter.

Whether or not medical or nursing students were to be included was to be decided later.

The successful operation of a psychiatric program requires the development of stable personal relationships between the staff and the patients. The Director of the Grace-New Haven Nursing Office realized that the standard policy of rotating nurses among the various services would therefore hinder the psychiatric unit, and she agreed to assign nurses permanently to Tompkins I. There was disagreement, however, over the number of nurses that were necessary. The Director of Nursing felt that since many of the routine chores on a medical service are not performed on a psychiatric unit, a normal nurse-patient ratio (about 1:6) would provide ample opportunity for patients to interact with the nursing staff. It was finally agreed that the nurses requested for Tompkins I to establish a higher nurse-patient ratio (approximately 1:4) would be assigned but that the psychiatric nursing staff would remain under the supervision of the Hospital's Director of Nursing rather than the psychiatric director. The nursing policy for Tompkins I provoked complaints from other segments of the Hospital's nursing community because of the shortage of nurses on other services, and repeated efforts were made to have it changed. With the support of the Nursing Director, however, these efforts were successfully resisted, and the policy for Tompkins I is now generally accepted.

Financial Arrangements

Because of the high expenses incurred by the hospital for the operation of the Psychiatric Outpatient Clinic, the question whether the psychiatric inpatient unit would be self-supporting or a "losing proposition" was one of the first taken up by the Planning Committee in January 1958. It was generally agreed that the service would operate at a loss unless a firm policy on admissions was instituted from the beginning. A policy of accepting only paying patients thus became the keynote of subsequent planning, but various alternatives were explored to provide coverage for the indigent.

The Welfare Department of the City of New Haven agreed, subject to later review, to accept financial responsibility for the hospitalization of welfare recipients for psychiatric treatment as it did for medical or surgical care. The only stipulation made by the Welfare Department was that it be informed at the end of a five-day stay of the patient's diagnosis and expected length of hospitalization. The Department did not wish to pay for long-term care in a local hospital when the less expensive state hospital was already available for this type of treatment.

The Connecticut Department of Mental Health was approached for a subsidy to cover the costs of care for patients who were neither eligible for welfare assistance nor able to pay privately. Although the Planning Committee and the Department of Mental Health held several meetings, no satisfactory financial formula was developed. In 1963, of 20 state Departments of Mental Health, three (California, Georgia, and New York) reimbursed general hospitals for psychiatric services. Both California and New York, under state laws, provide funds to county community mental health boards to defray up to 50 percent of the costs of general hospital care of psychiatric patients. Georgia, which has only one state mental hospital, pays general hospitals directly for psychiatric services for the indigent.

The basic hospital service charge of $25 per day to patients in the psychiatric unit was determined on the basis of the average cost per patient per day during the previous fiscal year for all other types of care in the hospital ($21–$23), the expected six percent increase in costs during the next fiscal year ($1.27), the estimated cost per patient per day for "routine supplies" ($1.50), and the estimated cost per patient per day for occupational therapy ($1.20). The per diem hospital rate for patients continuing therapy sessions with their own psychiatrists while in the hospital was set at $28 rather than $25. The fact that the basic hospital charge in the psychiatric unit was almost identical with that for other medical services did much to alleviate the fears of insurance companies that the costs of psychiatric hospitalization would be excessive. Almost all of the commercial companies contacted by the hospital, as well as Blue Cross, agreed to provide coverage for hospitalization on the new unit.

Shock therapy, X rays, laboratory examinations, other special services, and the services of the psychiatric staff were not included in the basic per diem rate. To cover the services of professional staff, patients were to be charged a flat professional service fee of $5 to $15 per day, depending on their financial resources, regardless of the scope of services they received. When a patient was treated by his own psychiatrist rather than by the unit's staff, the usual physician-patient contractual relationship was to apply, but the patient was also to be charged a professional service fee of

$7.50 for the services provided by the hospital staff. No professional service fee was to be charged welfare patients treated on the unit. The professional service fees are redistributed by the hospital's Clinical Practices Office and help meet the salaries of the entire staff of the Yale Medical Center. Thus basic scientists as well as clinicians benefit from this source of income.

The Opening of Tompkins I

In November 1959, two months before the opening of Tompkins I to patients, the Planning Committee considered the type of statement that should be made to the lay and professional community about the new psychiatric unit. The chairman of the Committee, Mr. Law of the Grace-New Haven Hospital administration, suggested that the purpose of the unit should be stated "because the purpose seems different at different times and perhaps different in the viewpoint of the various members of the Committee. Perhaps if we do not state the purpose others will supply their interpretation and measure the success or failure of the unit by the ability to meet the purpose they have set up." Other members of the Committee, however, felt that they could not make a precise statement of the unit's purpose at the time and that the purpose would evolve as the unit itself developed.

In 1963 when asked what he thought the original goal of Tompkins I had been, Dr. Detre stated that he considered it to be the "rehabilitation of the patient . . . permitting him to return to his occupation . . . and helping him to restructure his social environment." From the beginning, Dr. Detre had felt a deep conviction that the unit would in fact achieve the basic goals to which modern psychiatric treatment aspires.

As part of an effort to acquaint the New Haven community with the new psychiatric facility, an "open house" was held just before Tompkins I was opened in January 1960. Several hundred professional and lay visitors from the area attended, and expressed particular interest in the type of patient to be admitted for treatment. Many of the guests expressed astonishment when it was made clear that the staff intended to care for an acute psychotic population, and not just for patients with mild disturbances who needed rest. Many of the visitors thought that psychotic patients might be observed on the unit for a few days, but would then have to be sent to another institution.

The Operation of Tompkins I

The Administrative Structure

The administrative structure developed for Tompkins I reflected the personality and background of the psychiatric director, Dr. Thomas Detre, who was described as a "charismatic leader" in a sociological study of the unit's organization. In administering the unit, Dr. Detre has created multiple opportunities for the intimate involvement of all staff members — and even of patients — in the unit's program. From the day the unit opened, Dr. Detre presided over daily, hour-long conferences attended by all personnel, including nurses, aides, secretaries, and students. This policy, contrary to that of most hospitals where only the professionals attend staff meetings, was instituted so that each staff member would understand why various decisions were being made and would implement treatment plans in a consistent way. Believing that the constant clarification of underlying emotional feelings results in improved effectiveness and adjustment, Dr. Detre has encouraged all participants in these meetings, and in others where patients too are present, to express their views freely.

Observers comment that the various types of meetings held on the unit provided Dr. Detre with an excellent opportunity to exercise what they consider to be formidable powers of persuasiveness and show to best advantage the facets of his personality which give him considerable influence over his staff. It is thought that these sessions, coupled with the staff's intimate involvement in the unit's program, foster the creation and maintenance of enthusiasm and participation on the part of all staff members.

Routine ward procedures developed slowly because of the newness of the program and the lack of definition of what constitutes the most therapeutic procedures for a psychiatric unit in a general hospital. As time has passed and experience been gained in the operation of the unit, however, much of the trial-and-error approach characteristic of the early stages of the program's development has disappeared and a variety of routine procedures and programs has been established.

If the administrative structure of Tompkins I can be considered to have undergone any evolution since 1960, it can perhaps most aptly be described as having passed from a charismatic to a bureaucratic one. Although Dr. Detre's qualities of personal leadership are still very much in evidence, the daily functioning of Tompkins I no longer requires his close personal supervision. Occasionally staff members bring to him for solution crises that they are authorized to handle themselves, but for the most part Dr. Detre is now able to turn his attention more to administrative issues that concern the entire medical center and to regular consultation with other programs.

The Treatment Program

When it was initiated in January 1960 the treatment program of Tompkins I in many ways represented a serious departure from that of the Yale Psychiatric Institute and even from those of most psychiatric units in other general hospitals. The major principle that guided Dr. Detre's "Master Plan" from the outset was his attempt to "demonstrate how patient care should best be provided in the light of current knowledge." Because Grace-New Haven is a teaching hospital, Dr. Detre considered the transmission of this principle to residents and medical students to be one of the prime responsibilities of the program.

One principle of a therapeutic environment that has received considerable emphasis on Tompkins I is the assumption by patients of some responsibility for their own and the unit's functioning. From the time Tompkins I opened, weekly patient-staff meetings have been held. At first the emphasis was on such routine matters as the election of patient officers and the assignment of chores. With the passage of time, the staff decided that the meetings could be more useful to the patients if actual ward problems were considered. When patients reported harsh treatment by a kitchen maid, for example, she was invited to the next meeting to present her point of view, and efforts were made to work out the difficulty.

As a consequence of Dr. Detre's policies, patients on Tompkins I have been given greater responsibility than is usual in a psychiatric ward. A "patient-advisory board," for example, has responsibility for making recommendations to the staff concerning various patient privileges. The board is composed of patients from every resident's therapy group, and patients serve as chairman and secretary. The board meets twice weekly to review requests by other patients for weekend passes, room changes, permission to go on walks, and so on. The staff retains ultimate veto power but rarely uses it. Dr. Detre believes that this administrative procedure gives the patients an excellent opportunity to test their social reality independently, while at the same time relieving the staff of a chore which consumes a good deal of time and energy.

The extensive patient-staff communication, as well as the involvement of patients in various staff decisions, has led to the development of some rather unusual methods for dealing with problems. On the rare occasions when a patient has run away from the unit, Dr. Detre has immediately convened a meeting of all patients and staff members at which the facts of the case are fully explained. Dr. Detre believes that this procedure helps to prevent the spread of erroneous rumors. He further believes that it reassures patients who might have become upset at the thought that the staff had been incapable of handling the patient successfully, or that they had failed to help their fellow patient as much as they should, or that they too were so hopelessly ill that they would also have to resort to escape. Possible ways of dealing with future escapes are discussed at these meetings, and any new policies explained to the patients. In the majority of psychiatric units, similar decisions are made by the senior staff alone.

Recently "leaderless group therapy" sessions at which each resident's patients meet together have been initiated to increase patient involvement and responsibility in the treatment program. It was Dr. Detre's feeling that patients could beneficially discuss significant personal problems together in the absence of a therapist and that these sessions might on occasion be a highly desirable form of treatment. The leaderless meetings are apparently progressing satisfactorily, but an evaluation of their efficacy is being made. During these twice-weekly sessions the staff is free to attend one of the many teaching conferences that are held in a teaching hospital.

The most recently adopted technique for increasing patient involvement in the treatment program is the assignment at all times of two patient monitors to supervise the unit. Whenever the nurses change shifts, the patient monitors are present to hear a full report and to be briefed about patients who might be poorly controlled or depressed. The monitoring system has further reduced the number of incidents of bizarre behavior on the unit and has provided another opportunity for staff and patients to work together.

Dr. Detre has placed a heavier emphasis upon the involvement of the patient's family in the treatment plan than is the case in traditional private psychiatric practice, each patient's treatment being planned and conducted within the context of total family interaction. As a result, many members of the Tompkins I staff may have contact with members of the patient's family when they visit the unit or are interviewed. Rather than the social worker being almost the sole liaison with the family, as is usually the case in other programs, a variety of staff members get to know the patient's family, and their impressions are considered in evaluations of the treatment plan.

Each resident holds meetings twice a week which are attended by all of his patients and their families. These groups have shown a surprising degree of tolerance for severely disturbed behavior and have helped to reassure distraught relatives of newly admitted patients that almost all acute disturbances will subside.[8] The sessions are well attended by the families, and in many respects are the highlight of the weekly program. Discharged patients and their families are asked to return to the meetings for the first two weeks following discharge, and even though the staff cannot compel them to do so, attendance is at a very high level. Continued contact is considered to be reassuring to the discharged patients, and their presence at the meetings fosters discussion of readjustment in the community after discharge.

In addition to the large patient-family-staff meetings, "four-way" sessions are arranged regularly at which individual patients and their families meet with the psychiatrist and the social worker. The purpose of these sessions is to provide models for the more constructive interaction which the staff wishes to encourage between the patient and his family. An attempt is made at the meetings to work out some of the problems that necessitated hospitalization and to coordinate this effort with plans for discharge and follow-up care.

The recreation program of the unit is built around the participation of family, friends, and the community. The intention has been to reduce the isolation of the patient from his family and his community during his hospitalization by encouraging the extension of invitations to family and friends to visit the unit.

Because Dr. Detre has placed major emphasis on group and family treatment, individual psychotherapy plays a generally less dominant role in the overall treatment plan than it does in other psychiatric programs. Patients who can effectively profit by individual sessions focused on their personal problems are seen by a psychiatrist twice a week for one half to one hour. If they use

8. T. Detre, J. H. Sayres, N. M. Norton, and H. C. Lewis, "An Experimental Approach to the Treatment of the Acutely Ill Psychiatric Patient in the General Hospital," *Connecticut Medicine* 25:616 (September 1961).

the individual psychotherapy as a means of isolating themselves from the Tompkins I environment, however, the sessions are then directed at clarifying and overcoming their need for isolation and their difficulty in facing issues which arise in group meetings.

The environment which has been created on Tompkins I was described by the *New Haven Register* magazine in September 1960 as follows: "All in all something of a college dormitory air prevails with patients visiting from room to room and visitors and staff going in and out. But beneath this casual appearance lies a firmly disciplined psychiatric program."

The staff now believes that when the psychiatric program was initiated in 1960, massive doses of drugs were given to relieve not only the patients' anxiety but also that of the professional staff. Because the need to maintain a quiet ward in the general hospital loomed large in the minds of the staff, the Yale Psychiatric Institute practice of using very limited medication was not followed, and almost every patient admitted to Tompkins I was placed on a regimen of medication. As the months passed without a major crisis arising between the unit and the rest of the hospital, a more selective use of drugs was instituted, drugs being used not only to control grossly inappropriate behavior but also for more specifically focused purposes such as to lighten depression and increase appetite. Because of Dr. Detre's strong belief in the efficacy of drugs, however, considerable reliance continues to be placed upon medication, and over 90 percent of the patients receive some kind of drug during hospitalization and after-care.

Tompkins I is occasionally given financial support by pharmaceutical firms for research into drug efficacy. The staff cooperates because of Dr. Detre's interest in chemotherapy. Any staff resistance to use of the drugs under study would be immediately evident in so intimate an environment where close observations are made of the patients' behavior.

Although some early estimates based upon the experience of other psychiatric units in general hospitals suggested that electroshock treatment might be administered to as many as 50 percent of the patients on Tompkins I, only 12 of 167 patients were treated with electric shock during a recent year. This low ratio continues to be maintained.

In the light of the actual experience of Tompkins I, the initial decision to provide four seclusion rooms for the 24 patients is now viewed by the staff as another instance in which their own anxiety outraced patient need. Within a short period of time after the opening of the unit, three of the rooms were converted into offices because of the immediate shortage that developed for professional office space and the availability of other methods for controlling disturbed patients.

Although no real need was demonstrated for the remaining seclusion room, the nursing staff insisted that it be kept. Dr. Detre finally proposed that during a one-month trial period the room not be used for any purpose. The staff managed well without it, and the room was then used experimentally as an office for several months. By the middle of 1963 the safety lights had been replaced by regular fluorescent fixtures, and the unit is now operating without any special physical facility for violent patients. Some observers contend that the major purpose of seclusion rooms is reassurance of hospital personnel rather than control of patients.

The Staff

Many experts believe that extensive staff-patient contact is imperative in a psychiatric inpatient unit and that a high staff-patient ratio is therefore necessary. Goshen has even asserted that the administrator of a psychiatric unit should "Fight for as many as you can and then you'll be 20 per cent short." [9] Accordingly, the Yale Planning Committee approved an initial ratio of approximately one staff member (professional and nonprofessional) for every patient. Current staff-patient ratios in mental hospitals generally range from 1:2 on an acute treatment service to 1:10 on a chronic treatment service.

Although the number of patient beds on Tompkins I has remained stable at 24 since 1960, a veritable population explosion has occurred among the staff. There are now two permanent staff members for every patient, and in addition medical, social work, nursing, practical nursing, and psychology students rotate through the unit. On any given day a large proportion of the approximately 60 to 65 staff members and students associated with the 24-bed unit may be on the floor and create a critical shortage of office space. The following list specifies the number of staff and students by classification in mid-1963:

9. C. E. Goshen, "A Guide for Designing and Operating Psychiatric Units in General Hospitals," *Hospitals* 33:49 (February 16, 1959).

Permanent staff	Personnel in training
1 Psychiatrist in charge	5 Senior residents in psychiatry
2 Chief residents in psychiatry	5 Medical students
3 Psychiatric social workers	1 Psychiatric social work student
1 Clinical psychologist	1 Psychology intern
2 Recreational therapists	3–5 Senior nursing students
1 Director of psychiatric nursing	6 Practical nursing students
1 Head nurse	
9 Graduate nurses	
8 Licensed practical nurses	
4 Aides (male)	
3 Secretaries	
2 Division secretaries	
3 Housekeeping personnel	
3 Kitchen personnel	

The fact that Tompkins I is a teaching and research unit associated with the Yale Medical Center is certainly instrumental in making possible a ratio of almost two permanent staff members for every patient. Whether such a high ratio is necessary or desirable in other general hospitals is not known. After several years of experience at the University of Oregon Medical School Hospital, Saslow and Matarazzo[10] stated that the ratio of staff to patients needed for optimal diagnosis and treatment had not yet been determined.

Two full-time psychiatric residents were assigned to Tompkins I from January through July 1960 to gain experience on an acute treatment service. Their time was so fully occupied by the treatment program that in July the number of residents was increased to four so that supervision could be provided for medical students. At the same time, the residents' assignments were made rotational so that each spent only four months on Tompkins I.

This arrangement proved to be a poor one for several reasons. Most of the residents had already been exposed to the long-term care programs of the Yale Psychiatric Institute and of the West Haven Veterans Administration Hospital. The short-term treatment emphasis of Tompkins I, the extensive use of drugs, and the minimal development of individual therapeutic relationships be-

10. G. Saslow, and J. D. Matarazzo, "A Psychiatric Service in a General Hospital: A Setting for Social Learning," *Mental Hospitals* 13:217–226 (April 1962).

tween psychiatrist and patient were radically different approaches for them to have to integrate into their concept of their professional function. Because in 1960 and 1961 Dr. Detre was still administering the unit in a highly personal, informal way, the frequent change of residents made unit management extremely difficult. The new residents had no set of routine procedures available upon which they could depend for guidance, and learning the ropes involved much tentative groping and confusion. As a result, in July 1961 residents were assigned to Tompkins I for an entire year, and this system was still in effect in mid-1963. During this period there was a further increase in the number of residents. As noted in the list, by mid-1963 there were two chief residents — psychiatrists who have completed their formal residencies and are virtually junior faculty members — and five senior residents attached to the unit.

Many New Haven psychiatrists consider the psychiatric training program of Tompkins I to be of very high quality, and residency on the unit, which was originally resented, is now looked upon as a choice assignment. The permanent staff report that former residents are often regarded as experts in the use of psychotropic drugs and are sought out for consultation. They further claim that many Yale medical students trained on the unit during their clinical clerkships have been attracted to psychiatry as a career in spite of their prior selection of other specialties. Of the various goals Tompkins I was intended to serve, Dr. Detre currently considers its teaching and educational function the best fulfilled.

Dr. Detre and the chief psychiatric social worker originally believed that social workers should offer treatment to families rather than merely obtain information about the patient's history, as it is more often the social worker's major function to do. Because the psychiatric resident needed pertinent information quickly to formulate the treatment plan, he also saw the family. The staff and the relatives soon became thoroughly confused about their relationships with each other. Various schemes have been employed to simplify and integrate the respective roles of the resident and the social worker. Both of them, for example, participate with the patient and his family in the four-way meeting. It has been found in other psychiatric programs in which several staff members work with the same patient that the staff members' personal emotional security markedly affects their ability to work together comfortably.[11]

11. See A. H. Stanton, and M. S. Schwartz, *The Mental Hospital* (New York: Basic Books, 1954).

The frequent changes in routines on Tompkins I and the complex power struggle which revolves around Dr. Detre among the staff has left at least one social worker wishing that there were somewhat more structure in the unit's operation. The great involvement of the entire staff in patient care often has left the lines and areas of responsibility quite unclear. A more clearly defined role, which many social workers seem to want, would give those attached to Tompkins I an opportunity for more systematic involvement in the patients' treatment programs. The social workers on the staff remain responsible to the chief of social work in the Yale Department of Psychiatry rather than to Dr. Detre and thus can obtain external support should the need arise.

Of the various disciplines represented on the unit, clinical psychology had until very recently experienced the least development. The original clinical psychologist resigned for personal reasons during the summer of 1961 and was not replaced until February 1962 because of the great selectivity used by the Yale faculty committee. The absence of a psychologist while tightly knit personal relationships were developing among the staff created some difficulty when the newcomer arrived. Because the unit was governed by the personal leadership of Dr. Detre rather than by systems of routines, each of the staff had developed a unique personal relationship with him and there was some fear that a bright newcomer might upset the existing power structure among the staff. With the passage of time, however, the psychologist has become an integral part of the unit.

One of Dr. Detre's prime considerations when the psychologist was being selected was his desire to obtain someone with an active interest in research. The psychologist, with the help of several research assistants and senior medical students, performs or supervises much of the research directed at evaluation of the unit's program. Little emphasis has been placed in the Tompkins I program on individual psychological testing, and outside consultants have usually been employed when there has been a need for this service. Now that a psychologist is again on the unit's staff, the Yale graduate program in psychology has begun to send its students to Tompkins I for experience in the administration of psychological tests and, as a result, more psychological examinations are being performed.

Because extensive psychiatric resources are available to provide therapy to inpatients, the psychologist has been able to provide individual and group therapy for Tompkins I patients following their discharge. Dr. Detre is currently giving serious consideration to an expansion of after-care activities.

In the minds of many observers, the psychiatric nursing director is Dr. Detre's key assistant because of the vital role nurses play in ensuring that routines are adhered to, that a calm atmosphere is maintained, and that doctors' orders are followed. Dr. Detre has attempted to cultivate the nurses' self-esteem, dignity, and willingness to cooperate in order to make them aware of the significance of their involvement in the treatment program. Since they are expected to assume greater authority and responsibility than nurses generally have on other services, an inservice educational program is provided for both the permanent and the student nurses. The nursing staff meets regularly with Dr. Detre, and are carefully instructed in the nature, action, side effects, and toxic manifestations of any drug before it is used on the service. Through participation in various conferences on the unit, they gain further experience in the handling of patients and their problems.

From the beginning, the nurses have participated in staff conferences and attended group and family therapy sessions. The intense degree of their involvement in the treatment program has created problems for them and for other members of the staff as well. Most residents are not used to seeing nurses exercise the degree of responsibility they have on Tompkins I and have had to revise to some extent their concept of the nurse's role. Residents new to the unit rarely consulted with the nurses until Dr. Detre convinced them of his own point of view that it is both necessary and wise to include the nurse's observations of patient behavior in reports and decisions.

Although the nurses were proficient at one-to-one contacts with patients, they found it considerably more difficult to accustom themselves to active participation in group meetings with patients. Early in 1962 Dr. Detre decided that the patient-staff meetings should be conducted not only by the psychiatric residents but also by other staff members, including the nurses. Dr. Detre first presented this idea at a meeting of the senior staff where it met with intense resistance. When he raised it again a month later it gained some adherents, and the psychologist and the social workers agreed to serve as leaders. The psychiatric nursing director agreed in principle to the nurses' serving in a similar capacity, but her staff was reluctant, and some junior nurses even rearranged their schedules in order to be off duty at the time of the meetings. Dr. Detre, however, convinced the senior nurses that they would enjoy added prestige by conducting meetings, and the members of the nursing staff now take regular turns.

Recently an innovation has been made in the way the regular Monday morning staff conference is conducted. The nurse in charge of the unit over the weekend reports to the entire staff in the presence of all the patients about the activities and behavior of each patient. This method for bringing the staff up to date is designed primarily to help patients understand the nature of staff communication and decision making and thereby to dispel their fears of what the nurse might report behind closed doors. The procedure, which is different from that followed in most institutions where there is communication only between the head nurse and the director of the service, also has the purpose of improving communication among the staff.

The size of the nursing staff has grown steadily since Tompkins I opened as a result both of the general expansion of the unit's teaching program and its ability to extract more nurses from the Hospital administration. The cooperation of the Hospital's Central Nursing Office has been cultivated by the acceptance on Tompkins I of physically ill patients who have become emotionally disturbed during hospitalization and the retention on the unit of psychiatric patients who have developed physical illness. In 1963, 23 graduate nurses, licensed practical nurses, and male aides were assigned permanently to the unit, in contrast to the 13 assigned in January 1960. In addition, 10 senior nursing and practical nursing students rotate through Tompkins I, spending several months on the unit.

Nurses apparently find their participation in the psychiatric program rewarding. There is a low rate of turnover, and about 80 percent of the original nursing personnel are still on the staff. During 1962 four staff nurses participated in a fairly complex clinical investigation of sleep disorders, spending an extra eight to twelve hours weekly on the unit without any additional compensation. In mid-1963 there was a waiting list for assignment to the unit's nursing staff.

When vacancies do occur in the Tompkins I nursing staff, preference in hiring is generally given to recent young graduates of nursing schools who have had little or no psychiatric experience. The reason for the policy is the staff's wish to inculcate new staff members in the Tompkins I approach to psychiatric nursing without having to overcome previously developed stereotyped attitudes toward psychiatric care, patients, and programs.

The Cost

A firm policy of accepting only paying patients on Tompkins I was instituted by the Planning Committee in the belief that the unit would otherwise operate at a loss. After a careful analysis of the actual cost of operating Tompkins I, John Ives, the Assistant Director of Grace-New Haven, concluded that the psychiatric unit was paying for itself in every respect, including paying off of original construction costs.[12] One reason for the good financial position of Tompkins I is the fact that the unit has always been full, and there is often a waiting list.

A breakdown of average per diem Grace-New Haven charges to psychiatric and to medical patients in September 1961 shows the following:

Table 1. Per diem charges.

Patient type	Psychiatric	Non-psychiatric
Room and board	$27.03	$26.57
Laboratory	2.31	7.40
Pharmacy	0.71	1.36
X ray	0.30	2.90
Electroencephalogram	0.40	–
Electroshock treatment	0.03	–
Miscellaneous[a]	0.32	7.02
	$31.10	$45.25

[a] Includes charges for operating room, recovery room, delivery room, anesthesiology, and so on.

In a survey of 584 general hospitals, Bush found that the per diem charge in the majority of psychiatric units ranged between $15 and $22.[13] In some general hospitals, however, per diem fees for psychiatric care run as high as $60. Patient fees at state mental hospitals average approximately $5 per day, although such special state institutions as the Massachusetts Mental Health Center charge $23 per day. Fees to patients do not, of course, necessarily exactly correspond with costs incurred by the hospital for the care of those patients.

12. J. E. Ives, "Costs and Sources of Funds — Psychiatric Units in General Hospitals," paper read at Conference on Psychiatric Services in General Hospitals, Philadelphia, October 1962.

13. Bush, p. 1062

Ross has pointed out[14] that although an intensive treatment program may be expensive, it may be less expensive than state hospital treatment on a per-patient basis because the length of stay is shorter. The Assistant Director of Grace-New Haven believes that although the basic, day-to-day care of the psychiatric patient is more costly because of the large nursing staff that is necessary, this is offset by decreased need for medical facilities and equipment that are generally very expensive to build or operate.

The average length of stay on Tompkins I being six weeks, patients are confronted with a hospital bill of approximately $1,300 plus a professional services fee ranging between $210 and $360. The Connecticut Blue Cross plan, unlike most Blue Cross plans in other states and regions, provides psychiatric patients with the same coverage of up to 120 days of general hospital care that it gives medical and surgical patients. A major factor in Blue Cross ability to provide such extensive psychiatric coverage is the relative scarcity in Connecticut of general hospital psychiatric units. Connecticut Blue Cross officials indicate that if half of the state's general hospitals had psychiatric units, Blue Cross premium rates would have to be raised or it would become bankrupt.

Of 152 psychiatric patients discharged from Grace-New Haven during 1961–62, 67 percent were covered in part by Blue Cross and 22 percent by commercial insurance, 9 percent paid their entire bill out of pocket, and 2 percent were welfare patients.[15] The source of total payment for the bills of 31 patients sampled during this period was as follows:

Table 2. Source of financing.

Source	Amount	Percent
Blue Cross	$17,749.92	32.0
Commercial insurance	6,413.89	11.5
Patient	20,571.56	37.2
Allowances	365.66	0.6
Balance due	10,319.56	18.7
Total	$55,420.59	100.0

Although most of the patients had some form of insurance coverage, they met a significant proportion of their bills themselves.

14. H. A. Ross, *Hospitalizing the Mentally Ill — Emergency and Temporary Commitments*, Legislative Research Center, University of Michigan. Reprinted from *Current Trends in State Legislation*, 1955–56, p. 554.
15. Ives, p. 8.

Approximately half of the balance of $10,319 due Grace-New Haven is considered to be uncollectable. The hospital is collecting 90 cents on the dollar for its psychiatric billings, which is the same collection ratio that exists for its medical billings.

After reviewing the financial status of Tompkins I, the Assistant Director concluded that "the combination of making money and rendering service is one that the administrator and board very rarely are able to put together and when they are able to it makes them happy." [16]

The Impact of Tompkins I

Scope of the Program

Between the opening of Tompkins I in January 1960 and April 15, 1963, there were a total of 557 admissions to the unit. Of the 167 patients admitted from April 15, 1962, to April 15, 1963, 60 percent were female and 40 percent male, which is consistent with the usual male-female patient ratios of most psychiatric units in general hospitals. About 60 percent of the patients were between the ages of 15 and 35. The age distribution is shown below:

Table 3. Patient distribution by age.

Age	Number	Percent
Under 15	9	5
15–25	57	34
25–35	41	25
35–45	18	11
45–55	20	12
55 and above	22	13
Total	167	100

Although the Planning Committee made no official public distinction among the referral sources which would be given priority when patients were admitted, unannounced priorities have in fact existed from the outset. The top three priorities for admission to Tompkins I have been assigned by the medical staff to disturbed patients on other services of Grace-New Haven Hospital, students in the various divisions of Yale University, and members and families of the university community. It is Dr. Detre's view that since

16. Ives, p. 11.

Tompkins I is a teaching unit of the Yale Medical Center, its greatest obligation is to persons in these categories.

Of the 167 patients admitted between April 15, 1962, and April 15, 1963, 33 percent came from "internal" referral sources. The unofficial priorities, coupled with the Hospital's policy of accepting only paying patients, has meant that service has been given primarily to persons in the more affluent socioeconomic groups. Patients in the lower socioeconomic groups are rarely admitted, in part because they cannot afford the hospital rates. Another possible factor is the view widely held in the psychiatric profession that such patients have a poor prognosis. There are virtually no admissions from the Emergency Room, which is used primarily by the lower socioeconomic classes, because Tompkins I is always up to, and frequently over, full census.

Table 4. Patient referral source.

Source of referral	Number	Percent
Readmissions	18	11
Referred from non-psychiatric practice	68	41
Referred by psychiatrists	47	28
Emergency transfers from other hospital services	11	6
Yale students	23	14
Total	167	100

Psychiatric diagnosis, the significance of which is often a matter of professional dispute, was not given very much attention by the Planning Committee. Since the broad framework of the Tompkins I program is built on the expectation that a patient will benefit from short-term hospitalization, diagnosis continues to be irrelevant for purposes of admission. The distribution of patients by diagnostic categories during the year ending April 15, 1963, is shown below.

In a recent year, 27 percent of the patients from New Haven in Connecticut state mental hospitals were diagnosed as having chronic brain syndromes, for which the prognosis is poor. Only 3 percent of the Tompkins I patients had this diagnosis. On the other hand, 28 percent of the patients on Tompkins I were considered to have neurotic depressive reactions — a diagnosis rarely made for New Haven residents admitted to state hospitals — for which the prognosis is good. There are, of course, differences in the way diagnoses are reached at a state hospital and in a teaching

Table 5. Patient distribution by diagnosis.

Diagnosis	Number	Percent
Adjustment reaction to childhood	4	2.4
Adjustment reaction to adolescence	7	4.2
Phobic reaction	2	1.2
Psychosomatic reaction, respiratory type (intractable asthma)	1	0.6
Personality disorder, passive-aggressive type	4	2.4
Personality disorder, hysterical type	2	1.2
Sociopathic personality	3	1.8
Barbiturate addiction	1	0.6
Depressive reaction, neurotic	47	28.2
Depressive reaction, psychotic	10	6.0
Depressive reaction, involutional type	13	7.8
Manic depressive reaction	3	1.8
Borderline state	3	1.8
Anorexia nervosa	4	2.4
Postpartum psychosis	1	0.6
Dissociative reaction	1	0.6
Schizophrenic reaction	39	23.2
Behavior disorder associated with seizure disorder	8	4.8
Mental retardation	2	1.2
Brain tumor	1	0.6
Presenile dementia	1	0.6
Acute brain syndrome (other)	6	3.6
Chronic brain syndrome (other)	4	2.4
Total	167	100.0

unit. The statistics are striking, however. One conclusion of the 1957 Connecticut Mental Health Survey was:

> On the whole, the psychiatric inpatient units are seeing a different group of ill people than the state hospitals, many of whom would not otherwise receive any definitive psychiatric hospital therapy. In this regard it is fair to state that it is not likely that psychiatric units in general hospitals will materially affect the admissions to the state hospitals.[17]

The median length of stay on Tompkins I is six weeks, which includes a final period during which the patient must demonstrate that he can function effectively by going to work during the day, or going home to his family at night. Fifteen percent of the patients are discharged within one to three weeks — these are primarily patients suffering acute postpartum depressions or post-

17. Committee on Hospital Services for the Mentally Ill.

surgical reactions. Another 10 percent, principally patients with psychotic character disorders or adolescent schizophrenics of particular interest in a teaching program, may stay on Tompkins I for three to six months. Ross[18] reports an average length of stay of about three weeks in the psychiatric wards of 111 general hospitals. In the Connecticut state mental hospitals the median length of stay in 1955 was 75 days, in the West Haven Veterans Administration Hospital it was 56 days, and in the Hartford General Hospital it was 12 days.

Of the 167 patients admitted to Tompkins I in 1962–63, 78 percent were discharged to the community with the medical staff's consent, 7 percent were transferred to other private treatment facilities, 6 percent were transferred to state hospitals, and 9 percent were discharged against medical advice. Arrangements were made for 83 percent of those discharged to the community to continue to receive some form of psychotherapy. This unusually high proportion is indicative of the heavy emphasis the staff places on continued after-care, of the type of highly motivated patient initially admitted to Tompkins I, and of the number and variety of psychiatric resources available in the New Haven community.

Late in 1961 the staff wrote that "the overall rate of discharge and the very low readmission rate so far are encouraging indications of the initial success of the program." [19] At the Hartford Hospital approximately 15 percent of the discharged patients are readmitted within any given 12-month period; for the three Connecticut state hospitals the readmission rate is around 35 percent; statistics for Tompkins I indicate that the rate is 11 percent.

Dr. Detre is now making a serious effort to determine the post-hospital adjustment of Tompkins I patients. The clinical psychologist is developing a self-administered questionnaire which can be used to collect data from all discharged patients 9, 18, and 27 months after they leave the unit. The questionnaire will be supplemented by random visits to patients' homes to check on the validity of their responses. A preliminary pilot study of former patients indicates that of the 13 about whom adjustment could be learned, 12 were functioning "well."

Relationships with the Hospital and the Community

It has been hypothesized that the prompt availability of expert medical resources is one of the major benefits that accrues when a

18. Ross, p. 554.
19. Detre, Sayres, Norton, and Lewis, p. 619.

psychiatric unit is located in a general hospital.[20] Medical consultation is used extensively for the patients on Tompkins I, and X rays and electroencephalograms, which in a state hospital may not be completed for weeks, are given immediate attention. It is uncertain how essential such frequent medical consultation is to patient care.

The prompt medical consultation obtained for Tompkins I patients has been achieved in the face of a generally ambivalent, if not negative, attitude toward the psychiatric unit on the part of a number of physicians who have not fully accepted the role or value of psychiatric services in a general hospital. Concern over the potentially disruptive behavior of patients with mental illness has been one factor in these physicians' reluctance to accept the unit. Although Dr. Detre has taken the precaution of constantly warning his medical colleagues that occasional suicides or aggressive episodes must be expected on a psychiatric service, patients from Tompkins I have rarely caused any significant disturbances. On the infrequent occasions when the hospital has been upset by bizarre behavior, patients on the medical or surgical services were responsible. The rarity of disturbances on Tompkins I has served over time to calm the fears of other hospital staff.

In many general hospitals with psychiatric units, an assigned member of the unit's staff provides any necessary psychiatric consultation to the medical service. At Grace-New Haven, however, consultation is provided by a member of the Yale Department of Psychiatry who is not affiliated with Tompkins I. Because this psychiatrist is not administratively associated with the unit and cannot admit patients to it, the staff on the medical and surgical services have often had difficulty transferring disturbed patients to it in spite of the relatively high priority Dr. Detre has given to such requests. The problem is especially evident for the patients of medical residents. As a consequence, senior attending staff and chiefs of service usually request private consultation from Dr. Detre or his chief residents and thus ensure that, if transfer to Tompkins I is necessary, the administrative procedures will be simplified.

Generally, New Haven psychiatrists have reacted favorably to Tompkins I, and many psychoanalysts in the community immediately welcomed the new inpatient service and regularly referred patients who required hospitalization. A number of others, however, who have been described by a member of the Tompkins I

20. T. Detre, D. R. Kessler, and H. G. Jarecki, "The Role of the General Hospital in Modern Community Psychiatry," *American Journal of Orthopsychiatry* 33:691 (July 1963).

staff as "more orthodox than the high priests of the profession themselves," opposed the new program because of the violence its stress on family and group therapy did to the traditional one-to-one relationship between therapist and patient. In addition, these psychiatrists complained that the heavy use of drugs in the unit was alleviating patients' symptoms without getting at the underlying reasons for their illness as traditional psychoanalysis is intended to do. Over time, however, the range of referral sources has steadily increased.

An orientation toward family therapy has been introduced into the practices of some of New Haven's private psychiatrists, and by the summer of 1963 four psychiatrists were offering comprehensive patient-family treatment for the relatively modest fee of $5 to $15 per session. Thus a family can secure treatment outside the hospital in an emergency or arrange follow-up care after hospital discharge at reasonable cost. As more residents from Tompkins I go into private practice in New Haven this trend can be expected to increase.

Although the policy established for Tompkins I proposed that the full-time staff would have sole responsibility for the psychiatric management of the hospitalized patient, it also, as previously noted, provided that patients might retain their own psychiatrists if both Dr. Detre and the private psychiatrist agreed. By 1963, Dr. Detre estimates, not more than 5 percent of the patients admitted to Tompkins I had exercised the option of continuing therapy sessions with their own psychiatrists while in the hospital.

The Planning Committee had recommended that two private psychiatrists be included on a permanent committee that would act in an advisory capacity to the psychiatric inpatient unit and propose policies to the Medical Board of Grace-New Haven Hospital. This committee met rarely, and for all practical purposes has been nonexistent since 1962. As a result, responsibility for the formulation of policy relevant to Tompkins I has rested solely with Dr. Detre and other members of the Yale Department of Psychiatry.

New Haven private practitioners have not demanded the active role in the determination of Tompkins I policy which comparable groups play in other communities. One psychiatrist thinks that the explanation is the fact that his colleagues view Tompkins I as an economic asset rather than a threat. All patients referred by a private practitioner to Tompkins I for hospitalization are referred back to him for after-care, and those not previously under treatment are referred to a private psychotherapist. Because 83 percent of Tompkins I patients discharged in 1962–63 are being given some form of continued treatment, private practitioners are receiving a sizable number of referrals from the inpatient unit.

The former patients of Tompkins I show the community that it is possible to receive successful, short-term treatment for mental illness in a familiar local hospital. This success, in turn, helps to overcome the stereotypes of remoteness, isolation, and incurability that are usually associated with the treatment of the mentally ill. Unlike the much longer stays in remote state hospitals, local, short-term hospitalization prevents families from disentangling themselves emotionally from the absent member, and thus can facilitate the patient's return home and reintegration into his family.[21]

Probably the agencies and institutions serving the lower socioeconomic groups, who have been generally unsuccessful when they have tried to refer patients to Tompkins I, constitute the greatest source of negative reaction to the unit. The personnel of these agencies further complain that the Tompkins I staff display an attitude of superiority and disdain for the professional abilities of others. The impression given them is that Tompkins I has the only program capable of providing effective treatment and that the efforts of others are generally futile. This attitude is exemplified by the reluctance of Tompkins I staff members to transfer a patient to a state hospital. They believe that only they can successfully help the patient and that transfer to a state hospital is tantamount to sealing the patient's doom. Although in 1963 Tompkins I and various community agencies had some contact over the specific problems of certain patients, there was no evidence of any joint attempt to meet mental health needs in the community.

The Future

The most pressing problem confronting Tompkins I at this time is its inability to provide service to more than a very small part of the community. It was obvious, when the unit opened in 1960, that it could not begin to meet any substantial amount of the needs of the metropolitan New Haven area, and its founders so warned. However, the existence of even a minimal facility has further increased community recognition of the need for adequate

21. Joint Commission on Mental Illness and Health, p. 265.

psychiatric resources and stimulated demands for local inpatient services for the mentally ill.

Several solutions have been considered by the Yale Medical Center. The first possibility was an expansion of Tompkins I, and consideration was given to annexing the ward above Tompkins I so that the psychiatric unit would have two floors. Because of the pressure for space for other facilities and services within the building, this does not appear to be feasible at present. It is hoped, however, that at least some adjacent laboratories can be renovated so that already existing staff can be provided with office space. As part of the master plan for Grace-New Haven Hospital, it is intended to construct a variety of new buildings, one of which will contain a 50-bed psychiatric unit. This, however, is not scheduled for completion until 1970.

At the present time there is little that Tompkins I can do to extend the scope of its services. The suggestion has been made that the few patients who are not residents of New Haven be denied admission, but such a policy would have a minimal impact. It is conceivable that improved outpatient management on an antidepressant drug regimen plus supportive therapy could have obviated the need for hospitalization for many of the patients hospitalized on Tompkins I with a diagnosis of neurotic depressive reactions. In this connection Dr. Detre feels that his program has had at least an indirect benefit because "residents trained in this service are much more inclined not to hospitalize patients and their impact on the emergency room is already felt."

Of more immediate significance to the New Haven community is the plan of the Connecticut Department of Mental Health to construct and operate, in conjunction with the Yale Department of Psychiatry, a "mental health center" adjacent to Grace-New Haven Hospital. This project has been discussed for almost a decade and was one of the factors considered by the Planning Committee in 1958. Funds have now been appropriated by the State Legislature, a site has been selected, the center's director has been chosen, and the center is to begin operation in 1965 according to present plans. It has been designed to include 60 inpatient beds, facilities for 50 day-patients, and a large outpatient department. Because the patient population is to be drawn from the lower and middle socioeconomic classes, the present pressure on Tompkins I from this segment of the community will be partially alleviated.

The Medical Care Program of the United Mine Workers Welfare and Retirement Fund

November 1961

Revised September 1966

Marjorie Taubenhaus / Roy Penchansky

Genesis of the United Mine Workers Welfare and Retirement Fund

Both bituminous (soft) and anthracite (hard) coal are produced in the United States. The bituminous coal industry,[1] which accounts for over 90 percent of total production, reached its peak in 1947 when 630 million tons were produced. In that year 6,700 bituminous mines were operating with 419,000 employees who worked an average of 234 days per year and produced 6.42 tons per man per day. As a result of a decrease in demand for coal and an increase in output per man per day to 16.84 tons, only 130,000 employees working an average of 225 days per year were needed to produce the 487 million tons mined in 1964. Table 1 presents summary statistics on the industry from 1941 through 1964.

The three major areas in which coal deposits are found are the Appalachian Region from Pennsylvania to Alabama; the Central Region, which includes parts of Illinois, Indiana, Iowa, Michigan, and Kentucky; and the Western Region covering Colorado, Montana, New Mexico, Washington, and Wyoming. Bituminous coal is found in 33 states but production is significant in only 22 and, in fact, four states — West Virginia, Pennsylvania, Kentucky, and Illinois — accounted for nearly 75 percent of bituminous coal production in 1959.

Because coal deposits are often found in hilly or mountainous areas, mines are usually located in or near small and frequently isolated rural communities. Many of these were established only because of the mining activity.

Most coal production (two thirds) takes place in deep, underground mines, although an increasing proportion is surface-mined by stripping. A small number of large mines account for a major share of production, 3 percent of the mines producing 46 percent of the coal in 1964. A number of the larger mines have been owned by the large coal consumers of the past, railroads and steel companies. The number of mines in operation varies greatly over time

1. This report and the following statistics relate solely to the bituminous coal industry unless specific reference to the contrary is made.

Table 1. Summary statistics on the bituminous coal industry.

Year	Production — net tons (in millions)	Average price per ton	Number of mines	Employees (in thousands)	Average number of days worked	Net tons per man per day	Average hourly income
1941	514	$2.19	6,822	457	216	5.20	$0.88
1944	620	2.92	6,928	393	278	5.67	1.07
1947	631	4.16	8,700	419	234	6.42	1.64
1950	516	4.84	9,429	416	183	6.77	2.01
1953	457	4.92	6,671	293	191	8.17	2.48
1956	500	4.82	8,520	228	214	10.28	2.81
1959	412	4.77	7,719	180	188	12.22	3.25
1962	422	4.48	7,740	140	199	14.72	3.12
1964	487	4.45	7,630	136	225	16.84	3.30

Sources: Monthly Labor Review (Washington, D.C.: Bureau of Labor Statistics, United States Department of Labor, selected issues); *Minerals Yearbook II: Mineral Fuels* (Washington, D.C.: Bureau of Mines, Department of the Interior, 1964).

because small and marginal mines are brought into production to meet seasonal demands or when the price of coal is high enough to offset their marginal nature. The low cost of opening a mine and the general surplus of mines permit this fluctuation.

Mining Manpower

Although considered skilled workers, bituminous coal miners have no apprenticeship or formal training program. Traditionally, new employees have been trained while acting as helpers or in lesser mining jobs. With the increase in mechanization, the miners' work is changing, and there is now some feeling that a lower order of skill and younger men are required for the work.

Most active bituminous mine workers are members of the United Mine Workers of America (UMWA). Violence and bloodshed characterized the early history of labor relations in the industry. The owners of the coal mines bitterly opposed union organization, and the bitterness engendered in these early struggles carried over into the collective bargaining that followed recognition of the union. During the late 1930's, throughout the 1940's and into 1950 each negotiation was a battle, frequently involving long strikes and court action. The owners concede that John L. Lewis, president of the union, was the victor in most of these struggles, with the result that wages, hours, and working conditions for the miners improved greatly during the period.

In 1950 a "new look" in collective bargaining in the coal industry appeared with a change in leadership among the employers and a recognition by both sides that more was to be gained by cooperation than by conflict. Since that date all new contracts have been negotiated without strikes, and relations have been as cordial and cooperative as they once were bitter and combative. The union and the owners now lobby together to secure legislation favorable to the industry.

Although production per man-hour in the mines has been increasing over a long period of time, the increase has been especially rapid recently, largely because of increased mechanization, the growth of strip mining (with its greater efficiency of production of poorer quality coal) and higher management efficiency. As shown in Table 1, output per man per day has tripled since 1944.

The mechanization and modernization which have made possible the great increase in productivity have had the blessing and cooperation of the UMWA, which has demanded only that its workers share the benefits. In fact, the union's heavy demands for higher wages and for fringe benefits have driven the operators to adopt more modern methods in order to remain competitive. The demand for coal, however, has not kept pace with the increasing productivity of the workers, even though the average price per ton at the pit in 1959 was slightly lower than it had been in 1950. Consequently, there has been a great decrease in the total man-hours required. Utility companies used about half of the 500 million tons produced in 1965 with 52 percent of the nation's electricity produced in coal-fired plants. Coal consumption is certain to increase as electrical needs increase, but increased competition from nuclear power represents a new threat to the coal-mining industry.

Displacement from the mines has meant long periods of unemployment for many of the men because of the lack of other types of work in the isolated coal communities and the hesitancy of many workers and their families, particularly the older men, to move elsewhere. It was estimated in 1951 that more than 100,000 men were seeking work in the coal mining areas and that at least 50,000 of these are over 45 years old and would never be reemployed.[2]

The Welfare and Retirement Fund

The UMWA Welfare and Retirement Fund had its origin during the period of struggle and before the "new look" in collective bargaining in the industry. As far back as 1896 a district union convention in Morgantown asked the national office for a program of medical care, and every annual convention, both district and national, from 1928 on passed resolutions requesting the national office and the governing bodies of the union to explore and develop methods of providing medical care to union members. In the spring of 1946 Lewis included a welfare fund in a package of demands he presented to the operators. The operators vigorously opposed this demand, labeling the welfare fund "no more than a vast treasury to strengthen the union and build a social government within our public structure." [3] Negotiations were not successful, and the union struck when the contract ended on March 31.

After the strike had been in effect for over a month, Lewis

2. Michael Widmann, Assistant to the President and Director of Research and Marketing of the United Mine Workers of America, in a prepared statement before the United States Committee on Unemployment, October 1951.

3. *Coal Age*, April 1946, 51:127.

called a two-week truce during which the miners worked. When it became apparent that no agreement would be reached during the truce, President Truman ordered Julius Krug, the Secretary of the Interior, to seize the mines. At the end of the truce (May 25), the miners, following their old rule of "no contract — no work," again walked out even though the mines were being operated under government order through a Federal Coal Mines Administration established by the Department of the Interior.

Secretary Krug then entered into intensive negotiations with Lewis and on May 29, 1946, a new contract was signed which, in addition to an 18½ cent an hour wage increase and certain other benefits, provided for "a welfare and retirement fund" to be financed by "5 cents per ton on each ton of coal produced for use or for sale." The financing mechanism was one that had been used in Britain since 1920 when a National Miner's Welfare Fund was created for the purposes of improving the "social well-being, the recreation, and the living conditions of mine workers. It was financed by a tax of one penny per ton of output." [4] The agreement also called for a study and survey of hospital and medical facilities in the bituminous coal mining areas.

"The operators were thrown into consternation by the terms of the agreement," [5] and were especially critical of the royalty plan for the welfare and retirement fund. Krug and the Truman Administration were criticized for establishing a dangerous precedent that permitted the union to levy a tax of 5 cents per ton on the consumers of coal. Thus the miners' fund did not have its origin in the normal collective bargaining between management and labor but rather was forced on management by an agreement between the union and the government.

From 1946 to 1950 the Fund, already in operation, continued to be a point of controversy between the parties and one of the major causes of the strikes that plagued the industry during this period. The climax came in 1950 when the struggle over the Fund was waged not only in the economic arena but also in the courts. Following the strike and the court battle the parties reached an agreement for "cooperative administration" of the Welfare and Retirement Fund.

Since 1950 there have been no serious disputes between the parties over the Fund. Of course, as noted above, their general re-

4. Ludwig Teleky, *History of Factory and Mine Hygiene* (New York: Columbia University Press, 1948), p. 227.
5. *The New York Times*, May 30, 1946, p. 1.

lations have improved considerably. Some observers were of the opinion that the Fund, after its acceptance by the industry, would have a stabilizing effect on the relationship. Alinsky, a Lewis biographer, wrote in 1949, "The Welfare Fund is dependent upon coal production, and stoppage of the latter also means cessation of payments to the fund. The Fund has partially put the miners in the coal business, and now a strike against the operators is also a strike against themselves."

The Boone Report

The contract negotiated with the United Mine Workers by the Secretary of the Interior in 1946 contained one unusual and important provision, Section 5:

> The Coal Mines Administrator undertakes to have made a comprehensive survey and study of the hospital and medical facilities, medical treatment, sanitary, and housing conditions in the coal mining areas. The purpose of this survey will be to determine the character and scope of improvements which should be made to provide the mine workers of the Nation with medical, housing, and sanitary facilities conforming to recognized American standards.

Rear Admiral Joel T. Boone, Medical Corps, United States Navy, directed the survey. Five teams made up of Navy officers and enlisted men carried out the field work, with some technical assistance from civilians, during the summer of 1946 in each of the five areas[6] established by the Coal Mines Administration. The results of their survey were published in 1947.[7]

The survey team studied 260 mines, each producing 50,000 tons or more of coal annually and together employing a total of 71,856 workers. Labor and management agreed that conditions in these mines might be considered representative of the industry as a whole. Because of the omission of small mines, the survey team felt that their data tended to show a better picture with respect to housing, sanitation, and medical services than in fact existed.

6. Area I comprised Pennsylvania, northern West Virginia, Ohio, and Maryland; Area II: southern West Virginia, Kentucky, Virginia, Tennessee, and Alabama; Area III: Illinois, Indiana, Iowa, and Michigan; Area IV: Arkansas, Kansas, Missouri, and Oklahoma; and Area V: Colorado, Utah, New Mexico, Montana, Washington, Wyoming, and other Western states.

7. U.S. Department of the Interior, *Report of the Coal Mines Administration: A Medical Survey of the Bituminous-Coal Industry* (Washington, D.C.: U.S. Government Printing Office, 1947).

Housing and Health

The investigators found great variation in all types of facilities, and wrote, "So wide is the range in extremes with respect to housing, water supplies, and sanitary facilities that the median or average conditions are difficult to determine." Much of this variation was a result of marked differences in terrain from one area to another.

Where bituminous coal mines were remote from established communities, the mine operators supplied much of the housing and associated services. Rentals in camp houses, established by supplemental agreements between mine operators and the UMWA, in 1947 averaged about $2.50 per room per month or about $5.00 a month less than noncompany housing. Although some of these "camps" were modern and attractive, generally company-owned housing compared unfavorably with housing owned by the miner or by an independent real estate operator.

Company camps were most common in the Southern Appalachian area (II), where, because of hilly terrain and bad roads, mines were isolated and inaccessible. In the midwestern areas (III and IV), where the land was flat and the roads good, none of the mines surveyed were associated with company camps. But in Area II, 86 percent of the homes inspected were company owned and, although rents were cheap, facilities were often bad. The medical services available to miners reflected the same factors.

Although few facts on the incidence and prevalence of specific diseases were available to the survey teams, they did examine one index of health, the infant mortality rate, and such aspects of medical care as physician-patient ratios, hospital facilities, and methods of payment. Most survey conclusions relate only to the provision and financing of facilities.

Comparison of infant mortality rates in counties within a state showed a general trend toward higher rates in coal-producing counties. The high death rate among miners (in 1946 it was 15.1 compared to 10.0 for the United States as a whole) could be attributed to the hazardous nature of their jobs and was not necessarily related to the presence or absence of medical facilities. During the period 1941–1945, for example, an average of 1,120 fatal injuries occurred in the mines each year.[8]

8. P. Enterline, "A Study of Mortality Rates Among Coal Miners," *American Journal of Public Health* 54:758–768 (May 1964), published in 1964 and based on 1950 statistics found that "Death rates for coal miners are nearly twice those for all working males in the United States, ranging

Financing of Services

Prepayment systems for doctors' services were available in 60 percent and for hospitalization in 66 percent of the mines surveyed. The existence of prepayment plans followed the same regional distribution as company housing and for the same reasons. Over 100 years ago coal mine operators had found that some inducement was needed to persuade physicians to settle in the geographically isolated mining areas and that they could offer an assured income to the doctor through a payroll "check-off" system, under which his fee was deducted from the miners' pay by the operator.

Under the check-off system, the cost to the miner was low, averaging $1.36 a month for single men and $2 for married men. In most cases this covered unlimited office calls, house calls within a limited area, "ordinary medications," and routine immunizations. Obstetrical care and the treatment of venereal disease were excluded. The miner had no choice of physician and usually no contract stating the benefits to which he was entitled.

Originally the physicians had been chosen by the mine management but, as the UMWA gained power, the choice often became a union prerogative. Financial administration of the check-off plans rested in some cases with management, in others with the local union, and in still others with the physician himself.

The administration of the hospital prepayment plans followed the same geographical pattern as did the check-off contract for physician's services. In Area II, the Southern Appalachians, over 90 percent were administered by the hospitals and gave the miners no choice of hospital. Both the hospital and physician check-off plans were discontinued with termination of employment in the mine. When the unemployment was temporary, a retroactive check-off was imposed after the miner returned to work.

---

from a roughly 70 per cent excess at ages 20–24 and 45–54 to a 141 per cent excess at ages 60–64." When deaths from accidents are excluded the excess at the lower age groups is not so great, but the increase in excess mortality for diseases of the respiratory system is still striking (nearly eight times the expected at ages 60–64). A comparison of the U.S. experience with that of British coal miners leads the investigator to conclude that "The poor health which has prevailed in this important segment of our working population is not a 'necessary evil' for workers in the coal mining industry. The 15 per cent excess mortality reported for British coal miners does not appear large when compared with the 95 per cent excess for American coal miners. If subsequent studies support this differential, this comparison is of considerable epidemiological significance and may ultimately point to steps for the improvement of the health of coal miners in the United States."

Although the mining industry was the most hazardous in the nation in terms of severity of injuries and the second most hazardous in terms of frequency of injury, only 14 (about 5 percent) of the mines employed physicians for the treatment of industrial injuries. Under federal sponsorship, a program had been initiated in 1910 under which the miners themselves were trained in the techniques of first aid and mine rescue. By 1938 a peak of 83,000 miners a year were participating in the program. After that year the number gradually declined to 7,000 in 1945, largely because of disputes between management and labor over whether or not employees should be paid time and a half for hours spent in the first aid course.

The medical care of industrial injuries is a legal responsibility of the employer, but there was evidence that the operators were frequently evading it. A special study was made at seven mines in West Virginia where physicians accepted the check-off system to furnish care for nonindustrial injuries and illness. An examination of the claims submitted to the State Compensation Commission in 324 cases indicated that "company" or "check-off" physicians submitted claims in only 21 percent of the cases they treated while "noncompany" physicians submitted claims in 89 percent. The survey team noted, "The physician who receives the check-off for nonindustrial medical care by failing to submit claims for the care of industrial cases in essence furnishes medical care for the employer at the expense of the individual employee."

Nearly all physicians in the coal-mining areas were general practitioners whose offices usually were located in small frame dwellings supplied by management at low rentals. Well-equipped dispensaries were found at only 17 (6.5 percent) of the mines surveyed, and in 13 instances the survey teams noted that the doctor's office was "very disorderly" or "dirty." The team felt that the conscientiousness of the individual physician rather than the lucrativeness of his contract practice seemed to determine his maintenance of office and equipment.

Hospitals varied in character and quality from region to region. In Area I, where approximately 38 percent of bituminous coal miners were employed, there were many large cities and miners were not dependent upon the limited facilities of the mining camps. In Area II, however, where 43 percent of the miners lived, the coal-producing centers were remote from large cities. Here, where the check-off system of payment was most frequent, almost half the hospitals surveyed were small proprietary institutions, and more than one third had four or fewer physicians on the staff.

Of the 153 hospitals surveyed in all areas, 16 (10 percent) were not registered or approved by any accreditation body, and, although the remainder were registered with the American Medical Association, only 55 percent were approved by the American College of Surgeons. More than half the hospitals had no surgeon, internist, or obstetrician on the staff.

The standards for physical facilities used by the survey team were strict, requiring each hospital of up to 150 beds to have two surgical operating rooms and at least one delivery room, labor room, and nursery. According to these criteria, the team concluded, "The evidence is convincing that three-fourths of the hospitals are inadequate with regard to one or more of the following: surgical rooms, delivery rooms, labor rooms and nurseries, clinical laboratories, and X-ray facilities."

Physician and Hospital Supply

In the Appalachian area (Pennsylvania, West Virginia, Virginia, Tennessee, Kentucky, and Alabama), data were assembled on the availability of physicians and of hospital beds. Only one state, Pennsylvania, had physicians in greater supply than the national average used by the team of one doctor per 1,000 population. In the coal-mining counties of Pennsylvania, however, the supply of physicians was substantially smaller. Both Alabama and West Virginia had state averages of 0.9 physicians per 1,000 population, but in Alabama there was no difference between the coal-mining counties and other counties in the state. West Virginia had a range of 0.3 to 1.1 in the coal-producing counties.

The report states: "Observations made throughout the Survey in portions of Kentucky, Tennessee, West Virginia, and Virginia indicate that the mining population in many of the southern areas may have a slightly greater availability of medical services than non-coal-mining populations . . . Within the entire Survey, 96 percent of the mines were within 5 miles of a physician's office. This indicates that, in the southern areas, although physicians may be limited in number, nevertheless they are at least relatively close to the mines." The survey team felt, however, that there was a shortage of younger physicians in the mining areas. Because the number of patients a physician is able to treat may decrease with age, the physician-population ratio might not be a wholly adequate measure of physician availability.

Within selected areas in these six states, only eight of 125 counties (one in Alabama and the others in Pennsylvania and West Virginia) had hospital bed ratios equaling or exceeding 4.5 per 1,000 population, the target figure of the Hill-Burton Hospital Survey and Construction Act. Over half the counties had no hospital beds registered at all, and five of these were in the coal-mining area of West Virginia.

Other survey findings related to the lack of public health programs, particularly health education, and the absence of any comprehensive rehabilitation program. In view of the large number of disabling accidents in the coal-mining industry, rehabilitation programs would seem of primary importance.

The Boone Report was widely quoted to back John L. Lewis' claim that a medical care program was greatly needed by the bituminous coal miners. In 1949 the UMWA published a twelve-page pamphlet excerpting the report. The pamphlet concluded: "It is deeply regretted that the length of the Boone Report compels a digest, for as a whole it goes far beyond these excerpts in sustaining and confirming the justice of the case long pleaded by the United Mine Workers of America." [9]

Operation of the Fund

Although the UMWA Welfare and Retirement Fund was established in 1946, it did not begin continuous operation of the medical program and full provision of benefits until 1950. Legal action by the employers, their withholding of payments to the Fund, collective bargaining disagreements, and the inability of the parties to choose a third trustee combined to interrupt any major Fund activity during the interim period. The administrative mechanism and procedures were established, however, and during limited periods of time, certain benefits were provided.

The Fund is established as an irrevocable trust and operates as an entity separate from the employers and the union. Control of the moneys and full authority over benefits and eligibility rest with three trustees — one chosen by the union, one by management, and one neutral. In 1961 the neutral trustee was also Director of the Fund.

The Fund maintains a central office in Washington, D.C., and ten area medical offices scattered throughout the coal-producing

9. A *Digest of the Medical Survey of the Bituminous Coal Industry* (Washington, D.C.: United Mine Workers of America Welfare and Retirement Fund, 1949).

area. The Fund director is responsible for the executive medical offices, legal staff, field services and investigations, benefit applications and examining, comptroller's office, research, public relations, and administrative services. An executive medical officer directs the ten area medical offices. In 1960 the Fund had approximately 425 administrative employees, 225 of these in the area medical offices.

Total administrative costs, including those of the area offices, for the fiscal year ending June 30, 1965, were $4,313,458 or 3.6 percent of total expenditures by the Fund. The administrative burden is affected by the nationwide distribution of beneficiaries and by the use of local union offices to assist members in the filing of application forms.

The Fund operates on a pay-as-you-go basis. There was no attempt to fund the pensions or other benefits fully by developing actuarial reserves, because an immediate program was desired and it was thought that funding would require collection of funds for some time before services could be provided. Income is used to pay for current benefits, and any difference is added to or drawn from available reserves. For the fiscal year ending June 30, 1960, total income was $130 million, the Fund's expenses $148 million, and $18 million was drawn from reserves to meet the deficit. For the 1961 fiscal year, the Fund's income was $116 million and expenditures $133 million. The reserve balance at the end of the 1961 fiscal year was $100 million, of which $28 million was invested in long-term mortgages of the Miners' Memorial Hospital Association and $47 million in government bonds.

Except for interest on investments, all the Fund's income is derived from the royalty payments on coal tonnage mined under union contract. The initial 5 cents per ton royalty was increased in collective bargaining to 40 cents per ton in 1952 where it has remained. Because the income fluctuates with coal tonnage and benefits are not funded, the trustees have adjusted eligibility and benefits to maintain a sound financial position.

Benefits

The Fund provides three major types of benefits: pensions, medical care, and funeral expenses and widows' and survivors' benefits. These benefits cost $70 million, $55 million, and $3.6 million, respectively, in the fiscal year ending June 30, 1961.

The pensions, which are in addition to Social Security benefits, are available to miners 60 years of age or over who have had 20 years of service in the industry in the past 30 years and who were employed regularly in the industry immediately prior to the Fund's establishment (May 29, 1946). The pension was set at $100 a month in 1950 but was reduced by the trustees to $75 monthly in December 1960, because of a decrease in Fund income. On February 1, 1965, the benefit was raised to $85.

Although the exact form of the widows' and survivors' benefits has varied over the years, the amount of the total benefit has remained relatively stable at about $1,000. In 1961 it provided $350 for funeral expenses and a total sum of $650 over one year as well as medical care also for one year. These benefits were available to the survivors of active and retired miners and miners unemployed for up to one year. Earlier the widows' and survivors' benefits had been available to the families of unemployed miners for more than one year, but on July 1, 1960, a one-year limit was imposed because of the operating deficit of the Fund.

A maintenance benefit for widows and dependent children was provided in the early 1950's but later discontinued. The trustees have also authorized the payment of mine disaster benefits to meet the immediate needs of miners' families affected by serious mine accidents. Expenditures for this purpose totaled $56,000 in 1961.

Medical care services currently authorized by the Fund include:

Hospital care as long as the attending physician considers necessary, private or semiprivate accommodation and special duty nursing if medically necessary, and nursing home and rehabilitation services for convalescent cases. Personal phone calls and radio rental for hospitalized beneficiaries have been specifically excluded, and the Fund does not accept responsibility for custodial care.

Services of participating physicians in the hospital, specialist care in group practice units or in individual specialists' offices, and mental illness diagnosis and short-term therapy.

Pharmaceuticals for hospitalized patients and, under special administrative controls, certain nonemergency but expensive drugs, such as quinidine and epinephrine, needed over a long period by nonhospitalized chronically ill patients, prescribed on the basis of a special diagnosis.

Appliances and prostheses not available from another agency, eyeglasses following major eye surgery, and major mouth surgery.

Removal of teeth and ordinary dental procedures are not included in the program.

The Fund's philosophy is to avoid payment for any service available from another agency, although the strict observance of this policy is not always possible. "Actually, when a labor program pays for medical services which are obtainable from a tax-supported agency the worker is paying twice — once as a taxpayer and once through his program." [10]

In 1961 the Fund's medical care services were available to active and retired miners, miners unemployed for one year, and dependents. Until July 1, 1960, unemployed miners had continued to be eligible for benefits beyond one year unless they began work in another industry. According to the Trustees, the reduction in eligibility to one year was made because of the Fund's operating deficit. Another Fund ruling made in 1960 stated that any miner involved in operating a mine lost his eligibility for Fund benefits. This ruling was directed at those small groups of unemployed miners who banded together and tried to eke out a living from a "truck mine."

Administration of the Medical Program

The Early Medical Program

The Fund medical program began in 1947 with the appointment of a ten-member Medical Advisory Board to outline "a sound Medical, Health, and Hospital Program." R. R. Sayers, M.D., a long-time member of the United States Public Health Service and a specialist in occupational medicine, served as chairman until 1950.

Although conflict over the Fund made it impossible to embark immediately upon an extensive medical care program, Dr. Sayers and his associates started on a program of rehabilitation for the most seriously disabled miners. John L. Lewis had frequently referred to miners "ground up in the wheels of the mining industry and cast aside because they were no longer competent to earn a living or to produce a ton of coal." Aid for these men would relieve suffering after years of hopelessness; it might also

10. Lorin E. Kerr, "The Addition of Essential Health Services," *Papers and Proceedings*, National Conference on Labor Health Services, Washington, 1958.

serve to assure members of the union and of the medical profession of the validity of the Fund program.

Arrangements were made with special institutions capable of providing extensive medical and physical rehabilitation. Among these were the Kessler Rehabilitation Institute in New Jersey; the Institute of Physical Medicine and Rehabilitation in New York; and the Permanente Hospitals at Oakland and Vallejo, California. The first patient to be treated under this program was admitted to the Kessler Institute late in 1947.

By searching records at the union offices and questioning people throughout the coal-mining areas, the Fund located several hundred paraplegics and other disabled miners who had been bedridden without medical care for, in some cases, as long as twenty years.

In this crusade no effort was too great for the union and the Fund. Pullman cars were chartered and converted to hospital cars to transport patients to medical centers. Ambulances were hired to take patients to the trains. Where the lack of roads prevented the ambulance from reaching the patient's home, ten or twelve union members would be summoned to help the ambulance crew carry a stretcher patient several miles down ridges and across creeks. Ambulances bearing patients from different localities would arrive at the Pullman car or chartered plane at about the same time so that there would be as little delay as possible. Photographers recorded the poignant scenes at the railroad stations: stretchers drawn up in rows, miners lifted on to the train in chairs or hoisted through train windows on their stretchers.[11]

By October 1949, 496 miners had been admitted to the centers for physical rehabilitation. By June 1953, over 1,500 persons had been admitted. Although some of these were miners' dependents, crippled by nonoccupational disease or accident, the majority were coal miners themselves. The three major groups of patients, in that order, were paraplegics, amputees, and arthritics. The rehabilitation program was later expanded, and several thousand miners have since received physical and occupational rehabilitation services at other than the special centers.

No matter how extensive the rehabilitation program became, it never was, nor was it intended to be, the major part of the Fund's medical program. The ultimate goal was comprehensive prepaid

11. These photographs appear in *Rehabilitation of the Disabled* (Washington, D.C.: United Mine Workers of America Welfare and Retirement Fund, 1952).

medical care for all miners and their dependents. To create this service, Warren F. Draper, M.D., was appointed Executive Medical Officer of the Fund in September 1948.

Dr. Draper was a former Deputy Surgeon General of the U.S. Public Health Service. A Fellow of the American Medical Association, he had served in that organization's House of Delegates from 1924 to 1946, and was a member of the A.M.A. Council on Industrial Health. During World War II Dr. Draper served as major general in charge of public health on Eisenhower's staff in Europe.

Dr. Draper's office and immediate staff are located in Washington, D.C. where the responsibility for overall planning of Fund medical policy takes place. Soon after the program was begun Dr. Draper established a policy in the office of the Fund that encouraged the staff to carry out research on a wide spectrum of diseases. In one instance, he urged his assistant to make a study and review of the literature on pneumoconiosis, a relatively little known and little recognized disease of coal miners. This study was published in 1956 and stimulated interest in the subject which led to further research by the Public Health Service on the disease. Silicosis has traditionally been the only occupational lung ailment covered by state compensation laws, but the Fund's activities created enough interest and research to lead to administrative and legal changes. In 1965 the Pennsylvania legislature amended the Occupational Disease Act of 1939 to include "coal-miner's asthma" or pneumoconiosis as a compensable disease.

In 1953 the Fund office became disturbed about the large number of cases of shigella in children under the age of two. Again the Public Health Service was stimulated to send a study team into the field and, as a result, a monograph was published on the Relationship of Environmental Factors to Enteric Disease. No practical solutions have been forthcoming, however, as the proposed improvements in plumbing and waste disposal are related to housing and total sanitation control, both of which are beyond the capability of the Fund. Here the only course the Fund feels is practical is to try to stimulate the use of Federal funds. This was done in Lynch, Kentucky, in a slightly different way, when a grant was obtained from the Division of Dental Health of the Public Health Service to support a dental program for children, conducted by a local dentist interested in preventive dentistry.

In spite of these activities at the central office, much responsibility was delegated to regional offices. As Dr. Draper has said:

"Conditions differ widely over the far-flung area in which the mining communities are situated. The density of population, geographic location, proximity to medical centers, number and character of hospitals, the number of physicians in relation to the number of people and their distribution, the types of service that can be provided adequately — all present individual problems that require careful study to find the solution best suited to the area in which they exist." [12]

Ten area medical officers were established, each responsible for activities within a specified area. The area medical offices are located at Beckley, Charleston, and Morgantown, West Virginia; Johnstown and Pittsburgh, Pennsylvania; Knoxville, Tennessee; Louisville, Kentucky; Birmingham, Alabama; St. Louis, Missouri; and Denver, Colorado. Each office was put in the charge of a physician experienced in medical care administration. The area medical administrator was given sufficient flexibility in administrative detail so that he could adjust the general policies of the Washington office to meet the particular needs of his area. However, final decisions ultimately are made in Washington. Any beneficiary can appeal a ruling of an area administrator either through the fund or through the union. In fact, the Washington office has on occasion reversed the area administrator after review of the facts.

By December 1948, the ten area medical offices were staffed. Dr. Draper described the situation at that time in a talk given five years later to medical students in Boston:

> Here we were with money coming in and members of course knowing about Mr. Lewis' desire to have this Fund for his people, and naturally they want care without having to wait any great length of time. They wanted medical care right now and not six months from now. The problem was to provide it right now and the only way to do it was to use the facilities in existence. You have hospitals of certain kinds around these coal mining areas, and some doctors, and you develop a plan to use these people to the best advantage you can.

Thus the basic plan for provision of hospital and medical services was to use the facilities available, with the Fund paying for coverage.

The area medical administrators wrote to each physician in

12. Warren F. Draper, "Problems Encountered in the Operation of the United Mine Workers of America Welfare and Retirement Fund," presented before the 105th Annual Session of the Medical Society of the State of Pennsylvania, Pittsburgh, September 21, 1955.

their area, explaining the plan, and asking the physician if he wished to participate. In many areas, all physicians who expressed a desire to participate were placed on a list that was passed on to the local union. Lists of participating consultants were also developed, and these were circulated among physicians in general practice to facilitate referral in cases where specialist's care was considered necessary.

The operation of the program was simple. A beneficiary would present proper identification to any participating physician. After prescribed treatment the physician sent an invoice containing a report of the procedure to the area medical office. All bills were reviewed in the area medical office and forwarded to the Washington office for audit and payment. If hospitalization was needed, the doctor gave the beneficiary a note to the local union which then issued a hospitalization slip, and the presentation and the payment of the bill were handled in the same way as for physician's billings.

Payment was made to physicians on a retainer, a per session, or a fee-for-service basis, depending on mutual agreement between the physicians and the Fund. The retainer relationships established by the Fund amount to "fee-for-time." This retainer is agreed on only after Fund experience with an individual physician, who is then approached and asked to give a rough approximation of the proportion of his time he spends on Fund patients. On the basis of his income and overhead the retainer is calculated as a proportion equal to the proportion of time spent on Fund patients. This retainer is subject to renegotiation at any time. The physician keeps a register of Fund patients and sends a monthly report to the Fund office. In 1966 about 60 percent of Fund physicians were on retainers and this arrangement is also used with group practice units. In the opinion of the Fund staff the retainer system has a great impact on the quality of service performed by surgeons as it removes the monetary incentive for surgical procedures. It is also felt that the retainer system increases the willingness of physicians to refer patients to specialists when medically necessary. No fee schedules were requested from physicians who were to use their own discretion in charging for any individual case. The Fund has never used a fee schedule because the staff believes it is likely to become a floor, not a ceiling; neither does the schedule recognize differences in training or ability on the part of the doctor or differences in the difficulty of individual cases. The Fund accepts any fee equitable in the eyes of the doctor submitting it which is in line with the usual fees in the locality as witnessed by the area administrator who maintains the right to discuss with the physician any fee that appears excessive.

Arrangements were made separately with each participating hospital for the quality of service and for its cost. Most hospitals were paid an all-inclusive per diem cost, although in some instances incentive pay, such as additional payment per day for each additional nurse hired, was offered in an attempt to improve the quality of service.

In September 1949, payments were suspended by the trustees and physician and hospitalization services halted. By that time some 6,500 physicians and 600 hospitals had participated in the medical program. During 1949 over 55,000 persons received more than 500,000 days of hospital care and almost 275,000 home and office visits.[13]

Disputes between labor and management over the Fund were finally settled in 1950, and the Fund's medical care program was at last fully activated in July 1950, by which time Fund medical officers had accumulated much experience with the daily operations of their program. The fee-for-service program with free choice of physician for home and office visits was not reinstituted and new rules and control mechanisms were adopted. Table 2 presents summary information on the medical services of the Fund from 1950 to 1965.

Problems of the Fund

Certain problems arose almost as soon as the medical program began. Although the majority of physicians gave excellent service to Fund patients at costs that were reasonable and just, the area administrators reported many instances of excessive cost and bad service. Each bill submitted to an area office was accompanied by a report of the procedure performed, which enabled the area medical administrators to discover questionable performance or fees. Each area medical officer personally investigated the prob-

13. "An experiment in providing home and office care to a limited number of beneficiaries on a free-choice-of-physician fee-for-service basis was tried for about eight months. It was unsatisfactory in every respect and therefore discontinued." Warren F. Draper, "United Mine Workers of America Welfare and Retirement Fund Medical Care Program," *American Journal of Public Health* 43:757 (June 1953).

Table 2. Summary statistics on the United Mine Workers of America Welfare and Retirement Fund (dollar figures in millions).

Year	Total receipts	Total expenditures	Medical care expenditures	Days of hospitalization	Number of persons receiving benefits
1951	$130.3	$ 82.0	$25.3	–	–
1952	126.5	126.3	50.0	2,154,882	215,372
1953	131.5	139.0	56.4	2,325,921	230,678
1954	134.8	133.3	52.2	2,058,130	115,274
1955	129.2	119.2	42.8	1,615,486	95,824
1956	154.2	127.7	47.5	1,530,430	89,513
1957	157.1	141.9	59.6	1,631,144	93,679
1958	143.1	142.6	58.1	1,458,385	85,426
1959	132.9	144.2	57.8	1,343,893	81,132
1960	130.0	148.3	61.2	1,355,888	80,663
1961	116.7	133.0	55.0	1,034,921	–[a]
1962	124.1	118.2	50.7	905,691	–[a]
1963	125.0	117.7	50.5	878,288	–[a]
1964	135.8	118.7	52.2	832,189	–[a]
1965	145.1	118.8	48.8	832,749	–[a]

Source: Welfare and Retiremend Fund: Annual Reports (Washington, D.C.: United Mine Workers Welfare and Retirement Fund, 1951–1965).

[a] Since 1961 no figures are given as to the number of persons receiving benefits.

lems in his area and forwarded his findings to the central office in Washington.

The results of these investigations can be summarized briefly. It seemed that certain physicians were incompetent or were performing work they were incapable of doing properly, yet the Fund was often obliged to continue its relationship with these physicians because of personnel shortages in the area. In one section of eastern Kentucky, for example, there were 36 general practitioners, of whom eleven were over the age of 70. Two were known drug addicts, and one, in fact, had just returned from his third stay in the Federal Narcotic Hospital at Lexington. Three were practicing under limited licensure because they did not qualify for full licenses, and two had not graduated from any medical school.

There was also evidence that some otherwise competent physicians did not always consider the best interests of the patient or provide the best care that current knowledge would dictate. Unnecessary surgery was a major offense, as indicated by a study at one hospital where the pathologist's report confirmed a diagnosis of acute appendicitis in only 25 of 54 appendectomies. One physician was reported to have performed twelve appendectomies but to have obtained a white cell count in only one case.

A few physicians made excessive charges for procedures; in general, the administrators felt that they were physicians who handled relatively few Fund patients. There were also indications of excessive use of antibiotics, viewed with alarm by Fund medical officers not only because this wasted money but also because of the dangers inherent in the development of resistant strains of bacteria.

Problems arose with the hospitals concerning lack of proper facilities and improper hospitalizations. Many hospitals were poorly equipped and unable to give the quality of medical service the Fund was pledged to provide. Some lacked laboratories or had no registered nurses, and their general inadequacy was indicated by the fact that they were not listed with either the American Hospital Association or the American Medical Association. Closed-staff proprietary hospitals often urged their physicians to keep the hospital full, thus emphasizing quantity, not quality, of medical care. Although excessive hospitalization depends upon the physician's orders, Fund medical officers thought that the hospital itself often contributed to this major problem.

The area medical administrator is responsible for the quality of care purchased by the Fund and may, within certain limits, interpret the policies established by the trustees so as best to meet the needs of his own area. Insofar as was practicable, the area administrators attempted to meet and to know personally all physicians rendering service to Fund beneficiaries, and many questions of procedure and fees were resolved with physicians through discussion or correspondence. At one hospital, for example, 19 percent of the babies born to Fund beneficiaries were delivered by Caesarean section. After discussion and some education, the Caesarean delivery rate was reduced to 2 percent.

Where physicians seemed unscrupulous, or refused to negotiate with the administrator, the local or state medical society was often approached. The Fund expected the local society to act if evidence could be provided of unethical or incompetent practices. These expectations were not fulfilled, and experience with the county and state societies was usually unsatisfactory. One state medical society, after finding a member guilty of ghost surgery and fee-splitting, decreed a 24-hour suspension from the society, the suspension to be kept confidential.

In an effort to improve the standards of medical practice, consultants were brought to many mining areas to see problem patients, review clinical records, and suggest corrections. The liaison committees of the state and local medical societies aided and cooperated in this program.

Where an absolute shortage of physicians existed, area medical administrators tried to assist in the recruitment of young physicians. Elsewhere the area administrator might give moral support to the establishment of group practice units. In one instance, an Area Medical Office was approached by a delegation from a local mine workers' union for help in securing a replacement to the local check-off doctor with whom they were dissatisfied. The Office found a young general practitioner who was interested in the position only if he could practice with other general physicians and specialists. The Area Medical Office sympathized with this view and helped to set up a group under the sponsorship of a nonprofit corporation of local citizens. Neighboring local unions transferred their check-off to this group and specialists from nearby Pittsburgh began to participate on a part-time basis. The group began operations in February 1952 under the name of the Community Health Center of Russellton, Pennsylvania. This group later expanded with branches in other towns and in a sense established a pattern for Fund assisted group practice in mining areas.

Approach to Organized Medicine

From the start, the American Medical Association recognized the medical significance of the Fund, which was frequently discussed in the House of Delegates, and by the A.M.A.'s Council on Medical Service and Council on Industrial Health. The A.M.A. was primarily concerned with the protection of physicians dealing with the Fund and submitted statements concerning the desirability of free choice of physician with a fee-for-service method of payment, decentralization of control, and the establishment of local councils representing the county medical societies and the Fund. However, the Council on Medical Service and its Committee on Medical Care for Industrial Workers recognized the Fund's concern over the quality of medical and hospital services in some of the mine areas.

As a result of a presentation made by Dr. Draper to the Council in February 1952 the Council agreed to investigate and see what the A.M.A. might do to help improve "health conditions" in mine areas. A survey team was sent into the Kentucky, Tennessee, and West Virginia coal mine districts to meet with representatives of the local medical societies and UMWA medical administrators and to visit as many medical and hospital facilities in these areas as possible.

The survey team recommended expansion and strengthening of general practitioner services. Community hospitals were needed, but the team felt the prevailing pattern of proprietary hospitals should not be disturbed without much further study. They also said that liaison committees should be strongest at the state level and should work with the area administrators in developing postgraduate education programs for physicians. On a national level, they recommended that the A.M.A. standardization and rating services should be brought to bear to insure progress in attaining quality of care. Finally, the team recommended that a conference be held to encourage the states and communities to start on a program to carry out the recommendations.

The Committee on Medical Care for Industrial Workers did sponsor such a conference in Charleston, West Virginia, in September 1952. Attending were over 60 representatives from the medical associations of Kentucky, Pennsylvania, Tennessee, Virginia, and West Virginia, as well as representatives of the UMWA medical program and the A.M.A. Most of the two-day conference was spent in comparatively informal discussions although the five state medical societies presented written position statements at the end of the conference.

Similar conferences following the same pattern, including medical society statements, were held in 1953, 1954, and 1956. The reports of the conferences give an indication of the various concerns and approaches in different regions affected by the Fund's medical care program.

In Kentucky, for example, the state medical society reflected the growing concern of the state's medical practitioners with their own financial problems. During 1954 an economic depression followed the closing down of many eastern Kentucky mines, and the Fund program, with its guaranteed payment for service, took on increased importance in the economic life of Kentucky physicians. Most statements made by the Kentucky delegation relate to the fears of the physicians that the Fund might exclude them from its lists.

In Tennessee, the medical society accepted responsibility for both the quality and the quantity of medical care within the state. The society established a nonprofit medical foundation, empowered to accept financial gifts, to give continuity and permanence to its program. Reports of the Tennessee delegation are therefore primarily progress reports concerned with postgraduate physician education, recruitment of physicians, and possible expansion of Fund services to include office diagnostic procedures.

The position of the Fund's medical officers remained substantially the same from conference to conference. Area administrators presented documentation of their complaints and continued to stress over-utilization of hospital services, unnecessary surgery, and poor medical practice.

The Miners Memorial Hospitals

In certain mining sections the lack or inadequacy of hospital facilities seemed to be the most pressing problem. Dr. Draper in 1951 stated, "The availability of properly qualified physicians depends upon the adequacy of hospital and diagnostic facilities and provisions for housing." [14] Until these physical facilities were provided, Fund officials were convinced, the miners would suffer, both from the poor care given by a poor hospital and from the lack of physicians that is related to poor hospitals. The Fund therefore organized the Miners Memorial Hospital Associations of Kentucky, West Virginia, and Virginia to construct ten community hospitals in areas where the need seemed greatest.

In 1952 the trustees of the Fund authorized loans of over $28 million to the Memorial Hospital Associations. No federal funds were obtained under the Hill-Burton Act. On the basis of greatest need of the beneficiary population, sites were selected at Harlan, Hazard, Middlesboro, Pikeville, McDowell, and Whitesburg, Kentucky; Beckley, Man, and Williamson, West Virginia; and Wise, Virginia. The hospitals were planned and built to function as an integrated unit, with three central hospitals and seven satellite hospitals. Together they provide 1,045 beds under unified administration and policies. The hospitals opened variously from December 1955 to May 1956 and were dedicated as a unit on June 2, 1956.

Full-time specialists were recruited from all over the United

14. Quoted in *Welfare and Retirement Fund: Four Year Summary and Review for the Year Ending June 30, 1951* (Washington, D.C.: United Mine Workers of America Welfare and Retirement Fund, 1951), p. 15.

States. The hospitals were organized as open-staff hospitals, and all family physicians who applied for privileges were accepted. Schools have been established in several of the hospitals to train professional nurses, practical nurses, medical technologists, and nurse anesthetists. The hospitals' residency training programs in surgery, internal medicine, pediatrics, and pathology have been approved by the A.M.A. Committee on Medical Education and Hospitals.

Although the thousand additional beds could not meet all the medical care needs of potential patients, the hospitals and their staffs have helped to raise local standards of medical care. Key personnel are available on a 24-hour basis, and specialists' consultations can be had without delay. Ambulatory patient departments were developed by the hospitals, and by 1960 were handling over 1,000 patients a day. Offices were built in the hospitals for the use of full-time staff specialists.

The impact of the Memorial Hospitals was not confined to the quality of care. Many individual physicians in the areas involved bitterly resented the policies and practices of the hospitals. Some of the most frequently voiced complaints concerned the refusal of the Memorial Hospitals to admit indigent patients, thus placing the total burden of nonpaying patients on other hospitals in the area while siphoning off paying patients. The hospitals were also accused of taking nurses away from other hospitals by paying more than the average wage. And many physicians felt that the full-time staff specialists should not use offices in the hospital to see private, non-Fund patients even though their fees went to the Memorial Hospital fund. This feeling was reflected in the actions of four eastern Kentucky county medical societies which have refused membership to the full-time staff physicians in the Memorial Hospitals located in these counties.

The Memorial Hospitals were expensive for the Fund to maintain. In 1958, of the $58 million expended by the Fund on medical care $15 million were used to support the hospitals. This was at a time when a decreasing number of miners meant that a decreasing proportion of patients were Fund beneficiaries and the hospitals were serving as community rather than mine worker hospitals. Therefore, after prolonged consideration a decision was made to sell the hospitals. This decision was announced publicly by the Fund in October 1962.

The Fund takes great pride in the quality of care provided in the Memorial Hospitals and was careful in its choice of purchaser for the chain in order to maintain the high standards that had been set up. Bids from individual physicians were refused so that the creation of proprietary hospitals would be avoided, and in December 1962 the Fund began discussions with representatives of the Board of National Missions of the United Presbyterian Church, U.S.A., in order to work out arrangements by which the chain could be taken over and operated by a nonsectarian, nonprofit corporation.

The fiscal year ending June 30, 1964, closed with the completion of the sale of the Miners Memorial Hospitals to the Appalachian Regional Hospitals, Inc., the authority created by the Board of National Missions to purchase and operate the hospitals. The total price was $8 million, of which $3.9 million was paid in September 1963 for Harlan, Hazard, McDowell, Middlesboro, and Whitesburg Hospitals, and the remaining $4.1 million was paid on June 30, 1964, for the five hospitals at Man, Beckley, Pikeville, Williamson, and Wise. Loans from the Area Redevelopment Administration financed the purchases, but at first the Appalachian Regional Hospitals, Inc. was very short of working capital and there were some fears in 1964 that the hospitals would be closed. By the end of 1964, however, thanks to government aid, the financial crisis seemed to be over and the hospitals were breaking even. About 75 percent of hospital income still comes from the Fund and the Fund still exercises a great deal of influence on the maintenance of standards in the hospitals.

In the main, doctors recruited by the hospitals have stayed with hospital groups. Some have reorganized their groups into nonprofit associations with whom the Fund does business on a contract basis while paying per diem rates to the hospitals. It is not felt that the sale of the hospitals has affected the actual service provided. The facilities still exist and Fund officials feel that the hospital chain accomplishes as much for miners and their families as it did before.

The Fund has also continued the policy begun in the early days of the rehabilitation program of using any facility anywhere in the country necessary for the good of the patient. Over the years an average of 100 patients a year have been sent to the National Institutes of Health for highly specialized services. In general, the need for such referral has decreased as the quality of service provided by local physicians has improved and as local rehabilitation facilities have been established. Special arrangements have often had to be made on many levels. For example, it is obviously desirable for paraplegics to be transferred to rehabilitation centers as soon as possible, before the development of bed sores and other complications which mean prolonged hospitalization and convalescence. However, Workman's Compensation laws often did not permit payment to out-of-state facilities and the Fund had to develop means to make such arrangements for payment possible.

The attempts of the Fund to solve the problems of over-utilization and poor medical practice had limited success. The efforts of the area administrators were, of necessity, limited in scope and influence. The A.M.A. conferences were sincere attempts at understanding but were not empowered to do more than discuss and recommend, and their recommendations were acted on only sporadically. Although the Miners Memorial Hospitals eventually did much to raise standards of medical care, they were not in operation until 1956 and their sphere of operations was geographically limited.

Review of records had shown by 1953 that most surgery charged to the Fund was being done by general practitioners. Because surgical rates were thought excessive for Fund patients a ruling was made that only members of the American College of Surgeons, or doctors certified by the American Board of Surgery would be paid by the Fund. An immediate result of this ruling was a drop of two thirds in hospital admissions for surgery; this later leveled off at a rate one half of what it had been previous to the ruling. Although prompted by financial pressure, the ruling was in effect a measure to raise standards of care, and the result helped to convince Fund medical officials that if they would control for quality of care, then cost would take care of itself.

Hospital use remained high in spite of the decrease in surgery and the Fund finally issued a directive stating that, effective April 15, 1955, all beneficiary patients other than emergencies must be seen in consultation with an appropriate specialist in private practice to determine the necessity for hospitalization before admission at Fund expense. This measure had already been adopted in one area in Colorado where problems of hospital admission and stay had been particularly acute, and the Fund released figures to show that there had been a 36.8 percent reduction in hospital days as a result and a 16.5 percent reduction in all surgical procedures (appendectomies dropped by 59.4 percent).

This policy of preadmission consultation was bitterly opposed by the medical profession on the grounds that it discriminated against general practitioners and denied the patient free choice of physician. In West Virginia nine of the 28 county medical societies passed resolutions opposing the directive, and the Council of the West Virginia Medical Society instructed its delegates to the A.M.A. meeting in June to register the state's disapproval. In Pennsylvania the reaction was even more violent. The board of trustees of the state society, meeting at the end of May, notified Dr. Draper that they would recommend that physicians withdraw from the Fund program unless the policy were changed. Pennsylvania delegates to the A.M.A. meeting were instructed to support the West Virginia delegates and to introduce their own resolution condemning the directive.

As a result, the A.M.A. House of Delegates passed a resolution disapproving the requirement for consultation on all patients prior to hospital admission. The following day Dr. Draper withdrew the requirement rather than risk an open break with organized medicine.

The resolution of the West Virginia Medical Society was the most dramatic instance in that state of dissatisfaction with the UMWA Fund medical program. In Pennsylvania, however, there were many conflicts over the years. Some of these were directly with the Fund and some revolved around the group practice clinics at Russellton and Centerville. Charges of unethical conduct were brought in the local medical society against members of the Russellton group when a branch office was opened in a neighboring county and physicians of both groups were denied staff privileges at local hospitals.

Fund administrators, aware of these conflicts, tried to bring about better understanding and after months of meetings and discussions an agreement between the Pennsylvania Medical Society and the Medical Service of the Fund was drawn up. This agreement, adopted by the Society's Board of Trustees on November 17, 1955, spelled out the liaison procedure to be followed in arbitrating any differences between individual physicians and the Fund. It also enunciated principles dealing with the maintenance of quality in hospitals, unethical practices by physicians, and selection of physicians.

The agreement was printed in the *Pennsylvania Medical Journal* in April 1956, and Dr. Draper circulated copies of it to interested physicians all over the country. The text was also printed in the May 12, 1956, issue of the *Journal of the American Medical Association* with the following introduction: "All physicians can be encouraged by the fact that one medical society through diligent effort has faced up to a problem and through round-table discussion entered into a written agreement that seeks to accomplish resolution of a thorny problem facing its members."

Despite this official approval there was little effect on the concrete problem of hospital appointment. Members of the Russellton group were still denied staff privileges. The area administrator for the Fund felt that this not only discriminated against group practice units and the Fund program but prevented the hospital from instituting necessary improvements in service. The Fund would discontinue business arrangements with it unless changes in policy were made.

On October 1, 1956, the Fund informed the hospital in the Russellton area that participating agreements with it had expired and that the Fund would no longer assume financial responsibility for the admission of any Fund beneficiary. On October 17, 1956, the House of Delegates of the Pennsylvania Medical Society dissolved its agreement with the Medical Service of the Fund. No reasons were given at the time, but the A.M.A. Committee on Medical Care for Industrial Workers was later told that the action was taken in response to requests from physicians in the Russellton area.

In January 1957, the Illinois State Medical Society announced that it did "not look with favor upon any member physicians who include the UMWA Welfare and Retirement Fund in negotiations for medical, surgical and obstetrical care for any beneficiary of the Fund." Union officials in Illinois were informed that doctors would henceforth bill beneficiaries directly instead of the Area Medical Office.

Although most Illinois physicians did not follow this policy, it was still another sign of trouble. There were also many problems of long standing in Colorado that had not responded to efforts by either the Fund or the A.M.A. Dr. Draper therefore requested the A.M.A. Committee on Medical Care for Industrial Workers to use its "good offices" to help resolve the difficulties and avert harmful consequences.

The A.M.A. Guides

As a result, representatives of the state medical societies of Pennsylvania, Illinois, and Colorado met with the A.M.A. Committee in March 1957. The committee was requested to work out relationships and procedures that organized medicine and the

Medical Service of the Fund would follow. Although the Executive Medical Officer of the Fund was a member of the committee, he was excluded from participation in the formulation of these principles at the request of one of the state societies.

The *Suggested Guides to Relationships Between State and County Medical Societies and the United Mine Workers of America Welfare and Retirement Fund* were drawn up by the committee for submission to the House of Delegates at the June 1957 A.M.A. meeting. The introduction points out that the guides "surely will fail in their purpose if they are used by one party only." Medical society responsibilities are defined in one statement on good medical care and in eight statements on the functions of liaison committees, with the stipulation that the Fund refrain from unilateral action. The most controversial points are contained in the section entitled "General Guides."

1. All persons, including the beneficiaries of a third party medical program such as the UMWA Fund should have available to them good medical care and should be free to select their own physicians from among those willing and able to render such service.

2. Free choice of physician and hospital by the patient should be preserved:

a. Every physician duly licensed by the state to practice medicine and surgery should be assumed at the outset to be competent in the field in which he claims to be, unless considered otherwise by his peers.

b. A physician should accept only such terms or conditions for dispensing his services as will insure his free and complete exercise of independent medical judgment and skill, insure the quality of medical care, and avoid the exploitation of his services for financial profit.

c. The medical profession does not concede to a third party such as UMWA Welfare and Retirement Fund in a medical care program the prerogative of passing judgment on the treatment rendered by physicians, including the necessity of hospitalization, length of stay, and the like.

3. A fee-for-service method of payment for physicians should be maintained except under unusual circumstances. These unusual circumstances shall be determined to exist only after a conference of the liaison committee and representatives of the Fund.

4. The qualifications of physicians to be on the hospital staff and membership on the hospital staffs is to be determined solely by local hospital staffs and local governing boards of hospitals.

The Executive Medical Officer of the Fund testified to the Fund's point of view before the Guides were submitted to the House of Delegates. He served notice that the Guides were not acceptable to the Fund and would not be followed if adopted. Nevertheless, on June 6, 1957, the House of Delegates approved the Guides and several state societies followed suit.

In September 1957 a directive went out to area medical administrators from Dr. Draper which said in part: "To meet the mandatory requirements of conserving trust fund resources, and providing authorized services to beneficiaries, trust fund payments are hereby restricted to physicians and hospitals whose services are deemed necessary and essential."

By November 1957 approximately 29 percent of the physicians on the Fund's approved list had been dropped. The results of this in one state during the period September 1957 through June 1958 are described by the Fund as a reduction of 11.6 percent in hospital admissions, 14.4 percent in surgical operations, and 7.5 percent in total costs.

The annual report of the UMWA Welfare and Retirement Fund for 1958 states that, following limitation of the Fund's hospital and physician lists, payments for medical care showed a reduction of over one million dollars for the fiscal year July 1, 1957, through June 30, 1958. The number of beneficiaries served by the medical program during this period was 85,426 compared to 93,679 during the previous year.

The response of organized medicine was immediate. The Pennsylvania Medical Society vowed nonparticipation in the Fund's medical program and called upon its members to sever connections with the Fund. As in Illinois, this recommendation was ignored by most practicing physicians. In December 1957 the House of Delegates of the A.M.A. passed a resolution condemning the attitude and method of the Fund, and calling upon the A.M.A. to begin a broad educational program immediately to inform the general public as well as the beneficiaries of the Fund of the advantages to be derived from preservation of the American right to freedom of choice of physicians and hospitals. Shortly thereafter the A.M.A. point of view was aired in *Life* magazine (March 26, 1958), and *Fortune* carried a story in September of the same year. The *Fortune* writer reported that the A.M.A. had been unable to begin its proposed educational publicity campaign because "so far it has been unable to agree upon a policy statement."

The Fund had no difficulty with policy statements. Dr. Draper merely reiterated the many speeches and statistics he had been giving since 1950 and added three concluding sentences.

1. Every physician duly licensed by the state is not competent to perform any service that any patient may require, even if he claims to be.

2. Organized medicine, while insisting that it alone possesses the authority to judge and discipline its members, has thus far been unable or unwilling to establish and enforce effective means of doing so.

3. As matters now stand, the only way in which the Fund can insure the highest quality of care, and the maximum benefits that can be provided for the amount of money available, is through mutually satisfactory arrangements with physicians and hospitals whose services are necessary and essential.[15]

The A.M.A. Report on Medical Care Plans

The A.M.A. Commission on Medical Care Plans was appointed by the Board of Trustees in 1954 to review the many different types of plans through which persons received physicians' services. The Commission studied student health services, industry programs, "Medical Society Approved Plans," and miscellaneous and unclassified plans. The last category included group practice clinics such as the Group Health Association, Inc., and labor union negotiated plans such as the UMWA Welfare and Retirement Fund.

The long-awaited report of the Commission was submitted to the House of Delegates in December 1958 and published as a special edition of the *Journal of the American Medical Association* on January 17, 1959.

The report gave extensive information on many plans and made recommendations concerning activities of the state and county medical societies, the A.M.A., and medical care plans in general. The 24 recommendations contained many constructive suggestions, but two had particular significance for the Fund program.

Recommendation A–7 read:

"Free choice of physician" is an important factor in the provision of good medical care. In order that the principle of "free choice of physician" be maintained and be fully implemented the medical profession should discharge more vigorously its self-imposed responsibility for assuring the competency of physicians' services and their provision at a cost which people can afford.

Recommendation B–16, as amended by the House, read:

15. Warren F. Draper, "The Medical Care Program of the United Mine Workers of America Welfare and Retirement Fund," presented at the New England Hospital Assembly, Boston, March 25, 1958.

The A.M.A. believes that "free choice of physician" is the right of every individual and one which he should be free to exercise as he chooses.

Each individual should be accorded the privilege to select and change his physician at will or to select his preferred system of medical care and the A.M.A. vigorously supports the right of the individual to choose between these alternatives.[16]

There was no specific recommendation regarding the "fee-for-service" principle, although the report did say that physicians could "accept remuneration from any plan on any basis which is not in violation of the Principles of Medical Ethics." Violations included inadequate compensation (compared to prevalent fees), compensation so low that adequate service cannot be rendered, underbidding by physicians in order to secure a contract, denial of free choice of physician, and solicitation of patients.

The two recommendations and the policy statement cover most of the conflicts between organized medicine and the UMWA Welfare and Retirement Fund. What effect they will have on future relations between the Fund and local medical societies is unknown. The Commission report commented on the issues uncovered by their study of the Fund's medical program as follows:

The issues and problems are not new; they have existed ever since the Plan's medical program was instituted. Some of the problems have been resolved to the mutual satisfaction of the local medical profession and the Plan; others have merely simmered over the years and erupted when certain stimuli appeared.

16. *Action of the House of Delegates of the American Medical Association on the Report of the Commission on Medical Care Plans*, Atlantic City, June 1959.

Medical Practice in a Group Setting: The Russellton Experience

May 1964

Roy Penchansky / Beryl M. Safford / Henry Simmons

Group medical practice, however defined, is a growing phenomenon in American medicine. The number of physicians practicing in groups of three or more physicians, providing services in more than one medical field or specialty and pooling income according to some prearranged plan, increased 228 percent between 1946 and 1959. In 1946 they constituted 3.0 percent of all physicians in private practice, and in 1959, 7.1 percent. If single-specialty groups and those with fewer than three full-time physicians are counted, physicians in group practice constituted 9.2 percent of all physicians in private practice.

Group practice is characterized by a high degree of specialty practice. Although just less than half of all physicians in private practice are specialists, 76 percent of group physicians are full-time specialists and an additional four percent are part-time specialists. A higher proportion of the full-time group specialists are board-certified — 75 percent as opposed to 45 percent of all full-time specialists.

The virtues and vices of group practice are still being debated. Proponents hold that group practice provides better medical care. The reasons advanced for this view include the readier availability of consultations with colleagues, the more extensive diagnostic facilities physicians can acquire when they pool their resources, and the stimulation toward excellence that arises from both constant association with professional colleagues and the knowledge that one's work is always subject to observation and potential criticism. These claimed advantages for the patient are matched by advantages for the physician, including more regular hours of practice, the rotation of night and weekend duty, and the opportunity for vacations and continuing educational programs without neglect of patients or fear that they will turn to another physician.

To these claims physicians who are less enthusiastic about group practice retort that groups practice "impersonal" medicine, sacri-

The first few pages of this case and of the following case are the same. The remainders of the two cases — and their uses — are very different. Either case can be used first, or they can be used independently.

ficing a warm rapport between patient and physician to an alleged greater efficiency, and that the patient is subjected to unnecessary consultations and laboratory work. The advantages of professional association are easily available in hospital practice, they contend, and the opportunities for friction among group members may well outweigh any benefits to be derived from their close collaboration.

Certainly no one has claimed that all groups practice bad medicine, or that no solo practitioner practices as high a quality of medicine as the best group physicians. Dr. Caldwell B. Esselstyn, Director of the Rip Van Winkle Clinic and Chairman of the Board of the Group Health Association of America, has said: "There is nothing in the mere structure of a group, per se, which will guarantee a high quality of medical performance. There is nothing more lamentable than a poor single doctor, unless it is a poor group of doctors. But, a group does have some stimulating potentials." [1]

The Origin and Structure of the Russellton Medical Group

The Russellton Medical Group was established early in 1952 in the small town of Russellton, Pennsylvania, some 25 miles from Pittsburgh in Allegheny County, after a delegation from a mine workers' union had sought the help of the Pittsburgh Area office of the United Mine Workers of America Welfare and Retirement Fund in finding a new check-off doctor. Dissatisfied with their current check-off doctor, to whom a small amount of their wages was paid each month as prepayment for the medical care they and their families needed, they asked the Fund's area administrator whether he could suggest another physician to whom they could transfer their business.

The area administrator was willing to help the miners but was already finding it difficult to attract physicians to the generally isolated and relatively unprosperous coal-mining areas. One young general practitioner, who was already practicing in a coal-mining area that was becoming steadily more depressed economically, indicated that he would be willing to move to Russellton, but only if he could be associated with both general practitioners and spe-

1. Caldwell B. Esselstyn, "Controlling the Quality of Medical Care," *Proceedings, Tenth Annual Group Health Institute of the Group Health Association of America*, Columbus, Ohio, 1960, p. 97.

cialists in a group practice arrangement and could have diagnostic facilities available.

His point of view made good sense to the Fund's area administrator, who recently observed, "Some such arrangements seemed essential in order to attract doctors to the mining areas." [2] The Fund could not offer the general practitioner any help with the financing of routine home and office care — not among the benefits provided under the Fund's medical program — but it did assure him that it would extend participation in the Fund program to his group for specialist and diagnostic services and for inhospital care.

While the physician scouted for colleagues, the union delegation aroused the interest of two other mining locals in the area who agreed to transfer their check-off to the new group once it was established. Together they formed a nonprofit corporation to finance the facilities needed. Through a miner who owned real estate in Russellton, a building was acquired and equipped, and the Russellton Medical Group, consisting of two general practitioners and an internist, began to practice in February 1952. Since that time the medical staff has grown to consist, in the spring of 1964, of eight full-time general practitioners and one part-time general practitioner, three full-time internists, and twenty part-time specialists, and additional offices have been opened in the communities of New Kensington, Apollo, and Acmetonia.

The physical facilities and equipment used by the Group are owned and operated by the nonprofit corporation originally composed of five miners' union officials. As additional union groups have established check-off arrangements with the Group, the board has been enlarged until it now consists of twenty members. All the members have been coal miners at one time, but some are now employed in other industries.

The nonprofit board is considered to be analogous to a hospital board. It has the responsibility to operate and maintain the facilities "in such a manner as to make it possible for the Medical Group to provide medical services of the highest quality." [3] It determines the policies governing the facilities, and a qualified medical care administrator, selected jointly by the three parties — the board, the Medical Group, and the Mine Workers Fund — is appointed by the board to run the day-to-day operations of the

2. Leslie A. Falk, "Group Health Plans in Coal Mining Communities," *Journal of Health and Human Behavior* 4:9 (Spring 1963).

3. Falk, p. 8.

clinic. The board hires and pays all nonmedical personnel, and meets the expenses of building maintenance, supplies including medical supplies, and so on. Technical personnel are employed, however, only after the medical director certifies that they are technically qualified. The medical director may also recommend the discharge of technical personnel for just cause.

The Russellton Medical Group has agreed not to own or operate a medical facility or any major equipment needed for the practice of medicine in the area they serve. The Group retains for itself all responsibility for the "selection of physicians or termination of their services, the rendering of services by physicians, and supervision of the medical aspects of technical and nursing personnel. However, no physician is appointed to the medical group who is unacceptable either to the nonprofit board or as a participating physician in the . . . Fund." [4] The rules and regulations governing the Medical Staff of the Russellton Medical Group adopted in 1961 are included as Appendix A.

The Russellton office started very modestly in a quite small building. It has over the years been expanded and developed to include most of the equipment currently considered necessary for the practice of modern medicine. Until quite recently it had been the headquarters of the Group.

In the winter of 1953–54 the Group opened a second office in New Kensington, a trading center of about 35,000 persons across the Allegheny River in neighboring Westmoreland County, in answer to a request by another miners' union for a check-off doctor. The union had for some time tried to find a New Kensington physician willing to make home calls in a nearby mining community, and approached the Russellton Group when none could be found. The Group had planned, initially, to develop this facility as extensively as it had the Russellton clinic, but maintained it as a small physician's office when protests against the planned expansion were expressed by the county and state medical societies.

In the summer of 1956 the Group responded to appeals published in the *Pennsylvania Medical Journal* for a physician to serve the small town of Apollo quite a distance away on the other side of Westmoreland County. Originally quite small, the Apollo office has expanded to the point where three full-time physicians are needed, but it remains the Group's poorest physical facility, being located in the basement of the local hotel. Because of its considerable distance from the Russellton headquarters, it has been fur-

4. Falk, p. 8.

nished with somewhat more extensive equipment, such as an electrocardiograph and a unit for throat cultures, than the other satellite offices of the Group. Construction is to begin soon on a new building for the Apollo office, which will then be equipped with its own laboratory and X-ray facilities.

The Group opened one more office in the fall of 1957 in the town of Acmetonia, near Russellton in Allegheny County, again in response to appeals for a physician published in the *Pennsylvania Medical Journal.* At present there seem to be no plans for an expansion of the Acmetonia office, which has remained the Group's smallest and least extensively equipped facility.

In July 1963, the Group transferred its headquarters to an elaborate, modernistic, new structure in New Kensington, which is more nearly the center of the area it serves than Russellton. Completed at a cost of approximately $800,000, the new clinic contains offices, examining rooms, laboratories, X-ray facilities, physiotherapy rooms, a library, and a very extensive range of equipment. The Group has considered closing the other offices, since almost all of its patients live within a 25-minute drive of New Kensington, but has decided that its services should remain as close to the patients as possible. It therefore plans to make the other offices as nearly self-sufficient medically as possible by equipping them with all the basic diagnostic facilities.

Two hospitals exist in the area served by the Russellton Group. Allegheny Valley Hospital, with about 220 beds, is in Tarentum, within easy distance of Russellton. The Citizens General Hospital, with approximately 230 beds, in New Kensington, is the natural service hospital for Apollo, but is also easily accessible to residents of Russellton and Acmetonia.*

Perhaps largely because of the Russellton Group's identification with miners' unions, the clinic grew rapidly to provide all or most of the care for about 10,000 persons by the end of its first five years of existence. Since then it has grown more slowly, primarily, it is claimed, because of the difficulties its physicians have encountered in obtaining local hospital privileges. Nevertheless, by early 1964 some 35,000 patients had visited the Group's offices at least once, and close to 18,000 were using the Group for part or all of their medical care.

The majority of the Group's patients are beneficiaries of the United Mine Workers Welfare and Retirement Fund. Although three general practitioners on the staff of Citizens General Hospital also have participating arrangements with the Fund, some

* See map on page 219.

10,000 or so of the 12,000 Fund beneficiaries living in the area are patients of the Group. The principal services covered by the Fund are specialist and diagnostic care outside the hospital, comprehensive inhospital care, expensive drugs needed for long-term care of patients with chronic illnesses, and emergency care given by any physician. Over time the Fund has authorized a more liberal interpretation of benefits to reduce hospitalization and improve comprehensiveness and continuity of care, and the area administrator may approve payment for outpatient services needed for the "medical management" of chronically ill patients. Many Fund beneficiaries are elderly persons with chronic disease, and much of the care given them by the Group falls within the category of medical management.

About 6,000 persons use the Group for services covered under the check-off system usually handled by the employer for working miners and by the union for retired miners or widows who wish to participate. The check-off rate is $4.00 per month for married working miners, $3.00 for married pensioners and unmarried working miners, $2.00 for single pensioners, and $0.50 for widows. The check-off covers home and office care, including minor medications and simple remedies such as cough medicine which are dispensed at the clinic, routine injections of penicillin and the like, and immunizations for both children and adults. Probably more than 90 percent of the check-off arrangements in the area have been made with the Group. The check-off is voluntary, but working miners usually participate.

Although eligibility rules for Fund benefits have fluctuated over time, in recent years hospital and medical care benefits have been available to working and pensioned miners and their dependents, and, for one year only, to unemployed miners, widows, and survivors. Thus, most of the check-off patients treated by the Group are also beneficiaries of the Fund. Some 20 percent of the Group's patients are on public assistance, and many of these are said to be former miners.

The Russellton Group also sees a considerable number of "private" patients who pay for care on a fee-for-service basis according to an established schedule that is supposed to correspond with rates prevailing in the area. In Russellton perhaps 35 to 40 percent of the patients are private, at Apollo from 55 to 65 percent of the patients are private, and in Acmetonia, the percentage is about ten. Approximately 10 percent of the patients in the former New Kensington office were fee-for-service patients, but since the opening of the new clinic some 2,000 new patients, most of whom are private, have begun to use the Group.

The Apollo office provides the school health services for the township and operates a well-baby clinic for the town health department. Another township's school health services are handled by the Russellton office, which also provides routine and emergency services for patients in a nearby nursing home who do not have personal physicians.

The Group's major source of income is the United Mine Workers Fund, which in a recent month paid them $22,500 for the proportion of their time spent on Fund beneficiaries. The Fund's payment is based on a calculation, derived largely from figures of the Group's income from other sources, of the amount of the Group's time not spent on Fund beneficiaries. The check-off arrangements bring the Group approximately $6,000 per month, while the income from fee-for-service patients amounted, in a recent month, to about $11,000. The members of the Group pool all the income received, and from it draw annual incomes and pay rent of approximately $11,000 per month to the nonprofit corporation to cover overhead costs associated with the care of patients other than Fund beneficiaries. The nonprofit corporation also receives, directly from the Fund, an amount — approximately $30,000 in a recent month — covering the overhead expenses associated with the care of Fund beneficiaries.

The annual incomes of members of the Group range from $12,000 to $30,000, and are established according to a fixed schedule based on years of training, specialty status, experience, and years with the Group. A general practitioner, joining the Group upon completion of his internship, would receive $12,000. An additional $1,000 is paid for each year of residency training, another $1,000 for Board certification, and $500 for each year of experience. After joining the Group, members earn annual increments of $750 or $1,000. Part-time specialists are paid for the proportion of their time they give to the Group, and according to the same schedule, up to a maximum of $100 a day. In order to obtain the services of specialists in certain fields, however, negotiated adjustments have been made from time to time. Until recently the maximum income had been $25,000. Changes in the scale are discussed with the Fund's area administrator before being instituted because of their implications for the cost of medical care covered by the Fund. Members of the Group receive two weeks of vacation yearly during their first three years on the staff, three weeks' vacation for the next three years, and one month's vacation thereafter. They are now discussing arrangements for a pension plan. Apart from the costs of malpractice insurance, the members have few expenses.

Most of the full-time general practitioners of the Group are less than 35 years old, and the average age of the full-time internists is 40. Of the eight full-time general practitioners, four came to the Group directly from internships and one after a year of residency. The roster of part-time specialists includes 2 obstetrician-gynecologists, 2 urologists, 2 general surgeons, 2 specialists in chest diseases, 2 internists, one of whom has a subspecialty in rheumatology, 2 otolaryngologists, 1 pediatrician, 1 radiologist, 1 psychiatrist, 1 dermatologist, 1 ophthalmologist, and 1 allergist. The three full-time internists, and almost all of the part-time specialists, have teaching appointments at the University of Pittsburgh School of Medicine.

Since 1957 five full-time physicians have left the Group. The departure of one was not regarded as a serious loss. A number of those resigning have done so to undertake specialty training. There is said to be very little turnover among the part-time specialists.

The New Kensington office, which is expected to have approximately 24,000 patient visits per year, is the headquarters for the three full-time internists, two full-time general practitioners and one part-time general practitioner, and the administrator of the Group. The staff includes approximately 10 nurses, one public health nurse, a social worker, two physiotherapists, seven laboratory and X-ray technicians, four medical record personnel, four medical secretaries, two cashiers, an accountant, and other supporting personnel.

The Russellton office, which has approximately 13,000 patient visits per year and an estimated 4,000 patients, is staffed by two full-time general practitioners and one part-time general practitioner, four nurses, two laboratory and X-ray technicians, and seven other supporting personnel. The Apollo office, with about the same number of patient visits and estimated patients, is the headquarters for three full-time general practitioners, three nurses, and two nonmedical personnel. One full-time and one part-time general practitioner, with a nurse and a receptionist, staff the Acmetonia office, which has some 6,000 patient visits annually and an estimated 2,000 patients.

The Group's part-time specialists have offices in Pittsburgh but visit the Group regularly to see patients. Consultants in internal medicine and pediatrics spend one full day a week at the Russellton Clinic, and specialists in obstetrics and gynecology and in surgery spend one half day. Internists visit the Apollo clinic two days a week, but all other specialists' sessions are held in New Kensington. Each morning a technician visits the Apollo office to collect specimens for analysis at the New Kensington clinic, and a messenger visits each office twice a day.

Although the Russellton office still performs many of the laboratory and X-ray procedures needed by its patients, laboratory and X-ray work for patients at the other offices, and complex X rays for Russellton patients, are handled by the New Kensington clinic. In a recent month the New Kensington office had 535 patient visits to the laboratory and performed 1,047 procedures, 347 patient visits to the X-ray unit and 424 procedures, 182 patient visits for physiotherapy and 455 procedures, and about 130 patient visits for electrocardiograms. Although the clinic is equipped to perform a wide range of diagnostic procedures, patients are hospitalized for procedures, such as air studies and arteriography, which involve an element of risk.

All the offices have sessions on Saturday morning, and one physician has office hours each night at the New Kensington clinic. No evening sessions are held at the other offices, but a nurse is on duty at Russellton until ten at night for emergency calls. In addition, the Group has arranged for round-the-clock house call coverage. The three physicians in Apollo, and three in New Kensington, including one internist, rotate night-call duty. The two full-time general practitioners at Russellton and the one full-time Acmetonia physician rotate night-call duty on their side of the river. Because of the geographical dispersion of the Group's four offices, which have home-call radii of five to ten miles, the total home-call area covered by the Group is approximately 35 miles by 16 miles.

The Medical Program

Patients visiting the Group for the first time may select their own physician. If they express no preference, they are assigned to whichever physician is conveniently available and he is then designated on their records as the doctor in charge. They may subsequently switch to another Group physician if they wish. Insofar as possible, the Group also attempts to arrange that all members of one family use the same physician. If, however, one family member has a particular rapport with a different physician, no effort is made to induce the patient to change to the physician the rest of his family uses. Patients who have been hospitalized under the care of the two physicians who have local hospital privileges sometimes wish to retain them as family physicians, but this the Group discourages, feeling that these two members already have as heavy a workload as they can reasonably carry.

Early in its development the Group used a clinic system, the physicians holding office hours and seeing patients on a first-come, first-serve basis. In addition, as part of a deliberate emphasis on the continuing education of its members, the Group rotated physicians among the offices to prevent physicians in the smaller offices from becoming isolated and possibly falling away from the high standards of medical practice that the Group wished to maintain. A revised method to emphasize identification with a "managing physician" was instituted following an internal audit that pointed out the deterrents to continuity of care inherent in a system under which patient identification with a particular physician was almost impossible to establish. An appointment system has been introduced in every office, patients being urged by letter, personal contact, and signs to telephone and make an appointment with their physician rather than just drop by the office. The rotation of physicians among the offices has also been eliminated. It was planned to have each family physician work in only one office, but this has not yet been fully accomplished, and two of the full-time general practitioners practice in more than one office.

Despite the Group's efforts to encourage patient identification with a personal physician, members of the Group feel that this has been imperfectly realized. Patients are supposed to be given appointments with their doctors in charge but often cannot remember the name of the physician they last saw or may, in any case, be confused because they may have seen several different physicians at one office. And the person making the appointment, not having the patients' charts readily available, or any other listing containing this information, cannot ensure that patients always see their own physicians unless the patients themselves provide the names.

All new patients of the Group are supposed to be given complete physical examinations, whatever the presenting complaint, and this is now looked upon as the responsibility of the general practitioner. Until a few years ago, the full-time internists performed most of the comprehensive physical examinations because it was thought that the general practitioners had too little time. The appointment schedule has now been adjusted to give general practitioners more time — usually 15 minutes — with each patient, and they are expected to have completed a full work-up before referring a patient to an internist. One general practitioner attempts to do this on the patient's first visit, but the more usual practice is to schedule a second hour-long visit for this purpose.

The Group has attempted to stress the maintenance of continuity of care for all patients. The emphasis on identification of a doctor in charge is considered by the Group to imply the assumption by one physician of primary responsibility for the patient's care regardless of the number of consultants who may be called upon during the course of examination and treatment. The "consultation request" form used by the Group, in addition to specifying whether the consultation is an "emergency" (1 to 2 days), "urgent" (less than a week), or "elective" (anytime), also indicates whether the referring physician wishes the patient returned to him, wishes the consultant to follow the case with him, or wishes the consultant to take over the patient as managing physician. The patient's record, furthermore, is sent to the consultant when he sees the patient, and he enters in it his own findings, recommendations, and projected course of treatment. The consultant also completes a report for the referring physician, a copy of which is placed in the patient's record.

The record system was changed several years ago to promote greater continuity of care between managing physician and consultant. It was found that the former system, under which physicians who saw the patient made separate notes on separate sheets, left the loophole that managing physicians might not, while referring to their own notes, check carefully those that had been made by other physicians. Now records are maintained in strictly chronological order so that physicians reviewing the history of a patient will be less likely to miss notes made by other physicians.

The consultants in obstetrics and gynecology note that many patients in the child-bearing years come to look upon their obstetrician as a personal physician and that when they advise such patients to consult a general practitioner or internist in their private practice they have no particular confidence that the patients will in fact do so. Within the structure of the Russellton Group, on the other hand, they can arrange easily for a family physician to look into the problem. Furthermore, they claim, when they refer a patient they have seen in their private offices to an internist or surgeon, they may never be informed whether the patient made the necessary arrangements and, if so, what was discovered and what treatment given. At the clinic they need only refer to the patient's record to obtain this information.

A number of the specialists with the Group do become managing physicians for some of the patients. The consultants in obstetrics and gynecology, in addition to handling all obstetrical patients, have become, in a sense, "family" doctors for patients with infertility problems, while the full-time internists manage the medical care of patients with serious problems, such as severe cardiac disease. The Group's pediatrician has assumed responsibility for the care of virtually all children under three years of age as well as of older children with special problems.

Members of the Group generally agree that the family physicians call upon consultants more often than is the usual case in solo practice, partly because they are easily available and partly because no serious financial constraint exists for a large proportion of the patients. It is also agreed that some of these consultations are not really necessary, but that it is better medicine to have too many than too few. In the view of one specialist, some of the consultations may be a waste of the patient's time, but not of his own, if only because the patient load is not particularly heavy. The consultants in obstetrics and gynecology, for example, may see 30 or 40 patients during one day spent with the Group, but few of these will be new patients who have not yet had at least some of the necessary diagnostic procedures ordered and recorded by a family physician. The Group's medical director feels that fewer consultations are requested now that the appointment schedule for family physicians has been altered to give them more time with each patient, and that 80 to 90 percent of the additional diagnostic work implied by the frequent use of consultation is to the patient's advantage. A comparative study of diabetic patients at the Apollo and at the Russellton offices, he notes, suggested that those at Russellton, where more consultants were regularly available and where diagnostic facilities were much more extensive, were receiving more thorough care, such as periodic chest X rays and cardiograms and routine foot care, than were those at Apollo.

Some discontinuity of care, as well as inconvenience for the patients, has resulted from the Group's inability to obtain privileges in local hospitals. Early in the Group's history several of its members had privileges at the nearby Allegheny Valley Hospital in Tarentum, and the majority of patients requiring hospitalization were admitted there. In subsequent years the denial of hospital privileges to all Group physicians by both the Allegheny Valley Hospital and Citizens General Hospital in New Kensington has forced the Group to use Pittsburgh hospitals for patients requiring hospitalization. It is said that patients are for the most part content with this arrangement, in spite of the distance and travel time involved, because they like both the physicians who care for them and the Pittsburgh hospitals used by the Group. The Group has also, however, arranged consultations and surgical care for patients who insist upon being treated locally, even though it would prefer that its own specialists provide all needed inhospital care. As a consequence of the hospital privileges problem, the consultants in obstetrics and gynecology comment that a patient may come to them for one delivery, then go to a New Kensington community physician for the next, and then come back to them for a third.

Since July 1962 two Group physicians — the medical director who is an internist and a general practitioner — have had limited privileges at the Citizens General Hospital, and it is said that a larger number of patients than before now ask that they be hospitalized in New Kensington. The two physicians use selected members of the hospital's medical staff, whose skills they feel are of a high order, for consultation and surgery. At any one time, they estimate, the Group may have from five to ten patients hospitalized in New Kensington and twenty or so in Pittsburgh hospitals. Both physicians see all Group patients hospitalized at Citizens General every morning and usually alternate calls at the hospital in the evening and on weekends. Generally they feel that their relationships with other members on the hospital staff are amicable in spite of the long-standing dispute about hospital privileges. Although the Group uses a number of these community physicians frequently for consultation, it receives very few referrals from local physicians. Those it does receive the Group believes have been initiated by the patient.

The Group feels that its extensive diagnostic facilities, specialist participation, and roster of ancillary personnel have resulted in its using hospitals less than is the general case in the solo practice of medicine. The experience of the Mine Workers Fund has been that 160 of every 1,000 beneficiaries across the country will be hospitalized annually, 125 per 1,000 in the area served by the Fund's Pittsburgh office, and only 75 to 80 per 1,000 of the Group's Fund patients.

One Group physician comments that the lack of hospital privileges has resulted in his handling many more problems outside the hospital than he might otherwise. Even in cardiac emergencies, he states, he will do much more before sending the patient to the hospital than he did before in a different community where he did have hospital privileges.

The Group is consciously oriented toward the practice of preventive medicine, and many of the family physicians encourage their patients to have periodic complete examinations. Routine screening has also been given emphasis, and, according to their age and special risk factors such as family history of diabetes, obesity, smoking habits, and so on, patients are periodically supposed to be given appropriate diagnostic procedures. From the inception of the Group a Papanicalaou smear test has been performed for virtually all women who have used the clinic. This screening program was initiated and run for some years solely by the Group's consultants in obstetrics and gynecology, but for the past three or four years the family physicians have routinely included this test in their examinations of female patients. All reports on the tests are sent to the consultants as well as to the family physicians, and all patients with abnormal smears are referred to the consultant.

From time to time the Group has also arranged special immunization programs, even though the family physicians are supposed to see that appropriate immunizations are given to all the patients. In the spring of 1964 immunization sessions for administration of the new measles vaccine were scheduled at all four offices at no cost to patients on check-off, $3.00 to Fund beneficiaries, and $5.00 to fee-for-service patients. At the conclusion of the drive the Group expects to have vaccinated some 500 to 600 of the total of approximately 1,000 children included in the Group's patient population.

Believing that many of the patients are inadequately protected (only 20 percent of the miners, for example, who are in a high-risk group for tetanus, have been immunized) and that industrial physicians will not assume responsibility for this type of measure, the Group is now considering requesting the cooperation of management and union in a screening and immunization program to be held at the portals to the mines. It is also planning to hold sessions in the four offices during the late fall or early winter for immunization against diphtheria, tetanus, whooping cough, and possibly several other diseases.

One Group consultant sees as a potential danger of group practice and of emphasis on preventive medicine the possible neglect of the patient's presenting symptom. The family physician in solo practice, he contends, generally uses the approach of treating the patient's presenting symptom, on the theory that most symptoms are minor, and that any serious symptom will still be there the next time he sees the patient. In a group practice, where preventive medicine is stressed and consultants are readily available, the family physician may be more concerned that a patient has not had a particular immunization or a pelvic examination in quite a long while than in a presenting symptom of apparently negligible importance. The patient may, therefore, be relatively dissatisfied because of the failure of the Group physician adequately to treat the symptom which has brought him to the office. Nevertheless, another consultant comments, Group physicians display an amazing amount of concern for the personal needs of the patient.

Other physicians comment that, in any case, the thorough, preventive approach to which the Group adheres in principle is not applied uniformly to all patients. In a sense, one family physician contends, the Group's family physicians practice a double standard of medicine because of the different financial arrangements that apply to their various patients. Beneficiaries of the Fund and check-off patients are likely to be given a more extensive or searching type of care than are fee-for-service patients. If some part of the cost of medical care is covered, for example, a Group family physician may do cultures on all the members of a family in which there is a case of streptococcal infection. He will hesitate, however, to subject a family without prepayment benefits to the expense involved. Another family physician comments that he does practice more symptomatic medicine with his fee-for-service patients because he is more concerned about their ability to pay than he needs to be with other patients. He also contends that the Group's consultants, like consultants in solo practice, are less concerned than the family physicians about the financial constraints to which their patients may be subject.

Many members of the Group nevertheless state that they feel they are practicing better medicine as well as more "comfortable" medicine within the framework of the Group than they did in solo practice. Because in most instances the monetary factor is removed, patients are not denied needed tests because of their cost. And the physician has been relieved of the pressure of worrying about earning enough money, collecting his bills, and so on.

As part of the emphasis on preventive medicine, every family physician is supposed to complete a Health Needs Inventory for every patient that notes existing diseases, previous disease, injury, or surgery with continuing health implications, familial disease or constitutional defects with potential health implications, social and environmental health factors, medications requiring special surveillance, and completed immunizations. If patients are known to have allergies to particular drugs, vaccines, and so on, that fact is noted by a large stamp on the cover of their records.

The Group has planned to use the Health Needs Inventory to identify patients with the same types of health problems, and then to hold educational sessions for them. A number of years ago the Group held an educational program of about six sessions for diabetics with the help of the nutritionist of the Allegheny Valley County Department of Health. From 40 to 60 patients participated. Now that the Group is settled in its new facility in New Kensington, it hopes to be able to initiate other sessions of this sort and, through a newsletter it inaugurated in the spring of 1964, is exploring the interests of its patients in health discussion classes on home nursing, first aid, and resuscitation; basic facts for diabetic patients; health problems of women; cancer — facts and prevention; and bringing up infants and children. The nurses with the Group are said to be very interested in sessions of this sort and will be expected to take a considerable amount of responsibility for any that are initiated.

Since moving into the New Kensington building, the Group has instituted sessions for physiotherapy three times a week. Approximately 200 patient visits are made to the clinic each month for physiotherapy. One of the sessions is scheduled to overlap with the regular visit to the office by the Group's consultant in physical medicine, who routinely screens all patients in the program and provides any needed consultations.

Liaison with other community agencies is handled by the Group's social worker (now on extended maternity leave) or the public health nurse. The social worker also helps patients with emotional and psychosocial problems, and with interpretations of social security and public assistance benefits.

The public health nurse provides information to the patients on other available health services and handles liaison with such community agencies as Visiting Nurses' Associations. She is also now making the arrangements for the organization of a blood donor club open to members of the United Mine Workers unions in the area as well as the medical and nonmedical staff of the four offices. Benefits consist of total blood replacement without charge to members and their families, parents and parents-in-law, Fund pensioners, and widows. The public health nurse, with one of the Group's physicians, some years ago taught the firemen of four communities how to handle women in labor and deliver babies in an emergency.

With check-off funds the Group pays a nurse of the Visiting Nurses' Association to make home visits to patients in the New Kensington area. The rate paid by the Group, $2.00 per visit, is higher than the normal fee and costs the Group about $1,000 per year. Because home visits by physicians are covered under the check-off while nurses' visits had not been, patients had preferred to call physicians even when the service they needed could have been adequately given by a nurse.

The Group is now readying a grant application for a substantial sum of money to finance an expansion of mental health services. At present the Group's consultant in psychiatry sees at least 30 ambulatory psychotic patients regularly for treatment. A weekly psychiatric seminar is also held by the Group to increase the physicians' awareness of the psychological factors affecting illness. Should funds be obtained, the Group hopes to add psychiatric social workers to the staff to provide treatment for patients both at the clinic and in their homes. The Group claims that there has been a strong movement within the community in recent years for a mental health program but that opposition from physicians at the Citizens General Hospital has prevented its development. A social worker from a nearby state mental hospital holds a regular half-day session per week at the hospital, but Group members say that this session serves more as a screening mechanism for admission to state hospitals than as a mental health clinic.

Approaches to Quality Control

Although the Group has instituted various techniques, such as the appointment system, consultant request form, and so on, in order to promote good quality of care for its patients, its major effort toward this end is a constant attempt to elevate or maintain the standards of practice of its members. As stated in the rules and regulations governing the medical staff, one of the Group's major purposes is "To provide a continuing educational program for the Medical Staff." This has been particularly important for the Russellton Group, since most of its members have been denied the learning experience that hospital practice provides.

Each full-time member of the Group must devote one half day a week to an educational experience in a medical field of particular interest to him. Ordinarily, the physicians will work either with a participating specialist in the Group, or at a specialty clinic in Pittsburgh. One general practitioner is now spending his half day at the neurology clinic of the University of Pittsburgh Medical School because the Group feels that its coverage in this specialty is rather inadequate. In previous years this physician had worked in rheumatology, but changed to neurology because the Group now has a participating internist whose subspecialty is rheumatology. One of the general practitioners based in Apollo spent a year working with the Group's consultants in obstetrics and gynecology and now handles some problems in this specialty that are brought to the Apollo office. A third general practitioner has been working on cardiology for about three years and is able to use his learning experience since other Group general practitioners occasionally consult him about the interpretations of electrocardiograms and related matters. Over time, other physicians have worked in radiology, hematology, orthopedics, and so on.

Also compulsory for the full-time members is a two-week study leave during which they must take a two-week course or attend a serious ten-day meeting. Some 60 to 70 percent of the Group take courses and are often asked to report to one of the staff meetings on their return so that other members of the Group can share their learning experience. The Group's medical director, for example, in the winter of 1964 attended an advance course on metabolic disease offered by the American College of Physicians and reported on it to the staff early in March.

Twice each week the Group holds staff conferences at which, theoretically at least, attendance is mandatory. Although no disciplinary measures are used, attendance is at a very high level. At one time, when the conferences were held early in the morning, attendance was considered to be less than satisfactory. They have since been rescheduled as midday luncheon meetings, and attendance now approaches the 100 percent mark.

Several years ago the consultant psychiatrist initiated a psychiatric seminar for members of the Group. Currently held weekly, the seminar consists of a case presentation by one of the physicians followed by group discussion in which the psychiatrist now plays a minor role. One general practitioner, who reports that the seminars have changed his outlook and that he now goes into a patient's psychosocial history extensively when it seems to be relevant, seems to bear out the Group's general impression that the psychiatric seminars have had a definite impact on patient care.

On Friday the Group sees a closed-circuit television program transmitted by the University of Pittsburgh Medical School. Directed primarily at the "community practitioner," the program presents, usually in the format of "grand rounds," discussions of patient care problems of general interest, new techniques, or preventive medicine. Following the television program, the Group will take up additional subjects of special interest and concern. An effort is made to achieve maximum participation by various members of the Group, both as speakers and discussants, and broad representation of current cases.

Mortality conferences are held once a month, and X-ray conferences had also been held regularly until recently. These were suspended during the Group's move to New Kensington and have not yet been resumed because of the illness of the radiologist. Upon his recovery they will also be fitted into the schedules for the Friday conference.

Full staff conferences are held five times a year, and in this case sanctions are applied in an attempt to secure attendance. Members of the Group may miss one meeting a year without penalty, but are fined $25 if they miss more than one. At one of these meetings audit of the specialty and general practice work is discussed.

The Group has given thought to a further extension of the educational program to provide the full-time physicians with sabbatical study leaves, but has not as yet taken any formal steps in this direction. It has also considered instituting a formal program for the family physicians under which each would, for one year, spend his half day a week with a specialist in obstetrics and gynecology, for another year with a pediatrician, and for another year with an internist. Again, however, no specific action has been taken to put this into effect.

Members of the Group, although for the most part desirous of the learning experience that occurs in hospital practice, apparently believe that the Group's own educational activities are at least as valuable as the learning experience available at Citizens General Hospital. The hospital, the medical director reports, has a conference only once a month, and it is considered to be perfunctory.

In other less formal ways the Group has also stressed the continuing education of Group members. The Group has assigned to its specialists a more important role as teachers and consultants than as referral physicians. In their notes on patients' records, the consultants are supposed to discuss the bases for the diagnosis reached, explanations of differential diagnoses, and the principles underlying the indicated therapy, in order to increase the general information of the managing physician and his understanding of the management of problems within the particular specialty. Much informal consultation, during which treatment problems and philosophies are discussed, also takes place among the members of the Group. And a number of years ago the consultants in obstetrics and gynecology gave a series of evening talks on problems in their specialty at the homes of members of the Group.

The medical director himself exercises informal controls over the quality of physician practice through his regular but unsystematic screening of patient records at the various offices. He discusses those he screens with the physician and, on the records, raises questions concerning studies that are indicated, immunizations that are needed, and so on. When a physician is young or new to the Group, the medical director may also ask more frequently than with older physicians to see patients referred to him for consultation again after several months so that he can assess the intermediate care. In certain cases, the medical director may ask a member of the staff to prepare a memorandum to remind the staff of the availability and correct use of a new procedure such as the measles vaccine.

The Group does not, however, attempt to control the way its members handle particular problems. The medical director holds the view that ultimate responsibility must rest with the patient's family physician, but that he must be able to justify his treatment if called upon to do so.

The dispersal of the Group's full-time members in four different offices has constituted one barrier to the realization of a high degree of participation and cohesion among the members. This barrier was particularly evident before the Group moved into the New Kensington clinic, for the physicians stationed at Apollo were geographically quite remote from Russellton. On the other hand, the medical director notes, the physicians in Apollo have distinguished themselves among the members of the Group for their assumption of primary responsibility for patient care, perhaps largely because of their relative geographical isolation from the Group's headquarters. Their immunization record is excellent, more than 80 percent of their patients having been immunized against the major infectious diseases.

The medical director comments that the Russellton Group has experienced a problem which he feels is common to any group practice — the occasional inability of the physicians to submerge their own personalities sufficiently to become effective members of the Group. At times, he says, the specialists have been prone to operate as they would in their own offices, failing to maintain the degree of communication with family physicians which the Group feels is essential for continuity of care. Not all of them, furthermore, have fulfilled their function of educating the family physicians as consistently as the Group expects.

The problem of adjustment has seemed to be most pronounced for the internists. Although the Group would prefer to use internists rather than general practitioners as family physicians, many internists view their role in a group practice as that of consultation rather than provision of personal care. The inability of the Group to assure that internists will have hospital privileges, in any case, deters internists from joining the Group. In the past year, for example, the medical director says that eight internists were interested enough in the Group to come to New Kensington for an interview, but all finally decided against joining because of the lack of hospital privileges. The Group, in recruiting family physicians, therefore considers internists, pediatricians, or general practitioners, and tries to increase the general practitioners' technical skills through the continuing education program. The medical director has the impression that the practice of the Group's current general practitioners is in fact closer to that of an internist than to that of the average general practitioner in solo practice, but this impression has not been verified by a medical audit.

The Group finds recruitment even of general practitioners difficult, in spite of the fact that general practitioners are usually less concerned about the denial of hospital privileges than are specialists. Apart from the fact that a declining proportion of medical students are entering general practice, the annual income offered by the Group is generally lower than that possible in solo practice. Finally, many physicians are reluctant to join a group as closely identified with labor as is the Russellton Group and one that has been surrounded by a climate of (sometimes) bitter controversy since its inception. Indeed, the Group feels that it receives an unusually large proportion of applications from physicians who want to "retire" into group practice, or who are suffering from severe cardiac disease, drug addiction, or alcoholism.

In an attempt to assess the quality of the medical care actually being given by its physicians, the Group has had a number of audits made since 1952. Two audits were performed by the Area Medical Office of the United Mine Workers Fund, which in 1959 asked a consultant, Dr. E. Richard Weinerman, to undertake a third study. Dr. Weinerman was given two days in which to attempt

> . . . to measure to what extent the programs of the clinics approached the ideal model of comprehensive prepayment group practice with its preventive medicine and managing physician orientation. The principal short-comings were discovered to be in the realm of continuity and coordination of patient care, and in the weakness of the concept of the managing physician. The groups were characterized by Weinerman . . . as an inverted pyramid, top heavy with specialists and weakest at the general physician level. They compared in his opinion more favorably with the standard outpatient teaching model than with the "ideal" model of comprehensive prepayment group practice. Key weaknesses in educational programs, preventive medical services and ancillary staff organization were brought to light.[5]

At the time Dr. Weinerman visited Russellton, the Group was engaged on its own internal audit of the performance of both general practitioners and specialists. It was thought that records of patients who had only recently come to the Group and who had not been seen by any other Group physician would provide the most reliable guide to general practitioners' performance, and the sampling procedure was planned with this in mind. Later it was discovered that most of the records were for patients who were on public assistance or who had come to the office in an

5. Thompson A. Ferrier, "Appraising and Improving the Quality of Medical Care in an Ambulatory Group Practice," *Proceedings, Tenth Annual Group Health Institute of the Group Health Association of America,* Columbus, Ohio, 1960, p. 85.

emergency, and that they were thus not representative of the general practitioners' average practice. As a consequence no specific reports were prepared on the performance of individual physicians. A general review of the findings, however, was presented at a staff conference. No sampling problems existed for the patient records chosen to evaluate the performance of specialists, and a summary evaluation, as well as individual reports on each specialist's performance, were prepared. Copies of the evaluation form and of the reports on two specialists are included as Appendix B.

For the audit ten patient records of each specialist were selected and reviewed independently by two Group physicians. In addition to evaluation of the physicians' performance in handling the patients' medical problems, the auditors also examined whether continuity and coordination of care had been achieved, and whether the specialists, in their notes on other physicians' records, had adequately fulfilled their educational function. After the audit each physician was given a written report containing specific criticisms and comments as well as general recommendations.

Although the auditors noted and commended various examples of excellent performance, they also found examples of "virtually all known elementary technical and performance failures." These included:

1. Failure to document the chief complaint or reason for referral.
2. Failure to recognize and investigate significant collateral problems.
3. Failure to follow up collateral problems even when pertinent data were available elsewhere in the record.
4. Failure to perform elementary screening examinations.
5. Failure to include an etiologic diagnosis when possible, and sometimes failure on the physician's part to commit himself to a diagnosis.
6. Irrational and symptomatic therapy, and use of proprietary rather than generic terminology.
7. Failure to perform the educational function adequately.

The most common problem found was inadequate continuity and coordination of care. As noted earlier, in order to rectify this the Group promptly revised its operations to place much greater stress on the concept of a managing physician for each patient, and it changed both procedures and forms to facilitate coordination between family physician and consultant. Today the Group feels that its performance in this regard, while still not as perfect as the members would like, compares favorably with the standards to be found in solo practice.

The Group has discussed the possibilities of conducting continuing internal audits, but has not yet formulated specific plans. The conclusions drawn from the audit have been incorporated, however, as basic staff policy in the rules and regulations drawn up when the Group, formerly a partnership, established itself as a professional association in 1961.

The Future of the Group

The Group is now considering the desirability, and possibly the need for, an expansion of its entire operation. To an extent, it is already geared for quite a sizable enlargement in its patient population, for its new clinic in New Kensington is now operating at what the Group calculates to be only 60 percent of its minimal capacity, and a smaller proportion of its potential capacity. If all physicians held office hours in the evening, for example, many more patients could be accommodated with no increase in physical facilities. The building to be constructed soon for the Apollo physicians will also accommodate more patients than that office now serves.

Several very large industrial plants exist in the area served by the Russellton Group. The unions representing the employees of these concerns, an aluminum and a glass plant, have on a number of occasions approached the Group to discuss the formulation of a prepaid arrangement with the Group for their members. The Group has also considered the development of a voluntary prepayment mechanism similar to the check-off arrangement for families in the community. Nothing has yet developed from these discussions.

Should negotiations for another union-sponsored prepaid plan develop beyond informal discussions, the Board of Directors of the nonprofit corporation would be faced with the almost certain necessity of including representatives of these unions among its members. Although some members of the Board are no longer working miners, they understandably view the clinic for whose creation they are primarily responsible as a miners' facility. It is not certain how much they would welcome any threat to the now strong identification of the clinic with miners. Although discussions between the Group and representatives of non-miners' unions have been held at intervals for a number of years, the Board changed the name of the nonprofit corporation from Russellton Building, Inc., to Miners Clinics, Inc., in 1963. The Group's Medical Director, and the area administrator of the Mine Workers Fund, both feel that expansion is necessary and have expressed to the Board their view that a broadening of Board membership to create wider community representation would facilitate this expansion. For the present, however, it is considered unlikely that a major union group would be prepared to work out a formal arrangement until the issue of hospital privileges for members of the Russellton Medical Group has been satisfactorily resolved.

Appendix A

Rules and Regulations of the Medical Staff of the Russellton Medical Group

Article I. Name

The name of this organization shall be the "Medical Staff of the Russellton Medical Group."

Article II. Purpose

The purpose of this organization shall be:

1. To provide comprehensive physician services of high quality to coal miners and their families and to other persons in the community requesting such services, through the medium of medical group practice.

2. To develop and maintain regulations for the government of the Medical Staff.

3. To establish and maintain standards of professional performance of the Medical Staff.

4. To provide a continuing educational program for the Medical Staff.

5. To represent the Medical Staff in its formal relations with the Board of Directors of the Russellton Clinic facilities, the United Mine Workers of America Welfare and Retirement Fund and other similar consumer-sponsored medical care programs, other professional organizations and the public.

Article III. Membership

Section 1. Qualifications.

A. Members must have the professional and personal attributes compatible with the purposes of this organization. Membership will not be based upon factors of race, religion, creed or national origin.

B. Members of the Medical Staff must be licensed to practice medicine and surgery in the State of Pennsylvania.

C. Members of the Medical Staff must be Employees of the Russellton Medical Group (a Pennsylvania professional association).

Section 2. Procedure of Appointment.

A. Application for new membership shall be presented to the Medical Director who shall transmit it to the Professional Standards Committee of the Medical Staff.

B. The Professional Standards Committee shall review the application and submit a recommendation to the Medical Staff for its acceptance, deferral or rejection.

C. The Medical Staff shall receive the recommendation of the Professional Standards Committee and shall vote on the application at its next regular meeting. If at least three-quarters (¾) of the Staff members present vote for acceptance of the application, it shall be submitted as an application for employment to the Board of Governors of the Russellton Medical Group.

D. If the Board of Governors of the Russellton Medical Group engages the applicant as a professional employee, he shall automatically become a member of the Medical Staff and remain so as long as he is an employee of the Russellton Medical Group.

E. Within three (3) months of the end of the first year of membership in the Medical Staff, the Professional Standards Committee shall recommend approval or disapproval of permanent Staff membership to the Medical Staff. If at least three-quarters (¾) of the Staff members present at the next regular meeting of the Medical Staff vote in favor of permanent membership, this recommendation shall be transmitted to the Board of Governors of the Russellton Medical Group.

Section 3. Definition of Medical Staff Membership.

The membership of the Medical Staff shall consist of all professional employees of the Russellton Medical Group. The period of membership in the Medical Staff will correspond exactly to the period of employment.

Section 4. Ethics.

The principles of Medical Ethics as adopted by the American Medical Association shall govern the professional conduct of the Medical Staff.

Section 5. Dismissal.

Dismissal from employment by the Russellton Medical Group can be recommended to the Board of Governors of the Russellton Medical Group by the vote of at least three-quarters (¾) of the Staff members. Termination of membership in the Medical Staff will occur automatically with termination of employment by the Russellton Medical Group.

Section 6. Regulation of Membership.

All members of the Medical Staff shall be subject to the Rules and Regulations of the Medical Staff, the By-laws of the Russellton Medical Group and the conditions defined by their employment contract. Violation of the stipulations contained in these documents shall be cause for recommendation for dismissal from employment.

Section 7. Voting Rights.

All members shall have one (1) vote at meetings of the Medical Staff.

Article IV. Meetings

Section 1. Regular Meetings.

There shall be at least five meetings per year. These meetings shall take place on the last Monday of each month during the months of September, November, January, March and June. The membership shall be notified of the place and agenda of the meeting at least one (1) week prior to such meeting.

Section 2. Special Meetings.

. . .

Section 3. Attendance.

Attendance at meetings shall be mandatory for all members of the Staff except when absence is required by leave or necessary professional activities. A record of the attendance shall be maintained at each meeting. Absent members should inform the Secretary of the Medical Staff of the reason for absence from a meeting.

Failure to attend at least four of the regularly scheduled meetings without just cause may result in a $25.00 fine payable to the Russellton Medical Group within thirty (30) days of notice of such fine.

Section 4. Quorum.

. . .

Article V. Staff Organization

Section 1. Departments.

The Medical Staff may be organized into departments according to a table of organization established by the Medical Staff as the need arises. Department heads shall be appointed by the Medical Director, subject to the approval of the Executive Committee and a majority of the Medical Staff present.

Section 2. Medical Director.

A Medical Director shall be appointed by a majority of the Medical Staff, after review and recommendation by the Professional Standards Committee.

The Medical Director must be a practicing physician who participates actively in providing medical services as a member of the Medical Staff.

The Medical Director shall be responsible for:

A. Pursuit of the purposes of the Staff as defined in Article II.

B. Administration of the Medical Staff.

C. Liaison with other departments of the Russellton Clinic.

D. Official representation of the Medical Staff to the Board of Directors of the Russellton Clinic.

E. Representation of the professional function of the Medical Staff to consumer groups, medical programs, and other professional organizations.

Section 3. Chief of Staff.

A Chief of Staff shall be appointed by a majority of the Medical Staff, after review and recommendation by the Professional Standards Committee.

The Chief of Staff shall be a practicing physician who is a full-time member of the Medical Staff.

The Chief of Staff shall be responsible for the direction and supervision of the clinical services of the Medical Staff and for the program of continuing staff education.

Section 4. Officers.

. . .

Section 5. Committees.

Committees shall be standing and special. All Committees, except the Executive Committee shall be appointed by the President at the first meeting of the Staff in which the new President takes office.

A. *Standing Committees.*

1. *Executive Committee.*

The Executive Committee shall consist of the officers of the Medical Staff. The duties of the Executive Committee shall be:

a. To act for the Medical Staff in emergent situations between Medical Staff meetings, but such action to be subject to review and modification by the Medical Staff at the next regular meeting.

b. To review major problems confronting the Medical Staff and to make appropriate recommendations to the Medical Staff.

c. To assure that all provisions of the Rules and Regulations are rigidly observed.

d. To take disciplinary measures or to recommend such measures when appropriate.

e. To undertake other actions required by these Rules and Regulations.

2. *Professional Standards Committee.*

The Professional Standards Committee shall consist of five (5) members of the Medical Staff.

The primary responsibility of this committee shall be to take measures for the evaluation and control of the quality of medical care with the purpose of maintaining and improving the quality of medical care provided by the Medical Staff. Its duties shall be:

a. To investigate the qualifications of the applicants for employment by the Russellton Medical Group and to make recommendations for action to the Medical Staff on such applications.

b. To define the scope of professional activities of Staff members on the basis of training, experience and demonstrated competence.

c. To develop Principles and Standards of patient care in accord with the purpose of this organization. Such principles and standards may be established and revised by recommendation of the

Professional Standards Committee, subject to approval of the Executive Committee and a majority of the Medical Staff present.

d. To develop a table of organization of the Medical Staff which is appropriate to its size, needs, and responsibilities. Such a table of organization may be established and revised on recommendation of the Professional Standards Committee, subject to approval of the Executive Committee and a majority of the Medical Staff present.

e. To undertake a periodic assessment of the quality of patient care (Medical Audit) and to report the results of such evaluation to the Medical Staff.

f. To investigate charges of violation of these Rules and Regulations, By-laws of the Russellton Medical Group or of the employment contract or of professional misconduct of Staff members and to report its findings and recommendations to the Executive Committee.

3. *Medical Records Committee.*

The Medical Records Committee shall consist of three (3) members of the Medical Staff.

The Medical Records Committee is responsible for maintenance of adequate clinical records of patient care. Its duties shall be:

a. To establish standards for clinical records and to revise them when necessary.

b. To maintain supervision of the quality and completeness of clinical records.

c. To recommend action on any major inadequacy of records to the Executive Committee.

4. *Joint Conference Committee.*

The Joint Conference Committee shall consist of five (5) members of the Medical Staff and five (5) representatives of the Board of Directors of the Russellton Clinic.

The Committee shall meet periodically for discussion and review of matters of mutual interest to the Medical Staff and the Board of the Clinic. Such matters may include:

a. Policies and content of the medical care program.

b. Plans for long-term development of program and facilities.

Members of the Medical Staff shall represent the Medical Staff in meetings of this Committee.

B. *Special Committees.*

The Special Committees may include:

1. Library Committee
2. Laboratory Committee
3. Program Committee
4. Committee on Medical Staff Benefits
5. Therapeutics Committee.

Article VI. Responsibilities of Medical Staff

The responsibilities of the Medical Staff and its individual members shall include the following:

1. To provide medical care of the highest possible quality to patients of the Russellton Medical Group.

2. To confine professional activities to limits defined by the Professional Standards Committee (Article V, Section 5, A, 2, b).

3. To assure that each regular patient has a responsible personal physician on the staff of the Medical Group and that such physician is informed of, participates in, and approves of any major plans or decisions in respect to care of his patients.

4. To encourage the use of the resources of group practice by all patients.

5. To arrange for consultation as required by the Joint Accreditation Committee as well as in all instances where the diagnosis is obscure or where there is any doubt as to the best therapeutic measures.

6. To provide that emergency medical service is available at all times for all patients of the Russellton Medical Group.

7. To employ only drugs which are listed in the United States Pharmacopeia, National Formulary, New and Non-official Remedies and which are established as part of the Medical Group formulary, excluding exceptions which can be well-justified.

8. To maintain adequate records of medical care and to take personal responsibility for the completion of such records. The clinic record should include a Basic Health Record and Medical Need Inventory as well as a continuing record of:

a. Patient's complaints
b. History
c. Examination
d. Diagnosis
e. Therapeutic plan
f. Disposition
g. All correspondence
h. Communication by telephone with patient or his family containing significant medical advice.
i. Missed appointments and attempt at follow-up.
j. Reports of all clinical, laboratory and other diagnostic studies, hospital summaries, pathological reports, operative procedures.

9. To record in the clinical record all orders for treatments to be carried out by the Clinic Staff.

10. To become aware of the economic burden imposed upon each patient by needed medical care and to minimize this economic burden wherever possible without compromising the quality of services. Fulfillment of this responsibility requires knowledge of services, drugs, appliances and financial assistance provided by various programs and health agencies and direct assistance to eligible patients to secure such benefits.

11. To support the Staff educational program by attending all educational meetings and by participating in them.

12. To attend all Staff meetings, except when leave or professional duties prevent attendance.

13. To adhere to all provisions of the By-laws of the Russellton

Medical Group, Rules and Regulations of the Medical Staff and of the Employment Contract.

Article VII. Amendment of Rules and Regulations

1. Amendments to the Rules and Regulations may be proposed at one regular meeting and voted upon at the next regular meeting.
2. Amendments shall be adopted by approval of at least three-fourths (¾) of the Medical Staff members.
3. Votes on amendments may be conducted by mail, and will be valid only with the affirmative vote of at least ¾ of those entitled to vote.

Article VIII. Adoption of Rules and Regulations

These Rules and Regulations shall be adopted by affirmative vote of at least three-fourths (¾) of the Medical Staff members and shall be enforced immediately upon their adoption, and will supersede all previous by-laws of the Medical Staff.

Appendix B

Russellton Medical Group Appraisal Form and Specialist Appraisals

Russellton Medical Group

Appraisal No.

Appraisers — Appraisal date

Appraisal of Work in Specialty Departments

Physician__________ Specialty__________ Office: R Ac P Ap

Patient__________ Age___ Sex: M F — Payment: Co F NCO NF DPA Other — Origin Office: R Ac P Ap

Chart No.__________

Date of 1st visit to above M.D.__________

CODE: a-adequate, b-fair, c-poor

1. CC/REASON FOR REFERRAL
   Comment: — a b c

2. HISTORY
   Comment: — a b c

3. PHYSICAL EXAMINATION
   Comment: — a b c

4. INVESTIGATION
   Comment:
   Lab. EKG, BMR, etc. — a b c
   X-ray — a b c
   Consultation — a b c

5. IMPRESSION AND FINAL DIAGNOSIS
   Comment: — a b c

6. TREATMENT
   Comment: — a b c

7. CONTINUITY, COORDINATION, FOLLOW-UP
   Comment: — a b c

8. EDUCATIONAL FUNCTION
   Comment: — a b c

9. TIME INTERVAL FOR EVALUATION OR TREATMENT
   Comment: — a b c

10. GENERAL COMMENTS:

11. FINAL APPRAISAL — a b c

12. CC/REASON FOR REFERRAL:
    (1) __________
    (2) __________
    (3) __________
    (4) __________

13. FINAL DIAGNOSIS:
    (1) __________
    (2) __________
    (3) __________
    (4) __________

Physican Code J-101–110

Appraisal of Work in Specialty Departments

A. *OBSERVATIONS DERIVED FROM THE AUDIT*

1. *Chief Complaint and Reason for Referral*
   Almost always clearly stated.
2. *History*
   In one instance, the life history of the lesion for which the patient was referred was not stated. Example 101-J.
3. *Physical Examination*
   In only one instance, admission for major abdominal surgery, had no examination of the abdomen recorded at the Clinic. Example 104-J
4. *Investigation*
   In every instance where a histological study was indicated, it was recorded.
   Two patients were found to have internal hemorrhoids after presenting a complaint of rectal bleeding. In one instance, barium enema was not performed and in the other it may have been unduly delayed. Examples 106-J, 109-J.
5. *Impression and Final Diagnosis*
   There was an adequate definitive diagnosis in every instance.
6. *Treatment*
   In one instance, follow-up therapy and instructions were not recorded. Example 110-J.
7. *Continuity, Coordination, Follow-up*
   There were rare instances when follow-up after surgery was not recorded, and specific return and communication with the referring physician was not recorded. Examples 101-J, 110-J.
8. *Educational Function*
   The educational function was considered very adequate throughout. In one instance, a discussion of the differential diagnoses might have been helpful. Example 107-J.
9. *Time Interval*
   For evaluation or treatment.
10. *General Comments*
    Surgical consultation, particularly with respect to the level of continuity and coordination within the group, is worthy of emulation by other specialists in the group.

B. *COMMENTS AND RECOMMENDATIONS DERIVED FROM THE AUDIT*

1. The question is raised for discussion as to the necessity of including barium enemas in all instances of rectal bleeding, whether or not hemorrhoids are present.

C. *GENERAL COMMENTS NOT NECESSARILY RELATED TO THE AUDIT*

1. It is suggested that there be a general medical evaluation of surgical risk prior to hospital admission for major surgery.
2. Whenever possible, elective diagnostic studies should be carried out prior to hospitalization.
3. Summaries of hospitalization, plans for follow-up should be relayed to the referring or personal physician without undue delay.

PROFESSIONAL STANDARDS COMMITTEE RUSSELLTON MEDICAL GROUP March 18, 1960

Physician Code E-101–110

Appraisal of Work in Specialty Departments

A. *OBSERVATIONS DERIVED FROM THE AUDIT*

1. *Chief Complaint and Reason for Referral*
   In many instances, the record is inadequate with respect to the identification of the referring physician and reason for referral and the chief complaint of the patient.
2. *History*
   Historical information in these charts was generally considered inadequate with respect to the chief complaint or reason for referral. There was inadequate recording of details of the present illness, social history, family history and occupational history — see audit work sheets.
3. *Physical Examination*
   In most instances, physical examination was considered inadequate with respect to one or more of the following:
   a. vital signs and weight even when directly pertinent to the primary problem of the patient.
   b. funduscopic examinations.
   c. pelvic and rectal examinations.
   d. inadequate description of the physical findings related to one of the presenting problems.
4. *Investigation*
   Investigations are considered generally inadequate with regard to one or more of the following:
   a. routine screening studies.
   b. investigation of the primary problem with reference to diagnostic studies or indicated consultations.
   c. investigation of possible collateral problems.
   d. inadequate interpretation of data in the clinical records.

5. *Impression and Final Diagnosis*
In many instances, diagnoses are not justified or proven in the patient record.
In several instances, the diagnosis does not explain the chief complaint.
There were numerous instances in which the collateral diagnoses suggested by the clinical data were not included.
6. *Treatment*
Treatment was not described adequately and currently in several instances.
7. *Continuity, Coordination, Follow-up*
In a number of instances, plans for follow-up or return to the managing physician were absent or inadequate.
In addition, follow-up observations were inadequate with respect to the patient's primary problem. Examples 103-E, 108-E, 109-E.
There appeared to be no awareness of pertinent data in the clinical record in Example 106-E.
8. *Educational Function*
For the most part, the educational function of the specialist was not carried out by an adequate discussion of the differential diagnosis, and an adequate presentation of the rationale of therapy.
9. *Time Interval for Evaluation or Treatment*
No comments.
10. *General Comments*
In general, function as an internist was generally considered inadequate and appeared to be carried out in a perfunctory manner.

B. *COMMENTS AND RECOMMENDATIONS DERIVED FROM THE AUDIT*

1. In every instance, the chief complaint and reason for referral should be clearly stated and adequately presented.
2. Serious efforts should be made to provide a history which will serve as a meaningful basis for establishing a diagnosis relating to the chief complaint, present illness, and collateral problem.
3. Physical examinations should include in most instances a recording of pertinent vital signs, funduscopic examination and rectal and pelvic examination, and adequate description of the findings related to the presenting problems.
4. Investigation should include as a matter of routine, hemogram, urinalysis, serology and chest x-rays; as well as ECG, blood sugar and Pap smear in appropriate groups. Investigation should also be sufficient to establish the primary diagnosis, possible collateral problems and include an interpretation of such data.
5. Every internist's note should contain a diagnosis which attempts to explain the chief complaint, nature of the present

illness, and collateral medical problems; and such diagnoses should be justified by the available clinical data.

6. Therapy should be accurately and currently described in each progress note. In the initial note, the rationale of the therapy should at least be mentioned.
7. It is the responsibility of each physician to see that continuity and coordination of patient care is preserved by making specific plans for disposition, return to managing physician or return to the specialty. In each instance, there should be clear documentation of communication between the physicians. In addition, an awareness of all data contained in the chart is the responsibility of the consulting internist and it is his responsibility to take action appropriate to that data.
8. It is the responsibility of the consulting internist to provide in his note, sufficient discussion of the problem of the patient and justification of the diagnosis along with the discussion of the rationale of therapy and plans for management of the case to increase the knowledge of the referring physician.

C. *GENERAL COMMENTS NOT NECESSARILY DERIVED FROM THE AUDIT*

Strenuous effort must be made to elevate the quality of performance as a consultant in Internal Medicine.

PROFESSIONAL STANDARDS COMMITTEE RUSSELLTON MEDICAL GROUP March 18, 1960

Changing a Community's Pattern of Medical Care: The Russellton Experience

April 1964

Beryl M. Safford

The growth in group practices associated with prepayment, whether sponsored by private physicians, labor groups, or consumer cooperatives, has occurred in the face of, rather than with the blessing of, organized medicine. Particularly vehement has been organized medicine's opposition to prepaid group practices under lay sponsorship. It has been the contention of organized medicine that the quality of medical care is adversely affected by arrangements that include the limitation of the patients' choice of physician to those who are members of the group's "closed panel," the participating physicians' acceptance of other forms of payment than the traditional fee-for-service, and the possibility of lay control over the practice of medicine.

In its campaign against prepaid group practice, organized medicine has used a variety of legal devices, including pressure for such special state legislation as acts restricting establishment of prepayment organizations for physicians' services to physician-medical society controlled groups, assertion of the common law prohibition against the corporate practice of medicine, and charges of violation of state insurance statutes. Probably its most effective weapon, however, has been the right it claims to discipline members of the profession for what it considers to be "unethical" practice. And for many years denial of complete free choice of physician and acceptance in the ordinary practice of medicine of other forms of payment than fee-for-service were considered unethical. Not infrequently charges of soliciting patients were added to the other charges brought against group practices. The principal disciplinary action employed was denial of membership in, or expulsion from, local and state medical societies. This, in turn, in most areas meant ineligibility for specialty board examinations and ratings, and the denial to group physicians of hospital privileges, because the majority of hospitals required medical society membership of their staff members.

Organized medicine's punitive measures were challenged as early as 1919 in Great Britain and 1939 in the United States in the pioneer case of United States vs. the American Medical Association which concerned the Group Health Association of Washington, D.C. In the final appeal of the case, the United States Supreme Court dismissed the A.M.A.'s allegations of unethical practice by the Group Health Association and said, "The motivations behind the disciplines were purely economic." In this and a number of similar cases, the courts have decided that disciplinary action by medical societies on the grounds of unethical practice were in fact violation of anti-trust laws or restraint of trade in violation of the common law. One commentator has pointed out, "It is noteworthy that in every lawsuit against a Medical Society for using ethics as an economic weapon, the courts since 1939 have held against the Society." [1]

In the meantime, perhaps in part because of the court actions, the American Medical Association's conception of medical ethics was undergoing modification. When its Commission on Medical Care Plans, appointed in 1954 to "determine whether current medical care plans are effectively promoting 1) the highest quality of health services, 2) the welfare of the public and the medical profession, and 3) the ethical standards of the medical profession," issued its report in 1958, a new interpretation of free choice of physician apparently became acceptable. The Commission's recommendation, as amended by the Association's House of Delegates, read:

> The A.M.A. believes that "free choice of physician" is the right of every individual and one which he should be free to exercise as he chooses.
>
> Each individual should be accorded the privilege to select and change his physician at will or to select his preferred system of medical care and the A.M.A. vigorously supports the right of the individual to choose between these alternatives.

This more liberal position by no means terminated opposition to closed-panel, prepaid group practices at the local level. In some areas group physicians were still denied membership in local medical societies and privileges to practice in their local hospitals.

Because of the crippling effect on their medical practice of lack of hospital privileges, physicians have increasingly sought the assistance of the courts when denied hospital privileges. In a number of cases involving governmental hospitals, the courts have enjoined the directors from arbitrary discrimination against physicians associated with group practices. The issues with regard

1. Horace R. Hansen, "Summary of Argument for Appellant, Before the Judicial Council, American Medical Association, Matter of William D. Broxon, Trinidad, Colorado, Appellant," September 7, 1957.

to the rights and obligations of voluntary hospitals serving the entire community are more obscure. In a recent study, a former Assistant General Counsel of the United States Department of Health, Education, and Welfare asserts that "In the absence of a controlling statute or a hospital's own rule or regulation to the contrary, the doctrine prevails in most jurisdictions that in a private nonprofit hospital admission to, or exclusion from, hospital staff or privileges rests in the discretion of the governing board." [2] She also notes, however, that in a memorandum filed by the United States as *amicus curiae* in a case involving denial of hospital privileges to Negroes, voluntary community hospitals were equated with governmental hospitals because both serve as "general community hospitals." "If these assertions are correct," the author concludes, "it is to be expected that legal doctrines applicable to the control of public hospitals will more and more be found applicable to private (voluntary) community hospitals." [3]

The Origin and Structure of the Russellton Group

In the fall of 1951 a delegation of coal miners from the nearby town of Russellton appeared in the Pittsburgh office of Dr. Leslie A. Falk, area administrator of the United Mine Workers of America Welfare and Retirement Fund, to ask his help in securing a new "check-off" doctor. According to the miners, their current check-off physician, to whom a small amount of their wages was paid each month as prepayment for the medical care they and their families needed, was too much of a "company man" to represent their interests fairly. They believed that when the company's and the miner's interests clashed, as they might in a workmen's compensation case or when the required physical examinations were conducted after a lay-off period, the physician would protect the company rather than the miners. There were, in addition, rumors of fee-splitting circulating about the physician.

The Fund office was willing to help the miners but found it difficult to attract physicians to the generally isolated and relatively unprosperous coal-mining areas. Finally Dr. Thompson Ferrier, a young general practitioner who was practicing in a coal-mining area that was becoming steadily more depressed economically, told Dr. Falk that he would accept the check-off for the Russellton

2. Gladys A. Harrison, *Control of Medical Staff Appointments in Voluntary Nonprofit Hospitals* (Chicago: American Hospital Association, 1963), p. 11.
3. Harrison, p. 4–5.

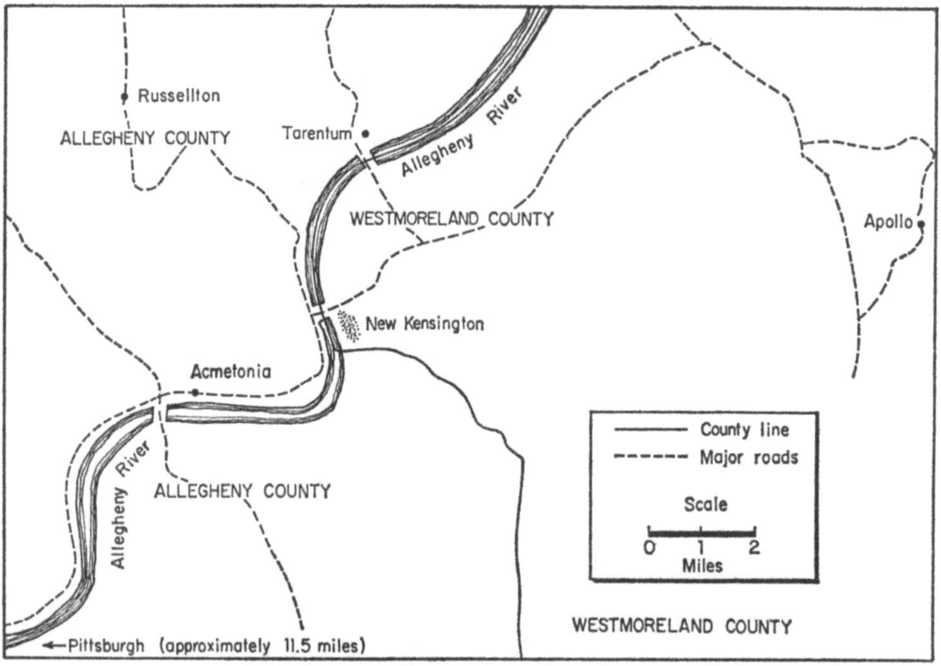

Geographical Area of the Russellton Medical Group

miners, but only if he could be associated with both general practitioners and specialists in a group practice arrangement and could have diagnostic facilities available.

Dr. Ferrier's attitude made good sense to Dr. Falk, who later observed, "Some such arrangements seemed essential in order to attract doctors to the mining areas. Its [the Fund's] strenuous attempts to help find doctors who would know when to seek assistance, would practice comprehensive medicine and avoid at least some of the unnecessary hospitalization and surgery to which the Fund and mining population was subjected had not been entirely successful when solo practice was the nature of the opening."[4] The Fund could not offer Dr. Ferrier any help with the financing of routine home and office care — not among the benefits provided under the Fund's medical program — but it did assure him that it would extend participation in the Fund program to his group for specialist and diagnostic services and for inhospital care.

While Dr. Ferrier scouted around for colleagues, the union

4. Leslie A. Falk. "Group Health Plans in Coal Mining Communities," *Journal of Health and Human Behavior* 4:9 (Spring 1963).

delegation aroused the interest of two other mining locals in the area who agreed to transfer their check-off to the new group. The miners formed a nonprofit corporation to finance the needed facilities, and the Russellton Medical Group, consisting of Dr. Ferrier, one other general practitioner, and an internist, began to practice in February 1952. By 1964, the Group consisted of eight full-time general practitioners, one part-time general practitioner, three full-time internists, and twenty part-time specialists. The full-time members have no practice outside the Group.

The facilities and equipment used by the Group are owned and operated by the nonprofit corporation, Russellton Building, Inc. All the members of the board have been coal miners at one time, but some are now employed in other industries. Although local union members serve in the capacity of community leaders, "there is psychologically a close tie to the union structure. Since more than 85 percent of the population of this community were members of coal mining families, its community acceptance was prompt, but it was, understandably, considered the 'miners' clinic.' "[5] Perhaps largely for this reason, the clinic grew rapidly to provide all or most of the care for about 10,000 persons by the end of its first five years of existence. Since then it has grown more slowly, primarily, it is claimed, because of the difficulties its physicians have encountered in obtaining local hospital privileges.

The board of the nonprofit corporation is considered to be analogous to a hospital board. It determines the policies governing the facilities, and a qualified medical care administrator, selected jointly by the corporation, the Group, and the Fund, supervises daily nonmedical activities and recommends for the approval of the board all ancillary personnel employed in the facilities. The Medical Group is responsible for the selection of member physicians and for supervision of the medical duties of technical and nursing personnel. "However," Dr. Falk has said, "no physician is appointed to the medical group who is unacceptable either to the nonprofit Board or as a participating physician in the . . . Fund."[6]

The Group has opened three additional offices since 1952 in response to the need of different communities for medical services. The first office was opened late in 1953 or early in 1954 in New Kensington, a trading center of about 35,000 persons across the Allegheny River in neighboring Westmoreland County. A miners'

5. Falk, p. 10.
6. Falk, p. 8.

union, unable to find a New Kensington physician willing to make home calls in a nearby mining community, had persuaded the Group to supply it with a check-off physician. In the summer of 1956 the Group responded to appeals published in the *Pennsylvania Medical Journal* for a physician to serve the small town of Apollo quite a distance away on the other side of Westmoreland County and in the fall of 1957 answered a similar appeal by citizens of Acmetonia, an even smaller community near Russellton in Allegheny County.

Until July 1963, the Russellton Clinic was the headquarters of the Group, and had been equipped with a very extensive range of laboratory and X-ray facilities. The Group has now transferred its headquarters to a much larger facility in New Kensington, which is more nearly the center of the area it serves than Russellton. Completed at a cost of approximately $800,000, the new clinic contains offices, examining rooms, laboratories, X-ray facilities, physiotherapy rooms, a library, and most of the equipment currently considered necessary for the practice of modern medicine. Although the Group has considered closing the other offices because all its patients are within a twenty-five minute drive of New Kensington, it has decided that its services should remain close to its patients and it therefore plans to equip the satellite offices with all basic diagnostic equipment. Construction is to begin soon on a new building to replace the Apollo facility, now located in a hotel basement and considered the poorest of the Group's present offices.

Two hospitals exist in the area served by the Russellton Group. Allegheny Valley Hospital, with about 220 beds, is in Tarentum, within easy distance of Russellton. The Citizens General Hospital, with about 230 beds, in New Kensington is the natural service hospital for Apollo but is also easily accessible to residents of Russellton and Acmetonia. Because for a large part of its history the Group's members have not had privileges at these hospitals, the majority of its patients requiring hospitalization have had to be admitted to hospitals in Pittsburgh. In spite of the distance and travel time involved, the members of the Group claim that the patients seem very well pleased both with the physicians caring for them and with the Pittsburgh hospitals used by the Group. The Group has also, however, in some cases arranged with local physicians for the care of patients who did not wish to travel into Pittsburgh for hospitalization.

The majority of the Group's patients are beneficiaries of the

United Mine Workers Welfare and Retirement Fund. Although three general practitioners on the staff of Citizens General Hospital also have participating arrangements with the Fund, some 10,000 or so of the 12,000 Fund beneficiaries living in the area are patients of the Group. The principal services covered by the Fund are specialist and diagnostic care outside the hospital, comprehensive inhospital care, expensive drugs needed for the long-term care of patients with chronic illnesses, and emergency care rendered by any physician.

About 6,000 persons use the Group for services provided under the check-off system, which covers home and office care, including minor medications and routine immunizations. Probably more than 90 percent of the check-off arrangements in the area have been made with the Group.

The Russellton Group also sees a considerable number of "private" patients who pay for care on a fee-for-service basis according to an established schedule that is supposed to correspond with the rates prevailing in the area. The exact percentage is not known, but it is thought that 35 to 40 percent of the Group's patients are private. Since the opening of the new clinic in New Kensington, some 2,000 new patients, most of whom are private, have begun to use the Group. Some 20 percent of the Group's patients are on public assistance, and many of these are said to be former miners.

The Group's largest source of income is the United Mine Workers Fund, which pays the Group monthly according to the proportion of their time spent on Fund beneficiaries. This arrangement, which has been called a "block-fee-for-service," "fee-for-time," or "retainer" method of payment, brought the Group in a recent month approximately $22,500. During the same month, income from check-off was about $6,000 and from fee-for-service patients about $11,000.

The members of the Group pool all moneys received and draw annual incomes starting at a minimum of $12,000 and reaching a maximum of $30,000 according to a fixed schedule based on years of training, specialty status, experience, and years with the Group. Part-time specialists are paid for the proportion of their time they give to the Group, and according to the same schedule. Until recently the maximum income had been $25,000. Changes in the scale are discussed with the Fund's Area Administrator before being instituted because of their implications for the cost of medical care covered by the Fund. The Group pays rent, now approximately $11,000 per month, to the nonprofit corporation to cover overhead costs associated with the care of patients who are not Fund beneficiaries.

The nonprofit corporation, which has recently changed its name from Russellton Building, Inc., to Miners Clinics, Inc., meets all operating expenses, including the salaries of all non-medical personnel, maintenance, supplies, including medical supplies, and so on. In addition to rent from the Medical Group, Miners Clinics, Inc., is paid by the Fund for the overhead expenses associated with the care of Fund beneficiaries. In a recent month, this amounted to approximately $30,000.

The Fund's relationship with the Russellton Medical Group and with Miners Clinics, Inc., has been explained by Dr. Falk.

> The U.M.W.A. Welfare and Retirement Fund has the responsibility to try to help assure the attainment of those goals [the provision of a high quality of medical services at a reasonable cost] on behalf of its beneficiaries, especially through financing services within its program at their full cost . . .
>
> All expansion of medical services or facilities is undertaken only after review and agreement among the three parties, the Area Medical Office needing to be sure that no unrealistic budgetary expectation is involved . . .
>
> The medical group and board exchange annual and monthly financial reports, which are also made available to the Welfare Fund . . . An annual budget of anticipated income and expenditure is submitted by the board and the medical group to the . . . Fund and to each other.[7]

Early Hospital Relationships

At the time of the Group's formation, the Fund had participating arrangements with almost all the physicians in the area later served by the Russellton Medical Group and with the area's two hospitals, Allegheny Valley and Citizens General. Nothing very complicated was involved. If a physician or hospital agreed to participate in the program, billing the Fund rather than the patient for any services rendered, they were added to a list that was passed along to the local union where beneficiaries might consult it. The members of the Group were added to this list.

Allegheny Valley Hospital appeared to be the natural service hospital for the Group in 1952, and the members promptly applied to it for privileges. Dr. Ferrier and two other group physicians

7. Falk, p. 8–9.

were admitted to the staff and used the hospital for the care of general medical patients. They also used the services of specialists on the hospital staff when appropriate. According to the Group's present medical director, Dr. Ferrier attempted to persuade these specialists to join the Group, but pressure from their colleagues prevented them from becoming formally identified with a prepaid group practice.

Late in 1953 or early in 1954, the Group opened an office in the Parnassus suburb of New Kensington, and Medical Society reaction was unfavorable. At the Third Conference on Medical Care in the Bituminous Coal Mine Area — an annual event started in 1952 and continued through 1956 under the sponsorship of the American Medical Association's Committee on Medical Care for Industrial Workers — the chairman of the Committee on Medical Economics of the Pennsylvania State Medical Society is reported to have said, "Our main problem stemmed from the UMWA sponsored Clinic Group practicing in Russellton, crossing over county lines and establishing a branch office (Parnassus) in New Kensington. This supposedly was done at the invitation of the UMWA unions and without the approval of, or even the knowledge of the county medical societies involved. It is impossible to evaluate the extent of the damage that resulted from this unprecedented attempt of the Clinic Group." He went on to say, "Here was a group of well-meaning, enthusiastic, young but uninformed, and ill-advised physicians floundering in a community already harboring an instinctive distrust of the U.M.W.A. intentions in the field of medicine." [8]

The new Parnassus office of the "Community Health Center," a name which the Russellton Group used for several years and which it eventually changed after vigorous protest apparently from the county medical society, was located several blocks from the Citizens General Hospital, to which members of the Group applied for privileges. Immediate opposition was forthcoming from the medical staff of the hospital. Charging that the Group engaged in unethical practices, including the acceptance of retainer rather than fee-for-service as a method of payment, "kicking back" to the United Mine Workers Fund, advertising in a local newspaper,

8. *Report of the Third Conference on Medical Care in the Bituminous Coal Mine Area,* sponsored by the Committee on Medical Care for Industrial Workers of the Council on Medical Services and Council on Industrial Health of the American Medical Association, October 1954 (Chicago: American Medical Association, 1954), p. 9.

and soliciting for additional patients among the workers at a nearby Alcoa plant,[9] the medical staff of the hospital petitioned the Pennsylvania State Medical Society to investigate the matter. In the meantime, they passed a resolution at a staff meeting on February 9, 1954, which was reported to have stated that no physician affiliated with the Community Health Center could be elected to the staff or continue as a member of the staff pending the report of the state society.

One physician affiliated with the Group, a young internist who was already on the staff of Citizens General, promptly resigned from the Group. In his letter of resignation he stated that he knew most of the Group's physicians very well, in fact, some were former classmates and teachers. He considered them highly motivated, well qualified and ethical. He felt, however, that as a member of the hospital staff he should abide by their decision, but this did not mean that he felt the Group's physicians were guilty of unethical practice.

In a prompt reply to the hospital staff's action, the secretary of the Russellton Medical Group requested copies both of the petition to the state medical society and of the resolution concerning denial of privileges to participants in the Group. He quoted the Chairman of the Medical Economics Committee of the state society, who had said: "It is our considered opinion that our society should now change from the critical to the constructive approach. We could and should stimulate community sponsored health facilities (clinics if you like), and man them by traveling teams of specialists who furnish better diagnostic and therapeutic assistance to the G.P. in the backward regions. We should strive to have our smaller hospitals staffed by qualified men representing the various specialties." The Group's secretary expressed the view that the action taken by the hospital staff hardly represented a "constructive approach." In reply, the president of the medical staff merely acknowledged receipt of the letter and said, "It will receive the consideration it merits at the proper time and you will be advised."

The President of the Board of Directors of Russellton Building, Inc., in turn wrote the president of the hospital's Board of Trus-

9. Over the years discussions have been held between the Group and representatives of the employees of the two major employers in the community, an aluminum manufacturer and a glass manufacturer. Although the possibility still exists that the Group may enter into some sort of arrangement with another employee group, nothing has yet developed from these discussions.

tees pointing out that the board of the hospital, like the board of miners, had been attempting in the past year to attract qualified physicians to the area and that the action of the hospital's medical staff appeared to violate the intent of that effort. He suggested that a meeting be held by representatives of the two boards, the medical staffs of the hospital and of the Group, and the United Mine Workers Fund. The president of the hospital board replied that the president of the medical staff had indicated willingness to participate in such a meeting as soon as the Medical Society of the State of Pennsylvania had made its report concerning the charges of unethical practice. By August, the state society had completed its investigation and had cleared the group of all charges. Nevertheless, members of the Group were still denied privileges at the hospital.

Conflict Arises on a Wider Scene

At the time, relationships between Pennsylvania physicians and the United Mine Workers Fund were becoming somewhat strained, and the situation may have affected the attitude of solo practitioners toward a group so closely identified with miners as were the Russellton physicians. Indeed, it was widely believed that the Russellton Clinic had been created by the Fund itself. At the annual meeting of the Pennsylvania State Medical Society in September 1955 Dr. Warren F. Draper, Executive Medical Officer of the Fund, was asked, "Why do you set up diagnostic clinics in areas where ample facilities exist in violation of your arrangements with the AMA (to create facilities only where none exist)?" Dr. Draper replied, "The Fund does not set up . . . clinics. Its financial arrangements with any type of clinic wherever located consist solely of direct payment for services rendered." [10]

Disclaimers of this sort apparently did not convince physicians. As late as 1964 the president of the medical staff of Citizens General Hospital — the same young internist who had resigned from the Russellton Group in 1954 — echoed this belief when he commented that the intent of the Fund program had been to provide better medical care in coal-mining areas that were without it. This aim, he said, and efforts toward this end had had the enthusiastic support of the American Medical Association, and there had reportedly been little opposition when the Group's office was opened in Russellton. The check-off system was held in low repute generally

10. *Pennsylvania Medical Journal* 58:1337 (December 1955).

and, in any case, only one physician was affected. But the office in New Kensington was an entirely different matter. One could hardly claim that good medical care for miners did not exist in a location only a few blocks from a hospital.

The Fund's area administrator had apparently felt otherwise. Like area administrators in other sections, he considered that there were serious problems involving both the quality and the cost of the medical care for which the Fund was paying, of which the most important were unnecessary hospital days and unnecessary surgery. At one of the Conferences on Medical Care in the Bituminous Coal Mine Area he compared the hospitalization record of the Russellton Group with the total hospitalization experience of the Fund in his area and noted that the Group's hospitalization rate was only 57 percent of the average rate for the area and that their average length of hospital stay was two thirds that for the area. He concluded, "These data tend to confirm our qualitative impression that dramatically less hospitalization, accompanied by an elevation in quality of care, has been effectuated by the medical group at Russellton." [11]

Citizens General Hospital figured in the area administrator's dissatisfaction with the medical care rendered Fund beneficiaries in his territory. According to his report, the chairman of the Pennsylvania State Medical Society committee that had investigated the charges of unethical practice lodged against the Group in 1954 had said: "The New Kensington hospital *can* make facilities available but they are not. The out-patient department is not functioning . . . The hospital seems to be a surgeon's paradise . . . A vociferous minority governs the majority of the medical staff of the Citizens General Hospital." Unofficially, it was claimed that the community of New Kensington, early in the 1950's, had had to intercede to persuade the hospital to provide coverage for its Emergency Room and to reestablish participation in the Blue Cross program which it had previously cancelled.

According to the Fund's own methods of analysis, which it called "conservative," at least 11 percent of the hospital days for which the Fund was paying Citizens General in 1953–54 were "questionably necessary." It compared CGH records in gynecological surgery with those of Magee Hospital in Pittsburgh, the regional gynecological teaching hospital, and found that the CGH had more than four times the proportion of uterine suspension cases

11. *Report of the Third Conference on Medical Care in the Bituminous Coal Mine Area*, p. 20.

and ten times the proportion of tubal ligation sterilization cases. "We concluded," Dr. Falk said several years later, "that the Citizens General Hospital was not keeping its house in order in gynecological surgery." [12]

Dr. Falk also claimed that in 1957 only 22 percent of the physicians on the CGH staff were Board-certified or eligible or members of the American Colleges of Surgeons and Physicians, whereas 70 percent of the members of the Russellton Group held such qualifications. The hospital, he said, had no physicians in a number of fields, including physical medicine and rehabilitation, neurology, and psychiatry, and none with formal training in such areas as allergy, chest diseases, and rheumatology.

At the time the Group was formed, other observers note, there was only one Board-certified obstetrician-gynecologist in the area, and he was on the staff of Allegheny Valley Hospital. Now there are three in New Kensington and two in Tarentum. One explanation offered for the relative scarcity of specialists early in the 1950's is what has been called the "provincial" character of the University of Pittsburgh Medical School at that time. It has been described by a number of physicians as having been a school that trained primarily boys from nearby communities, most of whom became general practitioners.

Early in 1964, the president of the medical staff agreed that Citizens General had not enjoyed a very good reputation in the past 15 or 20 years. "When you have local hospitals that have general practitioners doing surgery," he said, "you can make things look bad." Today, he contends, the hospital is adequate, with Board-certified staff in every specialty and excellent X-ray and laboratory services, including good pathology and radioisotope laboratories.[13]

While the area administrator felt that he had legitimate grounds for dissatisfaction in his territory, practicing physicians believed that they too had just grievances. One such grievance was the list of participating physicians. Physicians felt that the Fund was arrogating to itself the right to judge the professional qualifications of physicians and, in addition, claimed that the mere existence of

12. Statement to Medical Advisory Committee, Medical Service, UMWA Welfare and Retirement Fund, March, 1957.

13. The Guide Issues of *Hospitals*, Journal of the American Hospital Association, for 1958, 1959, 1962, and 1963 show no outpatient department for Citizens General. This information was not coded in 1960, and the 1961 Guide Issue reports an outpatient department at the hospital. Citizens General has no internship or residency programs.

the list meant that physicians not on it were damaged in the eyes of miners. Furthermore, they claimed, the list was getting shorter and shorter every year because the Fund was dropping physicians after disagreements over even small fees. The Fund usually explained that the physicians handled too few Fund beneficiaries to justify the bookkeeping expenses involved. Physicians also disapproved of a method of payment increasingly used by the Fund which involved block monthly payments to physicians for the amount of time they had devoted to the care of beneficiaries. According to the Fund, this method substantially reduced auditing expenses, kept the Fund's obligations more nearly current, and encouraged physicians to spend more time on the care of individual patients, and as a result less hospitalization and surgery were necessary.

Finally, physicians were angered by some of the letters sent out by the Pittsburgh Fund office. "As you know," one letter states, ". . . we are very concerned about cases which might represent medically unnecessary hospital admissions or unnecessarily prolonged hospital stays. Without benefit of medical summaries in these cases, it appears that we are justified in requesting further information about the following cases." One involved an admission for diagnostic purposes; a second involved a patient hospitalized for "severe malignant hypertension" whose record did not show that the physician, a surgeon, had obtained a medical consultation. "We are at a loss to know why a surgeon would treat a case of this type. Was 10 days' hospitalization, therefore, essential in this case?" [14] The last case involved a patient hospitalized for 42 days with a diagnosis of nucleus polposus, and the physician was asked whether this patient could not have been in a nursing home for the major part of the time.

When the Fund announced on March 1, 1955, that consultation by a specialist approved by the Fund would be required before beneficiaries could be hospitalized at Fund expense except in emergencies, an open breach between the Fund and physicians followed. County medical societies passed resolutions opposing the directive, and the members of several county medical societies in Pennsylvania subsequently officially withdrew from participation in the Fund program.

In June the problem was taken up at the annual meeting of the American Medical Association, whose House of Delegates

14. In John R. Lindsey, "Medicine by the Ton," *Medical Economics* 32:109–117, 342, 345–348, 351 (October 1955).

adopted a resolution expressing its disapproval of the specialist consultation requirement. Dr. Draper then withdrew the directive and informed the Chairman of the Pennsylvania Medical Society's Committee on Medical Economics that he would welcome the prompt opening of formal negotiations with the society. The result was an "Agreement Between the Medical Service, U.M.W.A. Welfare and Retirement Fund, and the Medical Society of the State of Pennsylvania." [15] One paragraph of the Agreement stated:

> We mutually endorse the basic principle that all qualified physicians be granted appropriate hospital staff privileges in order to ensure adequate medical care for the community. We also recognize that it is the prerogative of the individual hospital governing board to make final decisions on applications for staff membership.

Developments at the Local Level

The society's endorsement of the "basic principle that all qualified physicians be granted appropriate hospital staff privileges" had no effect on the situation in New Kensington. Russellton Group physicians were still denied privileges.

On August 17, 1956, Dr. Falk wrote the president of the Board of Trustees of Citizens General that "Fund beneficiaries are being denied the opportunity to be cared for in Citizens General Hospital by qualified physicians practicing in the communities served by your hospital. We have discussed this matter, both personally and through correspondence, with you and other members of your Board and with your hospital's medical staff. It has become abundantly apparent that our patient waiting for your Board and your medical staff to resolve this matter has been in vain." Dr. Falk listed eight physicians who had been denied privileges, four of them affiliated with the Russellton Group and four others who were on the staff of the Allegheny Valley Hospital in Tarentum. "All of these physicians," Dr. Falk said, "are highly qualified and respected practitioners of medicine. The Welfare and Retirement Fund has business arrangements with all of them and expects its beneficiaries to be able to utilize their services when they need them. The fact that these physicians are not permitted to admit and treat patients at Citizens General Hospital deprives Welfare and Retirement Fund beneficiaries, as well as other residents of your vicinity, of the opportunity to be cared for by these physicians in their own community hospital. We, there-

15. *Pennsylvania Medical Journal* 59:467–469 (April 1956).

fore, wish to notify you," Dr. Falk concluded, "that the Welfare and Retirement Fund will discontinue its business arrangements with Citizens General Hospital as of October 1, 1956, unless these matters are settled immediately."

In September a heated article entitled "Compromise of Free Practice of Medicine" was published in the *Pennsylvania Medical Journal*.[16] The author, Dr. David Katz, then president-elect of the Allegheny County Medical Society, started off by saying, "Physicians of Pennsylvania and elsewhere had better look around and come up with the right answer if they wish to continue the free practice of medicine." The culprit, in Dr. Katz's view, was the United Mine Workers Fund, and the Russellton Group a major source of complaint. According to Dr. Katz, "Information pointed to the fact that this clinic was dominated and regulated by the . . . Fund. There was no longer a choice of physician nor fee for service excepting for the small number of cases which were permitted to get away." Dr. Katz repeated the charges that the Group was "kicking back" to the Fund and that it had violated medical ethics by advertising in the newspaper for clients other than UMW patients.

"The . . . Fund has withdrawn its support to certain hospitals in order to gain control of these institutions. One must remember that they were originally built by public subscription and state funds. The United Mine Workers' representative has come to these institutions after they have been in distress and offered to resume sending their patients to these hospitals if they can get United Mine Workers' representatives on the hospital boards and have certain designated members of their clinics elected to the staffs of these hospitals. Here lies a great danger . . . They are attempting to raid public facilities supplied by public funds and limiting the practice of physicians who are given privileges to work in these hospitals within the range of their capabilities." Dr. Katz concluded his article by saying, "It is high time that the profession takes stock of such plans whose sole aim is a miniature socialization of medicine."

Several months later, the *Journal* published a letter by the medical director of the Russellton Group completely denying the allegations made by Dr. Katz. "The facts are," he said, "that the Russellton Medical Group is an independent partnership of physicians . . . The group consists of 23 physicians, all of whom are members of the county and state medical societies and of the

16. *Pennsylvania Medical Journal* 59:1166–1168 (September 1956).

American Medical Association. The majority of the specialists are board-certified; the remainder are board eligible . . . most of them hold teaching appointments at the University of Pittsburgh School of Medicine; two hold the rank of associate professor. All members of the profession are invited . . . to see . . . the ethical manner in which a high quality of medical service is provided and to note that this clinic is not (nor has it ever been) 'dominated and regulated by the . . . Fund.'" Taking up Dr. Katz's charges one by one, he concluded, "The most elemental standards of fair play to the physicians involved would have demanded that these facts be checked before they appeared in print, regardless of the author's personal opinion. We feel that it is deplorable that Dr. Katz experienced the compulsion to rush into print a compendium of rumors and hearsay in the guise of fact. Simple referral to the *Pennsylvania Medical Journal*, one telephone call to the Tarentum newspaper, and reference to tape recordings of the Allegheny County Medical Society Liaison Committee meetings would have saved him the embarrassment of bearing false witness." [17]

On October 1, Citizens General was notified that participating arrangements with the Fund had expired and that it was "not appropriate for the hospital to expect the Fund to assume financial responsibility for the admission of any Fund beneficiary" from then on. This action by the Fund has been described by the current president of the medical staff of Citizens General as an attempt to break the hospital. Other hospitals with which the Fund discontinued arrangements, he comments, were "knocked off" pretty quickly because from 50 to 60 percent of their patients were miners. At Citizens General, only 5 percent or so of the patients are Fund beneficiaries. "The Fund never dreamed it would have so much trouble with Citizens General," he claims.

The Russellton Board took quite a different point of view. In a statement made several months after participating arrangements had been terminated, their spokesman said: "After three years of getting nowhere negotiating with Citizens General Hospital we asked the . . . Fund to remove Citizens General Hospital from the list . . . A few years ago we were turned down by several local physicians when we asked them to make home calls to our families. Now that we have attracted well-trained physicians to this community to provide us with home calls, they are denied hospital privileges . . . The entire community is affected by this. The addition of well-qualified physicians would help improve

17. *Pennsylvania Medical Journal* 59:1462, 1464, 1466 (December 1956).

coverage in the emergency room . . . The community has been denied badly needed rehabilitation services. The . . . specialist . . . who was asked to set up this department (by the hospital's board of trustees) was told that he could not get privileges because he was a member of this medical group . . . If this were a private hospital, we would not raise any questions. But this is a community hospital, supported by community funds, to which the miners have contributed generously." During a fund-raising campaign for the hospital in the early 1950's, it is said that members of miners' unions in the area had contributed $36, one day's pay, each.

Turning to the charge that the Fund was trying to break the hospital, the Board member said, "The hospital staff has charged the United Mine Workers with an attempt to 'pack' the hospital and to take it over. How ridiculous can they get? Only a handful of doctors seek privileges on a staff that numbers over 60 members. According to the staff's own by-laws, these doctors could only obtain courtesy privileges without vote for a period of three years! In addition, the board has the right to renew appointments each year. How do you 'pack' a hospital under these conditions? . . . We ask that we be accorded the same rights which others in the community enjoy, including board members and doctors themselves—the right to be treated in our community hospital by doctors of our choice." [18]

According to Dr. Falk: "The Russellton Board and the Russellton Medical Group indicated that they had exhausted their ability to resolve the situation. We agreed to attempt to intensify negotiations. The Citizens General Hospital medical staff proved adamant, so the only alternative left was to ask that the Board of Directors at the hospital assume its responsibilities in righting a wrong situation. This was done numerous times verbally and by letter," the Fund invoking the clause concerning hospital privileges of the Pennsylvania agreement. "The Board at first showed some signs of being willing to tackle the situation. However, they had been made very much gun-shy by two previous clashes with the medical staff, and decided they did not wish to tackle them again. When this became evident, we felt that we had no alternative but to terminate our participating arrangements with the hospital." [19]

18. *Pittsburgh Post-Gazette*, March 6, 1957.
19. Statement to Medical Care Advisory Committee, Medical Service, UMWA Welfare and Retirement Fund, March 1957.

During the annual convention of the Pennsylvania Medical Society in October 1956, the agreement between the society and the Fund was terminated. The motion which culminated in the agreement's being called "null and void, terminated and ended," was made by Dr. Saul M. Fleegler, then staff secretary of Citizens General Hospital.[20] A physician "boycott" of the Fund, which was almost complete in the area served by the Russellton Group, followed. Although the Fund did not sever relations with any physician who wished to continue participating arrangements, the majority of the physicians themselves withdrew.

Efforts to resolve the hospital privileges issue in New Kensington continued, however, and in January 1957 the executive committee of the hospital's Board of Trustees met with representatives of the miners' Board to discuss the problem. Members of the hospital Board reportedly reiterated that, although the Board was responsible for the appointment of physicians, it acted only upon the recommendations of the Credentials Committee composed of members of the medical staff. To charges that affiliation with the Russellton Group was the sole reason for denial of privileges to the miners' physicians, several hospital Board members replied that in their opinion the physicians would be admitted if they severed their Group affiliation. One hospital Board member said that the Board backed the medical staff to ensure harmony, and another claimed to be in sympathy with the miners but said that the Board was in the middle of the situation. The hospital Board reportedly took the position that the first step in negotiations should be the reinstitution of Fund arrangements with the hospital. They noted that in the past ten years 18 new physicians, including specialists and general practitioners, had been appointed to the hospital staff, eight of them in the past two years.

One month later, in a public statement, the miners' Board claimed that the hospital Board had admitted that "their hands were tied by the medical staff."[21] At the January meeting, the miners said, they had been promised that further meetings would be held to discuss staff privileges for their physicians, but that the hospital Board had broken off negotiations. In a letter dated February 20, 1957, the president of the hospital Board had said, "It is our considered judgment that no further action can be taken by us at this time, and that further meetings would be unproductive . . . We also feel that it might be to the best interest of

20. *Allegheny Valley Daily News*, October 24, 1956.
21. *New Kensington Daily Dispatch*, February 28, 1957.

your members and their families to urge the Fund to put our hospital back on the participating list so that we may better serve you." Said the miners' Board, "They are saying, sure, we want you to use our hospital, but your doctors cannot. What kind of free choice is this?" [22]

While the miners' Board was waiting for the hospital Board to act, a further grievance against hospital physicians was chalked up by the miners — and in this they had support from some other segments of the community uninvolved in the hospital dispute. The Westmoreland County Medical Society ruled that its member physicians were not to participate in mass free clinics for the administration of Salk vaccine shots. According to one newspaper, the Society was also opposed to industries' buying vaccine for their workers and having their own plant physicians give the shots. In spite of a full-page advertisement in the newspaper that explained the reasons behind this ruling, which was signed by many physicians on the hospital staff, public opinion seemed generally to be unfavorable to the physicians' stand. An editorial in the *Pittsburgh Press* commented: "Unfortunately, one of the best arguments in favor of socialized medicine has just been supplied by our neighboring Westmoreland County Medical Society . . . The entire action of the . . . Society is incredible. It is hardly worthy of a distinguished profession dedicated to the service of humanity." [23] Letters to the editor of the New Kensington newspaper contained critical comments. "Crash! Down goes our knight in shining armor; down goes the hero on the white charger," said one mother. A businessman added, "The action by the Westmoreland County Medical Society confirms the ideas that many people have been getting of late that the Medical Profession has degenerated into a cold impersonal, commercial group that thinks only of money." "This is not the first time," said a third writer, "when doctors in our city and county have not acted in the best interests of the community. Our own hospital staff has kept doctors off the staff . . . They are apparently afraid of competition." [24]

By March 1957, the miners' Board had decided to "attempt to enlist the aid of the entire community in an effort to end discrimination against miners and their families at Citizens General

22. *New Kensington Daily Dispatch,* February 28, 1957.

23. *Pittsburgh Press,* February 12, 1957.

24. *New Kensington Daily Dispatch,* February 19, 1957. In subsequent years the Society revised its position. A news item in the *Daily Dispatch* of January 29, 1964, reported that a free Sabin vaccine immunization program was being sponsored by the Westmoreland County Medical Society.

Hospital." They also requested the Governor of the State of Pennsylvania to look into the situation. "We do not believe that our people can obtain good medical care when our doctors who treat us in our houses and in the office are not permitted to see us in Citizens General Hospital," they wrote. A spokesman for the Governor said that the state had no jurisdiction over the internal staff problems of local hospitals, but that this statement had prompted the Governor's office to ask the state Welfare Department to investigate.[25] In May the Governor proposed that a meeting be held at which representatives of the miners and of the hospital, and the state Secretaries of Health and Welfare, would be present. Said the Governor, "The situation the members of the UMW face in connection with obtaining care is a matter which apparently has developed through lack of understanding and one which very probably could be discussed reasonably with some hope of arriving at a mutually satisfactory solution." [26] The chairman of the miners' Board responded that even though the hospital did not come directly under the jurisdiction of any state department, it depended on the community for support. "We therefore feel that the state has appropriate interest in this matter and we firmly welcome your suggestion." [27]

A meeting was finally scheduled for early August. Several days before it was to be held (after having been postponed once), the president of the hospital Board wrote the state Secretary of Welfare, "Since our difficulties are with the United Mine Workers Welfare Fund, we can see no useful purpose in meeting with the . . . Local . . . , as we have already met with this group on several occasions with no fruitful results." [28] He added that the controversy had developed when the area administrator had removed the hospital from the participating list following its failure to add eight physicians to its staff. The Board of Trustees apparently placed a full-page advertisement explaining their side of the story in the New Kensington newspaper.

The chairman of the miners' Board issued an immediate rebuttal. "The hospital board's statement that the controversy was precipitated by the miners' fund in August, 1956, is absolutely false. They conveniently forget to inform the secretary of welfare and the public that this controversy has existed for more than four

25. *New Kensington Daily Disptach,* March 22, 1957.
26. *New Kensington Daily Dispatch,* May 18, 1957.
27. *New Kensington Daily Dispatch,* May 21, 1957.
28. *Allegheny Valley Daily News,* August 9, 1957.

years as a direct result of the hospital's staff and board's refusal to permit miners and their families to be treated by fully qualified doctors of their choice . . . Can (the board president) and the rest of the hospital board explain to the public how miners and their families and thousands of other citizens can obtain free choice of physicians and hospitals when physicians of their choice are denied hospital privileges? . . . "The real issue," he contended, "is that the board is running this hospital like a private corporation rather than like a community institution by its policy of excluding miners' doctors in order to maintain the economics of its medical staff." [29]

The Secretary of Welfare commented, "Certainly the least the hospital could have done was to go along with the meeting. I am very disappointed." [30]

Organized Medicine's Approaches to the Problem

While the factions in New Kensington were exchanging charges and countercharges, the American Medical Association Committee on Medical Care for Industrial Workers was attempting to resolve a number of thorny issues, including free choice of physician and method of payment, that had bedeviled relationships between the Fund and practicing physicians in a number of states. A *Suggested Guide to Relationships Between State and County Medical Societies and the United Mine Workers of America Welfare and Retirement Fund* [31] emerged from the Committee's deliberations and was adopted by the Association's House of Delegates on June 6, 1957. Even before its formal adoption, Dr. Draper said that the Fund would not follow the guides, largely because of clauses which read:

> Free choice of physician and hospital by the patient should be preserved.
>
> Every physician duly licensed by the state to practice medicine and surgery should be assumed at the outset to be competent in the field in which he claims to be, unless considered otherwise by his peers.
>
> A fee-for-service method of payment for physicians should be maintained except under unusual circumstances. These unusual circumstances shall be determined to exist only after a conference of the liaison committee and representatives of the Fund.

29. Ibid.
30. Ibid.
31. Published in the *Journal of the American Medical Association* 164:1113–1115 (July 6, 1957)

The guides also included a statement that:

> The qualifications of physicians to be on the hospital staff and membership on the hospital staffs is to be determined solely by local hospital staffs and local governing boards of hospitals.

Dr. Draper claimed that the Guides would return the Fund to all the problems of excessive surgery, excessive hospitalization, excessive length of stay, and so on, which it had experienced in the early days of its operation. In a statement to the Committee, Dr. Draper said that the Fund's efforts to ensure a high quality of medical care were again meeting violent opposition from some segments of organized medicine. Among the tactics being used, he said, were the charge that the "Fund is conniving to get control of the hospitals of this country by infiltrating highly qualified physicians, whom the miners like . . . Petty persecutions such as those by certain county medical societies which endeavor to prevent the Fund from providing medical care for its beneficiaries by denying membership . . . to physicians who do so, will be settled by legal means if other measures fail. Other petty forms of persecution have already failed."

It is questionable whether members of the Russellton Group could consider the denial of hospital privileges a "petty form of persecution." When Dr. Ferrier, who was on the staff of the Allegheny Valley Hospital, left the Group to become assistant area administrator at the Fund's Pittsburgh office in the late 1950's, members of the Group were without any local hospital privileges. Indeed, in March 1957 Dr. Falk noted, "Five of the physicians of the Russellton Medical Group have no hospital privileges anywhere, having been stalemated in applications for all hospitals, even those in Pittsburgh to which they have applied, as a result of the present epidemic of Citizens General-itis in western Pennsylvania." [32]

At some point during the history of the dispute between Citizens General and the Group, the hospital's bylaws had been amended to require that every application for privileges be signed by two hospital staff physicians. All hospital physicians refused to sign applications by members of the Group. Thus, the hospital was able to return applications by Russellton physicians with the comment that they were "incomplete" rather than rejected. The Allegheny Valley Hospital, to which members of the Group also

32. Statement to Medical Advisory Committee, Medical Service, UMWA Welfare and Retirement Fund, March 1957.

continued to apply during these years, had a different but equally effective policy. They insisted that members of the Russellton Group were not "residents of this community," a view that members of the Group considered unjustified, at least when applied to some of their members. According to the minutes of one Allegheny Valley staff meeting in mid-1956, "In the past, several applications have been refused for this reason and it has become Staff policy."

The denial of hospital privileges, serious as that was in the eyes of Group members, was not the only way in which other physicians made their disapproval of the Group apparent. It is reported that the Pittsburgh Dermatological Society disbanded solely in order to be able to reform without two members who participated in the Group. The Urological Society, it is said, attempted to expel any member who participated. And the Pittsburgh Society of Obstetrics and Gynecology passed a resolution requiring that all its members — except those in military, government, or teaching posts, or similar forms of activity — agree to accept only fee-for-service as the method of payment. One Group specialist, who was a member, refused to resign even though the resolution called for the resignation of any member who would not sign such an agreement. Another Group obstetrician-gynecologist, whose application for membership was then under consideration, withdrew it and is still not a member.

The two specialists in obstetrics and gynecology cite a number of other ways in which their affiliation with the Group has caused professional difficulties for them. Their advancement at their Pittsburgh hospital has been delayed beyond the normal time, one of them having been limited to courtesy privileges for three or four years longer than is the usual hospital practice. Even today, they claim, their colleagues at the hospital hesitate to propose them for advancement, fearing to cause them embarrassment should they be turned down. The application of one physician for his Board examinations was delayed for an entire year while the old, and disproved, charges of unethical practice against him as a member of the Group were once more "investigated."

The Russellton Group Expands

Early in 1959 the dispute between Citizens General and the Group erupted again when it became known that the miners' Board planned the construction of a new clinic for the Group in

New Kensington. The Parnassus office had been a focus of controversy in the past. The planned development was not merely a branch office operating under the general aegis of Russellton but a major facility which would become the central headquarters of the Group. A public battle ensued.

The Board applied for a building permit but was denied it by a zoning board which, a miners' union official charges, took orders from the mayor and his physician friends. Other labor and fraternal groups came to the support of the miners, and petitions were circulated which eventually collected some 6,000 signatures. The editor of the local newspaper, too, received large numbers of letters urging that approval be given for the clinic.

The physicians also marshalled their forces. The president of the Westmoreland County Medical Society wrote Dr. Falk on February 14, 1959, that there had been to date no correspondence with the Medical Society for prior discussion and approval of the establishment of the clinic and that this violated the "Standard Procedure for the County Medical Society and Lay Organizations for the Establishment of Medical Facilities as Recommended and Adopted by the Medical Society of the State of Pennsylvania in 1957 and Endorsed by the Westmoreland County Medical Society." Stating that the facilities of the society were available to assist communities and lay organizations in evaluating and discussing present and future medical needs, the president reported that the society's executive committee felt the matter should be presented for study and discussion and that a mutually beneficial solution could be evolved.

In March the staff of Citizens General prepared a series of articles explaining the bases for their opposition to the proposed clinic. Published in the New Kensington newspaper,[33] the series opened with a summary of the history of the Fund and the dispute with Russellton. Cited as points in the history were the Fund's gradual narrowing of the lists of eligible physicians, the establishment of the Russellton Clinic in an area served by two hospitals, and the creation of a branch in New Kensington only three blocks from Citizens General. Also mentioned was what the physicians claimed was a Fund program to force hospitals to place imported physicians on their staffs. "Some community hospitals were forced to give in," the physicians said, "and are now completely dominated by the UMW and are no longer truly community hospitals." The physicians concluded their first article with

33. *New Kensington Daily Dispatch,* March 16–27, 1959.

the statement: "It would seem from all the past actions of the UMW that they are following a preconceived plan to destroy the private practice of Medicine, and any compromise with existing concepts is merely temporary."

In their second article, the physicians attacked the 40 cents per ton tax that financed the Fund, suggesting that perhaps we should add 40 cents to the cost of a bushel of wheat so that farmers, too, could have free hospital and physician care, and so on. Where would this lead? they asked. To socialized medicine. "And 'what's wrong with that?' the members of the 'Fabian Society' (active workers for a Socialistic form of Government) and those of the ignorant (we can get it for nothing) citizen group ask." The allegedly sorry history of the British National Health Service was given as an example of "what's wrong." Turning to the Russellton Group, they said, "They would be here only because they . . . were subsidized by the large salaries those in control of the United Mine Workers Fund were willing to spend to have the job of undermining started."

The next article posed several direct questions to the miners: "If tomorrow you are told that starting Monday, 50 miners from Fairmont, W. Va. would be on hand to mine all the coal in the best section of Barking Mine and that they would displace, on a permanent basis, those who are presently mining that section, how would you react? Would you as individuals or a group accept this situation? Or would you do the same as your hospital (Citizens General Hospital) did in 1956 and refuse them the right to become members of your staff? Of course, you regular miners would be permitted to share or split up the remaining available work. But would that satisfy you?"

"The concept of medical clinics as developed by those entrusted with the management of United Mine Workers of America Welfare Fund looks to us like a deliberate attempt to undermine the very foundations of our American freedoms. We see in some of their tactics a repetition of those which have worked so well in some European countries. These are 'Control by minority group pressure and if you can't control, undermine to destruction.'" Thus did the next article open, and it went on to attack Fund efforts to control hospitals through the "blacklisting" technique and the duplication of facilities that a major clinic in New Kensington would represent. The final article was a defense of physicians' incomes on the basis of the cost of their education, the long hours they work, and the high percentage — 20 to 25 percent, the physicians claimed — of their fees which cannot be collected.

In addition to the articles, the physicians placed a full page advertisement in the newspaper under the heading, "We Definitely and Irrevocably Oppose Locating a United Mine Workers Clinic in Our Community." They also sent letters to their patients asking them: "Isn't the 'clinic idea' another creeping destructive force which, if allowed to continue, will ultimately lead to someone else telling you and your family what you shall do, where you shall earn your living, where and what you shall worship, who shall be your doctors, etc.?" "Without your consent as a customer," the letter continued, "you are now paying the 40 cents per ton tax on coal. If your local hospital must compete with a 'clinic,' it too would have to be subsidized. If you feel that a 'clinic' is contrary to the American principle of 'Free Democracy,' would you and your family sign and mail the enclosed card?" The card was addressed to the Medical Staff of Citizens General Hospital.

The battle for the zoning permit was carried on at a public hearing and then taken to the City Council where the miners' Board finally won. Reporting on the hearing at the New Kensington City Hall, the *Aluminum Workers Journal* said: "It was unreal; there were no past experiences to fall back on. Learned men of the medical profession battled to retain their monopoly of the market of human ailments of this region. One felt ashamed to be a witness to such a spectacle; where the highest ethics known to man, espoused by this group, were brought down to the level of the dollar . . . The generalities and emotion appealing phrases of the opposing medical practitioners caused acute embarrassment . . . Let us make this point clear however. We do not intend to desert our family doctors just because a clinic is available. The clinic will not harm any patient-doctor relationship that is on a healthy basis now." [34]

Months later — in October 1959 — the editor of the New Kensington paper wrote under the heading, "Rx for NK Physicians" that an economic consulting firm hired by the Pennsylvania State Medical Society had just told physicians meeting in Pittsburgh to "stop fighting the . . . Fund and to spend their energy on other problems and health plans," pointing out that there were only 38,600 members of the UMW in Pennsylvania and that doctors could afford to forget them as patients. "In New Kensington this year," the editor commented, "a great deal of time was wasted by private doctors and UMW physicians in thrashing out the

34. *Aluminum Workers Journal,* New Kensington 22:1 (March 1959).

future of a proposed UMW clinic here. The doctors could have used this time with their patients or in more constructive ventures. The report to the Medical Society pointed out that the union plan for medical care appeared to be working satisfactorily and 'continued attacks by the medical profession will not undo the program.' "[35]

The issue still rankled, however. The local newspaper reported that, in a letter to local physicians, the president of the medical staff had "described New Kensington Council's approval of a United Mine Workers Clinic in the city as a 'capitulation' to the United Mine Workers." "Whether you are registered Republican or Democrat," he is supposed to have written, "it should be obvious that your interest is served by the Conservative or Republican Party . . . It's time we began to act like citizens with backbones and make an effort to preserve our own way of life."[36] In a letter to the editor clarifying his stand, he said, "No criticism of the Council was implied. I was merely illustrating that when a choice is available, elected officials will support those people who support them."[37]

The State Medical Society Intervenes

During 1960, the disagreement between the parties apparently simmered, with little overt action by either side. The Russellton Board went ahead with its plans for the new facility in New Kensington, and a ground-breaking ceremony constituted a part of the April 1, 1961, Miners Day observances.

On April 25 the president of the medical staff of Citizens General wrote to the Westmoreland County Medical Society to protest the clinic development and to request that the society indicate that the Russellton Group's action was unacceptable. He said, however, that the hospital medical staff would not object to the clinic's treating miners and their families if the miners were guaranteed a free choice of any accredited physician. Copies of this letter with requests for support were also sent to the Allegheny County Medical Society and to the Pennsylvania State Medical Society. Since the clinic is located in Westmoreland County, whose society took no action on the letter, the Allegheny County Society tabled the matter. The Board of Trustees

35. *New Kensington Daily Dispatch*, October 26, 1959.
36. *New Kensington Daily Dispatch*, October 24, 1959.
37. *New Kensington Daily Dispatch*, November 2, 1959.

of the state society, however, requested its Medical Care Coordinating Committee to look into the matter.

On November 15, 1961, the Medical Care Coordinating Committee held its first meeting with representatives of the medical staff, administrator, and Board of Trustees of the Citizens General Hospital, the Westmoreland and Allegheny County Medical Societies, and the incumbent president of the state society. The staff of the hospital repeated the stand they had taken in April concerning free choice of physician, and the hospital Board said that the staff had their full support.

Approximately one week before the meeting, the Group's medical director had sent a letter to each member of the staff of Citizens General Hospital inviting inquiries in connection with the additional physicians' services the Group expected to need when the new clinic was completed in New Kensington. Dr. Falk later said (in a December 1962 letter to the hospital) that the hospital staff had not responded "to this invitation to any significant degree and, in fact, discouraged such response."

On December 6 the Coordinating Committee met with representatives of the Russellton Group, the miners' Board, and the Fund. The miners' Board repeated their position that the hospital was denying free choice of physician by refusing to accept their physicians on the staff; the Group physicians repeated that they desired staff privileges for their full-time members but that none of their applications had been considered, since they could not find two hospital staff members willing to sign the applications. Fund representatives indicated that they would be willing to determine physicians' qualifications through the Pennsylvania Medical Care Program[38] if a solution could be found to the problem of the Russellton Group.

Replying to a request from the Committee for a statement of their position in writing, the Citizens General Hospital staff said that they were prepared to grant temporary privileges for six months for the treatment of emergency cases to two Group phy-

38. The program, formulated in 1959, has as its core hospital utilization committees which are intended to function in every hospital for the review of prolonged, unjustified, or inefficiently handled hospitalizations. Blue Cross and Health Insurance and Blue Shield Review Committees, and a Physicians Qualifications Committee, form part of the structure. The basic objectives of the program are to make voluntary systems of health care financing more successful; to retain for the medical profession the responsibility for the quality, cost, and efficiency of care rendered under these plans; and to promote free choice by the public of physician, hospital, or system of medical care.

sicians in the hope that the problem could be solved within this period. In return, they requested that the Fund use the Pennsylvania program as a means for settlement of problems concerning fees, length of stay, and so on, that the Coordinating Committee act as a mediation board for the resolution of any subsequent differences, and that any agreements reached with the Fund be applicable to all other physicians in the four counties served by the state medical society's Tenth Councilor District.

In reply to the same type of request, the Russellton Group indicated that they felt a solution could be reached if their full-time members whose major practice was in the area served by the hospital were accorded staff privileges on the basis of their qualifications. They recognized that the granting of these privileges could justifiably be staged.

At the beginning of January 1962 the medical director of the Group and the new president of the hospital's medical staff were in communication concerning the issue of privileges. The latter said that he had recently put various suggestions for solution of the problem before his colleagues, and that he had already received a number of angry reactions. His suggestions included the following:

1. That the hospital and all its staff physicians be granted permanent participating arrangements with the Fund, and not be removed except with the approval of the Tenth Councilor District;
2. That the Russellton Group use the services of hospital specialists as much as possible when the need arose;
3. That approximately five Group members, particularly those living in the immediate area, might be given privileges at this time.

The Committee held a third meeting on February 22, 1962, at which representatives of the hospital and the Russellton Group were present. The Committee felt that agreement had been reached on two points:

1. Free choice as defined by the Report of the American Medical Association Commission on Medical Care Plans;
2. Participation in the Fund program by all physicians at Citizens General Hospital in accordance with Pennsylvania Medical Care Program Standards.

Hospital representatives attending the February 22 meeting said that they expected some commitment as to the number of physicians in the area who would be granted participating privileges, while representatives of the Group said that they could not speak for the Fund, even though they personally were in favor of wide participation of hospital physicians. The Group physicians also indicated that local physicians would be invited to participate in the Group. It was then agreed that two Russellton physicians would apply for courtesy privileges at the hospital, and that the hospital Credentials Committee would consider these applications at a meeting on March 13.

The fourth meeting was held on March 21 and included representatives of the Fund. Dr. Falk stated that he expected the hospital to grant privileges to all Group physicians solely on the basis of professional qualifications, and that he, for the Fund, was prepared to:

1. Place the hospital on the "approved list";
2. Grant participating arrangements to all hospital staff members in accordance with their qualifications and willingness to meet Tenth Councilor District standards of efficiency and cost;
3. Guarantee that any who chose to become participating physicians would not later be dropped for nonprofessional reasons;
4. Use Pennsylvania Medical Care Program criteria for qualifications.

The hospital representative reported that the staff had not acted on the offers that had been made at the last meeting and requested "clearer resolution of the issues." The Russellton Group then redefined free choice of physician, and the hospital representative indicated his staff would reconsider its position.

Late in May or early in June, the president of the medical staff of the hospital wrote to the Group indicating that temporary privileges for a period of six months for the admission of emergency cases to the hospital would be considered as a stopgap measure while negotiations were pursued. About one month later two physicians, including the Group's medical director, were formally notified that such privileges had been granted. As they wrote to a member of the Coordinating Committee, however, they accepted these privileges "only as an expression of good faith to you and your committee." They felt the hospital offer involved a deliberate bypass of the application of one Group physician who had openly and apparently severely criticized the hospital some months previously. They resolved, they said, that in further negotiation they would give the highest priority to the granting of hospital privileges to this physician, who has been described by the current president of the hospital's medical staff as "a devoted socialist" and "one bone sticking in the craw" of the staff.

On July 27 representatives of the hospital staff and Board, the

Group staff and board, and the Fund met. Dr. Falk repeated the offers he had made at the March 21 meeting. One hospital physician proposed that the two groups of physicians sit down together to resolve differences of opinion on medical ethics, and committees were chosen from among the hospital and Group staffs. A meeting was held on August 26. Apparently, from that time onward there has been haggling about the content of the minutes of that meeting — which are still not officially available — and no further meetings have been held.

In November one of the hospital Board members told a Group physician that he thought the Fund should act to try to break the stalemate that had followed the meeting of the physicians. He suggested that perhaps the Fund should restore the hospital to the participating list. Also in November, the Group wrote the Coordinating Committee informing them that negotiations had not progressed as expected, and requesting their further assistance. The staff of Citizens General Hospital told the Committee that, although they were not in favor of further joint discussions, they would gladly meet with the Committee to discuss their present position. A meeting was arranged for February 20, 1963.

Dr. Falk, in the meantime, wrote the hospital informing them that the Fund would reinstitute participating arrangements with the hospital on January 1 and that this arrangement would be continued for at least six months in the expectation that a final agreement could be achieved within that time. He pointed out that at that time there were five participating physicians on the hospital's staff — two from the Group and three others — who could thus hospitalize patients routinely at Fund expense. He reported that the Group assured him that their year-old invitation to local physicians to participate with the Group was still in effect and suggested that physicians from the hospital and the Group meet with him to prepare the specific detail for a final agreement.

When the Coordinating Committee met with hospital representatives in February, the hospital staff said that they felt that no significant efforts had been made by the Fund or the clinic to improve the situation. Dr. Falk's letter of December, they said, was a return to the 1956 situation, an attempt to dictate in the matter of staff privileges. They also expressed the view that the Group did not seem to them to be willing to adhere to the recommendations of the report of the A.M.A. Commission on Medical Care Plans. On the same day, Dr. Falk again wrote the hospital, pointing out that participating arrangements had been restored on

January 1 and expressing deep disappointment that the hospital Board and staff had failed to proceed with negotiations. He again stated the Fund's position:

> We are prepared to extend full participating privileges in the UMW Fund program to all of your staff physicians at the same time that you provide hospital privileges to all local physicians in accordance with their professional qualifications and moral character.

To this letter the president of the hospital Board of Trustees replied that the president of the medical staff was not only considering the appointment to the courtesy staff of the two Group physicians with emergency privileges, but was also considering other appointments to the staff "in the not too distant future."

Another meeting with representatives of the Fund and the Group was convened on March 6 by the Committee. Dr. Falk, expressing surprise that his letters had been regarded as dictatorial, said that the granting of participating arrangements to all hospital staff would, in his opinion, provide complete freedom of choice to Fund beneficiaries. The Group, for its part, said that they felt they should be informed in what way they were considered to have failed to abide by the recommendations of the Commission on Medical Care Plans. They urged the Committee to resume a more active mediating role in the situation.

The Medical Care Coordinating Committee issued a report on April 16. Detailing the history of the negotiations, it expressed the view of the Committee that "a reasonable solution is possible if each party will make further effort to understand and accommodate its point of view to the other interested groups." It added, however, "It is the considered judgment of the Coordinating Committee that further effective negotiations will be inversely proportionate to the degree of influence exerted on such negotiations by the Fund. The Fund, of course, must be legitimately concerned with its own relationship to the Russellton Group, the Citizens General Hospital, and the participating physicians practicing in New Kensington. It should, however, be apparent that these relationships are essentially, and might best remain, independent . . . The expressed willingness of the Fund to accept the practicing physicians of New Kensington as participating physicians could have the salutary effect of demonstrating that the sole concern of the Fund is in obtaining quality service for its beneficiaries, rather than the arbitrary favoring of a particular form of medical practice."

The Committee set forth recommendations for actions which, it said, would open the way for improved relations between the hospital and the Group if they were taken by the Fund, the Trustees of the miners' Board, and the Trustees of the hospital "in this order and on their own initiative." It suggested that continued liaison among all the parties be continued and that "unilateral action . . . should be avoided."

The recommendations, in the order given, were as follows:

United Mine Workers of America Welfare and Retirement Fund. The Fund should consider the requests of individual physicians on the staff of Citizens General Hospital to participate in the care of its beneficiaries on the primary basis of professional qualifications. Clinical Profiles and the assistance of the Qualifications Committee of the Tenth Councilor District will be at the disposal of the Fund and should be used when professional qualifications are unknown or in dispute.

The Fund should notify its beneficiaries of the availability of all physicians and hospital services in the community and clearly indicate the freedom of choice allowed between physicians, physician and clinic, and between available hospitals.

Regularly scheduled meetings between representatives of the Fund and the Medical Care Coordinating Committee should be considered for the express purpose of providing continuous consultation on all questions pertaining to medical care for Fund beneficiaries.

Board of Trustees — Russellton Building, Inc. The Board of Trustees . . . should indicate to the staff and the Trustees of Citizens General Hospital their willingness to refrain from solicitation of patients for physicians of the Russellton Medical Group or laudation of medical care provided at the Clinic.

It is ethical for any prepayment or insuring agency to indicate the advantages of its method of financing health coverages. However, care must be exercised in distinguishing between advertising a health care financing plan and solicitation of patients for particular physicians.

These problems can be minimized or avoided if both the . . . Group and Citizens General staffs can work out either joint or alternative solutions to the potential public demand for further prepayment of outpatient medical services.

Board of Trustees — Citizens General Hospital. The Committee recognizes the prerogative of the governing board of the Citizens General Hospital, in consultation with the medical staff, to make final decisions on applications for staff membership — such decisions to be based on their responsibility to bring the best possible medical care to the community. Professionally qualified physicians, including those full-time members of the Russellton Medical Group whose major practices are in the area served by the hospital and, particularly, those without hospital privileges elsewhere, should receive prompt and full consideration in order to assure the widest possible selection of qualified medical services to all of the citizens of the community, including beneficiaries of the Fund.[39]

Copies of the report were sent to the secretaries of the four county medical societies comprising the Tenth Councilor District, to the presidents of the Board of Trustees and the medical staff of the hospital, to the president of the miners' Board and the president of the staff of the Group, and to the Fund's area administrator.

On May 14 the Group's president acknowledged receipt of the report and said that its "recommendations in general provide an equitable basis for an early settlement of the dispute which has plagued the patients and medical community in this area." He urged that the Committee participate directly in efforts to obtain implementation of the recommendations.

Dr. Falk wrote the Committee's chairman on May 27, "We will accept the recommendations of the report. This is true despite the fact that the actions requested of us will probably entail serious sacrifices to the Fund." He suggested that the Committee call a meeting promptly, adding that this might help avoid any misunderstanding of the recommendations and loss of time in their implementation.

The president of the miners' Board replied on June 3, stating "We herewith accept the recommendations to our Board contained in this Report . . . We believe that this Report provides a basis for a prompt and permanent solution of this problem and we trust that all parties concerned will act quickly and simultaneously to effect this solution."

On July 1, apparently, the then president of the medical staff of Citizens General acknowledged receipt of the report, but, according to a member of the Coordinating Committee, indicated that "granting of staff privileges to . . . Group members would be staged — a recommendation not made by the Coordinating Committee."

The Board of Trustees of the hospital "did not acknowledge receipt of the Report." This matter was subsequently cleared up. The president of the Board on September 17 stated that the Board "assumed that it has acknowledged . . . in the reply offered by

39. *Summary, Findings and Recommendations of the Medical Care Coordinating Committee, Tenth Councilor District, Pennsylvania Medical Society: Citizens General Hospital, Russellton Medical Group, United Mine Workers of America Welfare and Retirement Fund,* Pittsburgh, Pennsylvania, April 16, 1963.

our Medical Staff. However, for the record, please be advised that our Board of Trustees acknowledges receipt of the report, and, furthermore, concurs with the recommendations contained therein." On September 23, the president of the medical staff informed the Committee that it was right about the failure of the Board to acknowledge, but "At that time I offered to acknowledge for them . . . This evidently was not made clear by me and I regret it."

A small meeting of all the parties was convened by the Committee on August 19 for further clarification of a number of points. An informal meeting held late in July had revealed that further definition was needed of the means by which the Fund might implement the recommendations satisfactorily, that further clarification of the recommendations to the miners' Board was necessary, and that a definitive reply and clarification of position was needed from the hospital Board. The representatives of the hospital Board, however, the president and the hospital administrator, failed to attend the meeting. In its minutes of the meeting the Committee noted that the Board president had telephoned the next day to apologize for his absence and to say that he had been "informed by a member of the Staff of Citizens General Hospital that the meeting was cancelled."

Both Dr. Falk and the representatives of the Group maintained their previously expressed views on resolution of the problem. The representatives of the medical staff of the hospital, however, said that they could not accept the recommendations without some modification. Their "stand was that to deny any U.M.W. beneficiary the choice of any physician or hospital in the state would be to deny him free choice." The Committee and the Fund opposed this view, the Committee maintaining that it was not their intention to achieve, at this point, more than a local solution, since it had been a local problem that had been brought to its attention, but that a successful local solution might later be applied on a broader basis. Dr. Falk indicated that the Fund could not afford a statewide arrangement. The hospital physicians finally suggested that some common meeting ground more inclusive than the local area of New Kensington might be a compromise solution, and that the area served by the Group would be more pertinent than the area served by the hospital. This raised questions concerning the Allegheny Valley Hospital in Tarentum, which was within the general service area of the Group. Group physicians indicated that, although they had repeatedly applied for privileges at that hospital, they had consistently been turned down. Citizens

General physicians indicated that they would suggest the resumption of meetings between their staff and Group representatives, but Group physicians expressed doubt that such negotiations would be very helpful from their standpoint. They said, however, that they would be willing to participate if invited to do so.

At the end of October, Dr. Falk, writing the hospital staff in connection with the minutes of this meeting, said, "I felt then, and I feel now, that the medical society report provides a fair basis for a peaceful compromise on this matter. Your Board, Russellton, and we have all accepted it — without conditions. Presumably all feel that they have made sacrifices in accepting it. I know that the Fund has. Why the recommendations have not gone into effect is really something of a mystery to me. If the Fund should be doing something specific, I shall be happy to be told what it is we are requested to do."

The Medical Care Coordinating Committee expressed itself as disappointed that agreement could not be achieved on the basis of the recommendations. They were also of the opinion "that a resolution of this problem is sufficiently important to merit further time and effort on their part, and that they should remain available should additional meetings be requested."

A Campaign Is Planned

At the annual meeting of the life members of the hospital on January 28, 1964, one member, an officer of a UMW local, presented a resolution directing:

> That the Membership of this Corporation at this annual meeting hereby instructs its Board of Trustees to assure prompt and full consideration of the applications of all professionally qualified physicians who practice or intend to practice primarily in the service area of this hospital; and
>
> That the Board of Trustees establish the policy that hospital privileges will be granted to physicians in accordance with their professional qualifications and moral character and without regard to their association with medical group practice.

In the resolution it was charged that New Kensington already suffered from a shortage of doctors. The president of the hospital medical staff countered with the charge that the clinic itself as well as the concept of "approved" doctors fostered by the Fund's maintenance of a list of participating physicians were deterrents to any influx of new young doctors into the community. To the resolution's statement that patients were denied the right to be treated in the hospital by physicians of their choice, he replied that true free choice implied a situation where any person could go to any physician he chose and have his bill paid by the Fund or any other prepayment plan.[40]

At the same meeting the president of the hospital Board reported that he had received a letter from the Northern Westmoreland County United Labor Council in which the Council requested the hospital Board to meet with it and representatives of the miners' Board to discuss the hospital's nonadmission of Group physicians. The Board president, then in his 33rd term of office, responded to the invitation, "We cannot expect any definite decision to be made at this meeting, but it is hoped that members of our medical staff can explain what action can be expected of them in the future." The meeting was scheduled for March 31, 1964.

In the meantime, the miners' Board appealed to the Hospital Planning Association of Allegheny County, pointing out that the expansion programs approved for both Citizens General and Allegheny Valley Hospitals would require generous community support in addition to the funds made available by the federal government. "The issues which divide this community in its attitudes to present hospital policy must be resolved if the broad community support needed for a successful fund drive is to develop," the president of the miners' Board said. "We would like to urge . . . that the Hospital Planning Association lend its good offices to the resolution of the present conflict, so that the community needs can be effectively met." The Association responded that it supported the report of the Medical Care Coordinating Committee, believing that implementation of the recommendations would be "in the interest of the public, the hospital, and the medical profession," but that it could not intervene in an internal hospital problem.

The Northern Westmoreland Labor Council also took the problem to the Governor of the State on March 20, asking the assistance of the Governor and of the executive and legislative branches of the state government in helping to resolve the long-standing dispute. Inasmuch as the state appropriates funds to the hospital, the Council said, the state should use its good offices in attempting to resolve the problem, and indicated that legislation should be passed if no other solution was found.

40. *New Kensington Daily Dispatch*, January 29, 1964.

The meeting called by the Council was held at the hospital on March 31, as scheduled. The president of the medical staff presented the hospital's position. First, he said, the Fund must define the area served by the Russellton Group, and then must grant participation to all physicians within that area regardless of their affiliations. If that were done to the satisfaction of the hospital, the staff would immediately grant privileges to one more Group physician. If Allegheny Valley Hospital then granted privileges to three Group physicians, he added, Citizens General would subsequently undertake to accept additional Group physicians on a staged basis. The representatives of the miners' Board and the Group were not at all satisfied with this proposal. They pointed out that an agreement was being offered to them that was wholly dependent on the actions of a third party — Allegheny Valley Hospital — which had never been involved in the dispute and which did not, presumably, even know what was being asked of it.[41] Representatives of the hospital suggested that another meeting be held, with the participation of the Medical Care Coordinating Committee but without that of the Northern Westmoreland Labor Council. After the meeting the Labor Council wrote the chairman of the Coordinating Committee that the Committee's recommendations apparently had been accepted at least in principle and that perhaps with some prodding from the Committee the issue could be finally resolved. They asked him to arrange a meeting and offered the services of the Council in any context in which the chairman thought they might be helpful.

As of April 1, 1964, the ten-year-old conflict appeared to be entering a new phase. Amid expressions of pessimism by the president of the medical staff, who says that he thinks community physicians will lose in the end although he, at least, seems to be prepared to fight to the finish, and of rather guarded discouragement on the part of the chairman of the Coordinating Committee, who apparently sees no prospect of an early settlement now that Allegheny Valley Hospital has been brought into the picture, the Russellton Group and miners' Board are mapping an extensive campaign. Among the steps whose potential effectiveness they are now exploring are legal action against the hospital Board and medical staff, and an attempt to achieve passage by the state legislature of a law barring hospital discrimination against group physicians.

41. A number of physicians are on the staffs of both Citizens General and Allegheny Valley Hospitals.

A sister group practice has already taken legal action. Like the Russellton Group, the Bellaire Medical Group, Bellaire, Ohio, is located in the area served by the Fund's Pittsburgh office and participates in the Fund program. The focal point of its controversy is an obstetrician-gynecologist, Dr. James E. Sams, who has been denied both membership in the county medical society and privileges at the voluntary Bellaire City Hospital since he joined the Group in the spring of 1962. Over its eleven-year history, the Group claims, most of its physicians have been denied medical society membership, which in turn has resulted in their being denied privileges at every hospital within their broad service area except Bellaire City. The City Hospital, although accepting some group physicians, has delayed their applications for as long as three or four years and, since Dr. Sams' arrival, refused privileges to him and two other group physicians. According to the Group, Dr. Sams is the only Board-certified specialist in obstetrics and gynecology in the entire county, and is clearly needed in a hospital whose maternity bed occupancy is only 36 percent because women go elsewhere for delivery.

In December 1963, after a long series of letters, petitions, and press releases had effected no change in the hospital's policy, the Bellaire group and a number of their patients instituted suit against the hospital, its trustees, the medical society, and various individuals, charging them with conspiracy in restraint of trade, violation of public policy, and violation of the Ohio Valentine antitrust act. Alleging in their brief that the main motive for the discrimination against group physicians is protection of general practitioners who "dominate" the City Hospital and who perform surgery and other specialized services "now deemed to be best handled by trained specialists," the plaintiffs seek admission to the county medical society, hospital staff privileges, and financial damages aggregating to nearly $2,500,000. Unless the hospital board capitulates, which seems unlikely, the legal battle will probably be a lengthy one.

One long-standing fight for hospital privileges was finally brought to an end early in 1963 when first Nassau County and then New York State passed laws barring hospital discrimination against group physicians. For years members of a number of the medical groups affiliated with the Health Insurance Plan of Greater New York had vainly attempted to obtain hospital privileges in several locations in and around New York City and had ultimately, after all other weapons failed, succeeded in interesting legislators in their plight. The State law, an amendment to the Public Health Law, affirms that:

1. It shall be an unlawful discriminatory practice for the governing body of a hospital

a. To deny to or to withhold from a physician staff membership or professional privileges in a hospital because of his participation in any medical group practice or non-profit health insurance plan . . . ;

b. To exclude or to expel a physician from staff membership . . . in a hospital because of his participation in any medical group practice or non-profit health insurance plan . . .

The Massachusetts Health Protection Clinics

February 1964

Marjorie Taubenhaus

In January 1950, the first of five multiphasic screening clinics in the state of Massachusetts opened under the sponsorship of the Massachusetts Department of Public Health, the United States Public Health Service, the Massachusetts Medical Society, the American Cancer Society (Massachusetts Division), and the Massachusetts Heart Association. By 1953 the Department of Public Health carried full responsibility for the clinics and the term "screening" was anathema to most Massachusetts physicians. This changed climate of opinion was not peculiar to Massachusetts. Reevaluation of multiple screening began elsewhere in the United States at approximately the same time, and various approaches are still being explored today.[1]

Origins of Multiphasic Screening

During the first half of the twentieth century there were remarkable achievements in the control of communicable diseases which transformed the frame of reference of public health practice in the United States. Success in controlling acute infectious diseases postponed death and added years to the life span of the average American, with a consequent drastic alteration of the age structure of the population. A sharp increase in the absolute number and proportion of aged people in the United States meant that care of chronic disease replaced control of infection as the nation's greatest health problem.

Soon after World War II professional attention was focused on this new problem. In 1946, a joint committee of the American Hospital Association, the American Medical Association, the

1. See, for example, Robert M. Thorner, and Quentin R. Remein, *Principles and Procedures in the Evaluation of Screening for Disease,* Public Health Monograph No. 67 (Washington D.C.: Government Printing Office, 1961). See also Charles M. Wylie, "Participation in a Multiple Screening Clinic, with Five-Year Follow-Up," *Public Health Reports* 76:596–602 (July 1961); Charles M. Wylie and Rose Mary Jacobs, "Opinions Expressed on Multiple Screening in Baltimore," *Maryland State Medical Journal* 10:675–677 (December 1961); and Theodore C. Krauss, "Medical Examination of the Well Person," *Health News* 40:4–19 (October 1963).

American Public Health Association, and the American Public Welfare Association, issued a statement: "Planning for the Chronically Ill."[2] Although much of this statement dealt with problems of treatment, hospital care, and nursing care, major attention was given to the first recommendation "The basic approach to chronic disease must be preventive." Unfortunately, much of the experience of the past in preventive medicine was not directly applicable to the problems of the present.

Communicable diseases had been attacked, in most instances, by measures directly involving the causative agent. This was done either by inhibiting dissemination of the organism (as through sanitary water supplies) or by building up individual resistance (through the specific protection of immunizations). Where neither of these direct methods would work, the time-honored solution of isolation was available. All of these techniques depend upon a known infective etiology to be successful.

Those chronic diseases (such as diabetes, cancer, and heart disease) which had no known infective etiology were not susceptible to these standard methods of prevention. In addition, chronic disease often involved long periods of usually increasing disability, and a need for complicated medical and hospital care.

One hopeful factor was the growing evidence that early diagnosis and treatment of chronic disease dramatically decreased severe disability, delayed permanent changes due to the disease, and often postponed death. This evidence was important to the practicing physician who dealt with people who were already ill or who suspected they were ill. To the public health practitioner it suggested that apparently healthy people could avoid some of the consequences of chronic disease if some practical means could be found to detect early signs of asymptomatic illness.

The idea of surveying a large population for disease with a technical device dates back to the hookworm surveys done in the southern United States early in this century. A definite diagnosis of the presence or absence of disease was made by a simple laboratory test. When mass Wassermann testing was used in Eastern Europe in World War I, the same principle was applied to another disease, syphilis.

In 1939, in Richmond, Virginia, the first linkage of more than one diagnostic test was made on a mass basis. Tests for syphilis

2. "Planning for the Chronically Ill," *American Journal of Public Health* 37:1256–1266 (October 1947).

and tuberculosis were carried out on the same individual at the same time. A year later, in North Carolina, simultaneous testing was done for syphilis and malaria. Both of these programs were in the field of communicable "curable" disease. They were new only in their suggestion that it was possible to carry on case finding for more than one disease in the same program.[3]

Early in this century it was recognized that an extensive case-finding program, using X-ray methods, was necessary if tuberculosis was to be effectively controlled. Until the development of the photofluorogram such a program was impossible because of excessive cost. By 1940 mass radiography was becoming available in the United States and the philosophy of mass detection of disease underwent a significant modification. The 35 mm film permitted only a presumptive diagnosis, to be confirmed or refuted by other laboratory and clinical tests. The mass diagnostic survey had been changed to a very effective screen, separating persons who probably had tuberculosis from those who probably did not.

Other chest conditions were frequently discovered during the mass radiographic surveys. Cardiac disease and lung cancer accounted for most of the nontuberculous chest conditions. Almost by accident, early diagnosis of tuberculosis became screening for several diseases.

The implications of this change did not go unnoticed. If one device could detect several chronic diseases, a combination of devices could detect even more. Spokesmen for the United States Public Health Service predicted several advantages for this combination, which was termed multiphasic screening. Costs of community education and organization would be minimized; fewer technical personnel would accomplish more work. A program could be flexible, expanding or contracting as resources permitted. Economy of administration and operation seemed assured, as well as better service to the persons screened.[4]

In May 1948, in San Jose, California, a small clinic was set up to test the desirability of "package" screening. Six tests were used on 945 industrial workers over a two-week period, and the conclusion was reached that "the value of the multiphasic screen-

3. E. M. Holmes and J. C. McCullough, "Health Screening," in Leavell, H. R. and E. G. Clark, *Textbook of Preventive Medicine* (New York: McGraw Hill, 1953), p. 359.

4. A. L. Chapman, "The Concept of Multiphasic Screening," *Public Health Reports* 64:1311–1314 (October 21, 1949).

ing procedure becomes even clearer." [5] The results of this experiment were still unpublished when health departments in several other parts of the country embarked on large-scale programs. In the first four months of 1950 multiphasic screening clinics were opened in North Carolina, Massachusetts, Georgia, and Virginia.

A Screening Clinic for Massachusetts

Dr. Vlado Getting was appointed Commissioner of Health for the Commonwealth of Massachusetts in April 1943. A large man with a forceful personality, he combined an imaginative approach to the problems of public health with a practical ability to get along with legislators. He has been described by people who worked for him as "brilliant" and a "born administrator." Dr. Getting was well aware of the new health problems created by an aging population. These problems were particularly acute in Massachusetts, where approximately 10 percent of the population was over the age of 65, and the median age in the state was more than two years older than that in the nation as a whole.

Several approaches to the chronic disease problem were activated by Dr. Getting. One of the most dramatic was the concept of a chronic disease hospital devoted to research, teaching, and rehabilitation. This resulted in the Lemuel Shattuck Hospital for the care of chronic diseases, opened in Boston in 1954. Dr. Getting was also interested in screening for chronic diseases and late in 1947 was working on a program for detection of heart disease which was conducted in Newton, Massachusetts, in 1948.

Sometime in late 1947 or early 1948, Dr. Getting approached Dr. A. L. Chapman, then with the Division of Chronic Diseases of the United States Public Health Service. Dr. Chapman indicated that fifteen thousand dollars could be made available to Massachusetts for a multiphasic screening clinic which would be one of the first in the nation. This clinic would demonstrate the obvious desirability of multiphasic screening and would be a coup for the administrator who succeeded in setting the precedent as well.

Dr. Getting accepted the challenge, and his enthusiasm was not dampened by the amount of time required to make a multi-

5. C. K. Camelo, D. M. Bissell, H. Abrams, and L. F. Breslow, "Multiphasic Screening Survey in San Jose," *California Medicine* 71:412 (December 1949).

phasic screening clinic operational. A comprehensive plan, and staff and facilities would be necessary. Financial support for the program would be needed to supplement funds from the Public Health Service.

A major question involved the use to which the screening would be put. There was obviously no point in picking up disease at an early stage, noting the fact that it had been picked up, and then filing away the note. Provision was necessary for follow-up, both for definitive diagnosis and for subsequent treatment. This aspect of the program, it was expected, would devolve largely upon physicians in private practice. Before any clinic could be started, the cooperation of practicing physicians would have to be assured. To this end Dr. Getting prepared a proposal for submission to the Massachusetts Medical Society, asking approval for "pilot" clinics.

It was suggested in the proposal that screening could be thought of as a substitute for an annual physical examination, since such examinations were not possible for many individuals. Research was needed, however, on the use of the various screening tools. The pilot clinics would be set up to do this research; they would establish proper methods of screening for chronic disease which could later be incorporated in the practice of the private doctor.

The Massachusetts Medical Society is made up of twenty district societies. Since the Society is chartered by the state, its constitution setting forth its powers and prerogatives and those of the district societies are a part of state law. According to the constitution, the district societies may not adopt policies or actions counter to the regulations of the state society, in matters where the general society is concerned.

The councilors of the state society are chosen by each district society. One councilor is elected for every 25 members, and there are no fewer than six councilors from each district. The Council sets and directs the policies of the state society, and a number of standing and temporary committees assist in studying and in implementing such policies.

The Committee on Public Health of the state Medical Society considered Dr. Getting's proposal on November 15, 1948. After considerable discussion a resolution was approved recommending the establishment of pilot clinics under the auspices of district medical societies to make examinations and refer the findings to family physicians. The Committee further recommended the appointment of a subcommittee to carry out this program. This resolution was formally approved on May 23, 1949, at the meeting of the Council of the Massachusetts Medical Society, and Dr. Getting had the official approval of organized medicine to move ahead with his program.

The Subcommittee on Pilot Clinics was set up with one representative from each district in the state. A five-man executive committee represented the full subcommittee, and in October 1949 the subcommittee's power to act was delegated to this executive committee. At that time, four of the five members of the executive committee were full-time specialists in public health.

A second advisory committee was set up by Dr. Getting himself — an advisory committee on screening to the Commissioner. This committee had representatives from the medical schools in the area, but it held few meetings, made fewer recommendations and decisions, and soon became defunct.

Organizational Development

Meanwhile, the position of the screening clinics project in the administrative structure of the state Department of Health had to be clarified. Dr. Herbert Lombard was Director of the Division of Cancer and other Chronic Diseases. On August 31, 1949, Dr. Lombard accompanied Dr. Getting to a meeting of the Subcommittee on Pilot Clinics and outlined the essentials of a screening clinic. But his main interest for many years had been statistical research in the field of cancer and he did not share Dr. Getting's boundless enthusiasm for the new project. Probably mindful of the pressures of time if Massachusetts were to pioneer in multiphasic screening clinics, Dr. Getting did not attempt to channel the program through Dr. Lombard. Instead he kept the main responsibility while delegating the day-to-day work to an administrator of his own choosing.

Dr. Claire Ryder, a 1943 graduate of Tufts Medical School, was then working in the Hospital Facilities Division of the State Department of Public Health. An eager, gregarious person, her temperament was ideally suited to complement Dr. Getting's forceful endorsement of new ideas. When Dr. Getting approached her to work on the new program she agreed readily and was therefore transferred to the Division of Cancer and other Chronic Diseases. Although a table of organization would have shown Dr. Ryder as responsible to Dr. Lombard, in fact her orders came directly from Dr. Getting. She was in effect on detached duty assigned to work directly under the Commissioner.

On October 5, 1949, the Subcommittee on Pilot Clinics voted to go ahead with one clinic and Dr. Ryder was appointed temporary administrator. With this approval she was now free to investigate practical matters with a view to concrete operation. Dr. Ryder anticipated that several months would be needed to make the physical arrangements for a clinic, draw up a budget, decide what tests to use, and educate private physicians as to their role in the follow-up of persons seen at the clinic.

Dr. Ryder visited many of the hospitals in the Boston area and found that the facilities of the New England Center Hospital, a Tufts teaching hospital, seemed best for her purposes. A list of screening tests was drawn up, and to check on false negative reports of the tests, arrangements were made for a twenty-minute physical examination to be performed by resident physicians at the hospital. Financial support for the clinic was obtained from the Public Health Service ($16,000), the Massachusetts Heart Association ($1,250), the American Cancer Society, Massachusetts Division ($1,250), with the balance of $16,500 to be supplied by the Department of Public Health.

Somehow Dr. Ryder received the impression that the Commissioner wished the opening date of the clinics to be advanced because of a rumor that a multiphasic clinic was to be opened elsewhere in the country. She therefore accelerated the pace of the preliminary processes, and on November 7, 1949, the Subcommittee on Pilot Clinics approved the choice of the New England Center Hospital and confirmed Dr. Ryder as administrator. The clinic was titled a Health Protection Clinic and members of the state legislature and employees of the Department of Public Health were invited to attend during a one-week trial period beginning December 1, 1949.

After this one-week trial in which about 100 persons were screened, the clinic was closed for a month. The results were analyzed with a view to finding bottlenecks to be eliminated before the clinic was opened to the general public. This was a useful function, but even more important was that served by screening members of the state legislature. The legislators, responsible for appropriations to support the clinic, were convinced at first hand of the valuable service performed by the clinic.

Shortly before the opening of the first Health Protection Clinic a brief announcement appeared in one of the Boston newspapers. Public response to this was so great that in three days all appointments for the next six months were filled. During the entire operation of the first clinic, January 3, 1950, through June 30, 1950, there was always a waiting list and all persons were seen by appointment only.

A summary of the screening procedures used is contained in Appendix A. Of the 2,620 persons screened, 1646 or 62.8 percent had positive findings. Although there were some persons with more than one positive finding, approximately one half were referred to their family physician because of overweight or hypertension. Written reports of findings were sent to the family physician. If a follow-up report was not received at the clinic a public health nurse contacted the physician to find out whether the patient had consulted him. If the patient had not done so, a medical social worker visited the patient to encourage him to consult his family physician. Approximately 70 percent of the physicians notified of suspicious findings on their patients sent reports back to the clinic. These reports indicated that there was about one case of disease for every two cases with suspicious findings. A finding of hypertension was confirmed more than any other cause of referral.

Drs. Ryder and Getting were elated at the apparent success of the Health Protection Clinic. Public response had been overwhelmingly favorable and private physicians were cooperating on follow-up of positive tests. Letters came in to the Department of Health from towns in many parts of the state, requesting local screening clinics. These requests were turned down with an explanation that Boston was being used at present for experimentation with techniques. Future clinics were promised for other communities.

Relations with the Medical Society were cordial. In February Dr. Getting spoke jocularly to the Council about the criticism he was encountering at the State House because of the Health Protection Clinic. It seems it was such a good thing that legislators were complaining that the Medical Society was getting credit for a good program that the state was financing. Legislators also objected because they said the Department of Public Health was acting as an agent to drum up business for private physicians. Dr. Getting said this was fine with him. He was happy to act as agent for the private physicians. He also mentioned that the legislators felt that more service should be provided for the large number of applicants to this worthy program.

Further communication with the Medical Society was made to the general membership at the annual meeting in May. The Preliminary Report on the Health Protection Clinics was read at the meeting and later published in the *New England Journal of Medicine.*[6]

After six months the clinic was closed to permit interpretation of results. Examinations of the records showed that such screening tools as hearing and vision tests gave more reliable information than did a clinic physician's examination. On the other hand, the physician was most valuable in picking up cancer and heart disease. It was therefore decided to cut the physical examination from twenty down to ten minutes, which also made possible a doubling in the number of persons the clinic would be able to handle.

Even though the avowed purpose of the pilot clinics was research on methods of screening, Dr. Ryder and others of the clinic personnel felt a strong responsibility towards persons attending the clinic. For this reason, if a small X-ray gave evidence suggestive of disease, the clinic arranged for a large film, or for stereo films if necessary. If blood samples were positive for sugar, glucose tolerance tests were done. Results of these added diagnostic procedures were included in the information forwarded to the family physician.

Occasionally the reaction of the private physician to this information was surprising to the clinic personnel. Sometimes, when potential cases of serious disease, such as cancer or diabetes, had been suggested by the screening examination, the clinic received no report of follow-up from the family physician. In a limited number of cases the clinic findings were ignored and Dr. Ryder and her staff felt that patients were suffering as a result. They were shocked and dismayed and did everything they could to convince the family physician that the findings were important. Although excellent cooperation was received from the majority of physicians, the few exceptions stood out for Dr. Ryder and her staff.

The second Health Protection Clinic was held at the New

6. Claire Ryder, and Vlado Getting, "Preliminary Report on the Health Protection Clinics," *New England Journal of Medicine* 243:277–280 (August 17, 1950).

England Center Hospital from October 3, 1950, through June 30, 1951. The number of persons screened was 5,057, twice the number screened at the first clinic. This second clinic was financed by funds provided by the Massachusetts Legislature and a continuation of the grant from the American Cancer Society—Massachusetts Division. The grants given by the Massachusetts Heart Association and the Public Health Service to the first clinic were not renewed.

Several of the standards and procedures used in the first clinic were changed for the second clinic. The physical examination was shortened; pulse, respiration, and temperature readings were omitted; and a one lead electrocardiogram and urine acetone examination were added. A complete description of screening procedures is given in Appendix B. Approximately the same proportion of persons screened had suspicious test results as had been found at the first clinic — 62 percent. However, informative reports on these persons were received from only 50 percent of the family physicians to whom they were referred.

In an attempt to evaluate the reliability of the screening tests, 521 persons attending the first clinic were reexamined by invitation at the second clinic. The results of this repeat screening have not been completely analyzed, but correlation coefficients were computed for the results of repeat tests for blood pressure, height, weight, and hemoglobin. It was difficult to differentiate between actual physical changes in a year and unreliability of the test. There is some indication, however, that the specificity and sensitivity of the screening tests left much to be desired.[7]

The first sounds of discontent were heard after the opening of the second clinic. If dissatisfaction with either the theory or practice of multiphasic screening existed it had not been publicly expressed up to then. But the *New England Journal of Medicine* of October 19, 1950, carried a letter from a practicing physician, Dr. Joseph Wassersug, and a reply from Dr. Brooks Ryder, Health Commissioner of the City of Quincy, husband of the clinic administrator, and newly appointed chairman of the Subcommittee on Pilot Clinics.

Dr. Wassersug criticized the clinics severely and called them "The Trojan Horse of Socialized Medicine."[8] He claimed that

7. Vlado Getting, and Herbert Lombard, "Health Screening Tests," unpub. ms., 1953.

8. Joseph Wassersug, "Criticism of Health Protection Clinic," Correspondence, *New England Journal of Medicine* 243:628 (October 19, 1950).

patients used the clinics to avoid the expense of private physical examinations and likened the clinics to the public services offered tuberculosis patients.

Dr. Brooks Ryder answered that the clinics were neither consultative, therapeutic, nor diagnostic, and thus in no way resembled tuberculosis services. By sponsoring the clinics, he felt that the Massachusetts Medical Society was effectively fighting socialized medicine.[9]

The correspondence reflects the great concern with the role of government in medicine which was current at that time in the ranks of organized medicine. On a national level, the head of the then Federal Security Administration, Oscar R. Ewing, was leading a fight for compulsory health insurance to be financed by a payroll tax. The American Medical Association, which violently opposed the program, levied an assessment on its members to finance a "National Education Campaign." The public relations firm of Whitaker and Baxter was hired in December 1948 to conduct a nationwide campaign on the issue.

Whitaker and Baxter used the state and local medical societies as distribution centers for promotional materials dealing with the cost and quality of medical care, free choice of physician, and socialized medicine. Federal administration of funds was equated with socialized medicine. One hundred million pamphlets were circulated, signs and pictures were placed in physician's offices, and doctors and their wives were recruited to speak to lay groups on these issues. The campaign lasted three and a half years, and cost a total of $4,678,157.[10] It covered approximately the same period of time as the Health Protection Clinics.

In addition to national issues, the problems of personal relationships within the State Department of Health were growing. Dr. Ryder was responsible directly to the Commissioner and her orders often came directly from Dr. Getting. Although she tried to clear all plans with the head of her Division, this soon proved meaningless. Dr. Lombard was not in line in an administrative capacity to issue any directives related to the clinics. The Division of Cancer and Chronic Diseases was housed separately from the

9. Brooks Ryder, "Reply to Criticism," Correspondence, *New England Journal of Medicine* 243:628 (October 19, 1950).

10. A transcript of testimony by Clem Whitaker and Leone Baxter before the United States Senate Special Committee on Political Activities, Lobbying and Campaign Contributions, San Francisco, California, January 22, 1957, p. 26.

Department of Health and three-way communication was awkward. The physical isolation of the Division (and of several other Divisions) had long been considered a barrier to smooth communications between the several divisions of the department.

Because the clinics were open in the afternoon, Dr. Ryder and her secretarial staff found that their greatest load of work came in the late afternoon and early evening. They therefore made a habit of working late most days and coming in two or three hours later in the morning than the rest of the Division personnel. Dr. Lombard was the target of many complaints from his divisional staff as a result, as others in his division accused the clinic staff of abusing special privileges.

Dr. Lombard and his statistical staff were directly involved in the collection and evaluation of clinic statistics. They prepared the material used by Drs. Getting, Ryder, and Lombard in reports on clinic activities, both for the Medical Society and for publication.

Dr. Lombard himself felt that the clinics were going much too fast and that private physicians had not been sold on the intent of the program. He was particularly disturbed by the difficulty of conducting research where standards were changed, procedures varied, and tests were added or discarded along the way. Although the Pilot Clinics were supposed to be a research project, in his opinion they had become a "mixed-up mess."

As far as the public was concerned the second Health Protection Clinic was as successful as the first, but the range of support was diminishing. Financial support was shrinking; the dissatisfaction of the medical profession was apparent in the lessening of cooperation from private physicians and the correspondence in the medical journal; the administrative conflicts within the Department of Public Health were intensifying. At this time Dr. Ryder was given a leave by the department to return to school in the fall for a degree in public health, financed by a grant from the department.

When the second clinic was completed (June 30, 1951), Dr. Ryder's first concern was to organize all the data from the clinics before she left in September. She was interested in operational research, what she calls "practical, on-going, how-to-do-it research." She prepared close to 7,000 records for transfer to IBM cards, but was unable to get authorization to pay to have the cards punched, and the card punching personnel of the Division of Cancer and other Chronic Diseases was not available to handle her material.

As far as she knows the information she was interested in was never completely analyzed.

Dr. Ryder recommended as her successor as administrator of the clinics Dr. Kathleen Shanahan Cohen, a 1948 graduate of George Washington University School of Medicine. Dr. Cohen had gone to work in the State Health Department in October 1950 in the Communicable Disease Division. In July 1951, she was transferred to Dr. Lombard's Division in order to work with Dr. Ryder for the summer.

By this time, it seemed to both Dr. Ryder and Dr. Cohen, the clinics in a hospital setting had proved themselves. It would now be possible to offer screening clinics to those communities which had been so anxious to have them the year before. Drs. Ryder and Cohen visited district medical society meetings in Worcester, Fall River, and New Bedford to discuss setting up local Health Protection Clinics. They were appalled at their reception. Although the Massachusetts Medical Society was formally supporting the clinics, the county societies did not agree.

Doctors at these medical meetings hardly bothered to be polite to the visitors, who were regarded as Oscar Ewing's government spies. Washington, D.C., license plates remained on Dr. Cohen's car from her medical school days and on one occasion served to confirm suspicion that multiphasic screening was part of a federal government plot. Dr. Ryder began to realize that some of the success of the first two clinics had been illusory. Certainly they had not succeeded in winning the confidence of practicing physicians over the state.

Discontent at the local level was soon reflected in the state society. On October 3, 1951, the Committee on Public Health presented a report on the first pilot clinic to the Council of Delegates of the Massachusetts Medical Society. The Committee recommended that the Subcommittee on Pilot Clinics be continued as an advisory committee to the Department of Public Health and requested the Commissioner to keep this subcommittee informed of developments and to give it an opportunity to review proposals.

The motion was discussed and a request was made from the floor that the Council advise the abolition of pilot clinics. The protesting doctor urged the Council to send a letter to the Commissioner stating that pilot clinics do not have a place in public health. His suggestion was ignored, but conditions were placed on the recommendation of the Committee on Public Health before it was passed. The proposal was amended to stipulate that the subcommittee would exist only if it were given the opportunity to review and approve proposals. It was further amended to limit the participation of the Medical Society to the advisory function of this subcommittee.

While relations with the Medical Society continued to deteriorate, the administrative conflicts within the department eased off. It was decided at this time to transfer the program from the Commissioner's Office, where new programs were usually carried during their development phase, to the Division of Cancer and other Chronic Diseases, directly under Dr. Lombard. Although Dr. Getting still expressed himself as being enthusiastically in favor of multiphasic screening, he no longer followed through on the detailed operation of the program. He worked on papers reporting the results of the clinics but had relatively little contact with Dr. Cohen. In many ways this made it easier for her to function in Dr. Lombard's Division.

The first two clinics had been held in a teaching hospital. This provided optimal facilities for testing materials and procedures. Now it was decided to branch out and experiment with other hospital and nonhospital settings. Accordingly, in the fall of 1951, Dr. Cohen approached the Director of Massachusetts General Hospital and suggested the creation of a multiphasic screening clinic in the outpatient department. This clinic would differ from the first two in that the State could not supply complete financial support, and the hospital was asked to contribute services and space. However, since it was now proposed that the examination by a physician be eliminated, this would minimize the hospital's contribution.

The Director of the M.G.H., Dr. Dean Clark, asked Dr. Earl Chapman, Chief of Medicine for the Out-Patient Department, and Miss Margaret Meehan, Superintendent, to investigate the desirability of a clinic. They were to act for the hospital's Out-Patient Committee which would consider the question. On November 15, 1951, the Out-Patient Committee went on record as unanimously unsympathetic to the principle of multiphasic screening. Some members of the committee felt that screening clinics were a step toward socialized medicine. The majority maintained that screening was poor medical practice, advocated by statisticians rather than clinicians.

Dr. Chapman and Miss Meehan obtained from Dr. Cohen a list of 41 persons, presumed to be M.G.H. outpatients, who had been screened at one of the previous Health Protection Clinics. They were able to find outpatient records for 19 of these patients. A review of these records indicated that nothing had been contributed to the medical care of these patients by the screening clinics (see Appendix C). The Out-Patient Committee felt that this finding substantiated their condemnation of the principle of multiphasic screening. Dr. Chapman informed the committee that he was meeting with Dr. Getting in December to discuss the matter and come to a final conclusion.

The meeting was cancelled by Dr. Getting because of the pressure of other business. Dr. Getting told Dr. Chapman he would set a date for another meeting, but none was ever set. Dr. Clark finally talked with Dr. Getting the following March and was told that a clinic was scheduled to open soon at the Peter Bent Brigham Hospital. As far as the M.G.H. was concerned, the matter was closed.

Meanwhile, the department opened negotiations with several of the towns that had requested screening clinics earlier. Dr. Getting reported to the Subcommittee of the state Medical Society on January 30, 1952, that the town of Chelmsford had requested a clinic. No action was planned on this request because of some opposition by local physicians. The department was exploring the possibility of a clinic in the town of Belmont. The International Fur and Leather Workers Union of the Lynn-Peabody-Salem area had also inquired whether a clinic could be set up for their members.

Reaction of the Subcommittee to Dr. Getting's report was mixed. The negative feelings of many private physicians were mentioned and ascribed to a lack of understanding of the research objective of the program. Physician education was called essential, and Dr. Getting replied that papers were being prepared which he hoped would serve this purpose. One member pointed out that the research aspects of the program were important, but that it seemed unwise at the time for the Department of Public Health to try to develop the clinics into what he termed wholesale health supervision of the aged.

Despite these reservations, the Subcommittee voted to endorse the Health Protection Clinic to be held at the Peter Bent Brigham Hospital. They also approved a clinic in Belmont, subject to prior approval of the local medical society, and said that they would approve a clinic for the union group only after the Council of Delegates or the local medical society had passed on it. The

Subcommittee felt, however, that such a clinic would be advisable as a step in establishing good public relations between the medical society and labor.

On March 18, 1952, the third Health Protection Clinic opened at the Peter Bent Brigham Hospital. The clinic ran through June 30, 1952, and screened 1,172 persons. There was no physical examination by a physician and the time given to each individual was thirty minutes (see Appendix D). Informative replies from private physicians were received on approximately 50 percent of the referred cases.

Early in April 1952, a fourth Health Protection Clinic opened in a school building in the town of Belmont. This clinic ran for six weeks and screened 1,004 persons. Jointly sponsored and conducted by the State Department of Public Health and the Belmont Health Department, its methods were the same as those used at the Brigham Hospital. However, informative replies were received from physicians on 76 percent of the referred cases. This good rapport with the practicing physicians is attributed by Dr. Cohen to the large number of specialists who practice in Boston and reside in Belmont. Dr. Cohen received support from many prominent specialists, including Dr. Paul Dudley White.

Evaluation and Dissent

Shortly after the clinic opened in Belmont, the Executive Committee of the Massachusetts Medical Society met and the representative from the Suffolk District Medical Society reported that the councilors in his district had voted to disapprove the clinics. There was a long discussion of the pros and cons of the pilot clinics, "all of which had been said before." The discussion was concluded by the statement of the secretary that legally there was no way to rescind the 1949 authorization of five pilot clinics.

At the full Council meeting on May 19, 1952, the clinics were again the subject of controversy. Supporters emphasized the research aspects of the program, while opponents reiterated their complaint that the clinics were an advance weapon of socialized medicine. Although no conclusion was reached, this was the first open debate of the merits of the screening clinics reported in the Proceedings of the Council of the Massachusetts Medical Society. Most of the previous argument had taken place in the relative privacy of committee meetings. Thus it was almost three years before the objections of some Massachusetts physicians to this particular program were discussed openly in their own state organization.

Open debate was not the only thing that came late in the history of multiphasic screening. In March 1951 a Conference on the Preventive Aspects of Chronic Disease had been held in Chicago. The deliberations of this conference were not published until 1952.[11] Definitions and criteria for screening tests and programs were worked out at that time by specialists in public health, preventive medicine, and chronic diseases. See Appendix E for list of definitions. Special emphasis was placed on the need for research and evaluation of these tests and programs.

When Dr. Getting reported to the annual meeting of the Massachusetts Medical Society in May on the progress of the screening clinics,[12] he stated that the Health Protection Clinics were carrying out the research suggested by the Conference on Preventive Aspects of Chronic Diseases. The physician's examination given at the first two clinics had been designed to determine the validity of the tests, and the recall visits of patients from the first clinic were intended to determine the reliability of the test.

Unfortunately, most physicians in Massachusetts were not familiar with these evaluative aspects of the clinics. The two reports given to the Medical Society had been published in the *New England Journal of Medicine,* but these seemed to stress the number of conditions detected rather than the evaluation of the tests. Other articles were published by Dr. Getting and appeared in journals less generally used by Massachusetts physicians. It is possible that Dr. Lombard might have succeeded in communicating to physicians the research intent of the clinics as his interest in research was well known, but he had been bypassed early in the program.

A *Shift of Divisions*

The pilot clinics had been from the first an activity of the Commissioner's office, later assigned to the Division of Cancer and other Chronic Diseases. Although they continued in the Division after Dr. Ryder left they were never integrated into the

11. Conference on the Preventive Aspects of Chronic Diseases, *Proceedings,* March 12–14, 1951 (Baltimore: Committee on Chronic Illness, 1952).

12. Vlado Getting, and Herbert Lombard, "The Evaluation of Pilot Clinics," *New England Journal of Medicine* 247:460–465 (September 25, 1952).

functioning of the Division. When Dr. Cohen discovered after the third and fourth clinics that she would be leaving the department in September because her husband was moving to a new location, there was little enthusiasm on Dr. Lombard's part to continue the program. It seemed logical to the department's staff to try to coordinate tuberculosis chest X-ray screening with other screening and to evaluate this type of organization of multiple screening. Dr. David Zacks, Chief of Clinics in the Tuberculosis Division, indicated to Dr. Cohen that he would be interested in working multiphasic screening into the operations of his units.

The Tuberculosis Control Section seemed ideally suited as a new base for multiphasic screening. Mobile X-ray units were already available and could be used as part of a screening program that could be established anywhere in a community. Dr. Augusta Law, a physician in Dr. Lombard's Division, requested a transfer to work on the screening program under Dr. Zacks, even though this transfer meant a considerable reduction in salary. She felt challenged by the possibility of carrying out practical research on costs, the fitting of multiphasic screening into existing programs, and the utilization of community resources.

After September 15, 1952, therefore, the pilot clinics were placed under the jurisdiction of Dr. Zacks, with Dr. Law as clinic administrator. Dr. Zacks proposed to offer clinic facilities to local communities on request, with some technical assistance from the department. Fewer tests were offered than at previous clinics, and a physician was used only for interpretation of the electrocardiogram. The first of the clinic sessions was held in January 1953, and there were eight other clinic sessions by June 1953 (see Appendix F).

One of these clinics proved to have disturbing consequences for the Department of Public Health. The International Fur and Leather Workers Union had maintained its interest in a screening program for its members and approached the department again with its request. Although there is some difference of recollection among the various persons involved in the clinic, certain events are a matter of record.

According to the published proceedings of the Council of the Massachusetts Medical Society, on February 25, 1953, the Secretary of the Essex South District Medical Society met with the Committee on Public Health of the State Society. He asked if the Massachusetts Medical Society or any appropriate committee had ever approved a screening clinic for the Fur and

Leather Workers Union. The District Society had not been consulted, was furious, and threatened to take action condemning the clinic at its next meeting.

Dr. Getting explained that a meeting on the subject had been held at the Department of Public Health on December 30, 1952, and he had received the impression that the union had already cleared its request with the Essex South District Medical Society. Plans had therefore been made to hold this clinic in early April 1953. The following motion was passed by the Committee on Public Health:

> On motion of Dr. Abrams it was voted to write to the Essex South District Society informing it that although there was no apparent intent on the part of the Department of Public Health to avoid receiving approval of either the state or local medical society, there had been serious misunderstanding and lack of good liaison; and that Dr. Getting indicated that this would not recur and that better communication would be set up with the component part of the Society, and that this should in no way be considered as establishing a precedent.

There is some reason to believe that at the December meeting Dr. Getting instructed Dr. Zacks to meet with the Essex South District Society and get their approval for the clinic. However, Dr. Zacks initially dispatched either a representative of the Union or a public health nurse in his stead. Whatever the background of this delegate, the Society was not convinced that they had been properly consulted and therefore made their formal complaint in February to the Committee on Public Health of the State Medical Society. It was after this that Dr. Zacks and Dr. Pope (Director of the Tuberculosis Division) met with the Essex South District Medical Society. Tempers were high, and many physicians felt that the department had sold out to labor. Unfortunately, about this time, an investigation of communists in Massachusetts splashed the name of one of the union officers and his wife on the front pages of the Boston newspapers, and the issue of communism in labor unions was joined to the general confusion.

The month of April was an important one for the Department of Public Health. Dr. Getting's reappointment to his third five-year term as Commissioner was due on April 1, 1953. In April the Governor of the Commonwealth attacked Dr. Getting in the newspapers because of a contract Dr. Getting had made with a federal program for providing technical assistance to public health programs in Pakistan. This was the first intimation that the

Commissioner had that he would not be reappointed. There are rumors that displeasure of the medical profession with the Shattuck Hospital and the Health Protection Clinics contributed to the Governor's decision not to reappoint the Commissioner.

Denouement

In April 1953 at the instigation of a member of the Essex South District Medical Society, the Executive Committee of the Council made a motion calling for further study of the Society's attitude toward multiphasic screening. The report to the Out-Patient Committee of the Massachusetts General Hospital, which was made early in 1952 when that hospital considered establishing a screening clinic, was resurrected for presentation to the Council the following month.

Meanwhile Dr. Law went ahead with small Health Protection Clinics at various institutions in the Boston area. A clinic was held for the Fur and Leather Workers during April and 3,575 persons were screened. However, Dr. Zacks sensed the deep schism between the Medical Society and the Department of Public Health, and he was concerned about the lack of a diagnostic set-up for following up suspicious findings of the screening tests. Even though all funds had not been expended, he suggested to Dr. Alton Pope, by then Acting Commissioner, that the program be discontinued.

When the Medical Society took formal action on May 19, 1953, they were actually belaboring a dead issue. The report of the M.G.H. Out-Patient Committee was accepted, and a proviso added that the Council be recorded as opposed to further screening clinics under the Massachusetts Department of Public Health.

The Subcommittee on Pilot Clinics was dissolved a year later, after the following statement had been released: "The Committee believes that this type of screening is not a substitute for a complete physical examination . . . We believe that the basic philosophy utilized in the pilot clinics was wrong and the method chosen was poor."

Appendix A

Tests and Results

Health Protection Clinic Number 1, New England Center and Joseph H. Pratt Diagnostic Hospitals, Boston, Massachusetts

Screening Tests:

1. Self-screener medical history
2. Blood test for serology, sugar, and hemoglobin
3. Urine test for sugar and albumin
4. Vision test
5. Hearing test
6. 70 mm chest X-ray
7. Measurement of height and weight
8. Blood pressure reading
9. Pulse and respiration recording
10. Temperature recording
11. Physical examination, including routine rectal with hematest, and pelvic and/or Papanicolaou where indicated.

Results:

1. Overweight — 29.1% at least 20% above ideal weight.
2. Vision defects — 12.5% with less than 20/40 near or far, either or both eyes.
3. Hypertension — 23.3% with systolic pressure 150 mm or over diastolic pressure 90 mm or over.
4. Heart disease — 24.4% with suspicious symptoms picked up by physical examination, X ray, or history.
5. Hearing defects — 8.7% with loss in either ear below screening level of 30 decibels at 500, 1,000, and 2,000 cy/sec.
6. Cancer — 1.4% with suspicious conditions found by examination, hematest, smear, X ray, or history.
7. Diabetes — 1.4% positive on the basis of blood sugar 180 mg/100 ml or above or positive glucose tolerance test.
8. Anemia — 3.6% males with hemoglobin level below 12.3 gm/100 ml; 2.3% females with level below 10.3 gm/100 ml. The original screening level was 11.0 for males and 10.0 for females. This was changed while the clinic was in operation.
9. Tuberculosis — 0.8% with positive findings based on 70 mm X ray checked by 14 x 17 film.
10. Syphilis — 0.5% with positive Hinton tests.
11. Albuminuria — 4.2% with any amount of albumin in urine.

    Other findings included positive conditions of almost all organ systems, picked up primarily on physical examination.

Appendix B

Tests and Results

Health Protection Clinic Number 2,
New England Center and Joseph H. Pratt
Diagnostic Hospitals, Boston, Massachusetts

Screening Tests:

1. Self-screener medical history
2. Blood test for serology, sugar, hemoglobin — glucose tolerance if indicated
3. Urine test for sugar, albumin, acetone
4. Vision test
5. Hearing test
6. 70 mm chest X ray — if positive, 14 x 17 film take
7. Measurement of height and weight
8. One-lead electrocardiogram — if positive 12-lead electrocardiogram done
9. Recording of blood pressure
10. Physical examination — including routine rectal, hematest and pelvic and/or Papanicolaou where indicated.

Results:

1. Overweight — 27.3% at least 20% above ideal weight.
2. Vision defects — 8.9% with less than 20/40 vision near or far, either or both eyes.
3. Hypertension — 23.3% with systolic pressure 150 mm or above or diastolic pressure 90 mm or above.
4. Heart disease — 25.1% with suspicious symptoms, picked up by physical examination, electrocardiogram, X ray, or history.
5. Hearing defects — 8.2% with hearing loss either ear below level of 30 decibels at 500, 1,000, and 2,000 cycles.
6. Cancer — 1.9% suspicious conditions found by physical examination, X ray, Papanicolaou, or history.
7. Diabetes — 1.9% diagnosed on basis of blood sugar at least 180 mg/100 ml or positive glucose tolerance test.
8. Anemia — 6.1% males with hemoglobin level below 12.3 gm/100 ml; 3.3% females with hemoglobin level below 10.3 gm/100 ml.
9. Tuberculosis — 0.2% positive findings 70 mm X ray checked by 14 x 17 film.
10. Syphilis — 0.2% with positive Hinton tests.
11. Albuminuria — 3.0% with any amount of albumin in urine.

Other findings included positive conditions of almost all organ systems picked up primarily on physical examination.

Appendix C

Excerpt of Minutes from the Committee Meeting

From the minutes of the Out-Patient Committee of the Massachusetts General Hospital on December 19, 1951:

Forty-one names were submitted by Dr. Cohen of which only nineteen could be identified as M.G.H. Out-Patient Department patients, due to the fact that unit numbers and other pertinent information were not available. Miss Meehan stated that Dr. Earl Chapman and Dr. Lezer had gone over the results of the survey and had agreed on the following tabulation of results:

6 — nothing added.
6 — disease missed.
3 — anxiety state.
2 — cancer suspects — not confirmed.
1 — patient with cystic ovary. Sent to Gyn. Clinic — appointment not kept.

Appendix D

Health Protection Clinic Number 3,
Peter Bent Brigham Hospital
Boston, Massachusetts

Screening Tests and/or Diseases Tested for:
1. Self-screener medical history
2. Blood test for serology, sugar, hemoglobin
3. Urine test for sugar, albumin, acetone
3. Urine test for sugar, albumin, acetone
5. Vision test
6. 70 mm chest X ray or 4″ by 5″ fluoroscopic film
7. Measurement of height and weight
8. Five-lead electrocardiogram
9. Recording of blood pressure readings
10. Papanicolaou smear on all women over 35 years or with symptoms
11. Hematest if examinee brought specimen.

Results:
1. Overweight — 23.4% at least 20% above ideal weight.
2. Vision defects — 13.9% with less than 20/40 vision near or far, either or both eyes.
3. Hypertension — 27.7% with systolic pressure 150 mm or above or diastolic pressure 90 mm or above.
4. Heart disease — 17.5% with suspicious symptoms, discovered by X ray, electrocardiogram, or history.
5. Hearing defects — 9.0% with hearing loss either ear below screening level 30 decibels at 500, 1,000, and 2,000 cy/sec.
6. Diabetes — 4.7% positive blood sugar screen (Wilkerson-Heftmann method).
7. Anemia — 8.3% males with hemoglobin level below 12.3 gm/100 ml; 2.8% females with hemoglobin level below 10.3 gm/100 ml.
8. Tuberculosis — 0.9% positive findings 70 mm X ray checked by 4″ by 5″ fluoroscopic film.
9. Syphilis — 0.5% with positive Hinton tests.
10. Albuminuria — 3.9% with any amount of albumin in urine.

The same procedures and criteria were used at the Health Protection Clinic number 4 held in Belmont, Massachusetts. The results were slightly different:

Positive Findings:
1. Overweight — 20.7%
2. Vision defects — 16.0%
3. Hypertension — 29.9%
4. Heart disease — 13.9%

5. Hearing defects — 13.6%
6. Diabetes — 3.1%
7. Anemia — 4.6% males, 5.5% females
8. Tuberculosis — 2.6%
9. Syphilis — 0.5%
10. Albuminuria — 0.6%

Appendix E

Definitions and Criteria Evolved at the Conference on Preventive Aspects of Chronic Disease held in Chicago, Illinois, March 12–14, 1951.

1. *Screening* is the presumptive identification of unrecognized disease or defect by the application of tests, examinations, or other procedures which can be applied rapidly.
2. *Detection* is the identification of ordinarily unrecognized disease or defect by the application of screening tests, examinations, and diagnostic procedures.
3. *Screening Tests* are procedures which sort out those who probably have abnormalities from those who probably do not.
4. *Mass Screening Programs* consist of the application of screening tests rapidly and economically to large population groups, to identify those who probably have abnormal conditions and refer them for diagnosis and, if indicated, for further medical care. The primary purpose of mass screening is to bring persons with disease to physicians at an earlier stage than otherwise would be the case.

Criteria for the evaluation of screening tests:

1. *The reliability of the test.* The test must be reliable in that information must be available concerning the reproducibility of results as limited by the technical procedure, the use of such procedure by technicians of average training, and the range or variation to be expected among specimens collected at different times under the same conditions from the same individual.
2. *The validity of the test.* The validity of a test is measured by the frequency with which the result of the test is confirmed by an acceptable diagnostic procedure . . . The ideal screening test would yield only true positives and true negatives, but no such test has been described.
3. *Yield of a screening program.* The yield of a screening program can be measured by: (a) the number of previously unknown verified cases of disease among the total population surveyed; (b) the number of persons with previously unknown verified diseases benefited by referral to medical care, and the number of previously known cases not under medical care benefited by return to it; (c) the number of individuals who believe they had the disease, have a positive screening test, but are shown not to have the disease by subsequent diagnostic examination; (d) the number of cases of communicable disease who are prevented from spreading their disease to the family or to the community.
4. *Cost.* The size of the yield of the screening program must be balanced against the cost. Cost must be measured in monetary

terms and in the relative amounts of time of professional and non-professional personnel.

5. *Acceptance.* Reliability, validity, yield, and cost are *essential* criteria for the evaluation of screening tests and programs. The measurement of acceptance of the program by physicians, individual laymen, and the community is a useful additional criterion of the effectiveness of a screening program.

Appendix F

Massachusetts Health Screening Tests Program
(Considered the fifth of a series of five pilot clinics)

Location	*Test Dates (1953)*	*Number Screened*
Women's Reformatory, Framingham	Jan. 12–16	323
U.S. Arsenal, Watertown	Jan. 19–Feb. 17	3,537
Boston College	Feb. 19–Mar. 13	1,615
Department of Public Works (State)	Mar. 16–27	1,048
Peabody (Leather Workers Union)	Apr. 1–May 1	3,575
Quincy (City Employees)	May 5–18	1,352
Weston College (Seminary)	May 19	211
Division of Employment Security (State)	May 25–29	886
Cambridge (City Employees)	June 8–16	585

Screening Tests and/or Diseases Tested for:

1. Chest X ray (4 x 5 photofluoroscopic)
2. One-lead electrocardiogram
3. Hemoglobin (screening level: 10 gm/100 ml in women, 12 gm/100 ml in men)
4. Blood sugar (screening level: 160 gm/100 ml on post-prandial blood specimen by Wilkerson-Heftmann method)
5. Vision (Screening level: less than 20/40 vision)
6. History — less than 50 questions

Health Services in Chile

May 1964

Roy Penchansky

Chile is a ribbon of land almost 3,000 miles long that is generally less than 100 miles wide. Its eastern border and a sizable section of the country consists of a range of gigantic barren mountains that are sparsely populated and relatively inaccessible. Its western border is the Pacific Ocean, a great resource which is only now being tapped as a source of food. Along the north, where Chile borders on Peru and Bolivia, there are barren, desert-like, sparcely populated areas which are rich in minerals and which support a large mining industry. In the south Chile borders on the Antarctic, and the southern section of the country is a large land mass, interspersed with bodies of water, which is quite inaccessible in winter and where, even in summer, the major means of transportation is boat. Because of these physical characteristics the country has a fairly small population, estimated in 1963 at slightly less than 8 million.[1] From 1950 to 1960 the population increased an average of 2.8 percent per year.

Chile's geography is said to affect it in another manner. The population, located on the southwestern tip of South America and almost 100 percent of European origin, unlike those of other countries of South America, is particularly concerned about its cultural and economic isolation from Europe and North America. For these reasons there has always been a great emphasis on "keeping up." This is manifested in education (80 percent of the people are literate), in social philosophy (a broad social welfare scheme was enacted as early as 1924), and even in such things as women's styles. One European observer who has been a resident of Chile for many years commented, "Chileans are so concerned about being isolated that in compensating for it they have become the leaders in South America."

Except for a civil war in 1891, Chile has had a relatively stable political life since its independence from Spain in 1810. It is a democracy with a federal government similar in structure to that of the United States. Unlike the United States, however, it has

1. Except where otherwise noted, the data presented in the Background Section of this paper are from *Servicio Nacional de Salud: Desarrollo Socio-económico y Planificación, Chile,* 1963, Impreso En Los Talleres De La Sección Educación Para La Salud, Servicio Nacional De Salud, Chile, 1963.

no history of strong local government, and political power and legislative responsibility are concentrated at the national level. The country is divided into 25 provinces for administrative purposes.

In spite of its relative political stability, progressive outlook, small Indian population, and early development of a large mining industry, Chile can be considered an underdeveloped country. The reasons include the country's geography, early reliance on foreign capital investment, dependence on international mineral markets, and heavy reliance on imports.

The country's economy is still largely agricultural, 25 percent of the working population being employed on the land. Approximately 65 percent of the population live in urban areas, primarily in three large cities located in the center of the country—Santiago, the capital, Valparaíso, and Concepción. In urban areas 73 percent of the population have potable water and 52 percent have sewerage. Only 5 percent of the rural population have potable water, and 40 percent have some sort of latrine or sewerage.

The working population is small. In 1960, 38 percent of the population, or 2.8 million persons, were children under 15 years of age, and another 4.3 percent of the population were 65 or over. Of the 4.5 million persons over 15 years old, only 2.4 million were "economically active"—working or available for work—in 1960. In the same year, unemployment was estimated at between 7 and 8 percent of the economically active population.

The national income of Chile rose from 124.5 million escudos in 1950 to 3,911.0 million escudos in 1960. The 1960 national income was 145 if the 1950 income, adjusted to its purchasing power in 1960, is used as a base of 100. Per capita income, in 1960 escudos, rose from 444 in 1950 to 510 in 1960. The average daily wage in 1960, when the exchange between escudos and United States dollars was approximately one to one, was 0.43 escudos for agricultural workers, 1.24 escudos for construction workers, and 1.49 escudos for industrial workers.

A number of studies have shown extremes in the distribution of income among different segments of the population. In 1960, according to *Servicio Nacional de Salud: Desarrollo Socioeconómico y Planificación*, 87.5 percent of the economically active population received 52 percent of the national income and 12.5 percent received the balance. The 87.5 percent made less than 2,000 escudos per year. The top 2.6 percent made 6,000 or more escudos per year and received 26 percent of the national income. Another study,[2] which divides the population into three groups — the working group, the employee group, and the ownership group — reported that in 1954 these groups represented 76, 15, and 9 percent of the population respectively, and that each group received 25, 25, and 50 percent of the national income respectively. Between 1953 and 1959 the share of national income and purchasing power received by the working class decreased while the share of the ownership group increased.

The country's general mortality was 12.7 per 1,000 population in 1960. Mortality had declined steadily from 1930 to 1953 primarily because of a decrease in the number of deaths caused by pneumonia, tuberculosis, gastroenteritis, and other infectious diseases. Since 1953 the rate of decline in number of deaths caused by tuberculosis, gastritis, duodenitis, enteritis, and colitis has slowed and the number of deaths from influenza, pneumonia, and bronchitis has risen. Deaths caused by accidents, malignant neoplasms, vascular lesions, and certain diseases of early infancy, which have remained relatively stable or increased, now account for a larger share of the mortality. Infant mortality, which accounts for one third of all deaths, has been declining steadily since 1930 when it was reported as 212 per 1,000 live births. It has, however, fluctuated considerably since 1953 when it was reported as 106. It rose to 118 in 1954, declined to the all time low of 105 in 1956, and stood at 120 in 1960. In 1959, when the infant mortality rate was 112, the neonatal rate was 35 and the postneonatal rate was 77. The major causes of death in children one month to one year old are respiratory infections, enteric infections, and malnutrition, in that order. In 1961 approximately 43 percent of the infants who died from respiratory infections had been under medical care. Approximately 70 percent of the infants dying from gastroenteric and certain major infectious and communicable diseases had been under medical care. The life expectancy in 1960 was 54.7 years for men and 59.9 years for women, somewhat lower than life expectancy in Argentina and Venezuela but higher than that in most other South American countries.

Early Development of Health Services

In 1552 the first medical institution in what is now Chile, the Hospital San Juan de Dios, was established. In subsequent years

2. Keith Griffin, Carlos Hurtado, and Pedro Paz, *Estrategia del Desarrollo*, Programa de Estudios Latinoamericanos para Graduados, Universidad de Chile, Santiago, June 1963.

religious orders and philanthropic citizens opened and operated other hospitals of the same type which were called "beneficencias." Staffed usually by nuns and practical nurses trained in the hospital, these institutions were the major source of medical care for people who could not afford private care. Eventually the beneficencias assumed the status of semi-governmental institutions as the federal government enacted national regulations for their operation. In 1927 they became part of the government welfare services under a national board of beneficencias supported by government appropriations. The board's authority was extended in 1932, and uniform medical standards, joint purchasing of supplies, fixed salary scales, and other features of coordinated administration were effected.

The government created a Dirección General de Sanidad within the Ministry of the Interior in 1918 following a series of epidemics. Limited public health activities had been undertaken in previous years. Organized primarily to combat typhus, typhoid, and smallpox, the Dirección gradually extended its scope, particularly in urban areas, to include programs in venereal disease control, environmental sanitation, epidemiology, maternal and child health services for the indigent, and so on. Its budget remained small, however. When a separate Ministry of Hygiene, Assistance, and Social Welfare was formed in 1924, the Dirección's activities were transferred to the new Ministry.

In 1924 a bill establishing a social insurance system was passed to provide protection against "disease, old age, and disability" for laborers, and health care for their wives during pregnancy and for their children under two years of age. The legislation, known as Law 40–54, established a Caja de Seguro Obrero (Fund for Worker Security) for manual workers in industry and agriculture. The benefits, financed by contributions from both employer and worker, included sick leave, unemployment compensation, hospitalization, outpatient medical care, and retirement benefits. Approximately 30 percent of the population were eligible for benefits under this Caja.

To provide ambulatory care for the insured workers, this Caja (CSO) first used the outpatient departments of existing hospitals and in 1932 began to establish its own clinics, known as consultorios, in cities and large towns, and small health stations, called postas, in rural areas. The CSO contracted with the beneficencia hospitals for the provision of inpatient care. Late in the 1920's attempts were made to unite the beneficencias and the CSO at the federal level but without success.

In the years following the creation of the CSO, similar social security funds were organized for other employment groups, such as employees of banks and retail establishments, but few of these Cajas provided medical benefits. For persons unable to finance their own care, or ineligible for benefits under the CSO or one of the other Cajas, the beneficencias remained the major source of medical care. To meet the growing demand for ambulatory services, these hospitals opened outpatient departments and a few established additional clinics in locations separate from the hospital.

In 1937 a Preventive Medicine Law was passed which required all Cajas to provide an annual physical examination for their members for the detection of syphilis, tuberculosis (and silicosis), and cardiovascular diseases. Cancer was later added to the list. If evidence of one of these diseases was found, members were to be given treatment as well as funds to replace salary lost during the period of disability. The country's health leaders promoted the legislation in an attempt to introduce preventive measures against diseases of high incidence detectable by simple procedures into the medical programs of the various social security schemes. Following its passage, all the Cajas initiated the minimum medical services it required, but the number of Cajas that offered broader medical benefits remained fairly small.

Some dissatisfaction with the segmentation of health services in the country began to arise in the late 1920's and 1930's, and, in addition to the unsuccessful efforts to unite the CSO with the beneficencias, a number of experiments directed at coordinating health services at the local level were undertaken. By 1939 the Colegio Médico, the Chilean Medical Association, became involved in the controversy, and some of its members proposed a resolution recommending unification of all health services in the country. It failed to pass primarily, it is claimed, because it was opposed by the chiefs of the various health units who were jealous of their individual positions. In later years motions recommending unification of the various health programs were passed by the medical association.

In 1941 the first Chileans to be sent outside their country for training in public health attended Johns Hopkins University, and in 1943 a School of Public Health was established in Chile. In that year 15 Chileans attended Johns Hopkins (constituting one quarter of the class), and in subsequent years additional Chileans were sent to North American schools for training. Although the

Chilean School of Public Health expanded steadily, students trained within the country were not regarded as having the same stature as those trained in North America.

The real birth of public health in Chile is said to have taken place early in the 1940's with the return to the country of the first group of personnel trained in the United States. In the years following, they were quite successful in implanting their orientation and concepts into the Chilean medical scene. According to current public health leaders in the country, the medical profession, and in turn the politicians, had held public health in low repute prior to the 1940's. The facts that the public health personnel had been trained in the United States, and that many of them were considered to be of very high caliber, helped to upgrade the status of public health in the country.

The objectives of the public health personnel of the early 1940's were to educate the medical profession in the need for broad public health programs and to show by experiments how the health standards of the population might be improved. Although the general emphasis was on national programs, many of the experiments focused on the local health unit. One project, which had United States support, attempted to relate health care to economic development in the area and united the efforts of the CSO, the Dirección General de Sanidad, and the Dirección de Protección a La Infancia y Adolescencia, which had been created in 1942 to take charge of the maternal and child health activities of the Dirección General de Sanidad. This experiment, which started in 1943, was the last of the local projects concerned with a coordinated, comprehensive program based on local conditions. Chilean observers feel that the experiments were not successful. One of the early public health leaders commented, "Our training and trials were too heavily weighted by North American experience." Nevertheless, the development of public health leaders and the trial programs had the total effect of giving public health greater importance and standing.

During the late 1940's pressure for unification of the various health services, for an extension of these services, and for greater stress on public health activities continued to grow. In 1952, after what was said to have been 15 long years of preparation and education of the medical profession, a broad national health service bill was enacted. Legislation with this goal had been introduced in previous years but had failed to pass. The success of the 1952 legislation is attributed to extensive lobbying among the nation's

45 senators by professional leaders, and to the fact that the president of the country was in his last term of office. Additionally, the duplication of services and the problems it caused were becoming more apparent every year, especially since each of the individual services was expanding.

Generally the medical profession actively supported the legislation but set certain conditions for their participation. First they insisted that membership in the Colegio Médico be made a legal requirement for medical practice and that the Colegio be represented on the governing body of the service. They also demanded that a civil service bill be enacted to establish uniform conditions of employment and compensation for professional groups — physicians, dentists, and pharmacists. These demands were met. Members of the medical profession comment that the salary set for them at the time was relatively high in comparison with wage rates for other positions and their own previous salaries.

The legislation established a Servicio Nacional de Salud (SNS) to provide comprehensive, integrated health services for the workers and their dependents covered by the Caja de Seguro Obrero (CSO) and for the country's indigent population. Although the legislation authorized the President of Chile to integrate into the SNS the health services financed by other Cajas under the general jurisdiction of the Minister of Health, only that for merchant seamen was integrated with the SNS.

The new National Health Service inherited the staff and facilities of the CSO health service and of the existing governmental mechanisms for the provision of health care in the country. These are listed below.

1. The beneficencias provided medical care for the indigent and inhospital care for beneficiaries of the CSO. Beneficencia hospitals existed in most cities, and contained close to 24,000 beds. The majority operated outpatient departments, and a few in the larger cities also ran separate clinics in other parts of the community. The beneficencia system employed approximately 15,000 people.

2. The Medical Department of the CSO provided ambulatory medical care through its own clinics and rural postas and inpatient care either through the beneficencias or one of its own two hospitals — one a general hospital and the other a tuberculosis hospital. The Department maintained approximately 40 consultorios in the cities and a larger number of postas in rural areas. Its facilities contained about 500 beds. The Department employed approximately 3,000 persons.

3. The Dirección General de Sanidad of the Ministry of Health was responsible for such public health functions as environmental health, epidemiology, and infectious disease control.

4. The Dirección General de Protección a La Infancia y Adolesciencia responsible for public health activities concerned with maternal and child health. A unit within the Ministry of Health, the Dirección maintained a number of maternal and child health stations.

5. The Industrial Hygiene Section of the Ministry of Labor was responsible for industrial health and safety. Its activities were very limited.

The Ministry of Health also operated a number of emergency stations, or Servicios de Asistencia Pública, for ambulatory emergency care which became part of the SNS. A National Bacteriological Institute, the public health laboratory of Chile, was another institution brought under the new SNS.

A statement prepared by the National Health Service in 1962 reflects the point of view that existed at the time the legislation was passed. Citing some of the successes that had been obtained in the control of infectious disease and in medical science by 1952, it noted among the achievements:

> Recognition that personal medical service, despite the perfection of its techniques, cannot significantly reduce the high rate of our morbidity and mortality . . .
>
> The attitude of the medical profession, as revealed in its conventions and congresses, that the problems of health care constitute a whole which must be solved upon the base of unification and integration of existing medical services into an integrated and national service.

Servicio Nacional de Salud

Scope and Eligibility

The Servicio Nacional de Salud is responsible for the public health of the entire nation, and for the provision of curative services to certain population groups. According to a statement prepared in 1963 by the Service, its functions and obligations are:

> 1. To protect and promote the health of the entire population of the country, through such activities as epidemiological control, food control, environmental health, and maternal and child health.
>
> 2. To provide medical care.
>
> a. comprehensively and freely to members of social security systems affiliated with the Service (manual workers covered by the

CSO and merchant seamen) and their wives and children under 15; to those who do not earn a living wage; and to the indigent;

b. to other members of the population who request care at a Service facility and are willing to pay for it;

c. to those injured at work.

3. To reimburse beneficiaries for wages lost because of temporary illness.

4. To reimburse insured women during pre- and postnatal periods for wages lost because of pregnancy, and to furnish nursing mothers who do not receive other supplementary aid with some further assistance.

5. To care for minor children "in unusual circumstances," in cooperation with other relevant agencies.

Both employer and employee contribute to the Service. To obtain benefits for themselves or their families, workers need only present a book which contains stamps representing the contributions made on their behalf. A major problem, however, has been the failure of some employers, particularly agricultural employers, to contribute and the resulting inability of employees to establish their eligibility.

Although the Service is intended to provide care for indigents, "indigency" has not been carefully defined, nor has a standard policy been consistently applied. In 1962 the Service supposedly followed the rule that persons earning less than 25 escudos per month were considered to be indigent. Some conflict has arisen between the physicians working for the Service and social workers and nurses because of the informal way indigency is established. A number of nurses and social workers comment that some physicians refuse to give free care to indigent persons who make an effort, by borrowing clothing, for example, to come to the clinic looking decently dressed. Dr. Milton I. Roemer noted one offshoot of this problem during a visit to a small rural hospital:

> On the wall of the out-patient waiting room of this rural hospital was a sign . . . posted by the Federación Médica de Chile, an association of doctors, and reads: "This establishment serves only the insured, indigents, and their respective families. Patients *not insured* will be attended *only* in case of extreme and serious emergency." The intention, of course, is to make it quite clear to the public that patients who are not insured and not indigent are expected to go to private physicians for their medical care. Despite this poster, the young doctor said that he never really turns anyone away. The poster is kept up, he explained, because of the insistence of a consultant pediatrician who comes to the hospital periodically.[3]

3. Milton I. Roemer, *Medical Care in Latin America* (Washington, D.C.: General Secretariat, Organization of American States, 1963), p. 204.

In mid-1963 the Colegio Médico and the Director General of the Service agreed that it was necessary to define "eligibility" and "indigency" more clearly and a study of the problem is being undertaken in an attempt to reach mutually acceptable definitions. The Federación Médica has made this issue one of its major concerns, and some observers feel that the problem is of such urgency that it might produce a physician's strike if it is not resolved.

The most frequently given estimate for the proportion of the Chilean population eligible to receive free curative services from the SNS is 75 percent. In 1962 it was reported that the Service was responsible for the medical care of 5,554,790 persons: 2,934,400 children under 15; 1,264,000 workers; 505,600 noninsured spouses; 32,000 personnel of the SNS; 12,800 wives of SNS personnel; 59,061 merchant seamen; and 755,925 indigent persons. Dr. Roemer has said, "It would appear . . . from these multiple sources of data, that the actual proportion of the Chilean population covered by the National Health Service lies somewhere between 45 and 70 percent and may possibly be closer to 50 percent than to 75 percent of the total." Dr. Roemer's lowest estimate (45 percent) is based on home interviews in Santiago which established the proportion of those questioned who actually used SNS Services when illness occurred. Utilization of the Service, however, cannot be used as a guide to eligibility because it is well known that many beneficiaries, particularly those in Santiago, pay for private care because of the long waiting periods at SNS facilities and their own negative feelings about the quality of care under the SNS. The beneficiary group may in fact be close to 70 percent of the population.

Although many Chileans not covered by the SNS receive some health benefits through other organized services established by the different Cajas or by particular organizations such as the armed forces, it is estimated that 20 percent of the population must purchase privately all or most of whatever care they receive. It has also been estimated that, at the most, 10 percent of the Chilean population can afford to purchase a full range of health services.

Structure of the Service

The legislation establishing the Servicio Nacional de Salud stated:

The National Health Service shall be the responsibility of a Director-General, without prejudice to the powers conferred on the National Health Council by the law.

In addition to the Director-General and the National Council, the National Health Service shall be organized into sub-directorates, departments, sub-departments, sections, sub-sections, health zones, health centers, and specialized services.

The Director General of the Service was to be a Chilean physician with at least ten years of professional experience. As required by law, the National Health Council was composed in 1952 of the Minister of Health, the Director General of the Service, two representatives of trade unions, two representatives of industry, and two representatives each of the Colegio Médico and the Faculty of Medicine of the University of Chile. The only members of the Council who were required to be physicians were the Director General of the Service and the members representing the Colegio and the Faculty of Medicine. The members are nominated by the groups which must be represented on the Council and appointed by the President of the country.

Below the level of Director General and Health Council, the legislation gave few guidelines to the organizational structure. One of the architects of the bill, Dr. Gustavo Molina, notes that three of the major leaders who drafted and supported the bill left the country soon after its passage. Although the people who assumed responsibility were considered to be extremely competent, they did not have a clear conception of the program that had been visualized by its creators and consequently had to think it through for themselves. It took them nearly two years.

The structure of the Service was eventually developed by Dr. Hernán Urzua, the first Director General, who later became Dean of the University of Chile School of Public Health. He comments that those responsible for implementing the legislation were not sure what type of structure would be most appropriate to Chilean circumstances. They reviewed steps taken by other countries, but concluded that foreign experience was not applicable to the Chilean situation. They therefore concentrated on evaluation of plans which they and other Chilean health experts designed. Dr. Urzua and Dr. Abraham Horwitz, now the head of the Pan American Health Organization, finally decided that responsibility for planning and establishment of standards should be separate from that for execution and supervision because of the magnitude of the undertaking and the limited experience of the people who were to operate the programs.

At the national level, a "Normative Sub-Directorate" was created to plan and to determine policy for the Service. Within it were eight subdepartments concerned with Medical Care, Epidemiology, Environmental Health, Health Promotion and Maternal and Child Care, Laboratories, Dentistry, Drugs, and General Technical Services.

The executive branch, called the "Sub-Directorate General," was given responsibility for the effective administration of the Service and for ensuring that the regional levels of the Service adhered to the policies and plans of the normative branch. It had four subdepartments concerned with Personnel, Architecture, Purchasing, and Inspection. Its staff included four inspectors who were to travel around the country to see that the Service was being run properly.

Below the national level, administrative offices were established in each of the 18 "health zones" into which the country was divided. Their major functions were coordination of areas and the provision of consultation for local programs. Below the zones the planners created 80 health centers, each under the direction of an officer trained in public health who was to be responsible for all public health activities and for the operations of all SNS hospitals, clinics, and postas which provided medical services and engaged in health promotion activities. At the time there were 675 such institutions in the country.

According to Dr. Urzua, the structure established for the national level did not work effectively, lack of communication between the policy-making and executive branches constituting a major problem. Another observer commented that the four inspectors were not out in the field often enough to know what was taking place at the lower levels.

Growing dissatisfaction with some of the problems that had arisen in the operation of the Service finally culminated in 1958–59 in what has been termed the "revolt of the clinicians." Different commentators cite different reasons for the revolt, but their conclusions seem to be quite consistent. The time lag of two years between passage of the legislation and development of a formal health service is said to have been an initial irritant to the clinicians. A group of nurses in high administrative posts summarized the situation in the comment: "The public health people ran the system from 1952 to 1958 and irritated the clinicians in the hospitals who blamed them for all the administrative difficulties. Since many physicians were originally unhappy with the SNS, negative attitudes toward the system developed readily."

Among the factors noted by other commentators are the following:

1. In organizing the Service and attempting to cope with various administrative difficulties, the public health professionals lost touch with the clinicians and a divorce between the leaders and the majority of the profession resulted.

2. In an attempt to attract good personnel for the administrative posts of the Service, the administrators' salaries were raised to compensate them for the loss of the additional income clinicians received from private practice. The clinicians' salaries for the portion of time they gave to the Service were not raised, and it is claimed that they were not given an adequate explanation of the reasons for the increase in administrators' salaries.

3. The clinicians were put under rather strict controls for the first time. In an attempt to achieve more efficient operation, administrative controls over such matters as length of hospital stay were instituted. These, it is claimed, alienated the profession. With the increase of administrative activities, particularly in planning and control in the "United States style," the public health administrators became known as the "American boys."

4. Not the least of the difficulties which administrators of the Service faced between 1952 and 1958 was the Chilean President's attempt to use the Service as a political arm of government and to fill its posts with political appointees. As a lever to obtain his way, the President could and often did withhold funds from the Service. This caused further administrative problems for the heads of the SNS.

In 1958, the President of Chile, using his executive power, reorganized the SNS. The major changes were replacement of the Normative Sub-Directorate and Sub-Directorate General by an Administrative Department and a Technical Department at the national level, and substitution of 53 hospital areas for the 80 health center areas as administrative headquarters at the local operating level.

Broad political considerations played a part in the reorganization. The 1958 election returned the conservative party to power, and a medical clinician was appointed Minister of Health. According to Dr. Molina, this conservative government was opposed to certain health service measures as a matter of principle. It did not want sanitary engineers to go into communities to promote self-help projects concerned with potable water, for example, because it thought this tended to encourage activities of a communistic

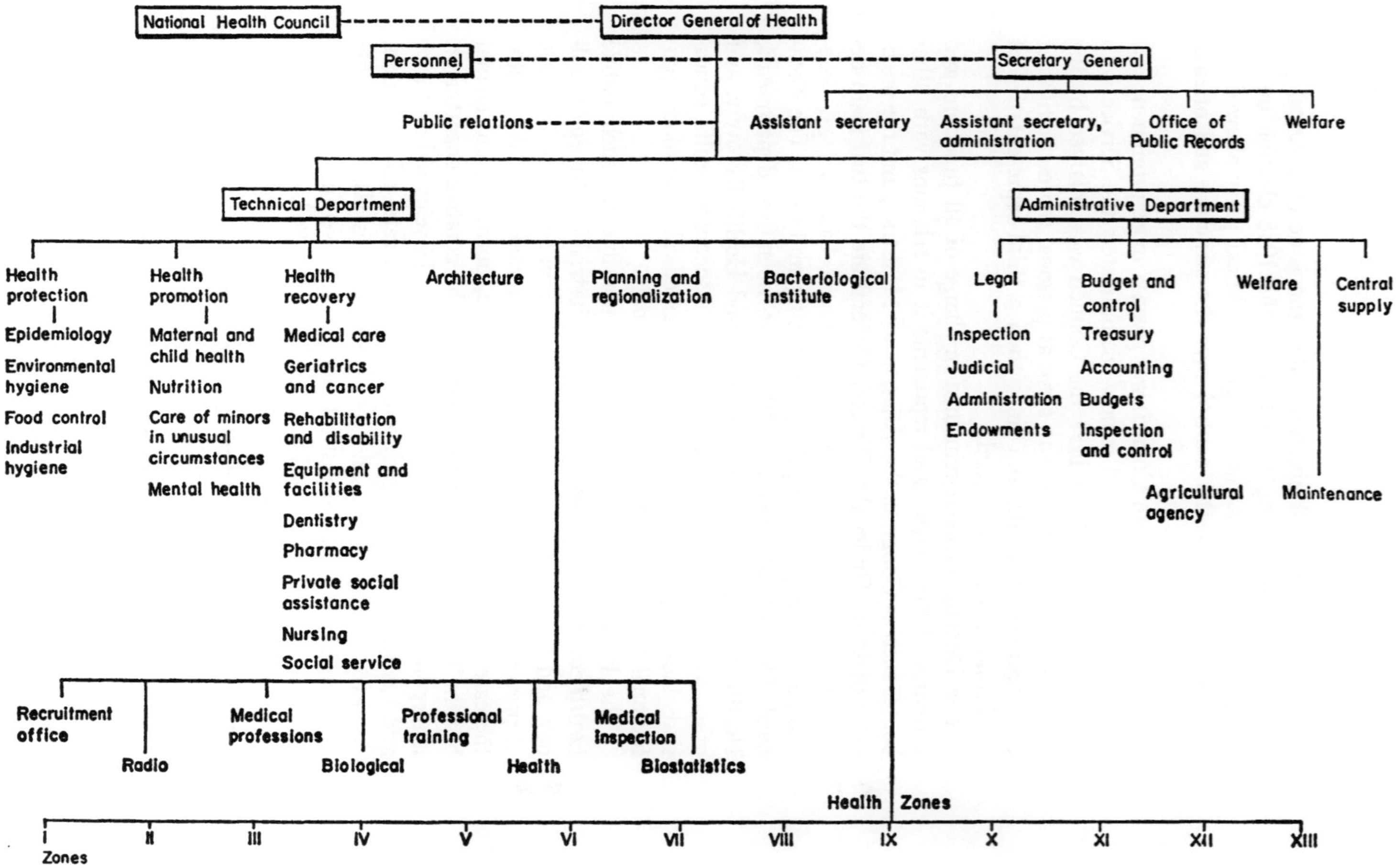

Figure 1. Servicio Nacional de Salud

type. Although not all observers cited the issue of political philosophy when discussing the effects of the 1958 election on the SNS, most agreed that the change of political party allowed the clinicians to gain greater control over the structure and orientation of the Service.

The National Health Council was given a more prominent role by the reorganization, and it now coadministers the Service with the Director General. In 1959 the Council was enlarged by the addition of two members who serve as personal representatives of the President of Chile, and since then a third representative of the President has been added.

The Director General remained in charge of all functions and activities of the Service and represents it in relations with other bodies such as Congress, the Cajas, other Ministries, and the medical profession. Under the Director General are the two main departments. The Administrative Department handles legal problems, accounting and budgeting, purchasing, and so on. The Technical Department contains the major operative departments, Health Protection, Health Promotion, and Health Recovery, and other sections concerned with planning, inspection, health education, biostatistics, the medical and paramedical professions, professional education, architecture, and so on.

The Health Protection section is responsible for such public health concerns as environmental and industrial health, epidemiology, and food control. The Health Promotion section is in charge of preventive measures concerned with maternal and child health, the care of children up to 15 years of age, nutrition, and mental health. The Recovery section, known as the curative department, is responsible for health services for persons 15 years old and over and has within it sections devoted to medical care, rehabilitation, dentistry, drugs, nursing and social service. It is also responsible for control over private institutions having government support, but this function had not been developed by 1963.

All policies and plans for the Servicio Nacional de Salud are determined at the national level. Programs are usually formulated by the heads of the major subdepartments of the Technical Department. Priorities are assigned to these programs and their coordination with the over-all operation of the Service is achieved through the office of the head of the Technical Department, the head of the subdepartment for planning, and a Planning Committee which is composed of the chiefs of the Technical and Administrative Departments and all subdepartment heads. During discussions held in mid-1963, senior personnel of the Service indicated that the basic principles underlying their plans were: an integrated health service; regional planning; orientation toward community public health; and the provision of ambulatory care. Undoubtedly these had been major considerations in the establishment of the SNS ten years earlier.

Although the Technical Department is divided into functional subdepartments, all communications between these subdepartments and lower levels of the Service are expected to go through the office of the head of the Technical Department on a line relationship. Supposedly, there are no communications between the subdepartments and lower levels except on day-to-day matters, all communications coming to the Department head's office, where they are sorted and then sent to the appropriate subdepartment. In fact, however, specialized staff members at the lower levels, such as experts in epidemiology and statistics, usually have direct contacts with their opposite numbers at the national level.

By 1963 the original 18 health zones had been reduced to 13, the major change having been the incorporation into one zone of the four zones that covered Santiago Province. In 1962 the 13 zones ranged in population from 2.5 million inhabitants and a population density of 150 per square kilometer to less than 80,000 inhabitants and a population density of less than one per square kilometer.

The major functions of the zone offices are coordination, consultation, inspection, and control. The zone has further executive duties, such as enforcement of the sanitary law, but in most zones these are not very well developed. The zone office also provides administrative services, particularly in accounting and the design and construction of facilities, for the institutions within it. The exact scope of the activities of any zone office depends very much on the size of the zone and the number and size of the hospital areas it contains.

The 53 hospital areas, each organized around a base hospital, constitute the operative level of the SNS. The hospital areas are set up on a regional basis, with smaller hospitals, polyclinics, medical stations, and postas attached to a base hospital which is also the headquarters for programs of water control, maternal and child health, food control, and distribution of free milk. In large hospital areas the base hospital may also contain sections in epidemiology and industrial hygiene. The director of the base hospital is the head of the hospital area and has ultimate responsibility for all service programs, curative, preventive, and promotive. Programs in which preventive, promotive, and curative activities overlap, such as maternal and child health and obstetrics and pediatrics, are directed by the chief of the relevant clinical service in the hospital. Responsibility for the day-to-day execution of the health prevention and promotion activities is often delegated to an assistant of the chief of service.

Depending on the size of the hospital area, the base hospital may be any one of the four different types, *A*, *B*, *C*, or *D*, into which Chilean hospitals have been classified on the basis of size and facilities. The *A* hospitals, which generally have 500 or more beds, are complete medical centers with a full range of specialties and services. Not all hospital areas have an *A* hospital. The *B* hospitals usually have between 100 and 400 beds and separate services in medicine, surgery, pediatrics, and obstetrics. The professional staff includes four or more physicians as well as dentists. The *C* hospitals have from 30 to 100 beds and at least two physicians, one for medicine and pediatrics and the other for surgery and obstetrics. A fourth type of hospital, the *D* hospital, serves rural areas. The *D* hospitals usually have between 8 and 15 beds and are staffed by a midwife and a practical nurse. Some of the larger *D* hospitals may have 30 beds and a physician on the staff. In 1963 SNS hospitals of these four types contained approximately 29,000 beds, which was close to 80 percent of the total number of beds in the country. In the same year almost 50 percent of all SNS facilities, including hospitals, were operating without either trained nurses or trained auxiliary nursing personnel.

The regional plan of which the base hospital is the core also includes definite schemes for the development of other facilities. In urban areas, where there is a high population density and easy access to hospitals, true ambulatory clinics are being created separate from the hospitals to supplement the facilities of existing hospital outpatient departments. In rural areas, where people travel long distances to reach a hospital, the health stations or postas are equipped with a few beds, mainly for emergency and maternity care.

The changes made in the national structure of the SNS in 1958–59 are rarely discussed today by Chilean authorities, who seem to hold the view that the previous system had not worked well and that the changes produced a better operating structure. Apart from any changes in orientation or philosophy that may have accompanied the organizational change, the new structure has resulted in a simpler and more efficient administration.

The implications of the changes at the local level, which have given the chief local officer responsibility for management of the hospital as well as for all programs of health protection and promotion, are more controversial. Some observers contend that the purpose was simply to remove one level of organization, the health center, so as to decentralize still further the operations of the Service — one of the stated goals for the reorganization. Others believe that the change has meant simply a new title for the local administrator, citing the facts that except in Santiago the health centers were located in hospitals, and that 40 of the 53 heads of hospital areas had formerly been heads of health centers. A former head of the Dirección General de Sanidad, Dr. Rene Garcia, who is now an officer of the Pan American Health Organization, is of the opinion that the transfer of primary responsibility from the health center to the hospital area was intended to achieve, and in fact has produced, a change in emphasis from prevention and promotion to curative medicine.

It is obvious that the area heads are heavily involved in the problems of hospital operation, particularly since they have few professional hospital administrators to help them. Before the reorganization, it is said, there had been considerable conflict between the head of the health center and the heads of hospitals over relative priorities for funds and personnel. Since the reorganization, this conflict has been replaced by a certain amount of resentment on the part of the staffs of the prevention and promotion programs, who feel that their work is being limited by the amount of attention that is given to curative medicine and hospital activities. Some observers now claim, however, that the clinicians who have acquired responsibility for health promotion programs are becoming increasingly aware of the need to prevent illness as a way of reducing the demand for clinical services which are limited by shortages of manpower, facilities, and equipment.

The members of the Faculty of the School of Public Health who are concerned with medical care administration express the following general view on the reorganization:

> The 1958–1959 change meant little to the over-all direction and programs of the SNS. An extra level was cut out of the structure, and, since the health center was an obstruction from the administrative point of view, this was an advantage. The hospital has become, of course, the major activity of the head of the hospital area, and he

cannot spent as much time on public health activities as did the head of the health center. Although many areas have maintained a fair balance between the various preventive, promotive, and curative programs, in other areas health protection and promotion have been forgotten.

Commenting further on the reactions to the reorganization, the nurses quoted earlier said:

> The clinicians began to understand the "why" of bad administration after the 1958–1959 changes. They had felt that once they started running the Service they would do a better job and problems would be minimized. Then they started to ask for more beds, more food, more nurses, and so on, and when the resources were not available to fill their requests, they began to understand the problems of their predecessors.

Operations in an Urban Area

Zone V of the SNS is coterminous with the Province of Santiago. It is the largest health zone in terms of population, covering 2.5 million of the country's eight million population. The zone, which includes the city of Santiago, has rural areas, high-income residential areas, and workers' residence areas. It is estimated that about 20 percent of the zone population live in "mushroom towns," a ring of shanties surrounding the city. About 300,000 of the zone's residents are rural inhabitants.

Zone V has within its organization 2,300 of the country's 4,500 physicians, and approximately 500 of its 1,300 nurses. For every 800 Service beneficiaries the zone is said to have one physician; in the extreme north and south of the country there is said to be one physician for nearly 10,000 beneficiaries.

The zone is divided into nine hospital areas. In 1963 they contained 37 hospitals of which five were type A and eight were type D. The number of beds in the zone ranges by hospital area from under two per 1,000 SNS beneficiaries to over six. The average for the zone is about 4.2 beds per 1,000. The occupancy rate is over 90 percent. Studies have shown that there is a great deal of beneficiary mobility among hospital areas because of the long waiting periods, and that the distribution of use is far more equitable than the distribution of beds. Although most large SNS hospitals contain a limited number of private beds which can be used by the public generally at a daily fee, SNS hospitals in Zone V have few such beds because of the relatively large number of private hospitals in Santiago.

The zone operates 28 medical clinics, 31 maternal and infant health stations, and 45 rural medical stations or postas. A number of the clinics and health stations are housed together; where these provide a full range of diagnostic services they are known as polyclinics. There are 10 of these in the zone. Santiago has half of the nation's 20 polyclinics and most of its 42 maternal and infant stations, but only about 10 percent of its postas.

The budget of Zone V constitutes nearly half of the total SNS budget. In addition to the money the Service spends directly in the Zone, it is indirectly responsible, according to Dr. Ayub, the Zone Director, for the expenditure of a further amount equal to 50 percent of its budget. This, he says, is the amount which SNS beneficiaries spend privately to avoid the long waiting lines and inadequate attention at SNS facilities and to purchase drugs that are not available in the Service. In the past Santiago has demanded and obtained more funds than other SNS zones. Now, under an agreement between the national office and the zone administration, Santiago is supposed to receive an amount calculated on the basis of the average per capita expenditure by the Service throughout the country. The national administration also pays the zone for specialized services given inhabitants of less well equipped zones who have been referred to institutions in Santiago. Dr. Molina, Chief Inspector of Zone V, comments that one of the goals of the national administration is to equalize benefits and services across the country.

Considerable emphasis is placed on the administrative aspects of the Service in Zone V. Discussions with Dr. Ayub suggest that he is far more concerned with issues of planning, priorities, and controls than with the medical aspects of the health service. In his opinion, many of the Service's problems are the result of inept administration. Dr. Ayub himself is widely regarded, with great respect, as an extremely competent administrator. He is also considered to be an administrative tyrant who wages a continuing battle to achieve what he considers to be appropriate for Zone V and the Service.

The zone office has what seems to be a relatively small staff for the magnitude of the operations within the zone. This reflects Dr. Ayub's desire to decentralize administration and authority within the zone, which is consistent with the avowed policy of the national administration. The heads of the zone's hospital areas are generally a stronger and more competent group than area heads in other zones, which has permitted greater delegation of responsibility and a smaller staff at the central zone office. The shortage of qualified staff personnel, the difficulties of the job, and the problems of working for Dr. Ayub were cited as deterrents to the development of a larger staff. Administrative expenses consume about 20 percent of the zone budget.

According to the head of one hospital area, planning at the zone office is excellent even though shortages of personnel and money limit what can be undertaken and accomplished. Dr. Ayub, the heads of the hospital areas, and certain of the technical staff meet weekly for three or four hours and once a year for as many days. At these meetings the needs of the areas as well as current problems and programs are discussed. Program priorities are established and any fights over allocation of resources settled. In addition to the coordination in planning, there is said to be excellent technical coordination — "real back and forth communication and advice with visits by the zone staff." A work team from the zone visits each area for a day or two at a time to review operations, discuss problems, and so on. In the Santiago zone, epidemiologists, statisticians, sanitary engineers, and other technical experts on the staff have direct contact with appropriate technical subdepartments in the national administration and advise and assist the staffs at lower zone levels. In addition, the head nurse in the national administration, the zone head nurse, and hospital area head nurses meet to discuss programs and problems of particular interest to them. This degree of communication and joint planning among the various levels of the Service is peculiar to the Santiago zone, and is possible largely because of the zone's location and size.

While discussing the decentralization of the SNS, Dr. Ayub noted that the objective had been to move authority for program and budget from the Director General to the zones and the hospital areas. He added that his major problem was the difficulty he was having in attempting to give the heads of his hospital areas power over key administrative functions. The national level has in fact delayed the transfer of certain administrative functions, and his hospital area heads, in spite of their generally high caliber, have been afraid to accept them, perhaps in part because SNS regulations stipulate that personnel within the areas report to the hospital area head only on technical questions. On administrative questions they are supposed to report directly to the zone head. When real decentralization is achieved, Dr. Ayub hopes that the area heads will increasingly challenge the allocation of resources among the areas, for he believes that each area should develop its own balanced program in the light of its resources and local problems. The areas within the zone vary, and those that have the greatest problems are those with the least resources.

Dr. Ayub is attempting to decentralize administrative power chiefly by giving the hospital area heads authority to allocate the hospital area budget, to propose personnel for all staff appointments, and to appoint, without consultation, one third of the lowest level staff. Once the spirit of independence is developed, the appropriate role of the zone office, coordination, will become primary, and its functions will be limited to the provision of technical advice, inspection of operations within the hospital areas, and assistance with administrative problems that are beyond the control of area heads. Such matters as problems of environmental sanitation that cross the jurisdictions of lower levels, and the enforcement of protective health legislation, are now handled directly by the zone office and will probably continue to be located there.

The Occidente Hospital Area is one of the hospital areas within the Santiago zone. It includes both urban and rural sections and has a population of 435,682. A good part of the population are low-income wage earners. The SNS is responsible for the medical care of approximately 66 percent of the residents over 15 years of age, or 187,576 persons. The area's base hospital, the 720-bed San Juan de Dios Hospital, is a rather modern *A* hospital and one of Chile's outstanding institutions in terms of size and scope of facilities and services. The area has four other hospitals, one *B*, one *C*, and two *D* hospitals. The *B* hospital, which had been a tuberculosis sanatorium, has 340 beds of which 140 are maternity beds. Seven clinics located apart from the hospitals provide maternal and infant care as well as adult care. Outpatient departments also function at each of the hospitals.

The base hospital provides a full range of inpatient services and operates outpatient clinics in both general medicine and surgery as well as all the major specialties. It is, as well, the center for coordinated medical care for the population of its area and gives selected special services to residents of less well developed hospital areas. Physicians located at the health centers refer patients to the hospital outpatient departments, but only to the general medical or surgical clinics. Even if a patient is to be sent on to the neurology clinic, for example, he is seen first at the general medical clinic. Almost all referred patients are in fact sent on to one of the

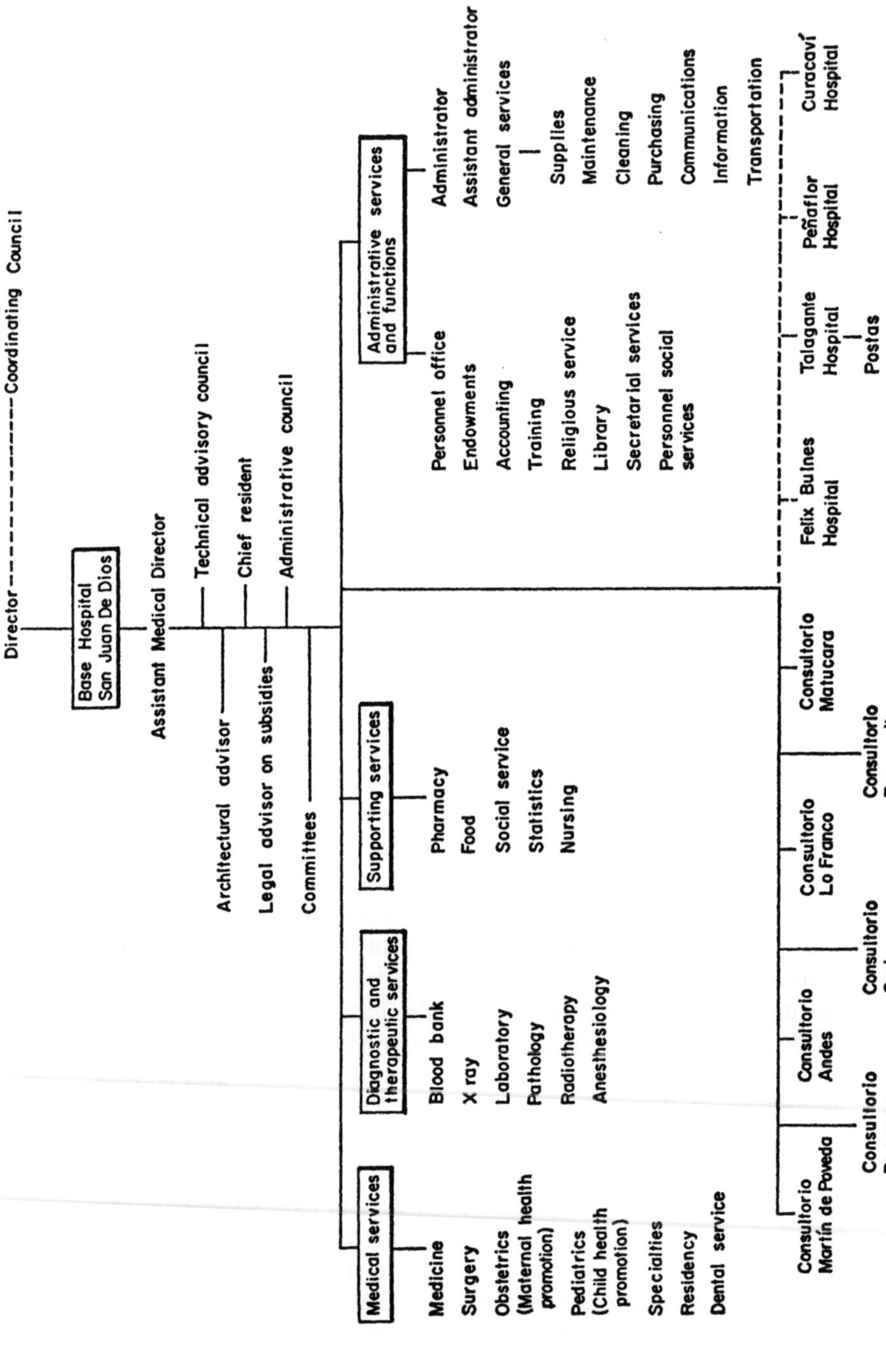

Director
Coordinating Council
Base Hospital San Juan De Dios
Assistant Medical Director
Technical advisory council
Chief resident
Administrative council
Architectural advisor
Legal advisor on subsidies
Committees
Medical services
Medicine
Surgery
Obstetrics (Maternal health promotion)
Pediatrics (Child health promotion)
Specialties
Residency
Dental service
Diagnostic and therapeutic services
Blood bank
X ray
Laboratory
Pathology
Radiotherapy
Anesthesiology
Supporting services
Pharmacy
Food
Social service
Statistics
Nursing
Administrative services and functions
Personnel office
Endowments
Accounting
Training
Religious service
Library
Secretarial services
Personnel social services
Administrator
Assistant administrator
General services
Supplies
Maintenance
Cleaning
Purchasing
Communications
Information
Transportation
Consultorio Martín de Poveda
Consultorio Barrancas
Consultorio Andes
Consultorio Garin
Consultorio Lo Franco
Consultorio Roosevelt
Consultorio Matucara
Felix Bulnes Hospital
Talagante Hospital
Postas
Peñaflor Hospital
Curacaví Hospital

specialty clinics for diagnosis. On a rotating basis the heads of the specialty services in the hospital act as coordinator of the work of the general medical clinic and of the various specialty services. Even though hospital specialists in certain fields, such as gynecology, hold sessions at the health centers on specified days, there is very little contact between the physicians who staff the hospital outpatient clinics and the physicians in the health centers. Limited dental services (confined for the most part to extractions) are available at the hospital. The base hospital is also the headquarters for all public health activities in the area.

Before 1960 most medical care in the area was given at the base hospital, and the demand for services greatly exceeded the institution's ability to provide care. With the conversion of the tuberculosis sanatorium into a general hospital, and the incorporation of ambulatory services for adults into the activities of health stations formerly confined to maternal and child care, more of the ambulatory care is being provided outside San Juan de Dios Hospital. Nevertheless, in 1963 it was reported that "about 1500 to 1900 patients a day are seen there, a load far exceeding its physical capacity." [4] Chilean observers often cite this area's experience to show the tremendous increase in demand for medical services which is taking place in Chile. In 1962, however, it was estimated that the adult population of the area made an average of one and one half visits to a clinic annually.

In this hospital area, as in one other, an experiment in the provision of personal care is being carried out. Instead of going to any center they choose and simply waiting to see whatever physician happens to be free, patients are being assigned to particular health centers as well as to particular physicians to whom they should go whenever they need care. Adults are assigned to internists, who would have a total list of no more than 1,200 to 1,500 assigned patients for each two hours they work for the Service. Children are assigned to pediatricians who would have a smaller total list since the patient load is based on an estimated utilization of two visits annually by adults and five visits annually by children. Physicians working with assigned patient lists do not follow the rule generally applied in the Service that physicians are to see no more than seven patients per hour. Under the beneficencia system physicians had been required to see 30 patients per hour. To date there has been a favorable reaction to the experimental system. Beneficiaries approve because the physician is

4. Roemer, p. 211

more readily available to them and they spend less time waiting to see him. The physicians like the arrangement because they have the patients' medical records available and can get to know them.

The Occidente Hospital Area was the site of one of the early experiments with a unified health service and continues to have a strong orientation toward public health activities, particularly maternal and child health care. The area also has major programs in environmental sanitation and communicable disease control and is developing a special tuberculosis control program.

San Juan de Dios Hospital operates both general and special pediatric outpatient clinics and has inpatient sections for the newborn, infants, preschool children, and children with infectious diseases. The area also has seven maternal and child health centers where clinics are held for ill and well babies. It is estimated that 80 percent of the infants in the area are under the care of the child health program.

During their first year children are supposed to be seen in a well baby clinic ten times: four times by a physician and the other times by a nurse or an auxiliary. The Service obtains a high level of participation because family allowances and milk for infants are given only to the mothers who bring their children to the clinic. In addition, since about 80 percent of the births in the area take place in hospital, the Service has a list of most infants which can be used to assure that the children are brought in for vaccination and general supervision. The lists are sent to the clinic of the area from which the mother came, and an auxiliary visits the home if the child is not brought to the clinic. The well-baby clinics, as they are called, in fact provide care for many ill children. At one time the pediatricians felt that they should see only children who were well, but this was considered unrealistic. As one pediatrician noted, "When you have an infant mortality of over 100 it's pretty hard to run well-baby clinics." The infant mortality was 86.8 per 1,000 live births in the area during 1962. The rates for the thirteen zones in the country range from 63 to 156. The death rate in the under-one-month age group is 24.8 per 1,000 births in Occidente. The general mortality was 11 in Occidente in 1962.

The head of pediatrics at the base hospital is the head of child health activities in the area, and since San Juan de Dios is a teaching hospital, he is also a member of the teaching faculty. He is responsible for services in the hospital and in the seven maternal and child health centers.

Working under him is a specialist in public health who is in charge of the clinics and the newborn service. The assistant chief, in discussing the goal of the program, said, "Our hope is to increase the number of centers and the amount of care given in them to reduce morbidity and in turn the demand on hospital beds. We are very short of inpatient facilities. Of course, this is just theory, and no matter how much we do on an outpatient basis it really won't reduce the demand to a level where we can meet it. We need more beds."

The maternal care program is separate from the infant services although both are a part of the area's Health Promotion Section. When a woman is pregnant she is first seen by a physician in a clinic. Then she is scheduled to see a midwife three times and to have a final visit with a physician. As has been noted, most women are sent to the hospital for delivery, and it is not unusual to find two patients in each maternity bed. In Occidente physicians are always available during deliveries, and all Caesarean sections and forceps deliveries are handled by a specialist. By law mothers are supposed to be given milk from their fifth month of pregnancy, but because of shortages in the area this was not being done in 1963. It is estimated that 70 percent of the expectant mothers in the area are under the care of the maternal and child health program.

Most of the physicians work six hours per day for the SNS. They generally greatly prefer hospital work, and especially ward assignment, and it is often difficult to get them to accept clinic assignments. The pediatricians in this area, however, usually rotate between hospital and clinic once or twice a year or work three hours per day in each. In the past there was said to be one physician hour per bed per day in the medical service at the base hospital. With the increased emphasis on coordinated preventive and curative activities geared to the local community, the physicians more readily accept clinic assignments and the staff time in the hospital has been reduced.

Operations in a Rural Area

Zone X of the SNS is located in the south of Chile about 500 miles from Santiago. It includes two provinces, Malleco and Cautín, and covers approximately 12,000 square miles. The zone had a population of somewhat over 600,000 in 1962, and the zone office estimates that it is responsible for the health care of 80 percent of this population. A large segment of the population, estimated at between 120,000 and 150,000 persons, are Indians. Cautín, the more southerly of the two provinces, is the center of Indian life in Chile.

Many of the Indians have land holdings of moderate size on which they raise sheep, preferring this to farming. They live in a primitive style, but the government has recently begun to replace their thatched roof huts with more modern dwellings in an attempt to improve their living conditions. The Indians' present health problems differ from those of the other inhabitants of the zone. They are less likely to use the Service for maternal and child health care and have a much higher maternal and infant mortality. They also have a much higher incidence of infectious disease. On the other hand, Chilean physicians claim that there is conclusive proof that the Indians are free of arteriosclerosis at the present time.

In Temuco, a city of 130,000 population and the major city of the south, some 75 percent of the people are said to have potable water. In the rural areas of the zone, it is estimated that less than 20 percent of the population has safe water. In 1963 the United Nations Children's Fund and the SNS were cooperating in a program of well drilling to improve the water supply.

The zone is divided into four hospital areas. Three are relatively small, their combined populations amounting to 300,000 persons. The large area, which includes most of the province of Cautín, is based in Temuco. The other areas are based in cities of 14,000 to 20,000 persons. The base hospital in Temuco is an A hospital; two of the areas have *B* hospitals as their base and one has a C hospital as the base. The zone has a total of 21 hospitals (one A, two *B*, seven C and eleven *D* hospitals) and 35 postas affiliated with the hospitals. Currently 12 hospitals are under construction in the zone. Some of these are additional facilities but others will replace outdated institutions.

The number of physicians in the zone is said to have increased by 50 during the last four or five years and to have reached 150 in 1963. In the Temuco area there are now 70 instead of 30 physicians, only five of whom work outside the SNS. Of the approximately 30 nurses in the zone, all but a few are with the SNS. The zone staff includes two physicians, one of whom is the director, a pharmacist, lawyer, veterinarian, social worker, nurse, civil engineer, and two sanitary inspectors. One person handles industrial hygiene activities in Zone X and its adjoining zone.

There is no epidemiologist. The budget for the entire zone was 3.5 million escudos in 1963. (In 1963, the exchange rate between escudos and dollars ranged from Es. 2.7 to Es. 3.5 per U.S. dollar.)

The Temuco Hospital, the base hospital for the Temuco Hospital area, is a new 550-bed institution which offers most health services, including a psychiatric clinic, but which is not equipped with units for neurosurgery, tuberculosis, or cancer. There are 25 private beds in the hospital. The only large X-ray unit in the zone is in the Temuco Hospital; the hospital also has a small chest X-ray unit but, in July of 1963, no X-ray plates had been available in six months. The Temuco Hospital provides patients from other hospital areas in the zone with laboratory and X-ray services, as well as specialized medical and surgical services.

The present Temuco Hospital replaced a small but relatively adequate old building which it is hoped will eventually be used for rehabilitation, cancer, and tuberculosis units. Construction of the new hospital was started in 1954 and finished in 1962. In 1963 there was an explosion in the boiler room which made it necessary to close part of the hospital. In July 1963, the hospital was without heat or hot water, and was functioning only partially because of the lack of equipment. None of the sterilizing equipment had arrived, and only two of the seven planned operating rooms were in use. The recovery room was not in operation and much laboratory equipment was still missing.

The hospital operates general clinics in surgery, obstetrics, pediatrics, and medicine that are staffed by general practitioners. A clerk asks patients for their symptoms, and then sends them to one of the four clinics. A limited history on the patient is kept and given to the physician when he sees the patient. Special clinics are held in urology, ophthalmology, psychiatry, cardiology, and neurology. In the general clinics about 200 patients per day are seen, and in the special clinics about 60 are seen per day.

The hospital area is divided into six sectors, each with one or more hospitals and postas. In all, the area has 12 hospitals and 25 postas, as well as two maternal and child health centers in the city of Temuco.

The staff of the protection section in the hospital area included two sanitary engineers, a veterinarian, a civil engineer, and seven sanitary inspectors in 1963. The core staff of the promotion section, which is concerned primarily with maternal and child health care, consisted of three nurses and 28 auxiliaries. Preventive health activities consist largely of vaccinations against whooping cough, tetanus, diphtheria, and typhus, and of food inspection and control. In 1963 an adjoining hospital area in the zone which was based in a 145-bed *B* hospital in a city of 20,000 population had, for administration and operation of all programs, a staff of seven physicians, five dentists, four midwives, five nurses, two pharmacists, two social workers, one dietician, three sanitary inspectors, and 51 auxiliaries.

About 20 minutes south of Temuco on the Pan American highway is a 14-bed *D* hospital. The hospital is an unheated frame building that serves approximately 5,000 persons from a small village and the surrounding countryside. The hospital's beds are usually fully occupied. One physician lives in the village and sees ambulatory patients at the hospital in the morning and afternoon. The hospital itself is manned by auxiliaries and a midwife. A dentist visits the hospital three days a week. Dental services are generally limited to extractions, although a small amount of restorative work is said to be done for children.

Another fifteen minutes farther south there is a thirty-year-old *D* hospital which has 32 beds, a delivery room, and a minor surgery room. It has no separate facilities for patients with infectious diseases, of whom there may be quite a few, and no laboratory facilities. The most seriously ill patients are sent to the Temuco Hospital. There are three or four deliveries per week at the hospital, which holds maternal and child health clinics as well as a general clinic. The head of pediatrics from the hospital area visits this hospital, as well as others in the area, periodically to check on the service provided to children. A dentist also holds several sessions at the hospital each week.

A new hospital is being constructed next to the old *D* hospital. Designed to contain 24 beds under ideal conditions, it can and will contain 36 beds. It will have four isolation rooms, an operating room, predelivery, delivery, and postdelivery rooms, central sterilizing facilities, and a laboratory. Residences for a physician, a midwife, and a nurse — the primary staff — are being included. The hospital is a single-storied, extremely modern, rather expensive unit. The walls are tile and ceramic, and in the center of the hospital is a glass-enclosed winter garden. In mid-1963 the hospital had been under construction for three and a half years and was expected to take another year. Three other hospitals of almost identical design are under construction in the zone.

In the rural area the posta is the primary health unit. Most are manned by an auxiliary, with one year of training, who lives at the site. Teams consisting of a physician, a nurse, and a midwife from the hospitals visit these units once a week or once every second week to hold clinics. The SNS green flag is flown at the posta when the physician is present just as the village stores fly a red flag when there is fresh meat and a white one when there is fresh bread. In the most isolated rural areas some of the postas are manned on a part-time basis by volunteers, usually the local school teacher, from the community.

The infant mortality rate (deaths under one year) in the Temuco Hospital Area is almost 200 per 1,000 live births. The director of the area stated, "Our biggest problem is maternal and child health. Because of lack of education, fear of hospitals, and a poor economic situation we have very high infant and maternal mortality." Hospital deliveries account for 80 percent of the estimated births in the City of Temuco and 30 percent in the rural areas. Most deliveries are expected to take place in the smaller hospitals. Only women who live locally or who have special problems are supposed to be delivered in the base hospital which has 60 maternity beds. The mothers are now kept two days instead of the planned four days because of a shortage of beds, but the area director has said, "Our hospital is so nice that the mothers don't want to go home." The average length of stay for adults and children in the Temuco Hospital is eighteen days. The long stays reflect the poor facilities for care in the homes as well as the fact that the patients, living in rural areas distant from the hospital and afraid of it, come to the hospital only when they are in serious condition.

It is estimated that about 40 percent of the infants in Temuco and only 10 to 20 percent of the infants in the rural sections of the hospital area are under child health care. In Temuco the maternal and child health clinics are separate from the other clinics. Approximately 260 children per day are seen in the three child health clinics in the city. The clinics have much the same program, including number of visits, as those in the Santiago zone, but the child is seen by a physician less often. Physicians assigned to maternal and child health care practice both in the separate health centers and in the hospitals. In rural areas the clinics are mixed, and general services provided on a first-come, first-served basis.

The director of the hospital area, who is trained in public health, commented on a number of interesting problems while discussing the operations of her area and of the SNS. Her comments are summarized below:

One of our real problems is that the doctors and nurses are so well prepared that they can't be sent to the rural areas to practice. Every year our physicians are better and better trained. The older doctors are broader in their practice. What we need are two-year nurses to do public health work. With more nurses we could get improvements, especially in public health measures. In Temuco we have only 20 nurses to 70 physicians.

The shift to an integrated plan based in a hospital has limited our ability to take care of public health. We now are heavily committed to operating the hospitals and cannot really do the public health job. Before, we at least had nurses and doctors working mainly in public health. The pendulum has swung from all public health to all hospital. Interestingly the doctors are becoming more oriented toward public health now, especially the pediatricians. The physicians who work in the field are much more involved in public health activities than the hospital staff.

The concept behind the zone organization, and one of the reasons for removing the health center level from between the zone and the hospital levels, was decentralization. However, such matters as employment and budget, and policies concerning particular public health measures, which should be handled at the zone, are still handled nationally. Many of these involve problems which should be adjusted to local conditions. There is no real decentralization. Furthermore, the SNS regulation that local staff report to the zone office on administrative matters but to the hospital area head on technical matters causes considerable operating problems. Frequently administrative and technical matters are intertwined, and whether a particular problem is an administrative or a technical one is sometimes a matter of opinion.

The director of Zone X commented that the change to hospital-based administration has benefited the Service. By removing a level of administration it has made the SNS more dynamic. Now the zone director is in direct contact with the operating units and the job is more action-oriented. The hospitals and zone director now work together more than they did. In discussing the goals of the Service and the increased emphasis on curative medicine that may have followed the 1959 reorganization, the director stated that his zone in fact has an integrated health service with no lack of balance among the program areas. The nurse and midwife, he stated, are the promoters of health. "The physician has turned these duties, vaccination, education, and so on, over to them."

Other Health Services

By law the Minister of Health of Chile is responsible for all health care in the country except the services provided to the members of the armed forces and the police (a national rather than local force in Chile). Probably close to 70 percent of the country's population is eligible for services from the Servicio Nacional de Salud. The balance receives varying amounts of care through one of the 49 other health services in Chile, or purchases care privately.

The majority of these other organized health care programs is based on type of employment and was developed after the passage in 1937 of the Preventive Medicine Law directed against tuberculosis, syphilis, cardiovascular diseases and cancer. Among the separate systems are those for bank employees (20,000 primary beneficiaries), white collar employees (500,000 primary beneficiaries), race track employees, and railroad employees. Many of the services provide only ambulatory care, and there is usually a slight charge. Under a legal provision authorizing the Minister of Health to return the social security contribution for medical care to industrial employers who spend at least as much on health services for their employees as would the SNS, and who report to and allow inspection by the SNS, separate services are maintained for such groups as mining and petroleum workers who often are located in isolated sections of the country.

Servicio Médico Nacional de Empleados

When the Preventive Medicine Law was passed, white collar employees of the government who were members of a Caja de Empleados Públicos had a small medical service which offered care primarily through a clinic in Santiago. Under a separate Caja, employees of retail merchants could go to three or four designated physicians in Santiago for care. White collar employees of other private companies, although covered by a Caja de Empleados Particulares, had no medical services. Following passage of the law, the medical programs for employees of government and retail merchants were expanded, and a program was created to provide members of the Caja de Empleados Particulares with the services it required. In 1942 the three medical services were united in the Servicio Médico Nacional de Empleados (SMNE), but each of the employee groups receives only the benefits provided by their former services. Thus, although all member employees are eligible for the services required by the Preventive Medicine Law, which include examinations and both outpatient and inhospital treatment for the specified diseases, curative care, limited to clinic care, is available only to employees of government and merchants.

The SMNE has about 500,000 primary beneficiaries for the required preventive services, and close to 1.5 million secondary beneficiaries (wives and children under 15) for additional maternal and child health care and vaccinations. Approximately half of this group is eligible for clinic care. Some 75 percent of the beneficiaries live in the cities of Santiago and Valparaíso. The contribution to the SMNE for employees who receive only preventive care is 5.25 percent of their salaries and is shared by employer and employee. The contribution is somewhat higher for employees who receive curative services.

The SMNE has separate cadres of physicians for the preventive and curative services. Usually the physicians give two hours per day to the Service. In mid-1963 approximately 300 physicians and 83 nurses were affiliated with the SMNE.

The examinations required by the Preventive Medicine Law are given at 16 locations. In several cities the SMNE maintains its own clinics, but in other locations it contracts with private physicians whom it pays according to an established fee schedule. Beneficiaries who suspect that they may have one of the diseases specified in the law visit a physician on the preventive roster for an examination that includes a chest X ray, blood pressure reading, serological examination, and a limited physical examination and medical history. Beneficiaries are said to have become quite sophisticated in their knowledge of the symptoms of the covered diseases. Should they be found to have a specified disease, they are given complete care at no cost at one of the SMNE's nine outpatient clinics or four hospitals, or from private practitioners and hospitals under contract with the Service. They are also reimbursed for any salary lost because of the illness.

Although all employees are supposed to have the preventive examination annually, it is estimated that only 12 percent of the SMNE beneficiaries actually come to the preventive physicians for this purpose. Those who do come are for the most part employees who require a certificate of health to obtain a new position or a bank loan. A smaller proportion of the workers covered by the Servicio Nacional de Salud are said to have this examination annually.

The two groups of SMNE beneficiaries who are also eligible for curative care may visit physicians on the curative roster and receive ambulatory care for any illness. A charge of 600 pesos (about 21 cents in 1963) is made for each visit to a clinic, and there are further small charges for diagnostic procedures and drugs.

SMNE beneficiaries usually use the private beds of SNS hospitals for inpatient care for diseases other than those covered by the Preventive Medicine Law and pay all the costs themselves. They can obtain loans from the SMNE to cover such hospital bills. Although the SMNE maintains four hospitals, three are specialized institutions for the treatment of the specified diseases. The fourth is a small general hospital which was recently constructed in Valparaíso and which will admit beneficiaries for all types of care if they pay part of the cost as well as the physicians' fees. A similar general hospital is being planned for Santiago.

The SMNE has developed an extensive program for expectant mothers and infants in which the only charge made is for any drugs that are prescribed. The program includes care and immunizations for children up to seven years of age. The child care program was started as a preventive service offered through well-baby clinics, but was expanded to include curative services since it was decided that mothers should not have to take their children elsewhere for care when they were ill. In theory the child care consists of visits with a physician at 15 to 30 days after birth, at three-month intervals thereafter until the child is one year old, and then at six-month intervals until the child is seven. Auxiliaries — nurses and midwives — give care only when physicians are absent on an emergency. In addition, the children are supposed to be brought in periodically for weighing and a general check-up by a nurse. When children are not brought in, a nurse is sent to the home. The nurse is also supposed routinely to visit the homes of beneficiaries at least twice a year primarily for purposes of health education. She may administer vaccinations during these visits.

Studies made by the staff of the SMNE indicate that, on the average, there are fewer premature births among SMNE beneficiaries than among SNS beneficiaries, that infant mortality is lower, and that children of SMNE beneficiaries develop faster. Approximately 80 percent of the children of SMNE beneficiaries are under routine care.

Like the SNS, the SMNE provides full maternity care for working women, and salary reimbursement for six weeks before and six weeks after delivery. Wives of employees are given free maternity care, but receive no payment beyond the family allowance paid after the birth of children. Currently the SMNE is planning to establish a birth control clinic for which it has obtained financial support from a voluntary organization in the United States.

In 1963 the budget of the SMNE was 22.5 million escudos. In 1960, when the budget was approximately 18 million escudos, the SMNE provided 222,470 medical consultations and 134,000 preventive consultations. Approximately 157,000 laboratory tests were performed, about two thirds by the preventive service, and 95,000 units of dental care were given.

Many SMNE beneficiaries, particularly the government employees, have organized "sickness clubs" to help finance medical services, both because not all services are available to them under the SMNE and because shortages of personnel and facilities make it difficult for them to obtain the benefits that are provided. Ordinarily these clubs are financed wholly by contributions from the employees, but in a few instances the government also contributes. The clubs are not compulsory. The leaders of the SMNE apparently consider them an aid to the Service and welcome their existence until the Service can provide more benefits. At present shortages of manpower and facilities limit the further expansion of SMNE services.

Many of the administrative personnel of the SMNE favor an alteration of the law which established it to permit integration of the preventive and curative services and an extension of curative services to the one group — employees of commercial establishments — which now has only preventive benefits. A bill which would accomplish some of these aims was awaiting the President's signature in mid-1963. The proposed legislation would authorize the extension of curative services to this group of employees through the use of private practitioners chosen by the beneficiaries. The costs would be shared by the beneficiaries, their Caja, and the SMNE. About 40 percent of the nation's physicians had agreed to accept the minimum fees listed in the Colegio Médico's fee schedule for service under the proposed program should the bill become law.

There has been considerable interest in and discussion of the possibilities of integrating the SMNE with the SNS. The director of maternal and child health of the SMNE, Dr. Bustamante, has pointed out, however, that "Although there has been considerable talk about an integration, the SNS cannot take us over because our beneficiaries are very status-conscious and do not want to be associated with workers. Our groups are very powerful politically, and will not permit an integration of the two services."

Medical Practice

All Chilean physicians are required by law to belong to the Colegio Médico, the professional association, whose activities include the establishment of a fee schedule for private patients, review of grievances relating to cost and quality, and the holding of professional meetings. Another medical group, the Federación Médica, is also active and is, supposedly, a dissident group which represents physicians' interests in negotiations with the Minister of Health and the various health services concerning such matters as salary schedules and the eligibility of beneficiaries.

Ninety-eight percent of all Chilean physicians are employed by a health service — approximately 75 percent by the SNS and the remainder by one of the other services. Physicians are allowed to work for only one service, even when they are employed on a part-time basis. From 60 to 70 percent of the country's physicians also have some private practice, but only about 30 percent are said to make a significant income from private patients. It is estimated, however, that in Santiago some 30 percent of the physicians earn as much privately as from a service.

Except for those on the administrative staffs, physicians work no more than six hours per day for a service and many work less. In 1962 the basic pay for the six hours per day was 300 escudos per month in the SNS. All physicians practicing in rural areas receive a bonus of from 30 to 100 percent of the basic salary depending on the remoteness of the area, and general practitioners in rural areas receive one and one half times the rural practice bonus. In addition, SNS physicians achieve a 20 percent increase every five years. Administrative personnel receive a minimum of an additional 30 percent over basic salary for the extra two hours they work per day but are allowed no private practice. Consideration is being given to revision of the usual salary arrangements for the physicians participating in the experiments with assigned patients so that they are compensated according to the size of their patient lists. The average SNS physician is earning a little more than 400 escudos per month as basic salary. After 30 years of service the professional physician, dentist, or pharmacist retires at the full current pay of active professionals.

In private practice the minimum fee is four escudos for an office visit and six to eight escudos, depending on the distance, for home visits. A physician with ten years of experience and some training in the United States might receive ten escudos for an office visit and 15 escudos for a home visit. Physicians apparently fall into the upper middle or possibly the lower upper income groups in Chile. Landowners and businessmen constitute the upper income groups in Chile. Many professionals are members of these families and have some outside income.

The original SNS salary schedule established in 1952 substantially improved physicians' incomes. Over the years, however, physicians' pay became relatively lower as the yearly adjustments in salary schedules failed to compensate for the inflation that was taking place. Pressure grew for a larger increase. Since professional salaries and conditions of employment are governed by a law passed in 1952, any change in salary schedules requires an Act of Congress and none was passed. In 1961 the physicians, working through the Federación Médica, attempted to pressure the SNS and the Ministry of Health into giving an increase which the Minister of Health is said to have promised. When no action was taken the physicians instituted a pen strike, refusing to fill out any forms, which continued for three months without government action. On May 18, 1962, the physicians decided to withhold medical services, manning facilities and giving emergency care but refusing to carry out normal duties. The strike continued for three weeks, and the public generally seemed to support the physicians. The demand for services was said to have declined, and it was thought that the health of the public had not been adversely affected. A salary increase was then promised by the Minister of Health and voted by the Congress. The Federación Médica had demanded a 90 percent increase in salaries while the government offered 40 percent. The final settlement increased base salaries by between 65 and 70 percent. In spite of the increase, the physicians in 1963 were supposed to be relatively worse off in terms of vital wage and purchasing power than when the SNS was established in 1952.

In discussing the necessity of a strike to obtain a salary increase, a number of observers pointed out that in Chile, as in many other Latin American countries, the strike is the only force to which politicians react. Strikes therefore become an overused economic weapon.

The low salaries paid physicians by the SNS and other services, and the physicians' consequent need for private practice, are said to be the underlying reasons for the limit of six hours per day that physicians work for a service. Under the beneficencia system, where most physicians had been employed, the pay had been quite low and physicians therefore began to see private patients on salary time. The physicians' need for private practice as a supplement to their still relatively low salaries is cited as one reason for the nondevelopment of a comprehensive national health service for all Chileans.

Today Chilean physicians are said to be taking a stronger stand against any further extension of prepaid curative services on any basis other than free choice of physician and adherence to the Colegio Médico fee schedule. One observer commented, however, that "Many people are medically indigent or in even worse economic circumstances. Physicians prefer not to have to charge these people for service or to attempt to collect fees from them. That is why Chilean physicians are not really opposed to socialized medicine."

There are three medical schools in Chile: at the University of Chile and the Catholic University of Chile, both in Santiago, and at the University of Concepción in the south. The University of Chile also offers the first two years of medical school in Valparaíso. Entrance to medical school is by competitive examination, and scholarships are available for those who require financial assistance. According to one estimate, 25 percent of the medical students are from upper-class families, 40 percent from middle-class families and 35 percent from the lower class. After graduation from high school the student has five years of medical school and one year of internship. The first two years consist of basic science studies. The third year is split between basic science study and clinical study. The last two years consist primarily of clinical study. In total, about 180 physicians are graduated each year. By historical precedent the University of Chile has the right to license physicians, and each year appoints a committee to design and administer the licensing examination to graduates of the three medical schools.

Medical education is said to be changing slowly. The Medical School at Concepción has altered its program and now teaches considerably more preventive medicine, the course beginning in the first year and continuing throughout the five years. At the University of Chile only a small amount of preventive medicine is taught and this is in the last year. Students from Concepción do less well in the licensing examination than the students from the other schools.

Consideration has been given to a shortening of the medical course and the creation of new medical schools as a means of providing more physicians to staff the rural areas. According to Dr. Urzua, these changes have been opposed by the Faculty of Medicine of the University of Chile.

Since 1956 physicians have been required to work for the SNS in a rural area at some time after graduation from medical school. A graduate may obtain a fellowship to specialize for a period of two or three years, but at the end of that period he must work for the SNS in the provinces for two years before he is free to seek employment elsewhere. A second choice is to take a two-year specialty program in internal medicine and pediatrics or surgery and obstetrics and then to take a post for two years in a *C* hospital of the SNS. A third alternative is to take a six-month to one-year residency in a major city hospital, studying largely obstetrics and pediatrics, and to become a general physician in a large *D* hospital or a small *C* hospital. After several years these physicians can return to one of the major hospitals (usually in Santiago) to specialize.

A clinician who is a faculty member of the Univerisity of Chile, like many other public health personnel in Chile, comments that the medical schools are not training physicians for mass or rural medicine but rather are turning out high level clinicians who are used to working with all of the instruments and advantages of modern technology — most of which are available only in the largest hospitals. In addition, these physicians dislike working in the consultorios where most cases are quite routine. They feel that they are prepared for better things and become frustrated in their work. The young physicians also have financial problems, it is said. Although it is difficult for them to make a living without private practice, the hours they must work for the SNS make it hard for them to practice privately.

The requirement of practice in rural areas, the bonus for all physicians in rural practice, and the extra 50 percent bonus given general practitioners in rural areas are intended to help correct the inequalities in physician-population ratio throughout the country. Although they are said to have brought about significant changes in the distribution of physicians, rural areas are still largely without physicians' services. One report referred to by Roemer states that the urban-rural distribution of physicians did not change between 1952 and 1959.[5] The large number of young physicians found practicing in rural areas in 1963 suggests that some progress is now being made in redistributing physicians.

Financing of Health Care

Total expenditures for medical care services constituted 4.9 percent of the Gross National Product of Chile in 1958 according to the study by Griffin, Hurtado, and Paz. Approximately two thirds of total expenditure was by government and the balance by the private sector of the economy. In the same year per capita expenditure for health services was, in United States dollars, $19.70 and per capita income was $340.

It is estimated that total national expenditure on health increased at least 90 percent in real terms during the period 1945–1958. The private sector's share increased 42 percent in real terms, while the share expended by the government increased 166 percent in real terms and approximately 100 percent per capita.

Expenditures for health constitute 9.8 percent of total public expenditures, and are the fourth largest item in the government budget. Larger amounts are spent for public welfare and security, transportation and communications, and national defense. An approximately equal amount is spent on education. The proportion of the total government budget spent for health services has fluctuated over time, but has remained fairly steady since 1953.

Two major health services, the Servicio Nacional de Salud and the Servicio Médico Nacional de Empleados, receive 82.7 percent of the government's expenditures for health. The balance goes to other health services, such as those for the armed forces, the police, railway workers, and so on, and for small miscellaneous items. Current operating expenses account for 72 percent of total government expenditures, salaries constituting 43 percent and purchase of goods and services 29 percent. Transfer payments for such items as maternity and sickness benefits, and subsidies to private philanthropic institutions, account for about 20 percent of total expenditures, and investment, including the costs of hospital construction and three fourths of the cost of professional training,

5. Roemer, p. 232.

is 7.3 percent of total expenditure. In other sectors of government expenditure, the average proportion devoted to investment is 18.2 percent.

In the private sector about 90 percent of total expenditures go to persons classified as independent professionals — physicians, dentists, nurses, and so on. It is estimated that manual workers spend 12 percent of personal disposable income on health care while white collar employees spend 4.2 percent and the self-employed 3.2 percent.

Servicio Nacional de Salud

The Servicio Nacional de Salud receives 75 percent of total government funds for health services. In 1963, when approximately three escudos equaled one United States dollar, the operating budget of the SNS was 157 million escudos, the capital budget was 3.5 million escudos, and the equipment import budget was, in United States dollars, $500,000. The total budget represented an increase of approximately 28.6 million escudos over the 1962 budget. In 1954, the first full year in which the Service had been operating, the budget was between 5 and 6 million escudos. Currently the budgets of the three major programs of the Service, as a proportion of the total budget, are 46 percent for Recovery, 21 percent for Promotion, and 2 percent for Protection. Almost one third of the Promotion budget is used to provide milk for infants and mothers.

The SNS has three major sources of funds. The central government provides funds for the salaries of SNS employees, which amounts to about half of the total budget, plus an amount that is supposed to be 5 percent of the salaries of the workers covered by the Caja de Seguro Obrero. The Caja, which is the second major source of SNS funds, is supposed to give the SNS 4.5 percent of the workers' salaries. Payments by the Caja have declined from over 30 percent of the Service's budget in the period 1954–1958 to less than 15 percent in 1960, 1961, and 1962. The amount transferred by the Caja was about 2.5 million escudos in 1954, rose steadily to about 18 million escudos in 1958, declined to 12 million in 1959, and has since been increasing slowly. It was about 20 million escudos in 1962. The third major source of SNS income is money derived from private patients, services sold, and holdings and endowments which the Service inherited from the beneficencias. This income totaled about 16 million escudos in 1962, of which about a third was patient fees. Other minor sources of income and the contribution for the Merchant Marine brought the SNS about 7 million escudos in 1962.

Theoretically, the budget of the SNS is supposed to be prepared on the basis of the Service's major programs. Each hospital area prepares a budget, usually for the six basic programs — administration, epidemiology, sanitation, maternal and child health, medical care, and dental care. In some areas food control and industrial hygiene are presented as separate budget items. At the zone office the hospital budgets are revised and combined into a zone budget which is in turn sent to the national level. At the national level special budget categories exist for national programs such as immunization and training.

In fact, observers claim, the budget is geared to the needs of the large hospitals and zones rather than to planned programs and is established on the basis of precedent, the Service simply being given each year a percentage increase over its previous budget. It is said that the Ministry of Health tells the Service that its new budget will be the same as the prior one but then gives it an increase when the Service claims that it "won't be able to feed the patients" unless it has more money. Dr. Ayub has said that "Medical care has such acceptance in Chile that relatively speaking we get lots of money." Even to operate at the same level as the previous year the SNS needs more money because of the inflation.

The amount that the Service receives directly from the Ministry of Finance for the salaries of SNS employees and as its contribution of 5 percent of the salaries of the covered workers is also the subject of annual haggling. At budget time the Service sends a letter to the Minister of Finance stating the amount which the Cajas have collected and requesting the Ministry's contribution but the Ministry objects and reduces the amount to be paid. In the end, it is claimed, the Ministry gives the Service only about two thirds of the amount it owes as the 5 percent contribution for workers' salaries.

The underpayment by the Ministry of Finance compounds the losses of income the Service suffers because of the failure of many employers, particularly agricultural employers, to make contributions for their employees or to make contributions on full wages. Aside from these losses of income, the government's payments to the Service are usually late, undoubtedly in part because of its own financial problems. In addition, however, many Chilean health professionals claim that the President has withheld payments as a lever over the Service.

Problems in Planning

Although Chilean health experts are concerned about the multiplicity of organized health services in their country, the lack of integration among them, and particular problems of structure within the Servicio Nacional de Salud, they see as their greatest problem the need for substantial expansion of both facilities and personnel. Not only are there present problems of overcrowding, waiting lines at facilities, and so on, but health personnel cite what they consider to be a spontaneous increase in utilization, currently low by the standards of other countries, as indicative of a steadily increasing demand which they must be prepared to meet.

To date, no general agreement has been reached on the priorities which should be assigned to different sections of the total health program in order to ensure the most effective expansion. At the time the SNS was created, Dr. Molina claims, the plan had been to assign priorities on the basis of five general criteria:

1. The magnitude of the damage to a community caused by a health problem;
2. The likelihood of achieving results;
3. The likelihood of the results being extensive and producing further improvements;
4. The locations where investment would have the highest yield;
5. The locations where community attitudes permitted and even fostered action.

In fact, observers claim, no real planning is being carried out, and priorities are set by tradition, legal requirements, immediate circumstances, politics, and community pressure rather than by a formal coherent plan. The present hospital construction program is cited as an example. Formulated late in the 1950's, the program calls for an expenditure of $6 million a year for a total of eight years. It was originally intended to provide hospitals in areas where they were most needed according to a regional plan and a system of priorities. Instead, it is said, local pressure and politics are determining the location of new hospitals, and construction is taking place even though the staff and equipment needed to make the hospitals operative do not exist. Starting out with about

24,000 beds which it inherited from the beneficencia system and the Caja de Seguro Obrero, the Servicio Nacional de Salud now has approximately 29,000. The President of Chile in early 1963 reportedly cited the rise in number of hospital beds as a major achievement of his administration.

Within the SNS itself, the 1958–59 replacement of the head of the health center by the head of the hospital area as chief local officer remains a controversial point. Instituted shortly after a change in political power in the country, the system is held by many public health personnel to make inevitable a much greater emphasis on curative activities than on preventive health programs. Yet Chilean health experts believe that preventive activities must reach at least a minimal level if health standards are to be raised — a level that Chile has not yet attained. Curative services for adults and maternal and child health programs consume approximately 70 percent of the budget of the Servicio Nacional de Salud, while the sanitary engineering and epidemiological activities needed to reduce overall morbidity receive only 5 percent. Health personnel in mid-1963 were awaiting the results of the 1964 national election with interest, anticipating that a change in governing party might well result in changes of senior personnel of the SNS, a restructuring of the Service, and a consequent strengthening of preventive health programs.

Nationalized Health Services: The British Experience

January 1963

William J. Curran

The British National Health Service, which began on July 5, 1948, is one of the most ambitious and all-inclusive medical and dental care programs in the world. Although at the time it received less publicity than the industrial nationalizations enacted by the Labour Government of the period, it now seems to many observers to be one of the most enduring and certainly the most popular of the Socialist legislative enactments of the post World War II era.

It is generally said in Britain that the National Health Service Act of 1946 was not a piece of party legislation advocated and enacted only by the Socialists. It was rather the least partisan of the Labour Party programs of 1945–1951, since the basic policies underlying it and the public impetus behind them were formulated and developed during the Second World War under the Churchill-Attlee Coalition Government. Furthermore, as the major political document of the period advocating a comprehensive medical care service was written by a Liberal, Sir William (later Lord) Beveridge, all of the major political parties of Great Britain were involved in the sponsorship of the essential characteristics of the National Health Service.

The Service is now firmly implanted in the social fabric of Great Britain. On all sides, and in every shade of political opinion, its essential features are accepted as an indispensable part of the nation's social security system. There are, however, differences of opinion among professional observers concerning the Service's effectiveness. A small minority of articulate physicians and economists, including J. B. Seale, and Professor and Mrs. John Jewkes, criticize the Service and are heard with sympathy in some quarters. Many others, such as Professor Richard M. Titmuss, defend it. The major question is the effect of nationalizing and rationalizing a health service on the goal sought by all these observers — better health for the British people.

Background

Medical Care Organization Prior to World War II

Public, or governmental, interest in an organized medical care system in Great Britain dates from the great social reforms of the 1830's. The first major program of a national character was created in 1911 with the passage of the National Health Insurance Act. Modelled after plans then operating in Germany, Austria, and Belgium, it provided for a system of small cash sickness benefits and domiciliary medical care by general practitioners. The plan covered all manual laborers, and other workers with annual incomes below a certain fixed amount, revised upward over the years. A compulsory, flat-rate contribution was required from all who were covered and from their employers. The plan did not cover the wives, children, or other dependents of the insured. In 1911 approximately one third of the British people were covered by the program; at the end of World War II, as a result of extension of eligibility over the years and maximum wartime employment, about one half of the total population was covered.

The cash benefits portion of the program was administered through voluntary nonprofit insurance societies ("friendly societies"), trade unions, and commercial insurance companies. Benefits were quite unevenly distributed among the insured because the various groups were allowed to accumulate their own surpluses, yet required to pay them out in additional benefits to their members. Larger, richer insurers were thus able to offer part-payment for such benefits as dental care, eyeglasses, and hospital and nursing care. The individual worker's selection of his group was limited not merely by such factors as geographical location, but by the group's right under the system to refuse membership applications. Poor risks therefore usually belonged to groups offering minimal benefits. In Wales, for example, the insurers offered only minimum benefits to their members, mainly coal miners, who were considered bad risks by larger, richer insurers.

The National Health Insurance Act also set up a mechanism for the provision of medical care, limited under the Act to general practitioners' services and medications outside the hospital. Doctors gave care to insured persons on their lists, and were reimbursed at a flat rate per year per patient no matter how much or how little medical attention the patient actually received.

The arrangement was essentially similar to that operated by the voluntary friendly societies before passage of the 1911 Act. Nevertheless, the organized medical profession, through the British Medical Association, fought against passage of the Act, and the government made liberal concessions to the profession's demands in order to gain its cooperation. Many of these revisions improved the operations of the plan. During the years the National Health Insurance program was in operation, the general practitioners listed with it achieved significant results in extending out-of-hospital care to beneficiaries.

The condition of general practice in Britain was also improved by the plan. Before the Act most general practitioners were under-compensated, and such competitive practices as price-cutting and patient canvassing were widespread. Many doctors were affiliated with various contract and "club" schemes for the provision of medical benefits. These schemes were operated for a variety of purposes which often bore little relation to the provision of good medical care, and they were not controlled by the doctors. With the coming of National Health Insurance, general practitioners were assured of an adequate income under ethical, professional conditions.

Before World War II Great Britain had two quite independent "systems" of general hospital care — the governmental and the voluntary hospitals. The governmental hospitals were operated by the local authorities, that is, counties and county boroughs, and the larger, richer authorities maintained some excellent institutions. Municipalities also maintained chronic disease and infectious disease hospitals. Local Medical Officers of Health, who were the local "public health officers" in charge of programs in preventive and social medicine, were also responsible for general supervision of the public hospitals in their areas.

At the same time, hundreds of voluntary charitable hospitals, varying widely in quality and size, were also operating. These hospitals were totally independent of one another and often provided services that directly overlapped those of other voluntary and public hospitals in the same area.

Planning During World War II

The threat of impending war led to a decade of planning for a reorganization of Britain's health services. The first step was the establishment in June 1938 of the Emergency Medical Service created to organize the hospitals and medical personnel of the nation to care for the casualties of air attack (substantially overestimated in the initial planning) and later of the battlefields. The Ministry of Health assumed general supervision and coordination of voluntary as well as government hospitals. The number of hospital beds had to be expanded effectively and quickly to accommodate trauma cases, and surgical facilities particularly were found to be clearly inadequate and had to be rapidly supplemented. London was divided into sections, each with its own evacuation area, and hospital regions were delimited in the rest of England, Scotland, and Wales. Regional organizations of blood banks and laboratory services were also formed.

The Medical Planning Commission

The medical profession of Great Britain took the initiative in studying the type of medical care organization the country would need in the postwar years. In August 1940 the British Medical Association in cooperation with the Royal Colleges and other leading medical organizations formed the Medical Planning Commission. It was composed of 73 leading physicians representing the sponsoring groups. Observers were appointed by the Ministry of Health, the Department of Health for Scotland, and the Ministry of Home Affairs for Northern Ireland. The Commission has been called the most representative body ever established by the medical profession in Britain.

The Commission published a Draft Interim Report on May 29, 1942. In it the physicians severely criticized "the existence side by side of two essentially different hospital systems — the individualistic voluntary hospitals dependent for their existence on voluntary enterprise . . . and the municipal hospitals." They called attention to the maldistribution of physicians, "said to be governed more by the economics of the medical profession than the medical needs of the various types of areas." They objected to the limitation of the National Health Insurance system to wage-earners when the needs of their dependents were just as great. They found also that, "the sense of isolation is one of the chief grievances of the general practitioner." In conclusion, the Commission asserted, "The foregoing criticisms can be summed up in the criticism that there has been no comprehensive national health policy to guide legislative and other developments in the sphere of medical service."

The Commission's recommendations followed directly from their criticisms. A central governmental authority (the type of organization was left open) should have responsibility for a comprehensive health service which would include general practitioner, hospital, and public health services. Regions of not less than 500,000 people should be established in which local medical services would be coordinated. These regional authorities apparently were to be concerned with all types of medical services in their areas, but details of organization were not given. General practitioners were to be encouraged to organize in groups to operate health centers which would provide various nursing, laboratory, and other ancillary services. Such centers were first proposed in the Dawson Report of 1920, prepared for the then newly organized Ministry of Health. The Commission made detailed suggestions concerning the organization of the centers and left little doubt that this was a key recommendation.

The Commission suggested that some hospital administration posts and certain clinical academic chairs be filled by full-time staff who would not have the right to engage in private practice. Another group of hospital practitioners would be on a full-time basis but would have a limited number of private patients within the hospital. Lastly, the majority of hospital posts in the specialties would be filled by specialists and consultants (the highest level of specialist in Britain) associated part-time with the hospitals.

The Medical Planning Commission's Report was probably the most influential and important resource document on medical care organization produced in Britain prior to the White Papers of the government in 1944 and 1946. As an interim report, it went into greater detail on alternative administrative arrangements and perhaps gave more critical analysis of contemporary conditions than a polished final report might have done. At the same time, however, it was primarily a technical document intended for professional consideration, and the mere fact that it was labelled an "interim" report was a handicap to its use in efforts to implement its recommendations.

The Beveridge Report

In 1941 the government established an inquiry into the entire field of social insurance, appointing the Interdepartmental Committee on Social Insurance and Allied Services under the chairmanship of Sir William (later Lord) Beveridge, a Liberal with a national reputation in the field of social welfare. The other members of the Committee were civil servants. Because the Committee was concerned with policy questions, its members were required to present their views *in camera* to Sir William. (Under the British system, career civil servants may give policy opinions publicly only as directed by their appropriate Ministers so that only one government position will be presented on important issues.) It was decided that the chairman would receive the views of the members and be guided by their advice and counsel, but that the report would be the responsibility of Sir William alone. The report, *Social Insurance and Allied Services,* was published by the government in November 1942.

The report received widespread attention and almost universal approval. The reader is not long left in doubt about its general tenor. As the first of three guiding principles, Beveridge states: "Now, when the war is abolishing landmarks of every kind, is the opportunity for using experience in a clear field. A revolutionary movement in the world's history is a time for revolutions, not for patching."

A substantial increase in social benefits was recommended for all the people on a comprehensive basis, to be covered by a "single weekly insurance contribution on one insurance document." Lord Beveridge went on to recommend a unified social security system; the abolition of the Approved Societies; the separation of medical treatment from the administration of cash benefits; and the establishment of a "comprehensive medical service for every citizen, covering all treatment and every form of disability under the supervision of the Health Departments."

The Beveridge Report goes beyond the Interim Report of the Medical Planning Commission in unreservedly advocating a comprehensive service for every person without exception. Although the Beveridge Report gives considerable attention to the administration and financing of the various social insurance programs it recommended be amalgamated into one, it states that the problems of organizing a comprehensive medical service are outside the scope of the report. Beveridge adds that the objectives of a comprehensive medical service outlined in the report are in accord with those of the Medical Planning Commission as expressed in its Draft Interim Report. He asserts that it is "not necessary to express an opinion on such questions as free choice of doctors, group or individual practice, or the place of voluntary and public hospitals in a national scheme" and concludes that the report cannot contain "final detailed proposals, even as to the financial basis, of this service." He leaves the actual planning to further "immediate investigation" in consultation with the professions and organizations concerned.

Wide press and radio coverage was given the report. A nationwide Gallup Poll taken two weeks after its publication indicated that 19 out of every 20 adults had some knowledge of it. When asked whether they favored the proposal that "doctor and hospital services should be extended, free of charge, to every person," 88 percent of those interviewed replied "yes," only 6 percent answered "no," and 6 percent were undecided. The government quickly announced its intention to prepare plans to implement the recommendations of the Beveridge Report, and initiated formal consultations with professional organizations concerning a comprehensive medical service.

The 1944 White Paper

In February 1944 the government released a White Paper entitled "A National Health Service." It was not intended to be a final statement of policy but rather to serve as a basis for discussion. No drafts of legislation were prepared to accompany it.

As outlined in the White Paper, the program was to provide comprehensive medical and dental care for all of the people. There was to be free choice of both doctor and patient, and no one was to be "dragooned" into any part of the service.

Hospital services would continue to be operated by local governments, with financial assistance from the Exchequer, but on a semiregional basis through Joint Hospital Boards which would represent combinations of various county and county borough councils. Voluntary hospitals could be associated with the plan within these areas, but only on their own initiative and on a contract or grant basis. The grants would not support the voluntary hospitals in full.

General practitioners would be under contract to a national body, the Central Medical Board, composed mainly of practitioners, which would have responsibility for organizing an equitable distribution of doctors throughout the country. Under contract to the Board, a doctor would be compensated on a per capita basis per patient on his list. Should the practitioner join a "health centre," however, a type of organization the White Paper viewed favorably, he would be placed on full-time salary or paid on some basis other than capitation fees, to eliminate competition among the physicians working together. He would, in a center, come under the supervision of the local government so that environmental and personal services, such as maternal and child care, health visitors, district nurses, and so on, could be "merged" with general practice as the Medical Planning Commission had recommended.

The government strongly advocated grouped practice in the White Paper, and placed it "in the forefront" of its plans for the service. It recognized, however, that separate practice would also continue. Because the concept of grouped practice found its most usual expression in the idea of the health center, the government intended to give full scope to the health center system in its design for the new service.

It was also said in the paper, albeit sketchily, that local authorities were to have responsibility for the general planning of health services in their areas in consultation with the Ministry.

Conservative Minister of Health Willink presented the White Paper to Parliament on March 16, 1944. He said the program would be supported by the Exchequer, the local authorities, and individual insurance contributions, and estimated the cost to the central government at £130 million per year.

The White Paper met with strong approval in Parliament. Mr. Alexander Walkden of Bristol, however, for the Socialists and Trades Union Council, indicated general support of the plan's objectives but asked why it was not proposed that the voluntary hospitals be taken over entirely. He said that he could not understand why the hospitals did not themselves want this reform so that undignified appeals to the public for funds could be eliminated. He saw no reason why medical students should be required to beg with tin cups on the platforms of the Underground for funds for the hospitals. He said that he could understand that some people seemed to like the idea of serving on the boards of governors of important voluntary hospitals, but dismissed this as silly snobbery. Mr. Walkden's comments received little attention in the press at the time.

The reaction of the British Medical Association to the White Paper was strong and unmistakable. They did not like it. In a detailed examination, Harry Eckstein describes the profession's reaction as having "all the earmarks of panic." [1] In particular, the B.M.A. did not like the prospect of a full-time salaried service

1. Harry Eckstein, *The English Health Service: Its Origins, Structure, and Achievements* (Cambridge: Harvard University Press, 1958), p. 143.

which they felt the plan implied. In addition, they did not like the great amount of power that would be given to the local authorities in every phase of the program.

The government was surprised by the profession's reactions. The B.M.A. had been consulted continuously during the preparation of the White Paper, and many of the technical medical aspects of the plan had been taken bodily from the profession's own Medical Planning Commission Interim Report. In any case, the Minister of Health resumed negotiations with the profession, but for some months only leaks and rumors concerning further compromises by Mr. Willink were published. The Parliament, the people, and particularly the Socialists, were growing restive for a definite plan.

The Labour Victory

At the end of the war in Europe in 1945, Britain went directly into a partisan national election. The Socialists campaigned strongly, appealing to the desires of the people for a better life, pent up during the long years of war. One of their major rallying cries was the pledge to install a comprehensive, free-to-all medical care program as soon as possible. They contrasted their firm position on this point with the slow, plodding efforts that had been made by the Conservative Minister of Health during the preceding year or two.

The Labour Party won an overwhelming victory in 1945, securing 393 seats to 213 for the Conservatives and an absolute majority of 146 over all other parties. The defeat of Churchill, the great war leader, and of the Conservatives was a stunning surprise to many in Britain, and certainly to most of the rest of the world. The Socialists, however, regarded their victory not as a repudiation of Churchill's leadership in the war, which they had shared, but rather as a mandate for a quicker, more radical social reform than had been offered by the Conservative Party.

The Labour Government moved along party lines to install their brand of "practical" British Socialism. Major attention was given to the industrial nationalization which had been the core of their platform since the party's creation. But the stage was also set for the new government to take responsibility for establishing the comprehensive health care plan which many of the British people, both lay and professional, seemed to want. The protagonist on this stage was the Welsh Socialist firebrand, Aneurin Bevan, who was appointed Minister of Health.

The Socialists' Plan for Health

The new Minister moved into office determined to formulate a comprehensive health service and to put it into legislative language as soon as possible. Bevan brought with him no very set notions as to how this task was to be performed. Labour Party policy, so articulate in other areas, gave no guidance. The Fabians, intellectual socialists who had contributed greatly to party theory, had been suspicious of doctors, regarding them as capitalist professional men possessed of often overrated skills. If the Fabians had a medical care philosophy at all, it was that greatly improved social conditions for the lower classes would eliminate ill health as a significant social problem. Only in later years, as the trade unions began to control national party policy, were expanded medical services for the working classes advocated by Labour. In Bevan's time, party principles were clear only on the points that the service should be without cost to the patient and that it should be as comprehensive as possible.

The Minister took a fresh look at the organizational structure which had been proposed for the health service by the Conservative Minister of Health. Along with the Labour Party generally, he did not consider as binding any "secret concessions" the former Minister might have made to organized professional groups. During these early months he produced the most significant new administrative and legal factor the Socialists were to add to the creation of the health service by advocating that the voluntary private hospitals be taken over and integrated directly into a national program along with the municipal hospitals. In the heady atmosphere created by the industrial nationalization going on around him, this did not appear to Bevan to be a drastic step, even though previous planning groups had rejected it. This course had already received some support from the trade unions.

Integration of the voluntary as well as the municipal hospitals into a single national system raised a wider range of questions about interhospital organization. One alternative was the establishment of a national hospitals board or corporation with regional constituencies — a structure similar to that used by the Socialists for nationalization of some industries. Another was the creation of a new government department, separate from the other medical services, under the Ministry of Health to supervise the hospitals. Both of these were rejected, however, in favor of a plan under which hospital regions were placed under the Ministry of Health as part of the general health care system.

The Ministry took another step away from the Conservative plan of 1944 by using the then existing structure of Insurance Committees of the National Health Insurance to administer general practitioner services. Under the Conservative plan, these would have gone out of existence as soon as the new system was installed. The Committees had worked well in the past, however, and had accumulated a wealth of experience in administering general practitioner services on the local level — services which would remain essentially the same under the new health scheme but which would be extended to the whole population. As in the past, doctors were to be reimbursed mainly by capitation fees for the patients on their lists, drugs were to be dispensed in the same way, and hospital referral would remain basically the same. Bevan therefore decided to retain the Insurance Committees, but to rename them "Executive Councils" and to give them jurisdictions coterminous with those of the local authorities so that cooperation with the public health services might be more easily developed. The Executive Councils were to remain creatures of the Ministry of Health, however, not of the local authorities. The only functions that would remain with the local authorities under the Bevan plan, then, would be traditional public health programs in environmental and preventive medicine.

The program of the new Minister of Health was now complete in its basic elements. At the same stage in program development, the Conservative Government of 1944 had opened discussions and negotiations with organized professional groups, principally the British Medical Association and its officially constituted Negotiating Committee. Aneurin Bevan, however, opposed the opening of formal negotiations, feeling that development of the new program was the responsibility of the government and that it was not a matter of compromise between the government and interested professional groups until it was before Parliament. In any case, he felt that his plan satisfied the major objection of the B.M.A. and its member general practitioners to previous plans by lessening the power of the local authorities, who, under former plans, would have had responsibility for both general practitioner and hospital services.

Bevan did seek the views of specialists and hospital officials, however. First, his changes in previous plans affected the hospitals more than they did other facets of health care and he felt that those who were involved deserved a hearing. Second, he was not faced with a formal Negotiating Committee and could therefore solicit views on a more informal basis, particularly from specialists with whom he was on friendly terms. These included Lord Moran, personal physician to Sir Winston Churchill during the war years, who was then President of the Royal College of Physicians.

Specialists and voluntary hospital officials did not greet the plan to take over the voluntary hospitals with strong opposition. Before the war, and even more during it, voluntary hospitals had become substantially dependent on public funds. In 1946 almost half their operating income came from governmental sources, and even so, the great majority were running up growing deficits. The teaching hospitals of London had a cumulative deficit of £751,000 in 1947, compared with an estimated £77,000 in 1938, the last full operating year before the war. An additional factor was the very great difference in quality among the voluntary hospitals. The London specialists and hospital officials could see no reason to fight to keep the struggling smaller hospitals operating by means of the alternative contract basis outlined in the 1944 White Paper that would not even cover their costs, let alone reduce their deficits.

About the teaching hospitals, however, there was disagreement. The specialists argued that these institutions, whose primary functions were teaching and research, should not be subordinated to regional organizations whose paramount responsibility must be patient service. In any clash, they believed, the teaching hospitals would be the losers under this arrangement. Bevan, who had had experience as a member of a hospital board, recognized the importance of the teaching institutions in providing educational resources and facilities for the new health service as a whole and agreed to leave them out of the regional organizations. Instead, they were to be nationalized, but placed directly under the Minister of Health. Each was to have its own Board of Governors.

In Scotland where, unlike England and Wales, the teaching hospitals provide a significant number of the total hospital beds, they were brought into the regional system. Some commentators have taken this to mean that Bevan's concession to the specialists in England and Wales was a political maneuver designed to gain their support, not an objective recognition of the special status of teaching hospitals.

The Minister of Health was now ready to draft appropriate legislation. He felt assured of the support of the Royal Colleges, the specialists, and the hospital authorities. And, although the local governments might be losing their hospitals, they were at the same time shifting sizable tax burdens to the central government. The B.M.A. and general practitioners might still oppose the plan, but much of their argument against the administrative structure of the service had been satisfied, and they had lost many of their allies among the profession.

The Legislation in Parliament

The National Health Service Bill was presented to Parliament in March 1946, slightly less than a year after the Labour Government assumed office. It was part of a package of bills concerned with social services (cash sickness benefits, retirement pensions, maternity grants, children's allowances, and unemployment relief) which together constituted the Socialists' program of comprehensive social security. With the Bill the government submitted a financial memorandum estimating the yearly cost to the Exchequer for the Health Service at £110 million.

The Conservatives expressed their opposition to the inclusion of the voluntary hospitals, but admitted basic agreement with the overall objectives of the legislation. In the major address for the Opposition, Mr. Richard Law said that his party was committed to a "100 per cent comprehensive service with the fullest possible benefits to all the people." The Conservatives having accepted this, he continued, understood the necessity for "a far greater degree of coordination, or planning as it is usually called, than we have ever had before."

The Bill moved smoothly through Parliament; although there were amendments, none were considered to be fundamental changes. On July 26, 1946, the House of Commons passed the National Health Service Act by a strict party vote of 261 to 113. After receiving the agreement of the Lords, it was accorded Royal Assent and became law on November 6. The date when the Service was to go into operation was not set and was to be determined by the government and the Minister of Health.

The government selected July 5, 1948, as the beginning date for the new social security programs, including the health service, so that they would coincide with a new fiscal year for the employer-employee insurance contributions to existing programs that had been incorporated into the new plans. In spite of bitter and open opposition from the B.M.A., which was eventually fairly well compromised (with substantial help from Lord Moran and the Royal Colleges), the Health Service got under way on the appointed day in full, not in stages as some had advised.

Structure

Central Administration

Under the 1946 Act a highly centralized national health service has been established. All basic powers and authority are derived from the Minister of Health. Administratively and legally, this situation has been achieved as follows:

1. The property of all hospitals is transferred to and vested in the Minister.
2. The Minister directly appoints almost all important officials of the National Health Service.
3. New administrative bodies are established within the Ministry to operate the hospitals and the general medical services. (Under alternative plans, responsibility for both hospital and general medical services would have been delegated to independent local government authorities.)
4. A prohibition is imposed on the buying and selling of general medical practices.
5. The Minister's authority over local government units is extended in the area of public health and preventive medicine services.
6. The Minister has broad discretionary authority and wide power to adopt administrative regulations having the force and effect of law in nearly all areas of the Service.

The Act established a Central Health Services Council composed of representatives of the major medical, dental, and other professions to advise the Minister in his responsibility for direction of the Service. The presidents of the three Royal Colleges, the British Medical Association, the General Medical Council (the medical licensing board), and the Society of Medical Officers of Health are members *ex officio*. The remaining 35 members are appointed by the Minister after consultation with such organizations as he considers appropriate. Fifteen of the 35 must be medical practitioners; the others are drawn from hospital administration, local government, dentistry, mental health, nursing, midwifery, and pharmacy. They are not, however, representatives of specific organizations and are neither selected nor nominated by such groups. The organized professional groups attempted to have this provision amended in Parliament so that they would have greater control over the appointments, but Minister Bevan stood firmly against any change.

Over the years the Council has rendered good service, conducting a number of studies in specific areas of concern to the Service. There is evidence that the Minister has acted upon its advice on many occasions.

To operate the Health Service, which has a budget exceeded only by that of the Armed Forces, the Ministry of Health has developed a relatively small administrative staff at the national level. Under the Minister and the Permanent Parliamentary Secretary is the chief civil service medical administrator, the Chief Medical Officer. (His services are shared with the Ministry of Education and the Home Office, which makes him the generally acknowledged head of the medical civil service throughout the government.) The Chief Medical Officer has his own division at

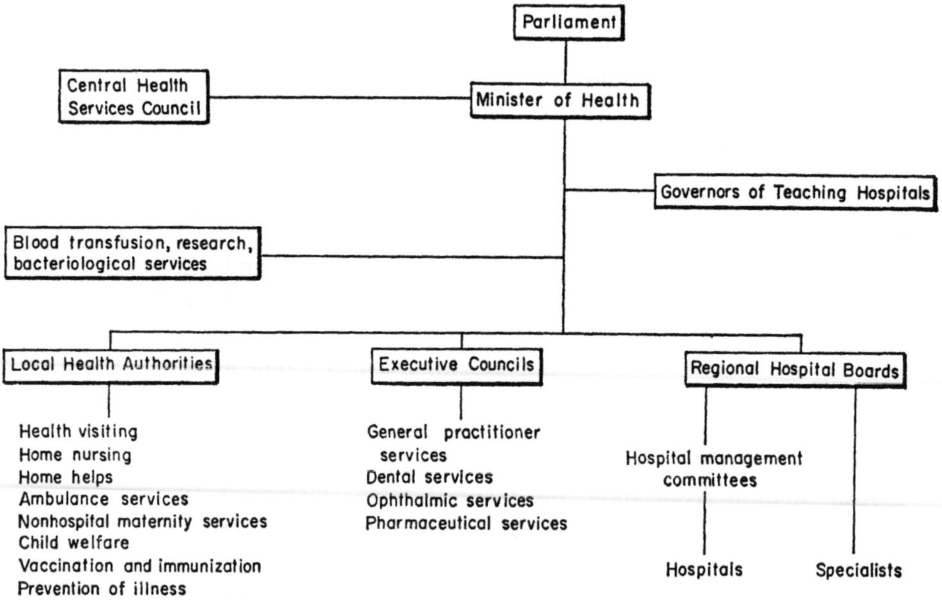

Organizational Structure of the British National Health Service

the Ministry for general administration, and there are also "line" or operational divisions in the Ministry concerned with the administration of services.

Administratively, the Service is divided into three main branches: hospital and specialist services; general medical practitioner, dental, pharmaceutical, and ophthalmological services; and Local Health Authority services. The Ministry also has authority over the Boards of Governors of the teaching hospitals, and over blood transfusion, research, and bacteriological services.

In rejecting a more coordinated arrangement for the provision of services, such as the Medical Planning Commission's Interim Report had recommended, Bevan created a tripartite system whose units have remained relatively isolated from one another. Although the structure has been much criticized for this reason, it has remained almost unchanged since 1948. A committee appointed by the British Medical Association to review the country's medical services strongly recommended in its 1962 report that the three major branches of the Service be brought together under new "area health boards" to achieve closer coordination.

Hospital and Specialist Services

Coordination of the Hospitals. The major contribution made by the Socialists to the organizational structure of the health services was the consolidation and coordination of all hospital services, not just the public hospitals, in the national plan. Public hospitals formerly owned and operated by local governments were united with voluntary private institutions nationalized by the Act. In actual numbers, the Ministry took over 2,800 hospitals with slightly more than 500,000 beds. Approximately 250 hospitals remained outside the system.

The hospitals were grouped originally in 14 regions, and later in 15 when one region was divided. All types of hospitals except teaching hospitals are consolidated under Regional Hospital Boards. The Act requires that the Minister, in establishing the regions, must assure, in so far as is practicable, that each region "can conveniently be associated with a university having a school of medicine."

The Regional Hospital Boards are unpaid, volunteer groups of about 25 persons appointed by the Minister after consultation with the university of the region, practitioner organizations, local health authorities, and such other groups as the Minister deems appropriate. They are responsible for administering the hospitals and specialist services in their areas on behalf of the minister and under his general direction.

The objective of coordinated services is largely achieved through the Hospital Management Committees that have been established throughout each region. The committees, also composed of unpaid volunteers representative of interested groups in the area, are appointed by the Regional Boards and given charge of a group of hospitals on a functional, planned basis, and are expected to work with the hospitals to promote coordinated services. The Management Committees rather than the Regional Boards are concerned with general supervision, including budget administration, for the individual hospitals. Each hospital has, in addition, a "house committee" appointed by the Management Committee to discharge "non-policy" duties on behalf of the Management Committees.

The large mental hospitals remain outside the grouping of hospitals under Management Committees. Each mental hospital is operated by its own Management Committee, and coordination is left to the Regional Hospital Board.

As with any other voluntary board structure acting as a policy-making body, the British hospital system has full-time salaried administrators who carry a great part of the day-to-day responsibility. The Regional Boards have two principal executives, the Senior Administrative Medical Officer and the Secretary, or business manager. Many of the Senior Medical Officers have been drawn from the ranks of the former Medical Officers of Health of local governments who, when the hospitals were taken away from the municipalities, chose to remain in hospital administration rather than in the public health activities of the local health authorities. The Hospital Management Committees have a secretary, a deputy secretary, and various other officers.

Hospital Finances. The Ministry maintains quite strict financial control over the Regional Hospital Boards. It was thought at first that they would be given a good measure of autonomy in financial matters. Parliament's full realization of the substantial cost of the combined hospital services (grossly underestimated previously), coupled with the general national "austerity" of the early 1950's, led to the imposition of close central supervision which has never been lifted. The Regional Boards submit annual budget estimates in October for the fiscal year beginning April 1. After consultation with the Treasury and Parliament, the Minister of Health determines the allocation for each region and the budgets are set in final form. The Regional Boards then submit financial reports to the Minister each month. The Boards and Management Committees are held to expenditures within budget categories, and transfers of funds among accounts are very rare. Unexpended balances in all accounts must be returned to the Treasury at the end of the year.

The Regional Boards and Management Committees have some freedom in the use of endowment funds formerly held by the individual voluntary hospitals. These may be spent for hospital and research purposes by the Boards and Committees. The Act also allows Management Committees to receive gifts through charitable trusts and to administer these funds in accordance with the trust instruments. For most hospitals, however, neither of these supplementary sources of income is an important factor in their budgets.

Most of the hospitals in Britain are of the large, open-ward variety, having been built originally to serve primarily charity or low-income patients in the days before the National Health Service. The more well-to-do patients tended to use "nursing homes," small proprietary institutions maintained by or on behalf of specialists. When the National Health Service was instituted, a small number of "amenity beds" and "pay beds" were set aside in National Health Service Hospitals for patients who wanted private or semi-private accommodations. Amenity beds, of which there are about 5,400, are semi-private or small-ward beds available to Health Service patients at an extra per diem charge. An additional 5,800 pay beds are used by private patients of specialists attached to a particular hospital, and patients must pay the full cost of these beds as well as their specialist's fee. National Health Service patients who need private or semi-private accommodations for medical reasons pay no extra charge.

Organization of Specialists' Services. The traditional separation between specialists and general practitioners in Britain has been firmly institutionalized by the National Health Service. General practitioners in Britain have never had close associations with hospitals, medical care requiring hospitalization having always been the province of the specialists. A recent survey,[2] for example, indicated that only about 20 percent of the general practitioners

2. M. D. Warren, "General Practitioners in Hospital: Report of a Study-group at the London School of Hygiene and Tropical Medicine, 1961–62," *The Lancet*, Vol. 2 of 1962, pp. 601–602 (September 22, 1962).

questioned had access to beds in National Health Service hospitals. A slightly smaller percentage of the general practitioners held hospital appointments, and almost all of these had completed or were still undergoing specialty training.

The specialists are employed by the Regional Boards and the Hospital Management Committees. A hierarchy of hospital-based physicians and surgeons has been established in terms of years of training and experience. House officers, registrars, and consultants correspond roughly to interns, residents, and Board-certified specialists in the United States. "Consultants" are the highest ranking specialists with senior hospital medical officer being a specialist position between registrar and consultant.

Attractive salary schedules have been established for all the ranks of specialists. Three graduated merit or special distinction increments are given to 20, 10, and 4 percent of the consultants to reward high professional achievement. In 1958 it was calculated that all full-time consultants of at least three years' standing were in the top 1.6 percent of all British income getters.[3]

To encourage specialists to move out of the big population centers, particularly London, and to staff hospitals throughout the country, salary schedules are uniform in all areas. By moving out to the provinces, a doctor could more rapidly become a high-ranking consultant than he could in London with its heavy concentration of physicians. In a relatively few years, the National Health Service, according to Lord Moran and other commentators, has achieved a better distribution of specialists than had previously been thought possible.

General Medical and Related Services

Under the second major branch of the National Health Service four types of services are provided:

1. General medical services;
2. Drugs and other medicines prescribed by general practitioners;
3. General dental services;
4. Ophthalmic services (eye tests and eyeglasses).

Supervision of these services rests with Executive Councils, successors to the local Insurance Committees created by the National Health Insurance Act. Their jurisdictions are coterminous

3. Paul F. Gemmill, *Britain's Search for Health: The First Decade of the National Health Service* (Philadelphia: University of Pennsylvania Press, 1960), p. 87.

with those of local counties and county boroughs, but they are not a part of local government.

The councils are composed of 25 members: five appointed by the Minister, eight by the local government body, seven by the medical practitioners of the area, three by the dentists, and two by the pharmacists. The doctors, dentists, and pharmacists each have a "professional committee" which represents the group in matters of concern to the Executive Councils.

Like the Insurance Committees they replaced, the Executive Councils are primarily payment agencies. They disburse funds to the general practitioners, keep records of the doctors' patient lists, arrange for transfers of patients, and so on. The administrative staff is headed by a Secretary or Clerk who is usually a lay person. Many have stayed on from similar posts with the Insurance Committees.

General Practitioners' Services. The organization of general practice has changed little from the National Health Insurance arrangements. Practitioners are paid a flat yearly fee, currently about £1 per person on their lists. There is an additional "loading" payment of 14s. for the 401st to 1,600th patient on the list of a doctor practicing alone, and for the 501st to 1,700th patient of a doctor in partnership.

An upper limit has been set on the size of general practitioners' lists, but this limit is seldom reached. A doctor practicing alone is permitted to have no more than 3,500 persons on his list, and a doctor in partnership may have 4,500, so long as the average for the partnership is not above 3,500 patients per partner. If a doctor employs an assistant, an additional 2,000 patients are allowed. In fact, however, only one third of the practitioners had more than 2,500 patients on their lists in 1958, and another third had 1,500 or less.[4] According to the Ministry, the average number of National Health Service patients on a doctor's list was 2,280 in 1960. There has been pressure from both lay and professional groups for an official reduction in the maximum allowable number of patients.

With the capitation fee of 19s. 6d. per patient per annum, and the additional loading payment, the annual gross income from capitation fees alone is £3,063 for a doctor practicing alone with an average size list. After deducting the expenses of practice, estimated by the Ministry to be about one third of gross income,

4. Almont Lindsey, *Socialized Medicine in England and Wales: The National Health Service, 1948–1961* (Chapel Hill: University of North Carolina Press, 1962), p. 207.

the average physician has a net income before taxes of £2,022 from capitation fees, or approximately $5,660. A physician with a full panel has a net income after expenses but before taxes of about $7,910 from capitation fees.

Physicians may earn additional income from the National Health Service by treating temporary residents, giving emergency treatment, dispensing drugs, and so on. They also benefit from a government contribution of 9.5 percent of their net annual receipts to a superannuation fund. They contribute 6 percent of their net receipts to the fund.

Private patients, which all National Health Service doctors are permitted to have, constitute another source of income, and four fifths of Health Service doctors do treat private patients. According to Gemmill, however, four fifths of the general practitioners he questioned in 1956 received at least 90 percent of their income from National Health Service practice, and this income was made up overwhelmingly of capitation fees.[5] An official estimate of general practitioners' average net income from all sources was $6,530 in 1958. In the same year, general practitioners with patient lists of the average size, and with no income other than capitation fees, were in the highest 2.8 percent of British income-getters.[6]

Patients are free to choose any general practitioner they wish, and doctors are free to reject patients if they so desire. Some doctors voluntarily maintain small lists, and others reject certain types of patients they do not wish to serve. Since all persons are entitled to general practitioner services, however, Executive Councils are authorized to place with a general practitioner in their areas patients who have been unable to secure general practitioner services on a voluntary basis. Normally, the general practitioner must keep the assigned patient on his list for at least six months, after which he may request that the patient be passed on to another doctor. Over the years, the number of patients who have had to be assigned has remained very small.

Distribution of General Practitioners. When the National Health Service went into operation, there was, according to the Ministry, a maldistribution of general practitioners, with too many in large metropolitan centers and seaside resorts and too few in rural areas and industrial towns. To help relieve the problem, and to control it in the future, certain provisions were incorporated into the Act:

5. Gemmill, p. 84.
6. Gemmill, p. 87.

1. The sale of general practices is prohibited.

2. A doctor must have the permission of a special national committee — the Medical Practices Committee — composed of seven doctors and two laymen, before starting a new practice or taking over the practice of a deceased or retired physician.

3. An "Initial Practice Allowance" is paid to doctors setting up in single-handed National Health Service practice in areas designated as needing more doctors, or filling vacancies in small single-handed practices in these areas. (The allowance is £1,250 the first year, decreasing to £250 in the fourth year, subject to certain conditions.)

4. Inducement payments are made to encourage doctors to practice in sparsely populated or otherwise unattractive areas. (The payments vary by the type of practice, and range between £250 and £650 per year.)

According to the Ministry, in 1952, 51.5 percent of the population of England and Wales lived in areas designated as "underdoctored," 4.5 percent in areas with too many doctors, and 44.2 percent in intermediate areas. By July 1960 the percentage of the

Table 1. Changes in the distribution of principals providing unrestricted medical services (applying the Medical Practices Committee classification of areas) 1952–1959.[a]

	Percentage of patients in areas			Average number of patients per principal in areas		
Year	Designated	Intermediate	Restricted	Designated	Intermediate	Restricted
1952	51.5	44.1	4.4	2,851	2,184	1,581
1953	38.9	56.5	4.6	2,726	2,183	1,594
1956	21.7	73.4	4.9	2,711	2,234	1,548
1958	18.6	76.4	5.0	2,672	2,247	1,594
1959	19.9	74.9	5.2	2,745	2,251	1,575

Source: John and Sylvia Jewkes, *The Genesis of the British National Health Service* (Oxford: Basil Blackwell and Mott, Ltd., 1961), p. 60.

[a] The Ministry of Health produces regularly statistics in which the whole country is divided into "areas": designated (i.e. under-doctored); restricted (i.e. over-doctored); and intermediate (i.e. the rest) . . . By and large, all Medical Practices Committee areas where the average number of patients per doctor exceeds 2,500 are classified as designated and all areas where the average falls below 1,500 are classified as restricted. It appears that in part the judgment of the Medical Practices Committee in any particular Medical Practices Committee area is a qualitative one. Some of the changes in the figures above, therefore, may be due partly to variations in the standards adopted by the Medical Practices Committee (Jewkes, p. 60).

population living in "under-doctored" areas was reported to be 20.1.

Group Practice. The Ministry has actively encouraged general practitioners to enter partnerships or group practice. Interest-free loans for the construction of premises are available to practitioners who enter into group practice agreements. Furthermore, doctors in partnership or group practice are allowed to carry up to 4,500 patients on their lists (the single-handed practitioner may accept no more than 3,500), so long as the average number of patients per partner is no more than 3,500. Finally, doctors in partnership may apply to have the number of "loading" payments to which they are entitled calculated on whatever division of the aggregate number of their patients produces the greatest income.

Group practice, the Labour Government believed, would find its ultimate expression in the "Health Centres" to be provided and maintained by Local Health Authorities for coordinated practitioner, consultant, and preventive phases of medical care. For a variety of reasons discussed later, the health centers have never developed to any extent.

Partnership and group practice have, however, come to be the pattern in Britain. In 1960, 70 percent of all physicians with practices were partners, and 80 percent of all partnerships comprised two or three physicians. A larger proportion of rural than of urban doctors were in partnerships.[7]

General Dental Services

Comprehensive dental as well as medical services are provided to the people of Britain under the National Health Service. Although this aspect of the program did not receive either the attention or the publicity given to the medical services plan in 1946, it was actually a more novel feature of the Service. Dental care had been offered to only a small number by the Approved Societies under the National Health Insurance, but only certain types of dental care were covered, and the insurer never paid more than half the cost. It was estimated that only about 7 percent of the eligible insured made use of the dental benefits during any one year.

Under the National Health Service, patients are free to go to

7. Lindsey, p. 165.

any dentist registered and patient lists are not maintained. Dentists may use their professional judgment in supplying patients with relatively inexpensive, routine procedures, but must obtain approval of a Dental Estimates Board composed of dental practitioners before undertaking expensive work such as multiple extractions, partial plates, or full dentures.

Some of the restrictions imposed on physicians under the Service do not apply to dentists. No limit is set on the number of patients they may accept; they may engage in practice at any place they choose; there is no prohibition on the sale of dental practices; and there is no method by which a dentist can be forced to take any Health Service patient he does not wish to treat.

Dentists are reimbursed on a fee-for-service basis and are among the highest paid practitioners in the Health Service; only some medical specialists have incomes higher than the £2,290 averaged by dentists in 1955–1956.[8] The schedule of payments to dentists fixed in 1948 was set quite high in order to attract dentists to the Service. In spite of this, original estimates of average income to the dentist proved to be very low. The committee that set the fees underestimated the number of chair-side hours dentists can work, and there was an unexpectedly great demand for dental treatment, particularly for dentures.

In an effort to stem the demand, patient charges were imposed in 1951. These charges are now the highest, both in amount and in proportion to total costs, in the entire Service. Patients now pay up to £1, or the full cost if less, for any treatment except a routine examination. A further and larger charge (about one half of cost) is now made for dentures.

Pharmaceutical and Supplementary Ophthalmological Services

Prescription drugs are distributed by both the hospital and the general medical services branches of the Service. In the general medical services branch, however, the pharmaceutical service is a separate administrative unit under the Executive Councils, and almost all dispensing is done by retail pharmacies. Eye-testing and the supply of spectacles are also administratively separate.

Both of these services proved to be much more costly than had

8. Lindsey, p. 415.

been anticipated. New and costly drugs like the antibiotics, increasing use of proprietary drugs, and an increase in total amount of drugs prescribed combined to make the Pharmaceutical Services extremely expensive. In an effort to stem "the torrent of drugs flowing down British gullets," as Minister Bevan put it, as well as to produce additional revenue, a charge of one shilling per prescription was imposed on patients in 1952. This was later increased to one shilling per item on the prescription and later to two shillings per item.

The problem of high costs for spectacles arose almost immediately after inauguration of the Service. The Ministry grossly underestimated the probable demand (based on experience under the National Health Insurance when 75 percent of the cost was borne by the patient). Anticipated costs for the first year were set at £3.5 million; actual expenditures during the first nine months were nearly £15 million. In 1951 charges were imposed for spectacles — full cost of frames and part cost of lenses. As a result of these charges and of the fact that demand had been largely satisfied in the first few years, expenditures for ophthalmological services have been reduced and now are under relatively good control. The numbers of sight tests and of spectacles provided have risen slowly, however, by 3 or 4 percent a year in recent years.

Local Health Authority Services

The third main branch of the National Health Service is the Local Health Authority of the counties and county boroughs. Under Medical Officers of Health the municipalities operate programs in social and preventive medicine, environmental sanitation, and such personal services as visiting nurse and midwifery programs. They also operate ambulance services for the hospitals in their areas.

Although all these services were provided prior to the National Health Service, the 1946 Act assigned them exclusively to counties and county boroughs, taking them away from the few municipalities which had previously offered them. The 1946 Act further made all of the services mandatory; some had formerly been optional. Under the Health Service, the national Ministry has been given more authority over local health programs than had ever before been permitted in legislation.

The Act of 1946 contemplated the establishment by Local

Health Authorities of health centers in which general medical, dental, and pharmaceutical services, as well as such Local Health Authority personnel as district nurses, midwives, mental health counsellors, health educators, and so on, would be located. The centers, it was suggested, might also be used for outpatient services of hospitals and specialists. The centers themselves were to be buildings constructed or renovated by the Authority to house any or all of these services. The Authority, through the Executive Council, would recover from the physicians using the center rent for the space they occupied.

The idea of health centers dates back to the Dawson Report of 1920. Centers were also advocated in the Medical Planning Commission's Interim Report, viewed favorably in the 1944 White Paper, and adopted by the Socialists as a main feature of the White Paper accompanying the 1946 Health Service Act. The idea had struck the imagination of many people, both lay and professional, as one way to raise the quality of general practice and of medical care generally. Doctrinaire Socialists, including the Socialist Medical Association, were among the strongest backers of the plan.

The plan for health centers has nevertheless been the largest single concept in the 1946 Act which has almost totally failed to develop. The cost of building centers to serve every 10,000 to 20,000 people was prohibitive, and in any case, construction was strictly controlled in the postwar years and priority given to the replacement of housing damaged or destroyed during the war. Practitioners, particularly older established doctors, were unenthusiastic about the prospect of entering such centers.

Perhaps most important, the official position of the Ministry has been somewhat equivocal. Although Local Authorities were instructed to submit plans for the centers by November 30, 1947, the Ministry first postponed this deadline to the end of December and then cancelled it. Finally, in January 1948 the Ministry asked the authorities to postpone their plans, giving as reasons the shortage of building materials and the view that "the extensive provision of health centers should wait on the experience to be gained from the use of a limited number of experimental centers."

A few of these have been established over the years and appear to be operating well. A conspicuous failure, however, was the center constructed by the London County Council at Woodbury Downs at a cost of nearly £200,000. A fine, new building functionally designed as a model health center to serve 20,000 patients, it has never operated as a total health center. It is occupied today by various public health and social services conducted and coordinated by the Local Authority.

As the National Health Service operates, the Local Health Authorities are almost wholly divorced from the other branches. The hospitals formerly operated by municipalities have been absorbed into the Regional Hospital Boards, and the Authorities and Medical Officers of Health participate in other branches of the Service only through some overlapping committee and board appointments.

Experience

Utilization

Within a very short time after inauguration of the National Health Service, 97 percent of the population had been enrolled as National Health Service patients—a figure that has remained stable. Among the professions, only an estimated 700 of Great Britain's approximately 46,000 physicians are today wholly in private practice, and almost all dentists, pharmacists, and opticians have also registered with the Service.

In the first years of the Service, statistics showed increased utilization of general practitioner services, particularly, as might be expected, by the groups not covered under National Health Insurance—unemployed women, children, and persons over the age of 65. After examining a variety of studies of physician-utilization rates before 1939 and after 1948, however, Professor Titmuss concluded that "on average and contrary to public belief, demand has not increased under the National Health Service and may indeed have fallen." [9] W. P. D. Logan, after comparing data from a survey of sickness for the twelve months following the introduction of the Service with the twelve preceding months, found a 13 percent increase in physician consultations. Data from the British Survey of Sickness, 1943 to 1952, show an increase of 20 percent in the number of women, and of close to 16 percent in the number of persons over 65, who were ill or injured and who saw a doctor during the month. Tables 2 and 3 present data on both the proportion of persons ill or injured who saw a doctor and on the

9. Richard M. Titmuss, *Essays on "The Welfare State"* (New Haven: Yale University Press, 1959), p. 174.

intensity of use for periods preceding and following the start of the service.

According to the Ministry of Health, the number of visits to general practitioners rose from an average of five per year per patient under the National Health Insurance to a little less than six per year per patient in 1951 under the National Health Service. Surveys of their own practices by several British physicians show a range from 3.7 to 5.45 in the number of annual visits and consultations per patient. The General Register office reported in 1952, however, that the busiest general practice studied had an average of only 4.7 calls annually.

Between 60 and 75 percent of a doctor's patients use his services at least once a year, and women, children, and persons over 65 con-

Table 2. Mean monthly percentage of persons ill or injured who saw a doctor during the month, England and Wales, October 1946 to June 1951, according to age group and sex.

	Persons 16 years of age and over[a]		Persons 16–64 years of age		Persons 65 years of age and over	
Period (July–June)	Male	Female	Male	Female	Male	Female
Before NHS (1946–48)	23.7	22.5	22.7	21.6	28.7	27.0
After NHS (1948–51)	25.3	27.4	23.8	26.5	32.5	32.0
Percentage change	6.8	21.8	4.8	22.7	13.2	18.5

[a] Ages 21 and over, starting in February 1951.

Table 3. Mean monthly visits per person ill or injured who saw a doctor, England and Wales, October 1946 to June 1951, according to age group and sex.

	Visits/person 16 years of age and over[a]		Visits/person 16–64 years of age		Visits/person 65 years of age and over	
Period (July–June)	Male	Female	Male	Female	Male	Female
Before NHS (1946–48)	2.736	2.628	2.742	2.623	2.699	2.647
After NHS (1948–51)	2.666	2.425	2.649	2.410	2.730	2.480
Percentage change	–2.6	–7.7	–3.4	–8.1	1.1	–6.3

Source for Tables 2 and 3: William H. Stewart and Philip E. Enterline, "Effects of the National Health Service on Physician Utilization and Health in England and Wales," *New England Journal of Medicine* 265:1188 (December 14, 1961).

[a] Ages 21 and over, starting in February 1951.

sume the largest part of his time. A study of one practice, reported in the *British Medical Journal,* indicated that one sixth of the patients accounted for one half of the work, and that chronic diseases accounted for one third of all the work.

In early complaints about the National Health Service it was alleged that there were long waiting lines in doctors' offices, and that, in consequence, harassed physicians were rendering low quality care on an assembly line basis. The removal of all financial deterrents, it was charged, had resulted in heavy demands being made by persons who really did not require medical attention.

Long waiting periods in doctors' offices were relatively common under the National Health Insurance, perhaps in part because it was and still is the custom in British medical practice to keep office hours but not to fix specific appointments. In 1956, the doctors and patients questioned by Gemmill apparently did not feel that long waiting periods were a significant problem. Of the patients asked how often they had to wait as long as one and a half hours in a doctor's office before being seen, 6 percent answered "usually," 15 percent "occasionally," 64 percent "almost never," and 15 percent "never." Only 25 percent of the physicians questioned thought long waiting periods were a problem.[10]

According to a British Medical Association survey among 12,879 general practitioners in 1951, 53 percent of the physicians felt that patients were making "excessive numbers of unnecessary demands." Another survey by Dr. Hadfield, Assistant Secretary of the Association, reported that only 30 percent of the physicians felt this to be the case. A physician has some recourse against patients who continue to make what he feels to be unjustified demands in that he can refuse to keep them on his list. They are then put to the inconvenience of seeking another doctor, sometimes with the additional public notoriety of passing before the local Executive Council. The Social Surveys in 1956, however, indicated that, excepting the instances when doctor or patient moved away, only eight percent of the patients had had a change of physician since the beginning of the Service.

In the early years of the National Health Service there was very heavy utilization of the dental, pharmaceutical, and ophthalmic services, with a resultant cost to the government much higher than had been anticipated on the basis of National Health Insurance experience. Small charges to the patient were introduced in these services in 1951 and 1952 primarily to deter what was considered

10. Gemmill, pp. 54–56.

to be excessive utilization. The charges initially reinforced the already downward trend in use of all three services, but in recent years utilization is again rising. Although the number of prescriptions declined appreciably after the introduction of deterrent charges, the cost of the pharmaceutical service continued to rise. In its final report, dated 1959, the Committee on the Cost of Prescribing concluded that "the deterrent effect of the shilling charge, whether per form or per item, has not been particularly marked."

Considerable disagreement still exists concerning the deterrent charges. Some believe they are needed in order to bring actual utilization closer to real need. Others hold that they discourage those who need care the most — the poor and those who are not well educated about or motivated to obtain medical care — from seeking it. Certain groups of patients, however, including those on National Assistance, pensioners with war disabilities, hardship cases, and so on, are either reimbursed or exempted from some or all of the charges imposed in the three services. All students and all children under 16 are exempted from the ophthalmic service charges, and dental care is given without charge to all persons under 21 and to women who are pregnant or who have had a child within the past 12 months. Any patient for whom the charges would constitute a serious burden may apply for reimbursement.

Table 4. Expenditures for dental, pharmaceutical, and supplementary ophthalmic services, selected years, 1950–1961, in millions of pounds.

	Dental		Pharmaceutical		Ophthalmic	
Year	By patient	By service	By patient	By service	By patient	By service
1950–51	–	37.7	–	38.5	–	18.4
1953–54	6.3	22.3	6.0	39.5	4.3	7.1
1957–58	8.1	34.5	10.8	53.3	5.2	8.9
1960–61[a]	8.9	43.0	11.0	66.9	5.4	10.0

Source: Ministry of Health, mimeographed material.
[a] Estimated.

Although adequate statistics measuring hospital utilization do not seem to be available, the waiting period for admission to hospital is still felt to be a problem in Great Britain. Hospital surveys conducted for the Ministry of Health just before the establishment of the National Health Service estimated that a 30 to 40 percent increase in hospital beds was needed—an estimate which has since been thought to be too high. Because of the severe limitation on capital expenditure, however, most of the funds available for this purpose were used for remodeling, for new operating units, and so on. The Minister of Health informed Parliament in November 1959 that since the beginning of the Health Service, three new mental deficiency and three new general hospitals had been opened and that nine others, mostly general hospitals, were then under construction.[11]

The Ministry of Health estimates that, primarily by reducing the number of unstaffed beds and by shortening the length of stay of patients, the British hospitals were able at the end of ten years to accommodate almost 30 percent more patients than they could when the Service began. Substantial reductions in tuberculosis morbidity have also eased the hospital bed shortage by freeing tuberculosis beds for other uses. The population of Great Britain has remained quite stable since the end of World War II.

In December 1960, 465,000 persons supposedly were awaiting admission to hospital, but some observers thought this figure might be inflated by as much as 25 percent because of duplication of lists which are revised infrequently.[12] Logan and Forsyth in 1958 believed that at least 60 percent of the patients awaiting surgery in provincial hospitals, where the waiting period is generally more of a problem, were admitted within three months.

The waiting period before admission to hospital varies with the nature of the complaint as well as with the hospital region. It does not affect those who are urgently in need of hospitalization. Of the doctors interviewed by Gemmill, 98 percent said that emergency cases were always promptly admitted to the hospital. To the more generalized question, "When you refer patients to hospital for examination or bed occupancy, do you have difficulty getting them admitted promptly?" 73.5 percent of the physicians answered "no" and 26.5 percent answered "yes," but many of the latter group added, "unless very urgent." [13]

As concern over rising costs has lessened, and as the country's prosperity continues to grow, new attention has been given to hospital construction. In January 1962 the Ministry released a new "Hospital Plan" in which it revealed that more money had been available for capital expenditures since about 1955, and that con-

11. Lindsey, pp. 301–302.
12. Lindsey, p. 280.
13. Gemmill, pp. 61–62.

tinued increases were expected. It therefore offered to Parliament a detailed, fifteen-year "Long Term Plan" for the hospital regions, of which a major feature is the concept of a 600- to 800-bed district general hospital serving a population of 100,000 to 150,000 and offering, in addition to general medical services, a maternity unit, short-stay psychiatric unit, geriatric unit, and isolation facilities for infectious diseases. Costs of the program are estimated at £200 million for the first five years and £300 million over the next five (with five more years needed to complete construction). The hospital plan received wide and generally favorable comment in the British press and was greeted sympathetically in Parliament.

Quality

When the National Health Service was established, all political parties were in agreement that it should provide the best possible medical care for the entire population. The Royal Societies, the hospital groups, the Local Health Authorities, and the members of the British Medical Association — after their defeat in the battle against the Service — seem to have agreed with this principle from the start. The general practitioners, however, more than any other group, insisted that they be free from "bureaucratic control," and to a large degree seem to have achieved this objective.

The quality of hospital care is said to be imposed and maintained by the rigid hierarchical system of training and experience requisite for all professional advancement. Specialists now supervise patient care to a greater degree than they did before the Service began, when most of them, particularly in voluntary hospitals, gave only unpaid or limited part-time service to some patients.

The situation of the general practitioner, however, is a matter of controversy. In 1950 Collings, in a classic report on general practice in England, concluded: "The over-all state of general practice is bad and still deteriorating. The deterioration will continue until such time as the province and function of the general practitioner is clearly defined, objective standards of practice are established and steps are taken to see that these standards are obtained and maintained." [14] Fears about the deterioration of general practice are still often expressed in Parliament, the press, and professional surveys. It is said that the status of the general practitioner has declined because he has become only a small cog in a huge

14. Joseph S. Collings, "General Practice in England Today," *The Lancet* 258:555 (March 25, 1950).

machine. He is pictured as merely a conduit for patients to the inpatient and outpatient wards of the hospitals. Nevertheless, a survey by Brotherston, Cartwright, and Martin, reported in *The Lancet* in 1957, disclosed that patients prefer the general practitioner over the hospital outpatient department by a vote of almost four to one.

The relationship between the general practitioner and the specialist is also subject to controversy. It is widely held that general practitioner and hospital services should be better coordinated than they are at present. Lindsey states that almost all reports and surveys take the position that family doctors who wish access to hospital work should have it, in view of the need for more fruitful cooperation between general medical practice and hospital and specialist services.[15]

In spite of the considerable freedom of the general practitioner, certain checks on substandard practice and inducements to improve quality of care do exist within the Service. Both general practitioners and dentists are subject to disciplinary action under a mechanism that is largely a legacy from the National Health Insurance Act. Patients may complain to special committees of the Executive Councils which are empowered to hold hearings and recommend appropriate disciplinary action to the Executive Council. Complaints relate mainly to such things as failure to answer a house call or alleged negligence in treatment, and the disciplinary action may consist of a warning, a fine, or, in serious cases, dismissal from the Service. An appeal may be made to the Ministry from the decision of the Executive Council. The Ministry considers all appeals by either doctor or patient except a decision to discharge a doctor or dentist from the Service. These appeals go directly to a special National Health Service Tribunal composed of a physician or dentist as appropriate, a representative of the Executive Councils, and a lawyer who serves as chairman. An appeal from the Tribunal may be made to the courts.

Much of the Parliamentary discussions of 1946 and later negotiations with the British Medical Association dealt with the nature of the disciplinary proceedings and the structure and jurisdiction of the Tribunal. General practitioners were very concerned that there be safeguards against improper disciplinary action by the Ministry. No comparable disciplinary machinery for hospital-based specialists was created in the legislation.

Executive Councils, acting independently or through the local

15. Lindsey, pp. 192–193.

medical committee, were given the right to inspect the premises of any doctor and to enforce compliance with certain minimal physical requirements — a lavatory for patients, a separate or screened-off area for examination, a sufficiently large waiting room, and so on. A survey sponsored by the Ministry and the General Medical Services Committee in 1956 reported that the overwhelming majority of the offices visited were satisfactory and that, where they were not, the fault often lay not with the doctor but with such external circumstances as building restrictions. Dr. Hadfield, in 1951–52, found that two thirds of the doctors' premises he visited were adequate for the maintenance of a high clinical standard, and that 91 percent of the practitioners had all the necessary equipment.

Dr. Hadfield also attempted to evaluate the quality of the care rendered by practitioners. He decided that 69 percent of those he saw adequately examined their patients, and that only 7 percent needed to revise their methods of diagnosis. All in all, he concluded, "Over 90 per cent of the practitioners that I saw are undoubtedly interested and careful in the treatment of their patients." Under the sponsorship of the Nuffield Provincial Hospitals Trust, Dr. Stephen Taylor also evaluated the work of general practitioners, rating one fourth of the doctors as very good and another half as good.

The National Health Service Act empowers the Minister to arrange postgraduate and refresher courses at the universities and to help finance the expenses incurred in taking them. The courses include short weekend sessions, intensive two-week courses, and extended courses covering weeks or months. Physicians taking them receive a daily subsistence allowance and funds to pay a substitute. In 1960 about 2,600 physicians were enrolled.

Since the inception of the Health Service, extra fees have been paid to general practitioners in maternity cases. A larger fee was paid to physicians who met specific standards of experience or training. In 1959 a Maternity Services Advisory Committee reported unfavorably on maternity care in general practice and recommended that the standards of admission to the obstetric list for extra payment be strengthened. It further recommended that the more stringent standards be applied to practicing physicians as well as to doctors entering practice. The Committee concluded that no extra fee should be paid to practitioners not on the list who nevertheless accepted maternity cases, and advocated that the minimum requirements of care be increased to include six mandatory prenatal examinations, attendance at labor or shortly afterward if a midwife had been used, and five postnatal examinations in the two weeks following delivery.

The Ministry opened negotiations with the British Medical Association after receiving the report and announced late in 1960 that agreement had been reached and that the report would therefore be implemented. General practitioners, however, objected vigorously to all phases of the recommended program as interference in medical practice and as unrepresentative of accepted medical practice in England. Negotiations were reopened, and the Minister agreed to delete the proposed requirement for a specific number of physician visits, to postpone for five years the application of the new standards of eligibility for the obstetric list to practicing physicians, and to continue the extra fee for general practitioners not on the obstetric list but taking maternity cases.

More recently, in April 1962, the Ministry announced that an effort would be made to reward and encourage general practice of high quality in accordance with the recommendations of the Royal Commission on Doctors' and Dentists' Remuneration. The plan has three parts:

1. The sum of £500,000 per year would be used to reward "distinguished general practice" under arrangements similar to the merit award system available to consultants in the hospital service. A special Selection Committee, aided by local assessors personally acquainted with the practitioners under consideration, would select the recipients. The names of the doctors selected for awards would not be revealed.

2. The sum of £250,000 per year would be used to encourage general practitioners to attend refresher courses. Practitioners who attended a certain minimum number of courses in each five-year period would receive an added £60 each year during those five years.

3. The sum of £750,000 per year would be used to increase the remuneration of general practitioners for each 1,000th to 1,500th patient on their lists. This increased "loading" payment is intended to encourage smaller lists, to which it is felt more attention can be given. It is also said that it will encourage additional practitioners to enter partnerships.

The Ministry hopes to obtain the agreement of the medical profession to the plan, although many general practitioners are opposed to any merit award system. The British Medical Association has already indicated that it tentatively approves the second and third of the Ministry's proposals, but that it has strong doubts about the first "differential payment" proposal. In a press release issued the same day as the Ministry's proposals, the Association said "the whole concept (of differential payments) is highly contentious."

Cost

The greatest single problem of the National Health Service has been its unexpectedly high cost. Over-all expenditures were grossly underestimated in the Beveridge Report, in the 1944 White Paper, and in the planning for the program in 1945 and 1946. Efforts to stem the expense and keep it within bounds have affected the Service ever since.

In 1946 Minister Bevan gave Parliament an estimate of £110 million for the annual cost of the Service to the Exchequer. At the end of 1947 the Ministry set a figure of £179 million for the cost during the first operating year, July 5, 1948, to July 5, 1949. By the beginning of 1949, however, supplementary estimates had added another £71 million. In Parliament Winston Churchill described these estimates as "the most wild miscalculation." Net costs to the Exchequer for 1948–49 eventually turned out to be £242 million.

In 1949–50, net costs of the Service to the Exchequer jumped to £305 million. Sir Stafford Cripps, the Socialist Chancellor of the Exchequer, announced that a ceiling was being placed on the next year's costs, which were estimated to be £352 million. Actual net costs to the Exchequer in 1950–51 were £335 million, and £348 million in 1951–52.

As a part of the new policy, charges for dentures and spectacles were introduced in 1951. After the election of the Conservatives in 1952, the new government announced that it would continue to set a ceiling on the cost of the Service, and to this end further charges, including the prescription charge, were introduced in June 1952. The new Chancellor of the Exchequer said that utter bankruptcy was the real threat to the Service at that time.

Expenditures continued to rise, however. In 1952–53, the net cost of the Service to the Exchequer had risen to £384 million, partly because general practitioners were given their first general remuneration increase since the Service had begun. Table 5 shows the gross cost of the National Health Service during the five years 1949 to 1954.

During these years there were constant outcries against the "fantastically high cost" and great "waste" of the Service. There was also fear that the cost spiral could not be stopped — that, with an aging population, expenditures would continue to rise. In May 1953 Parliament authorized an official "Enquiry into the Cost of the National Health Service." The task was given to a small committee headed by Professor C. W. Guillebaud, a Cambridge economist. The committee asked the National Institute of Economic and Social Research to prepare a memorandum on the present and prospective costs of the Service, which was done by Mr. Brian Abel-Smith and Professor Richard M. Titmuss of the London School of Economics. The committee held extensive hearings concerned with almost all aspects of the Service, and its report, as well as the memorandum by Abel-Smith and Titmuss, were published in January 1956.

The results of the Enquiry were a surprise to many. Instead of finding great waste and heavy increases in cost, the committee said:

1. No apology need be made for the underestimation of costs before the Service began. These had been the mistakes of inexperience, and they should not influence the analysis of the actual cost situation.

Table 5. Gross costs of the national health service in England and Wales, 1949–1954, in millions of pounds.

Category	1949–50	1950–51	1951–52	1952–53	1953–54
Gross current cost[a] of the National Health Service					
In actual prices	376.6	395.7	411.7	436.7	453.4
In 1948–49 prices	376.6	393.1	383.6	391.9	406.6
Capital expenditures	13.7	15.3	16.5	9.8	8.8
Patient charges	5.0	5.2	9.6	19.8	23.1
Gross current cost per head	8 14s.	9 2s.	8 17s.	9 0s.	9 7s.
Net current cost per head	8 12s.	8 19s.	8 13s.	8 11s.	8 15s.
Gross National Product	9,907	10,539	11,560	12,487	13,273
Gross current cost as a percentage of Gross National Product	3.80	3.75	3.59	3.50	3.42

Source: Brian Abel-Smith and R. M. Titmuss, *The Cost of the National Health Service in England and Wales* (Cambridge: Cambridge University Press, 1956).

[a] Does not include capital expenditures or take patient charges into account.

2. In actual current costs to public funds, not including capital costs, expenditures under the Service had risen by about £15 million each year to a high of £430.3 million in 1953–54.

3. When the general inflation in prices during these years is taken into consideration, the "real" increase in the cost of the Service between 1949–50 and 1953–54 totaled only £11 million.

4. During the same years, population increased by nearly two percent. If this increase and changes in age structure are taken into account (again at 1949–50 prices), the cost per person remained almost constant.

5. Expressed as a proportion of the Gross National Product, the net cost of the Service actually fell from 3.75 percent in 1949–50 to 3.25 percent in 1953–54.

6. In the words of the committee, "The widespread popular belief that there has been an increase of vast proportions in both the money cost and the real cost of the National Health Service is not borne out by the figures."

Public debate about the costs of the National Health Service has quieted down since publication of the Guillebaud Committee report. Perhaps the most significant contribution made by the committee was its analysis of costs in terms of Gross National Product rather than absolute pounds-sterling totals.

There are some significant differences in the cost structures of the three major branches of the Service. In the first seven years expenditures rose most steeply in the hospital service, rose slightly for the local health services, and remained relatively stable for the general medical services rendered through Executive Councils.

Three fourths of the increase in hospital expenditures was the result of additional personnel — primarily nurses and domestics — rather than of wage increases. Few of the charges imposed in the

Table 6. Gross expenditures in the three major branches of the national health service, England and Wales, selected years, 1950–1961, in millions of pounds.

Year	Hospital and specialist services	Executive council services	Local health authority services
1950–51	229.2	139.2	31.2
1953–54	262.3	122.8	40.3
1957–58	365.0	163.2	53.0
1960–61	446.3	193.7	(70.0)[a]

[a] Estimated.

Service have affected hospital patients. In 1953–54, for example, direct payments by patients for amenity and pay beds, as well as for supply and repair of appliances, drugs, and medicines provided through the hospital service amounted to only £3 million, or slightly more than 1 percent of total expenditures in the hospital and specialist service.

The most important result for the hospitals of the early imposition of a general ceiling on costs has been the severe limitation on capital expenditures. Relatively little building or capital renovation has taken place, and the number of total available staffed hospital beds increased by only about 6 percent between 1949 and 1959, largely because of redistribution, repair of bomb-damaged facilities, and additional staff. The hospital construction program announced in January 1962 is intended to increase the number as well as to improve the distribution of hospital beds at an estimated cost of £500 million over a fifteen-year period.

In the early years of the Service, some heavy expenditures were made in the Executive Council services, notably in the dental, ophthalmic, and pharmaceutical services. The very conspicuousness of these services, and the ease with which they can be isolated in a financial statement, led to widespread publicity over their cost, not only in Britain but elsewhere as well. It is in these services that patient charges which bring in additional revenue have been imposed.

The drop in expenditures for Executive Council services noted by the Guillebaud Committee between 1948 and 1953–54 is probably a result of the leveling off of expenditures for dental, ophthalmic, and pharmaceutical services and the relative stability of the budget for general practitioner services. The number of general practitioners is increasing, but not greatly, and their remuneration is controlled by the limitation on the size of their patient lists and by the slow population growth in Britain. Although hospital expenditures have increased sizably because of additional patient services and although the capitation payment has been raised since the start of the Service, the capitation payment system and the limitation on the number of patients a general practitioner can accept operate as checks to increases in income.

The cost of the local health services, of which 85 percent is for personnel, has grown largely because of added staff and services, particularly district nurses, domestic aides, and ambulance services.

Costs in the midwifery program have decreased, both because

of a lower birth rate in Britain and a growing preference for hospital deliveries. Whereas before 1940 less than 40 percent of the births took place in hospitals, by 1960 about 70 percent of deliveries occurred in hospitals. Although the government has from time to time attempted to encourage home confinements, the number of hospital confinements has steadily grown. In the hospital mother and child receive all care, including meals, for ten to twelve days without charge, while at home the family must pay for food and other expenses as well as part of the cost of any drugs or confinement incidentals. The limited available hospital maternity facilities appear to be the major factor keeping down a further rise in the proportion of hospital deliveries. The 1962 Hospital Plan uses the actual 1960 figure of 70 percent of births occurring in hospitals in its calculations for future facilities.

Until April 1959 the Service made grants to the Local Health Authorities that met approximately 50 percent of their expenditures after patient charges. Since then these grants have been absorbed in the General Grant to County and County Borough Councils. In 1950–51 the National Health Service grants to Local Health Authorities totaled £15.6 million, in 1953–54 £20 million, and in 1957–58 £26.4 million. Payments by persons using the Local Health Authority services totaled £2.6 million in 1950–51 and £3.3 million in 1953–54.

The National Health Service is financed by a variety of sources. In 1957–58, for example, 81.25 percent of the funds were provided by national and local taxes, 5 percent by patient payments, 4.75 percent by the superannuation contributions withheld from Service salaries, and 9 percent by transfer payments from the National Insurance Fund and direct Health Service contributions required since September 1957 from employers, employees, and self-employed persons. These direct contributions reached almost £100 million in 1960–61 and met almost 14 percent of the total cost of the Service. In the years before the direct contribution was required, the National Insurance Fund met a decreasing proportion (9 percent in 1949–50 but less than 7 percent in 1956–57) of Health Service costs by transferring about 6 percent of its annual total income, or £36 million, to the Service.

Effect

From the beginning, the National Health Service was intended not only to meet the needs of the population for medical treatment, but to operate as a preventive service as well. Statistics for 1946 through 1951 gathered by Stewart and Enterline, however, indicate that the Service probably did not favorably affect sickness rates.[16] To Gemmill's question: "Under the National Health Service, are the medical needs of the country as a whole being better met, less well met, or cared for 'about the same' as before NHS?" 87 percent of the physicians replied "better met," 3 percent "less well met," and 10 percent "about the same." [17] In a 1958 issue of the *Spectator*, an English physician wrote: "The sharpest critics of the National Health Service have got to admit that the service provided for the ordinary citizen is better than it has ever been. The man who earns his living has been relieved of the fear that grave illness in one of his family may eat into his savings. He knows that he, and his dependents, can have a consultant opinion, and any treatment they may need, in hospital, or out-patient clinic, not as charity, but as a public service to which they have contributed by tax payments."

Table 7. General mortality and mortality by selected communicable diseases, England and Wales, United States, and Sweden, 1931 and 1957.

	General mortality[a]			Mortality by selected communicable diseases[b]		
Country	1931	1957	Percent decrease on 1951	1931	1957	Percent decrease on 1951
England and Wales	12.3	11.5	8	109.4	11.1	67
U.S.A.	11.1	9.6	1	88.8	8.3	62
Sweden	12.5	9.9	0	132.9	8.9	62

Source: Satya Swaroop, ***Introduction to Health Statistics*** (London: E. & S. Livingstone, 1960), pp. 258–289.

[a] Crude death rate per 1,000 population.

[b] Deaths from selected infectious diseases per 100,000 population.

In 1931 there were 66.4 infant deaths per 1,000 live births in England and Wales, 61.6 in the United States, and 56.6 in Sweden. By 1948 the infant mortality rate in England and Wales had

16. William H. Stewart and Philip E. Enterline, "Effects of the National Health Service on Physician Utilization and Health in England and Wales," *New England Journal of Medicine* 265:1187–1194 (December 14, 1961).

17. Gemmill, p. 141.

dropped to 34, and by 1957 it had dropped still further to 23.1. The rate was 26.3 in the United States in 1957 and 17.8 in Sweden.

The maternal death rate per 1,000 births was 1.02 in England and Wales in 1948. By 1960 it had dropped to 0.39. The drop in the United States, however, was even sharper — from 1.17 to 0.36. The maternal death rate in Sweden in 1960 was 0.24, the lowest in the world. In Italy the rate was 1.08 and in the Irish Republic it was 0.66.

World War II, continued shortages and rationing in the postwar period, as well as changes in medical technology, undoubtedly have affected the impact on the health of the British people of the National Health Service. In any case, more than the fourteen years the Service has been operating may be required before its effects can become clearly evident.

A final word of appraisal was given to Gemmill in 1956 by a Conservative Member of Parliament: "We do not have a first-class, but only a second-class health service. However, before 1948 it was only fourth-class. It has been improving ever since, and by and by we shall have a Service that is truly first-class." [18]

18. Paul F. Gemmill, "The British Health Service Today," *New England Journal of Medicine* 259:23 (July 3, 1958).

Drug Costs and Utilization: The Massachusetts Public Assistance Experience

February 1963

Philip D. Berlin

Public assistance programs were established in 1935 as part of the Social Security Act to provide for those persons who would not be covered by social insurance or for whom social insurance would be inadequate. It was anticipated that the public assistance programs would decline in importance as time passed. Since then, however, payments for public assistance have increased, particularly payments made directly to providers of medical care services to recipients.

In 1950 an amendment to the Social Security Act was passed which for the first time permitted the states to pay vendors directly for medical services provided beneficiaries under the federally supported programs. Previously, only cash payments to beneficiaries had been allowed.

A further amendment, the Kerr-Mills, passed in 1960 not only established a new group of beneficiaries, the medically indigent, but required that the states pay vendors rather than beneficiaries for medical services authorized under the program.

In 1952, the first full year in which vendor payments were made, nationwide expenditures under all public assistance programs for vendor payments were less than $100 million. In 1960 total vendor payments were $400 million, and in 1962 the figure was expected to reach $680 million. In 1962 only two states spent more for vendor payments under public assistance programs than Massachusetts.

Vendor payments generally fall into four categories — hospitalization, nursing and convalescent home care, practitioners' services, and drugs and supplies. The last has generally constituted about 9 percent of the national total. In 1960 Massachusetts' vendor payments for drugs and supplies amounted to 11.5 percent of total payments, a larger proportion than is reported by any other major state, and considered on a per capita basis for the entire population, were nearly 50 percent higher than those of the next state reporting these expenditures. Furthermore, Massachusetts was the only state which spent significantly more for drugs and supplies than for physicians' services.

Legislative Background

The Social Security Act of 1935 established a system of federally aided public assistance grant-in-aid programs to the states, as well as several social insurance programs to be administered directly by the federal government.

The major social insurance plan was the Old Age and Survivors' Insurance Program (OASI) which required contributions from the earned income of a major part of the working population as well as from their employers. The program, called OASDI after 1956 when disability provisions were added, was designed on an actuarial basis to be self-supporting, with the administrative costs minimized by the widespread participation for which OASDI provided. Since 1936 many groups originally excluded, including the self-employed, have been added, and payments have been considerably increased. Today more than 90 percent of all civilian workers in the country are covered by OASDI, and 17,000,000 people now receive payments in excess of $13 billion a year.

The public assistance programs established by the Social Security Act cover persons who are ineligible for OASDI or for whom OASDI payments are inadequate. In 1962 almost 30 percent of the 6.3 million people receiving public assistance payments also received OASDI benefits.

The OASDI program is designed to provide payments for some average projected need based upon prior earnings. Once eligibility is established by age, death of primary beneficiary, or disability no tests are applied to determine whether or not need actually exists. Under public assistance a person's financial position must be reviewed before state payments can be federally supported, even though the individual state is allowed to set the criterion for need. Need can be interpreted to include payments for medical care as well as for maintenance, and many states include allotments for medical costs in the cash payments.

Public assistance also differs from social insurance in that federal funds for its financing do not emanate from any special tax, as is the case with OASDI, but rather are appropriated from general revenues. Furthermore, the level of federal appropriations to each state is not fixed by the federal government, but depends rather upon each state's level of expenditures. Federal appropriations made according to this mechanism are known as "open ended."

The Social Security Act, with its subsequent amendments, attempted to differentiate between federally aided public assistance programs in the states and special state general assistance programs which receive no federal subsidy. First, it required that cash payments be made directly to eligible recipients, not to the vendors of goods and services to those recipients as had often been the case in state programs. (A 1950 amendment to the Act permitted the use of the "vendor payment" system for the medical care expenses of beneficiaries.) Secondly, the Act tried to standardize the treatment of welfare recipients within each state, as well as to minimize the social stigma attached to welfare programs. Finally, it required that federally aided programs be equitably and impartially administered and that welfare records be kept confidential.

State general assistance programs, maintained to provide for those persons in need who do not qualify for any of the federally assisted programs, are financed entirely by the states and localities and are often simply "poor relief." Frequently payments are made in voucher form rather than cash. Because general assistance may be administered by local units of government, there may be no uniform program throughout a state. In some states, Massachusetts among them, general assistance programs are financed entirely by local communities.

Federal grants for state public assistance programs are made for certain classes of recipients and for the costs associated with the administration of welfare payments and services to these classes. The original Social Security Act assured the states of financial aid for three types of assistance: Old Age Assistance (OAA); Aid to Dependent Children (now called Aid to Families with Dependent Children or AFDC); and Aid to the Blind (AB). Aid to the Permanently and Totally Disabled (APTD) was added by amendment in 1950, and Medical Assistance to the Aged (MAA), was added in 1960 by the Kerr-Mills Amendment.

OAA was designed to cover the needs of indigent persons aged 65 and over who for some reason did not qualify for OASDI payments or for whom OASDI payments were not sufficient. States customarily apply a "means test," and a common definition of need is "an amount necessary to maintain a standard of decency and health." For AFDC, federal law defines an eligible person as a needy child under the age of eighteen "who has been deprived of parental support or care by reason of the death, continued absence from the home, or physical or mental incapacity of a parent." Parental unemployment has since been added as a basis for eligibility. Closer interpretation of the criteria is left with the states.

The purposes of the Aid to the Blind program is to enable "needy blind individuals to secure the essentials of living and to provide them with the opportunity to continue to participate in the life of the community." Provisions for need are similar to those for OAA, except that the states are required to exempt from consideration the first $85 of the recipient's earned income per month. The decision as to the degree of blindness and minimum age is left to each state.

Aid to the Permanently and Totally Disabled, added in 1950, is intended not only to provide maintenance, but also to encourage the states to help needy disabled persons to attain self-support or self-care. Otherwise, federal regulations are similar to those for other programs.

The program of Medical Assistance to the Aged, added by the Kerr-Mills Amendment, was brought into being "to furnish medical assistance on behalf of aged individuals who are not recipients of old age assistance but whose income and resources are insufficient to meet the costs of necessary medical services," that is, the "medically indigent." Although the general requirements for federal participation in MAA were the same as those for Old Age Assistance, vendor payments rather than cash payments to beneficiaries were required. The states were assured of federal assistance for a full range of comprehensive medical benefits but were left free to decide the exact scope of their own programs. With the passage of the Kerr-Mills Amendment, a full cycle away from the original blanket prohibition on the use of vendor payments was completed, and such payments are now regarded as a necessary instrument in the administration of medical care under public assistance.

Under the original Social Security Act, the federal government was to match assistance payments made by the states to recipients of Old Age Assistance and Aid to the Blind, up to a maximum of $30 per month per person. For Aid to Dependent Children, the Act provided for a federal grant of one third of the total amount paid to the first child up to a total of $18, and up to $12 for each additional child.

In 1946 an amendment to the Social Security Act introduced a new approach to federal financing in an attempt to achieve a more equitable balance of the public assistance burden between the richer and poorer states. It specified that the federal government was to pay a major portion of the first part of the total payment to a beneficiary and a smaller portion of the remainder (for OAA, two thirds of the first $15 and half of the balance, up to a total of $45). It was assumed that a state's public assistance payments would be roughly proportional to its per capita income and consequently that, under the new arrangement, federal grants would cover most of a poorer state's public assistance burden. It was hoped that this procedure would give poorer states the incentive to broaden their programs by making the incremental cost of expansion less to them than to the more prosperous states.

In 1963, maximum amounts of individual monthly payments subject to federal participation are $65 for OAA and APTD, $30 for the first child in AFDC (plus $30 for one needy relative with whom the child lives), and $21 for each additional child. The federal share of expenditures within specified maximums is four fifths of the first $25 and one half of the balance for OAA, AB, and APTD, and four fifths of the first $15 plus half of the balance for AFDC.

Under the Medical Assistance for the Aged program, the state may be reimbursed for from 50 to 80 percent of its total expenditures on vendor payments for the medically indigent, the percentage depending on the state's per capita income relative to the national average. Another amendment effective October 1, 1961, provides that the states be reimbursed a maximum of $15 per recipient for the amount above $65 expended on medical vendor payments for each recipient. Table 1 summarizes the sources of funds for federally aided public assistance categories.

Early Drug Payment Plans in Massachusetts

In 1952 the Massachusetts Department of Public Welfare first permitted local welfare agencies to make payments to vendors for drugs supplied to recipients of public assistance. No uniform statewide program for the administration of these payments was developed at that time, and each locality was allowed to make its own arrangements. The Department indicated, however, that a program would be worked out with the Massachusetts State Pharmaceutical Association.

Local public welfare agencies handled payments within their communities and were reimbursed by the state for two thirds of the difference between their total expenditures on vendor payments for drugs dispensed to welfare recipients and the federal funds provided to meet part of these expenditures. Although the

State Department of Public Welfare exercised little or no direct control over expenditures for drugs provided to public welfare recipients until August 1960, some of the cities attempted to control costs by fixing certain maximum allowable mark-ups for drugs prescribed.

Table I. Source of funds for federally aided public assistance categories, including vendor payments for medical care, fiscal year ending June 30, 1961 (dollar amounts in thousands).

Source of funds	Program: Old Age Assistance	Medical Assistance to the Aged	Aid to Dependent Children	Aid to the Blind	Aid to the Permanently and Totally Disabled
Federal	1,159,941	21,355	665,872	44,992	166,669
State	649,820	14,377	348,465	42,195	101,121
Local	105,185	7,167	114,654	6,804	33,570
Total	1,914,946	42,899	1,128,991	93,991	301,360
	Percentage distribution by source				
Federal	60.5	50.0	59.0	48.0	55.0
State	34.0	33.5	31.0	45.0	33.5
Local	5.5	16.5	10.0	7.0	11.0
Total	100.0	100.0	100.0	100.0	99.5

Source: Release from the U.S. Department of Health, Education and Welfare, Bureau of Public Assistance, Division of Program Statistics and Analysis, December 28, 1961.

The Boston Welfare Department began the development of its own drug plan in 1954. Its drug pricing formula, which went into effect on August 1, 1956, established the fair trade minimum price as the maximum to be paid for fair traded drugs.[1] For non-fair

1. Fair trade laws first came into being as a result of the Miller-Tydings Amendment to the Sherman Act in 1937, which exempted from antitrust laws vertical agreements between manufacturers and distributors to maintain resale prices of branded items. The federal amendment also allowed states to pass a "nonsigner clause," under which all sellers are required to maintain the contractual terms which exist in a single agreement between any retailer and manufacturer. This amendment was struck down by the Supreme Court, but the McGuire Amendment making the nonsigner clause explicitly legal was passed immediately thereafter. In 1963 fair trade agreements were legal in Massachusetts, as was the nonsigner clause. These amendments were passed in order to alleviate the difficulties of small retailers whose markets were being invaded by large and efficiently organized chain sellers operating with large turnover and volume. As defined by the National Association of Whole-

traded drugs, unit cost plus 33⅓ percent was allowed, plus 35 cents if the prescription called for a standard packaged amount, or plus 50 cents if the prescription required that the standard size package be broken. A minimum charge of 75 cents for welfare prescriptions was allowed.

About one half of all drugs are fair traded. The remainder are sold under free competition or come to the retailer bearing a "manufacturer's suggested price."

Under the Boston plan, prescriptions were not to be refilled after 60 days. "Medicine chest items" were not reimbursable, but no definition of these was given, and Boston has in fact made vendor payments for items such as "Empirin Compound" and "Maalox." Prescriptions were limited to drugs that were not "expensive, experimental, or unproved," but these terms were left undefined.

The administrators of the Boston Welfare Department held internal discussions in order to define these terms more specifically. They gave some consideration to requiring prior authorization for all drugs costing more than $10.00 and to establishing a formulary and requiring prior authorization for the prescription of any unlisted drug. In the end, however, it was decided to leave the definition of "expensive, experimental, or unproved" to the discretion of prescribing physicians, who would thus be subject only to the implicit check of disapproval by the Department. The Boston plan explicitly ruled out consideration of any scheme under which drug prices would be established on the basis of competitive bidding.

Although Boston accepted the fair trade price as a basis for reimbursement, the Brookline Drug Plan, which was established late in 1958 and copied with some modifications by several other Massachusetts communities, made no provision for payment of the fair trade minimum price in its formula. Brookline based its reimbursement formula on the American Druggist *Blue Book*, allowing a mark-up of 66⅔ percent on drugs whose unit cost to the druggist was less than $4.00 and to 50 percent when the unit cost was $4.00 or more. The minimum prescription charge was fixed at $1.00. Under the Brookline plan, then, the reimbursement allowed for a particular drug might fall short of the fair trade minimum price established for it.

---

sale Druggists, the fair trade prices were to be sufficient to "afford the average retailer adequate gross profits to cover his operations and leave a reasonable margin of net profit."

Drug Payment Plans in Other States

In several states the state welfare agency has developed a statewide program to administer and control drug expenditures. One of the most comprehensive is that which evolved in Connecticut in the late 1950's. This plan incorporates a number of regulations relating to all phases of the supply and cost of drugs dispensed to welfare recipients. It provides for a fee schedule allowing a minimum prescription charge of $1.00 but, unlike the Boston plan, makes no provision for an additional "professional fee" when the original package must be broken. For prescriptions whose unit cost to the retailer is from 60 cents to $2.99, a maximum of 66⅔ percent may be added. If the unit cost is $3.00 or more, a maximum of 50 percent may be added. If the fair trade minimum price is lower than the price determined by this formula, then the fair trade price is used. If it is higher, it is ignored.

Under the Connecticut Plan, regulations limiting the prescribing authority of the physicians are broad and may be grouped into three different categories: those relating to total prescription price or amount over time, those relating to the nomenclature required in the prescription, and those relating to the nature of the drugs for which payment will be made.

Any prescription for drugs costing more than $10.00 or for supplies costing more than $5.00 requires prior authorization from a District Office, of which there are eight in Connecticut. Prescriptions may be refilled only for patients with chronic diseases requiring continuous therapy, and refills for such patients may be made only within a period not to exceed 90 days. Refills of sedatives and tranquilizers are not allowed.

Secondly, physicians are required by regulation to write prescriptions for 17 of the most important drugs, representing perhaps 90 percent of the most commonly prescribed trade-name preparations, in terms of generic names — for instance, instead of "Serpasil," welfare prescriptions must read "reserpine, U.S.P." These 17 drugs were listed after consultations between the Welfare Department and the state medical and pharmaceutical societies. Physicians are urged, but not required, to use generic terms for all other drugs as well.

Finally, the Connecticut State Welfare Department Drug Plan does not permit payment for any "medicine chest" or proprietary items. This rules out prescriptions for cathartics, first aid supplies, preparations such as Bufferin, Vicks Vaporub, aspirin, sodium bicarbonate, and so on. Allowance for the supply of these items is included in the monthly payment to welfare recipients. Furthermore, the Connecticut Welfare Department will not pay for anything of an "unproved, experimental, or research nature."

In 1961 Connecticut added a provision under which contracts for the supply of drugs to welfare patients in convalescent nursing homes, rest homes with nursing supervision, and boarding homes are allocated by competitive bidding. Connecticut's Welfare Commissioner has estimated that over 75 percent of the drugs given welfare patients in these institutions are supplied under this system. Much thought has been given by Connecticut authorities to extending this system to cover drugs needed by all welfare recipients, but no actual steps have been taken.

Several other states have considered establishing a formulary or selected list of drugs and limiting the physician's prescribing authority to those drugs unless he obtains special authorization to prescribe others. The New York State Department of Welfare has recommended that each local welfare district establish a formulary which would consist of a list of drugs taken from the *U.S. Pharmacopeia* and *New and Non-Official Drugs*. The formulary would be based on the therapeutic efficiency of the drugs and mixtures recommended only when it was clear that they provided a substantial advantage over their individual components. These recommendations have not as yet been implemented on a statewide basis.

Under the Washington State Drug Plan a formulary has been established which is similar to the system recommended in New York. Drugs not in the formulary and all single prescriptions costing more than $10.00 require prior authorization. Drugs allowed by the Medical Plan of West Virginia are limited to those listed in official published national formularies; all others require prior authorization, as in Washington.

The Statewide Drug Plan in Massachusetts

Beginning in 1952, the Massachusetts State Pharmaceutical Association (which represents approximately one third of all retail druggists in the state) and its legislative representative, Mr. Sam Silverman, tried to persuade the Commissioner of the Department of Public Welfare, Mr. Patrick Tompkins, to enter into negotiations leading to a statewide drug payment plan. Commissioner

Tompkins, who was appointed in 1946, had been kept on as a holdover without reappointment since the end of Governor Herter's first administration in 1954, and he discharged his duties with the knowledge that he could be dismissed at any time. (A new commissioner was appointed late in 1962.) Silverman explained that he was anxious to see a statewide drug plan established because, in his opinion, local druggists were being unfairly and arbitrarily treated by local welfare boards, which evidently did not consult them when local drug payment plans, if any, were established. Nevertheless, these pharmacies only rarely actually refused to serve welfare customers.

During the period that the Massachusetts State Pharmaceutical Association and Silverman were attempting to bring Commissioner Tompkins to the bargaining table, several studies were made of the level of prices that various local welfare departments were paying for their drugs. During the early 1950's, Mr. Lawrence Collins, then of the Boston Welfare Department, undertook several studies of the drug costs of Boston, Winthrop, Lynn, and Brookline, and in 1955 some brief studies were undertaken by the State Department of Public Welfare. The studies undertaken by Collins led to Boston's drug plan, which was instituted in 1954, and to Brookline's, which was instituted late in 1958, and copied, with some modifications, by Lynn and Winthrop.

The Massachusetts Department of Public Welfare, to ascertain actual drug expenditures at the time when it was under increasing pressure from the State Pharmaceutical Association to enter into negotiations for a statewide drug plan, in 1959 studied drug expenditures for Old Age Assistance recipients in twelve of the largest communities in the state. The study covered all prescriptions paid for in May 1959, in 11 communities and a 10 percent sample of all bills for drugs paid in Boston from January to August 1959. Of the total of 30,000 prescriptions reviewed, prescriptions actually compounded by druggists amounted to less than 5 percent. Prescriptions for supplies (which are counted as drugs when the recipient's condition necessitates heavy use) amounted to 2 percent of the total.

During the periods studied, 1,607 different prepared drugs, many of which differed only in brand name, were prescribed for OAA recipients. A large proportion of the drugs were sedatives, tranquilizers, and anti-hypertensives. The average cost per prescription was $3.19, and the average expenditure per OAA drug recipient was $10.86 during the period of study. Instances of the same person being charged different prices for the same item by the same vendor were occasionally noted.

In an analysis of 225,345 prescriptions made by Abbott Laboratories in 1955, the average price per prescription to the general public was $2.56. The increase in drug prices since 1955 and the fact that the aged may require more expensive drugs may account for some of the disparity between the Abbott Laboratories and the Department of Public Welfare figures.

In Table 2 the relative magnitude of payments under federally assisted public assistance programs in 1958, and of expenditures for drugs under those programs, is shown. In Table 3 the average

Table 2. Percentage distribution among public assistance programs of total welfare payments and of drug expenditures in 1958.

Program	Percentage of total welfare payments	Percentage of total drug expenditures
Old Age Assistance	67	76
Aid to Dependent Children	18	8
Disability Assistance (Aid to the Blind and Aid to the Permanently and Totally Disabled)	8	12
General assistance	7	4
	100	100

Table 3. Average prescription cost per old age assistance case in twelve Massachusetts cities and in the state excluding Boston, 1957–1959 (in dollars).

Locality	1957	1958	1959
Massachusetts, excluding Boston	4.03	4.47	4.75
Boston	2.21	2.33	2.96
Brockton	5.56	5.82	6.39
Brookline	4.39	4.81	4.03
Everett	5.50	6.10	6.42
Fall River	3.39	3.97	4.49
Fitchburg	4.30	4.87	5.18
Haverhill	6.56	7.01	5.61
Holyoke	4.64	5.01	5.22
Quincy	2.93	3.73	3.98
Somerville	3.12	3.75	4.20
Springfield	4.19	4.53	4.95
Worcester	3.75	4.25	4.66

Table 4. Mark-ups over cost and over fair trade price for the quantities and strengths most commonly prescribed of the fifteen most frequently prescribed drugs.

Drug	Number of pre-scriptions	Total cost to Massachusetts (dollars)	Total cost to druggist (dollars)	Mark-up: Over cost (percent)	Mark-up: Over fair trade price (percent)
Digitalis					
1½ gr., 35	602	671.45	48.16	1,295	–
1½ gr., 50	65	96.15	7.80	1,133	–
Diuril					
0.25 gm, 30	127	331.70	154.94	141	50
0.50 gram, 30	127	514.84	271.78	89	50
Insulin					
NPH-40, 10 cc	205	311.59	202.95	54	50
NPH-80, 10 cc	103	293.41	194.67	51	50
Raudixon					
50 mg, 50	73	219.80	109.50	101	67
50 mg, 100	101	519.35	303.00	104	67
Equanil					
400 mg, 30	65	230.15	126.75	82	–
400 mg, 50	124	664.46	403.00	65	–
Phenobarbital					
¼ gr., 100	109	135.67	9.81	1,181	–
½ gr., 100	58	70.50	9.25	662	–
Serpasil					
0.25 mg, 50	94	393.95	211.50	86	67
0.25 mg, 100	75	566.25	337.50	68	67
Orinase					
tab., 30	29	136.30	91.35	49	29
tab., 50	254	1,799.92	1,333.50	35	29
Darvon Compound					
pul., 30	68	176.45	82.28	115	50
pul., 20	63	121.80	50.40	142	50
Maalox					
12 oz.	228	409.78	239.40	71	67
8 oz.	24	38.80	16.80	131	67
Campazine, 5 mg					
Spansules, 50	37	193.00	106.56	81	–
Spansules, 30	33	248.84	141.90	75	–
Donnatal					
tabs., 100	32	75.58	36.80	105	50
elixir, 4 oz.	53	79.90	31.80	153	50
Seconal					
1½ gr., 24	39	56.40	17.16	229	50
1½ gr., 30	66	105.95	36.30	192	50
Nembutal, sodium capsules					
1½ gr., 30	47	73.32	28.20	160	50
1½ gr., 24	30	38.83	14.40	170	50
Thorazine					
25 mg, 50	39	202.70	113.10	79	–
25 mg, 30	29	97.90	50.46	94	–
Total	–	$9,017.37	$4,840.87	88.3	–

Table 5. Weighted average mark-up for the twenty most expensive drugs.

Drug	Number of prescriptions	Weighted average mark-up (percent)	Mark-up over fair trade price (percent)
Orinase	353	47.9	28.6
Achromycin	68	103.9	33.3
Achromycin V	87	74.7	50.0
Serpasil Apresoline	91	107.3	66.7
Liver Extract	75	63.1	-
Medrol	65	57.2	28.7
Chloromycetin	65	73.1	50.0
Ilosone	62	68.5	50.0
Meticorten	62	80.3	66.7
Rauwiloid	53	81.7	66.7
Decadron	47	91.0	50.0
Deprol	47	76.4	66.7
V-Cillin K	42	92.4	50.0
Panalba	41	42.0	28.6
Furadantin	36	73.8	66.7
Cordex Forte	36	96.1	28.6
Combid	37	89.3	-
Aristocort	35	69.4	50.0
Diupres	31	120.8	50.0
Mysteclin	28	65.5	50.0
Gerilets	31	108.5	50.0

expenditures for drugs per case in 12 communities and in the state excluding Boston are given for 1957, 1958, and 1959.

In Table 4 the cost and mark-up given for the most frequently prescribed drugs refer only to the most commonly prescribed strengths and quantities of those drugs but may nevertheless give a fair indication of the mark-ups for less frequently prescribed amounts of the same drugs. The figures may be consistently lower than actual charges, since the data for Boston were included and the average prescription cost for Boston was significantly lower than that for the other 11 cities studied.

For the 20 highest priced drugs — those whose unit prescription cost was highest — disaggregated data were rarely available, and a weighted average of percentage mark-ups for all quantities of each drug was computed for Table 5. In both Tables 4 and 5, when fair trade or suggested prices were available, the average percentage mark-up allowed by these prices is given as a basis of comparison.

The purpose of the earlier studies made by the State Department of Public Welfare, and of the 1959 study, was not so much simply to ascertain what prices the state was paying for drugs for welfare recipients and what reforms to institute, but rather to strengthen the state's bargaining position vis-à-vis the State Pharmaceutical Association and to put the Association's allegations that local druggists were being exploited into what the Department felt was the proper perspective.

The years before the negotiations actually took place were fraught with acrimony, particularly between Commissioner Tompkins and Mr. Silverman. Charges and countercharges were exchanged, and the press was often enlisted by both sides. Tompkins firmly resisted opening negotiations, believing that the state would come off second-best once they began. Finally Silverman was able to convince Governor Furcolo that the Commissioner was being unreasonable in refusing to negotiate, and pressure emanating from the Governor's office brought Tompkins to the bargaining table in 1960.

It is not clear whether Tompkins approached President Shea of the Massachusetts State Pharmaceutical Association before pressure was brought to bear directly by the Governor's office or as a result of that pressure. In any case, in July 1960 a settlement was negotiated between Tompkins and Shea under which it was agreed that the state would establish a price formula binding on all communities except Boston.

Tompkins had originally offered the same payment schedule that Boston had been using since 1954 but without the "professional fee." This was not accepted, however, and he acquiesced in a more liberal payment plan. The State Pharmaceutical Association argued against introducing the less liberal Boston plan on a statewide basis, asserting that the local Retail Druggists Association had accepted it in Boston because the volume of drugs dispensed to Boston's welfare recipients was larger than that dispensed in the rest of the state. Too, supply conditions in Boston were asserted to be more efficient than in the rest of the state which permitted more efficient retail operations.

According to Commissioner Tompkins, Mr. Silverman objected to the settlement which had been negotiated between Tompkins and Shea (he had not been present during these negotiations), even though it had been approved by the Executive Board of the State Pharmaceutical Association. Through his connection with the Governor, Silverman was able to have the negotiations reopened, and this time he took the place of Shea at the bargaining table. Although he fought for a "broken container" fee of $1.50, he finally acquiesced in a fee of $1.00 and a $1.00 minimum prescription charge. Later Silverman admitted that Massachusetts had, with the $1.00 broken container fee, the highest such charge of any of the states. The fee ostensibly reimburses the pharmacist for the expense of breaking an original container and repackaging its contents in the course of filling a prescription.

The series of negotiations between Tompkins and the State Pharmaceutical Association resulted in a formal drug plan. This plan incorporated a number of features of the Boston plan but in several ways is somewhat more liberal, especially in its "broken container" fee and its schedule of allowable markups.

In detail the final plan provides that:

1. No prior approval to purchase drugs is required so long as the recipient is accepted for public assistance. A physician's prescription is necessary, however, before the local board will pay for the drug.

2. The medical advisor to the local welfare agency may review the prescription but no controls are stipulated in the event that he finds that the prescription is improper.

3. The local board will accept for payment only the amount of medication and the number of refills specified in the written prescription of the physician. Prescriptions which do not call for a specific number of refills will not be honored for payment if refilled by the druggist. Further, neither the notations "ad lib" or "PRN" (allowing for refills upon request of the recipient) nor refills made after 90 days from the date of issuance will be honored.

4. In general, "medicine chest items" are provided for in the welfare recipient's budget, and prescriptions for them will not be honored.

5. Payments for drugs will always be made to the vendor, not the recipient, and reimbursement will always be on the basis of an itemized monthly bill to which copies of the original prescriptions must be attached.

The program for payment by the state for drugs furnished to public assistance recipients involves the following procedures:

1. Drugs compounded by the druggist are to be paid for at a price which represents a reasonable profit on the item, including compensation for professional skills and time involved in the compounding. What represents a "reasonable profit" is not defined, nor are any criteria given for determining compensation for professional skills.

2. All drugs prepared by the manufacturer which have a fair trade price, as indicated in the latest edition of the American Druggist *Blue Book*, shall be paid for at that rate when dispensed in the original container.

3. Payment for all prepared drugs not bearing a fair trade price shall be in accordance with the *Blue Book* wholesale price plus 50 percent when dispensed in the original container, and in all cases the minimum charge shall be $1.00.

4. Drugs which are dispensed in quantities less than the original container are to be paid for according to the proportion of the amount in the original container, plus a $1.00 "professional fee" for the broken container. If more than one size of container is available to the druggist, administrators, in approving reimbursement, are instructed to base their calculations on "the size most likely to be used by most druggists."

5. Payment for medical supplies prescribed by a physician shall be made in the same way as for prescribed drugs.

The plan provides that these shall be the maximum prices paid; if a local welfare department is able to negotiate a lower fee schedule with the relevant professional group, it is free to do so. It is not evident from the wording of the plan whether this extends to the professional charge for the broken container as well.

The Administration of the Drug Plan

The explicit regulations of the Drug Plan seem to be generally observed, insofar as this is administratively feasible. Local welfare department staffs are often small, and larger towns can check only samples of the payment claims they receive from retail druggists; all others are paid automatically, even though they may not happen to adhere to the established payment schedule.

The apparatus for reviewing claims used by individual towns or cities is thus not altogether dependable. In towns or cities where samples of claims are audited (in Boston each welfare district selects a 15 percent sample of all drug stores in that district each month), druggists whose claims exceed that which is allowable under the drug plan are not reimbursed for those claims until the reimbursable amount is settled. There is only a small chance, however, that excessive claims will be found, and there is no penalty for overcharging. Thus there is little to prevent a druggist from making claims in excess of the amount allowable under the established payment schedule. Should he be caught, he loses no more than the excess. As yet, no druggists have been "blacklisted" for overcharging, and charges exceeding the allowable level are frequently discovered in the sample.

The provision made in the Massachusetts Drug Plan for review of welfare prescriptions by the medical advisor to the local welfare department is generally interpreted solely in the light of medical propriety and not of cost. In Boston, however, the medical advisor may indicate to the prescribing physician that a less expensive drug be used, if an identical or nearly identical therapeutic drug is available at lower cost.

Even in Boston, catching prescriptions for drugs that are "expensive, experimental, or unproved," which are officially proscribed by Boston's Drug Plan, is likely to prove difficult. In the first place, these terms are left undefined, and the clerk who checks the claims from the druggist is given no explicit criterion for what is "expensive, experimental, or unproved." Although the social worker is expected to remind the physician what sorts of drugs may not be acceptable, she is not likely to have much specific understanding of the particulars involved. Medical social workers check a number of prescriptions in each district, but it is not clear how they interpret the restrictions, which are apparently more of a deterrent than a prohibition. Outside Boston, few local boards will challenge a prescription on the basis of its expense if it has been written in accordance with the regulations set down by the state.

Before the institution of the State plan, the informal study by Lawrence Collins of the Brookline Welfare Department disclosed that many of the smaller communities had no real conception of how to administer their drug payments efficiently. Many local welfare directors apparently had not even thought about the problem. Since the inception of the State plan, these communities have been allowed by law to pay no more than the established fee schedule. However, the Department of Public Welfare reimburses them automatically on the basis of their stated drug expense for each month, requiring no proof from them that they have in fact adhered to the established schedules.

Although field representatives are sent by the Department to each of the local welfare departments, the field office is understaffed and an audit of a town's welfare records may occur only infrequently. Even when the field officer does check local records, he may not review drug payments, and in any case, it would be difficult for him to discover many cases of drug overpayment. If, however, it should become evident that a community has regularly been paying excessive amounts for its drugs, the state may refuse to reimburse it until it brings its payments into line with those required by the State Drug Plan.

Another administrative problem has arisen from the tendency of some doctors to prescribe drugs for welfare patients in amounts which often necessitate breaking the original container in which the drug was packaged. Each time this has occurred the state has been obliged to pay the extra charge of $1.00, even if the prescription called for several refills. The professional fee for broken containers is regarded by the State Department of Public Welfare as particularly iniquitous, since containers can be and frequently are changed with relative ease.

In order to avoid the unnecessary expense of the broken container fee, the State Department of Public Welfare has made several strenuous attempts, both through personal contact and letters, to "educate" physicians who treat welfare patients to prescribe drugs in terms of the original container. No studies have been made of the success of these efforts, but the experience of Brookline may be relevant. Brookline's original drug payment plan allowed diminishing mark-ups for three different unit cost classifications, and although its plan allowed a $1.00 minimum prescription charge, it made no provision for a broken package fee. When its plan was superseded by the State plan, its drug costs immediately rose, and in 1961 they were still rising, in spite of the State Department of Public Welfare's efforts to educate physicians to write prescriptions in such a way that this professional charge could be avoided.

At one time the Department also sent a mimeographed letter to each doctor known to treat welfare patients urging that, whenever possible, he prescribe drugs by their generic names. This was not followed up, however, apparently because of a division of opinion among the Department's administrative officers.

Commissioner Tompkins believed that prescriptions written in terms of proprietary names were legitimate and reasonable, and that no effort should be made to force physicians to prescribe in generic terms for welfare patients no matter how great the savings in cost. He was of the opinion that the Massachusetts Medical Society would consider such a measure an infringement of the physician's professional autonomy and therefore submitted no proposals to them on the matter. The Secretary of the Society, however, has indicated that Massachusetts physicians might be willing to write welfare prescriptions in generic terms. As the Department has never approached it on this matter, the Society has not formally considered such a step.

Perhaps for the same reason Commissioner Tompkins also rejected the introduction of a drug formulary and a requirement that physicians obtain explicit authorization from medical advisors to local welfare departments when they wished to prescribe nonlisted drugs.

Prior to his replacement in 1962, Commissioner Tompkins had been anxious to disallow prescriptions written for drugs and remedies which can be obtained without a prescription, such as aspirin, bufferin, Maalox, and so on, contending that allowance for these items is included in the regular welfare payment. It is difficult to estimate the effect of his stand. As yet, no explicit restriction is made on payment for these items.

In 1961 Mr. Sam Silverman, legislative representative of the Massachusetts State Pharmaceutical Association, was active once again in legislation concerned with the Massachusetts Drug Plan. A statute proposed by him was passed which requires that each welfare recipient be allowed a free choice of pharmacist.

Many welfare administrators, who are often trained social workers, believe that welfare recipients have as much right to choose their own pharmacist as they have to choose their own physician. Furthermore, as some 80 percent of all welfare recipients are aged, many administrators feel that it would be an unnecessary hardship for them to have to go more than a few blocks from home to obtain drugs.

Nevertheless, Commissioner Tompkins fought strenuously at a hearing before the Joint Committee on Public Welfare to prevent passage of the statute. There is, however, no evidence that the Department of Public Welfare had ever considered a program under which it would purchase drugs directly from manufacturers and distribute them, through the local welfare departments, to welfare recipients upon the presentation of a prescription. The possibility of its instituting a centralized drug purchase and distribution system has now been effectively blocked for so long as the statute remains in force.

Part Two
Case Method

The Case Method and Training of Health Service Administrators

December 1966

Roy Penchansky

How should we be training health service administrators for useful future employment? I contend that our objective must be to provide the following in our programs:

Comprehension of the disciplines underlying health services — economics, sociology, social psychology and statistics — and of their application to health, specifically material on such areas as medical economics, medical sociology, and biostatistics;

Knowledge of administrative and organizational fields, both quantitative and behavioral, such as managerial accounting, personnel administration, administrative practice, operations research, political science, community organization, and their appropriate application;

Knowledge of the health system — the personnel, programs, organizations, institutions, laws, and processes; the disease, diagnostic, and treatment processes; the objectives, history, problems, and attitudes; and the approaches to organizing, controlling, financing, and evaluating; and,

The development of problem-solving and decision-making skills, the ability to plan for implementation, and the ability to synthesize and apply theory to specific problems, the development of skills in group process and verbal communication, and the development of an action orientation.

This listing of areas of education does not imply any conclusions regarding their priority or the weighting which should be given them, but rather provides what I feel is the general order in which the subject areas should be presented to students. There would be, of course, some overlapping in time, and the medical care content would probably overlap the most with the other areas.

A not dissimilar statement of educational objectives has been made by George Bugbee in describing new curriculum developments in the Graduate Program in Hospital Administration at the Graduate School of Business Administration of the University of Chicago.

The Graduate School of Business at the University has firm convictions about the teaching of management or administrative behavior. Essentially, they hold that schools of business should do those things wherein they have a distinct comparative advantage. This means teaching primarily the basic disciplines which underlie operations and their applications in management — not the details of current practices which will be outmoded tomorrow — and conducting basic research which will contribute to the understanding and solution of existing business problems and new ones as yet unknown. What the university can do well is develop the student's critical, analytical, problem-solving, and decision-making capabilities. It can equip the student with the basic knowledge and analytical tools which will enable him to profit most from his experience and enable him to cope most effectively with the changes and situations which lie ahead. In short, the university can equip him for life-long learning.

This they attempt to accomplish via a pyramid — like curriculum. The base of the pyramid is the basic disciplines — quantitative and behavioral subjects. The second level is the operations, or "applied" areas including personnel and financial management. The apex of the pyramid consists of a sequence of related courses in the field of specialization — in our case, Hospital Administration.[1]

It is my thesis and the basis for the development of this case book that the case method of teaching is particularly suited to the presentation of a number of these areas of education and is most useful, and superior to alternatives, in realizing the objective most difficult to achieve — the development in students of problem-solving and decision-making skills, the ability to plan for implementation, the ability to synthesize and apply theory to specific problems, skills in group process and verbal communication, and an action orientation. For this reason, the case method should be employed in training programs for health services administrators.

What is the case method? Because individual teachers use a wide range of specific approaches, the case method is difficult to define. Malcolm P. McNair, editor of *The Case Method at the Harvard Business School,* stated in the preface to that book:

> The decision to have a book written by many men rather than one man is a logical consequence of the fact that the case method is so varied, so diverse, so adaptable to the nature of the individual course and to the personality of the individual instructor that no single person can portray it accurately.

1. George Bugbee, "New Curriculum Developments in the Graduate Program in Hospital Administration at the Graduate School of Business Administration of the University of Chicago," presented at the Annual Meeting of the Association of University Programs in Hospital Administration. Durham, North Carolina, April 1966.

McNair does go on, however, to begin to describe the case method:

Indeed, the only discernible common thread running through these varied dissertations on the case method is the emphasis on student participation in the educational process, on the extent to which the student is expected to carry the ball — assessing the facts, making the analysis, weighing the considerations, and reaching a decision." [2]

Donald David, former Dean of the Harvard Business School, described the case method in a similar way:

The distinguishing characteristic of the case method in the classroom is the extent to which the responsibility for this analytical sifting of pros and cons and for arriving at a definite decision is undertaken by the student himself.[3]

In an article with the interesting title "Because Wisdom Can't Be Told," Charles Gragg presents a somewhat more analytical description of the case method: "Independent, constructive thinking on the part of students is essential to the sound operation of the plan. This result is achieved in two ways." [4] First, Professor Gragg says, students must be given materials that make it possible for them to think purposefully; and second, free channels of communication must be opened between students and students, and students and faculty.

Gragg's word, "materials," rather than the possible alternative "cases," has been retained deliberately. As I shall discuss in more detail below, the case method requires a specific focus for discussion and this focus should have certain attributes. Usually the focus is a case, such as those provided, which has been prepared specifically for this purpose, but specially prepared cases are not always necessary. Many things — a movie, a newspaper story, a piece of legislation, or a part of a novel — can and have been employed as a basis for *meaningful analysis by students,* and that is the case method or, in the words used in 1908 in the first catalogue of the Harvard Business School, the "problem method."

It is only because the item to be discussed must have specific attributes and a descriptive setting and because discussions should

2. Malcolm P. McNair, ed., *The Case Method at the Harvard Business School* (McGraw-Hill, New York, 1954), p. xi.

3. Donald K. David, "Forward," in McNair, p. viii.

4. Charles I. Gragg, "Because Wisdom Can't Be Told," in McNair, p. 6. Also found in Kenneth R. Andrews, ed., *The Case Method of Teaching Human Relations and Administration* (Cambridge: Harvard University Press, 1960), p. 4.

cover various administrative tools and techniques as well as problems for analysis and decision, that documents, usually called cases, need to be specifically prepared and used. Although I use the term case, I have the broader connotation in mind. My primary focus here is on the case method, not on the cases to which the method is applied.

I should like to add my own description of the case or problem method, and in part begin to define the manner in which I see these cases employed. As I see it, the case method has five elements:

First, there should be material, for which I am using the generic term case, as the focus of class discussion. In addition to providing a relevant setting, the case should generally allow the student to know the different roles of the persons mentioned in the case and perhaps to identify himself with one of those roles, and to adopt, or to be able to analyze, institutional or program goals or objectives. Not every case has to have all three attributes, but when a case does, the discussion can be focused and directed within some given boundaries and the student can learn to evaluate the particular circumstances of each person and each situation involved rather than operate on the basis of generalizations inappropriate to the setting or people. Although we seek similarities and useful generalizations, we must stress the differences and the implications of differences in settings for definition of appropriate action.

Second, it must be the students who attempt to delimit the problems or issues for discussion. To tell them the questions to be discussed and what is important in the case does not provide exercise in the development of their ability to perceive and to define problems nor an atmosphere in which they feel they have free range for thinking. The most effective administrators are those who can see the problems, define them operationally, and separate the important considerations from the unimportant ones or the policy issues from the individual decisions. We should promote the development of such skills.

Third, there must be discussion between students, not solely discussion between individual students and the instructor. It is easy for a student to think that a faculty member's answers are better, or that he need not reevaluate his own approach after he has missed some important aspect of a problem — after all, he says "the professor should know more." Approaches and ideas presented by his peers may cause a student to be more critical of himself. Moreover, it is difficult for some students to challenge a faculty member. They may be more willing to be critical — and possibly constructive — with their classmates. Attempts to influence peers, and at times to disagree without causing hostility and strife, are an important learning experience in persuasion, group process and communications.

Fourth, the discussion should be as concerned with the approaches to analysis and to reaching a decision as with the material itself, and the student should have some influence over the pattern of the discussion. The attempt by students to direct or control discussion of a complex problem is an exercise in analysis as well as in group process, and it should form a part of classroom activity.

Fifth, the students must be forced to deal with the question at issue — whether it be making a decision, developing a plan for implementation, or outlining a proposal. Even if the case material leads them to a decision to postpone action or to seek more information, the decision must be a positive one the consequences of which are noted — not a decision that is backed into passively or by default. Students must learn that decisions and action are necessary, even at times when, as is usually the case, information is incomplete. They must learn that even a decision to obtain further information has a cost, and that there are consequences to inaction as well as to action.

My own conception of the case method and the use of these cases may become somewhat clearer if I discuss a number of current interpretations of the use and effect of the case method which I believe to be inappropriate applications of the technique. First, the case method is sometimes seen as an attempt to provide specific information from which students can generalize and thereby develop theories. I do not think this is an appropriate role for the case method. Other pedagogical methodologies can provide the student with more knowledge in less time and in a more organized fashion. Professor Hamilton, in the introduction to his casebook on hospital administration, states, "It must not be assumed that from cases one can easily derive generalizations of overall usefulness. In fact, this method tends to recognize and point up the dangers of broad generalizations." [5] The proper role of the case method, as it relates to theory, is to help students learn how to translate the theory of individual disciplines into a meaningful analysis of problems which takes into account the specific char-

5. James A. Hamilton, *Decision Making in Hospital Administration and Medical Care: A Case Book* (Minneapolis: University of Minnesota Press, 1960), p. 9.

acteristics of each situation. The generalizations to be drawn from cases relate to the processes of analysis, decision-making, and implementation, and, in turn, to the development of a framework or frameworks for use in approaching problems.

Another frequent interpretation of the purpose of the case method holds that it is to present students with examples: they are given a theory or an administrative tool, and then they read a case to see how it applies.[6] To an extent, the case method may do both of these. After a series of cases in which there are recurring issues or problems, the students individually, or the class collectively, may try to generalize. The cases may also provide students with examples of proper and improper application of some technique. Neither of these results, however, should be equated with the case method, nor, I think, should the case method be introduced primarily for these ends as other teaching techniques would accomplish them with a more efficient use of the students' time.

How can the case method contribute to the educational goals of programs in health services administration outlined earlier?

In the teaching of the disciplines underlying medical care, the more usual techniques, such as lectures, seminars, and library work, seem much more appropriate than the case method. The case method can play an important role, however, in the specific application of the theories and techniques of these disciplines to medical care. Let us take, as an example, the use of economic models and statistical techniques to predict the demand for some health service. To hear a lecture and to read articles on how to predict demand is very different from being placed in the role of a hospital administrator who is confronted with a specific problem concerning expansion of facilities, or of a consultant to a planning council who is evaluating the need for additional beds in a community ("Medical Care Planning in a Small Urban Area I"). We are not interested in making economists, statisticians, or sociologists out of our students; but we must be concerned that they know when and how to use the techniques of these disciplines in the solution of actual problems. Case studies presenting such situations can provide the basis for analysis, application of techniques, and, where appropriate, decision making.

Case studies can be presented as part of the "applied discipline

6. Such a use of cases is noted in Edwin Bock's article "Case Studies About Government: Achieving Realism and Significance," in *Essays on the Case Method*, by Bock, Edwin A., James W. Fesler, Harold Stein and Dwight Waldo.

courses" — the term I use for courses such as medical economics and sociology — or as part of an integrative policy course to be discussed later. Assuming that they are used in the applied discipline courses, and that the case method is employed concurrently in other courses or that the students have had previous experience with the case method, it may be effective to intersperse cases with didactic material. One problem associated with this approach is that students may view the cases as examples. The cases must be used rather as drills for the students, and the primary emphasis placed on their selection of the technique and adaptation of it to the given setting. Another alternative is to reserve one section of the course, probably near its end, exclusively for case studies. The advantage of this approach is that the didactic material and the cases are not so closely identified, and more emphasis can be placed on definition of the problem at hand and choice of the proper analytical process. When the students do not have other case method courses at the same time, or do not have experience with the case method, the second alternative may make their adaptation to the method easier and more effective.

In developing knowledge of administrative and organizational tools and techniques and their proper application, the case method plays a similar role. Here, however, the case method not only provides a drill for the students in the use of appropriate technique and its adjustment to the particular circumstances presented, but it can have a far more fundamental effect. The classroom discussion of a specific problem that forces the students to see through their own analysis the need for some form of budgeting or control procedure, for example, makes them far more receptive to learning about such techniques. And the problem that faces many students when they are being taught specific organizational and administrative tools of not really knowing why they are needed or how to apply them does not then arise.

In trying to define some tool or procedure they think needed, the students may be able, depending on their background, to go a long way toward outlining the attributes desired. The instructor can then, if he wishes, lecture on the specific technique in question. Readings on the technique — or technical notes written specifically for use in conjunction with the cases — are then assigned. When cases prepared to make students see the need for some form of analysis or procedure are used, a number of different techniques can be presented in sequence. Cases can then be used which drill the students in the use of the techniques and force them to apply a number of the techniques in one situation, to decide on which technique is appropriate, or to adapt the techniques to specific settings. It should be pointed out that even in this sort of case approach there is an action orientation. The technique is used in a specific way for the solution of a problem; it is not discussed for its own sake.

Does the case method have a role to play in the provision of information about the health system? I don't think that it is efficient to try and provide students with basic information about the institutional aspects of health services through case method courses. Nevertheless, the use of cases written about actual health situations in other sections of the training program can add tremendously to the students' store of information and reduce the amount of time needed for courses concerned primarily with substantive material on health services. In addition, and more important, the type of information conveyed through cases is different from that conveyed by lectures and readings. The actions of persons concerned with health services as described in cases portray their attitudes in a way far more appropriate than could be achieved through a lecture. Use of case studies on, for example, the United Mine Workers Welfare and Retirement Fund, the Saskatchewan conflict, and a group practice where group physicians have been denied hospital privileges ("Changing a Community's Pattern of Medical Care"), can do more to give students a history of the attitudes of physicians and of the areas of conflict in medical care than can alternative teaching methods. Not only can the student develop his own impressions of attitudes, but the specific circumstances in which those attitudes have arisen and the variations they have taken become a part of his thinking rather than some inappropriate generalizations.

The case method also has a special role to play in the provision of information on actual operating procedures used by agencies or institutions. (See especially "Medical Practice in a Group Setting".) These are seldom presented in class, and are probably not worth discussing as a separate subject. But case studies frequently contain considerable material on these points through which the student can become aware of the way in which different organizations operate. They can begin to develop benchmarks upon which to base evaluations or ideas for application in other settings.

Let me conclude these remarks on the role of the case method in the transmission of information with a quote from a discussion of the use of cases in public administration by Dwight Waldo;

One inevitably learns from reading the cases a wide range of facts about the governmental system, about social affairs, about economic life, about the arts and sciences. These facts one could quite possibly learn by other means of pedagogy. But in studying the cases *he does learn them,* inevitably and relatively painlessly. He learns them in context and as they endlessly and subtly interrelate; but of special importance, he learns how the technology of administration relates to the society in which it is practiced.[7]

The case method can make its greatest contribution in the development of skills in problem solving and decision making, in planning for implementation, and in the synthesis and application of theory, and in the provision of an action orientation. These are the skills and the orientation which the student must have but which lectures or seminars do not seem to develop. Through the more traditional teaching techniques, we may be able to provide students with theory, analytical and administrative tools, and goals or direction. But it is also necessary for them to see how a variety of factors involved in a particular situation influence a decision, or why they should be taken into account in the decision; that no patterns of action or solutions are uniformly applicable and that the generalizations of any one discipline must be modified in an actual setting. Students must learn how to recognize the important determinants and how to analyze them for a "useful" solution in a given situation. These ends are not usually effectively achieved through lectures or seminars.

In somewhat of an overstatement, but one which has an important underlying truth, Gragg said, in talking about the need for the case method: "No amount of information, whether of theory or fact, in itself improves insight and judgment or increases ability to act wisely under conditions of responsibility." [8]

The emphasis on field experience and residencies in training programs is an attempt to provide this most important part of an administrator's education and to give him exposure to actual operating procedures. If the desired skills could be developed in class, then time-consuming field experiences could be shortened or eliminated. Moreover, and more important, there is considerable question about the effectiveness and the controllability of field placements as an educational process.

7. Dwight Waldo, "Five Perspectives on the Cases of the Inter-University Case Program," in Edwin A. Bock, ed., *Essays on the Case Methods in Public Administration* (Brussels: International Institute of Administrative Science, 1962), p. 44.

8. Gragg, in McNair, p. 10; in Andrews, p. 7.

In an academic setting, the most meaningful way to develop the skills and orientation desired is through student analysis and decision making on actual situations and problems where the complexities of real life are presented. One focus for such broad student exercises is what I call integrative, policy-level cases through which the student can be given exposure to a wide range of problems and settings and can be brought to analyze more situations and make more decisions than in years on a job. This should not be taken to mean that case method courses in the "tool" or applied discipline areas do not develop the same skills. But the integrative policy course has a somewhat broader orientation and set of objectives than do the tool or discipline areas. The cases presented in this volume are meant for such use.

The objective of the integrative policy course is to put the students into a setting where they must analyze and solve problems in which:

There is a need to integrate theory, tools, and information;

There are a complexity of factors — economic, social, and political — which create the problem and which must be dealt with in its solution;

There is a need to define the problems at hand in an operational way and to differentiate policy from individual decisions;

There are issues of goals, direction, and social policy which are at times in conflict within or between institutions and agencies.

Four interrelated factors determine whether the skills outlined will actually be developed and these should be considered in planning the use of the cases. These are the timing and planning of the course, the performance of both the students and instructor, and the social process in class. These factors are important in all case method courses, of course, but I shall discuss them in terms of an integrative policy course.

First, the proper ordering of courses, the curriculum planning process, and the proper choice and ordering of cases or material, the course planning process. The integrative policy course should come at the end of the curriculum, after courses providing the students with theory, tools, and basic descriptive material. The students will then know the analytical and administrative tools they must select and apply and should have some benchmarks against which to measure the specific situations found in the cases.

The cases themselves should be ordered to foster the objectives of the course. In an integrative policy course, the sequence in which the cases are presented should support an administrative framework. One approach is to start with cases where the objective is definition of the problems or issue and then to progress to those in which the key objective is identification of the reasons for the problem or the issue. The next objectives might be delimitation of alternatives, weighing of the factors which need to be taken into account in reaching a decision, and finally planning for implementation, control, and evaluation. The setting of the cases can also be controlled to move from cases set within one institution with a single set of objectives, to broader settings involving multiple pressures and objectives and in which decisions or analysis may be more difficult. Thus, while still allowing a free range of discussion, the instructor can program the scope of discussion and the development of an analytical framework.

When the cases do not permit such an orderly progression — because they are in short supply or because they deal with multiple and complex problems, as is true of most of those in this volume — the instructor can encourage the development of analytical frameworks by allowing or forcing the class to spend time discussing how the case should be approached.

Second, the proper role of the student. The development of the skills desired depends upon the free exchange of ideas by students, the testing of one's ideas against those of one's classmates, and self-analysis; the use in class of the wide range of experience and education possessed by students in most graduate programs; and the honest involvement and motivation of the student.

A considerable amount has already been said about the need for and the effect of student analysis and discussion. A number of additional points should be noted here. It takes time for the students to learn how to deal with cases and for the class to develop into a social unit in which the students begin to control not only the direction of the class discussion but individual participation as well. If classes are not held frequently enough, neither process takes place. Additionally, more than a few active participants are needed if there is to be meaningful discussion, and since not all students can be expected to participate in each class — nor should there be pressure for daily participation by all — the class must be of a good size, probably no less than 25. With groups of this size and larger, the physical arrangements in the classroom, such as the students' ability to view each other with ease, become important in influencing the discussion and interaction among the students.

What is expected of the student? If the case method is to function effectively, the student must be prepared to analyze and to defend his analysis in class. This means he must come to class with a completed analysis and be willing and able to present and defend it and, where appropriate, adjust it on the basis of other analyses. The student must feel that each analysis is important, and that he is making a responsible analysis and decision. At first students tend to read a case only once and to feel ready then to talk about it in class. Generally, this leads to confusion and disagreement on facts, absence of any complete, integrated analysis, and unreadiness to present solutions or plans. As a way of promoting careful preparation for class early in the course, each class can be started by the instructors calling on a student to present his or her analysis.

Another basic student function is listening — careful attention to and evaluation of the discussion is an important ingredient of the case method. To promote this, the instructor can at times ask a student to summarize the discussion to date; to synthesize a number of comments; whether another student's comments are consistent with his own; or to interpret another student's comments for the class.

Third, the functioning of the instructor in guiding the class. This in good part determines the class' progression and cohesiveness and the students' willingness to discuss and test ideas, and whether the class time is spent on irrelevancies or analysis of the key questions. The key to leadership in the case method is the ability to guide a class through a meaningful analysis and possibly to a decision while allowing a free range of discussion.

The most difficult challenge of the case method for the teacher is to become comfortable and effective in a situation where direct control should not be exercised. To accomplish this requires: (1) a thorough familiarity with the content of the case, from the factual data and what is stated as opinion and what as fact, to the various approaches that can be used to analyze the problem, so that no matter which way the discussion moves the instructor is prepared with pertinent questions, knows where the discussion can lead, and does not fear that the class will get beyond his control; and (2) the development of skill in knowing when and how to intercede to move the class forward or to refocus the discussion without disrupting its flow of discussion or making the students feel that they are being manipulated. The types and numbers of situations that an instructor faces in the case method are so numerous that it is not possible to describe them all, and certainly there is no one prescription for dealing with them. The only way the proper leadership role can be described is by saying that the instructors must have an accurate concept of the objectives of the method and of the course in terms of the effect of the process on students and must become sensitive to the means by which they can foster these objectives not by "telling students" but rather by guiding the discussion and having the students "experience the process."

Last, the social process that develops in a case class. If the instructor has developed an atmosphere that encourages free discussion and that motivates the class toward responsible action, the social process will keep the class moving in a given direction, promote analysis of what is wrong when the class functions poorly, and discipline class members who disrupt the discussion or whose participation is considered superficial. Such action by the class provides a learning experience in group processes for the students.

Some of the general advantages and disadvantages of the case method are outlined below:

Disadvantages

1. Cases are not in fact the real life situation and they cannot provide the students with a complete picture.

2. Generally the students do not have an opportunity to see the consequences of their decisions. Some cases have been developed, however, which provide the students, after they have faced a decision and made it, with another part of the case in which the action of the person faced with the problem and the effects of his decision are described.

3. The case presents a prescribed amount of material. The students learn to select the relevant from the irrelevant information, but this means that unnecessary information must be provided so that the important is not made obvious. Generally the students do not have to seek information, which is an important part of the administrative process. It may be appropriate to allow class discussion of other data that might be desirable or needed as long as the students do not use this as an excuse for not committing themselves to a decision or course of action where appropriate.

4. Continual concentration within the confines of a case can cause excessive orientation to specific incidents and inadequate attention to outside sources of information and theory.

5. It is difficult to develop the skills needed by the faculty. In integrative policy courses the faculty must have an extremely broad orientation. Even when they do, the instructors probably cannot be expert in many areas arising in the cases. If careful preparation is not undertaken, superficial discussion can result.

6. The technique is very time consuming for both faculty and students. Two or three hours of outside work per class hour are not unusual for students, and the instructor can easily expect to double this amount.

7. It is costly to keep case material up to date.

Advantages

1. Case studies are a very pleasant form of education. There is considerable student involvement and interest, with students using their experience.

2. The case method promotes an active rather than a passive orientation.

3. Case studies come close to duplicating the work situation in a number of ways. There are real life problems; interaction among people in reaching a solution; incomplete information; and a need for action.

4. Because the focus is on processes rather than content, the case method develops an approach or attitudes which foster acceptance of changing technology.

5. The focus on the processes of analysis and decision making forces a synthesis of the underlying disciplines.

6. Students develop at their own pace and to the limit of their own ability. The instructor does not have to set a level of presentation that may be above some and below others.

Are there any specific advantages or disadvantages in the use of the case method in programs of health services administration? The particular advantages and disadvantages of the case method are in part a function of the characteristics of individual programs and of the size, type, and quality of the student body. The following observations are drawn from my experiences in the Harvard Interfaculty Program on Health and Medical Care at the Harvard School of Public Health where, for a number of years, I was responsible for a case course. The Harvard program was, in effect, a partially integrated public health administration and medical care program. Each of you can interpret these comments in terms of your own type of program and your own student body.

The classes at Harvard tended to be a little too small, having usually only about twenty students. This disadvantage was exaggerated by the fact that in the early classes an even smaller group participated in the discussion. Most of our students at the School of Public Health were physicians, although there were also a few nurses and social workers, and in the Interfaculty Program courses, a few economists. The students' previous status and roles were carried into class. Until the class developed its own social system and the full student group could be involved, the physicians and the economists tended to dominate the discussion — and there was only limited involvement of the other groups. In addition, the social workers and nurses seemed reluctant to challenge the physicians' opinions. However, one very real advantage of the variation in academic and work experience of the students was the variety of information and experience they brought to class. Moreover, the differences in attitudes and points of view, especially among different professional groups, make a very real contribution to discussion and at times can be related to the case being analyzed.

Another problem in the Harvard Program was the limited time available for the case course. The class met only once a week for two hours and, since it was the only case course, students found it difficult to become accustomed to the case method or to develop a social system in the class. If the case course is to be effective, assuming that it is the only one given, probably at least two classes per week of about one and a half hours each are required. It seems preferable to have a shorter course which meets a number of times per week than one that covers a longer period but meets only once a week. Because of changes in the curriculum at Harvard, the case course will now meet twice a week over a shorter period and I think this means a more effective course. During the summer semester here at Michigan we plan to have an integrative, policy level case course which will meet three times a week for two hours each time.

Another limitation to date has been the shortage of good material to use as the basis of class discussion. Not only is the quantity limited, although this problem is being reduced because of Public Health Service efforts, but our case studies have been written not for a specific teaching purpose but because of current interest in or the general applicability of the situation described. Many are not good cases for class discussion, but because of a lack of real understanding of the case method or a true commitment to it, there has always been pressure to prepare cases on big or current issues. For development of effective case method courses, the objective in the future must be to prepare cases needed for specific teaching purposes. I might add that shorter, more effective cases can be prepared less expensively and often by faculty members on the basis of their own consulting or work experience.

How successful has the case method been? I have no valid basis for any conclusions on whether our students have changed or developed because of our case course. We would have to know the competence of the students when they enrolled and the contribution of other courses. Can we, in fact, measure the effect of education in the short run? These questions cannot be answered. I can, however, provide you with the basis for my own judgment that the case method has been successful, in spite of the problems noted, in developing the skills desired and in motivating the students and of my conviction that with larger classes, more case course time, and more and better cases, the case method can be highly successful in accomplishing the objectives outlined earlier.

During the course of a semester, we observed a notable change in the students' ability to analyze the cases, reach meaningful decisions, interact in class, and discuss approaches to analysis. The students themselves seemed to enjoy the process and to become fully involved. Enrollment in the course in each of the past two years grew during the term, and a very active and cordial atmosphere existed.

Graduates of the Harvard Program, about half of whom I have had occasion to discuss it with, have generally spoken highly of the case course. Many have been much less complimentary about another course with which I was involved so I do not feel that they are merely trying to be pleasant. Student responses fall into two patterns. The small number of students who were candidates for doctorates in economics considered the course to be of limited usefulness; they do not have an administrative and decision-making orientation and generally used the cases as a way of showing the accuracy of economic theory by fitting it to the case incident. Our master's degree candidates who have become administrators, on the other hand, have expressed a feeling that they gained considerably from the course.

To summarize, I do not believe that the case method is appropriate for all aspects of the training of health service administrators

— but, I do believe that there are some essential elements of training that can best be accomplished through the case method. New and better training is needed, and there should be a willingness to try any technique which may make a contribution.

The potential for case courses in many schools and especially for an integrative, policy course including students majoring in medical care, public health, and hospital administration who have differing academic backgrounds and experience, would permit effective employment of the technique. Students in these fields will have to work together in the future, and joint learning in class, with a problem-solving orientation, may give each group broader perspective and greater future effectiveness. It must be remembered, however, that the case method will not be successful unless the teacher understands it and uses it appropriately.

Charles Gragg has stated:

> No method is foolproof. A badly handled case system cannot but be an academic horror. Improperly handled, a case is merely an elaborate means for confusing and boring students. If, moreover, the teacher insists on being a patriarch — if he is sure he has the right and only answers and visualizes his task as one of forcing the students, the case facts, and his answers into an affectionate rapport — it will be found that the out-and-out lecture system is infinitely less costly and less straining to everyone concerned. Such use of cases perverts the unique characteristics of the system. The opportunity which this system provides the students of reaching responsible judgments on the basis of an original analysis of the facts is sacrificed.[9]

9. Gragg, in McNair, p. 13; in Andrews, p. 11.

Course Development

December 1966

Robert W. Merry

The central issue in course development is "How does an instructor wish his students to be different because of having taken his course?" Necessarily, therefore, the beginning of all course development should be the establishment of goals in terms of the student, not in terms of the teacher, nor of the subject matter. The practice of treating what is taught or what is assigned as equivalent with student learning is extraordinarily prevalent in higher education despite its widely known fallaciousness. Effective course development avoids this pitfall.

Effective course development involves selection of methods for particular purposes that within the resources and capacities of the institution and the instructor will most facilitate the learning experience on the part of the student. Hence, any attempt to determine in advance that a course will be a "lecture course," a "discussion course," or a "case course" is ordinarily undesirable.

The following discussion of course development will deal with the subject in terms of:

Proposed goals
Components
Constraints
Selection of components
Sequence of components
Revised goals
Teaching experience
Reevaluation and evolution
Case course development

The development of these topics will be sequential. The actual process, however, as conducted by a professor, involves much simultaneous evaluation and decision making. His intuitive knowledge of his students, his institution and his subject field often make it possible for him to block out quickly certain elements for inclusion and certain elements for exclusion. The consideration of method should be subjected to considerably more thought and experimentation than it ordinarily receives, however. Unfortunately methods are all too often selected intuitively, largely by following habitual or traditional practices.

Proposed Goals

Proposed goals may be equated to desired changes in students. These changes may be thought of in terms of two sets. The first set would include types of changes. The second set would constitute degree of change. The variety of types of changes can generally be subsumed under three headings: knowledge, skills, attitudes.

Knowledge, for this purpose, may be thought of broadly as not only information to be learned but relationships, significance, critical understanding, and the like. In other words, everything from specific data to a rather full comprehension of a subject area may be thought of as knowledge.

Skills may be thought of as the development of personal capacity to utilize techniques for the accomplishment of specific purposes, whether analytical or synthetic. Such techniques might range from as simple physical skills as learning to manipulate and read a slide rule or slicing tissue for microscopic examination to a behavioral capacity for nondirective interviewing to as intellectual an activity as drawing from a novel its basic plot structure or analyzing an administrative problem to determine the major elements of significance and to project a proposed plan of action.

Attitudes involve the development of values, personal priorities, a basic philosophy of life. A course goal may be to help individuals develop their own values. Other courses may have the goal of seeking to inculcate specific values, such as tolerance for others, particular points of view, a belief in social responsibility, a desire to contribute to the welfare of others as well as to one's own welfare.

Each of these changes may be very slight in amount or may be quite extensive in amount. Or the level to which one wishes to bring students, regardless of the level at which they begin, may be quite modest or may be quite high. For example, it may be a course goal simply that students should be aware of the existence of certain data or of certain techniques. A somewhat higher level would require that they have some familiarity with the major elements of the data or the major elements of a technique. A still higher level of achievement would involve a sufficient understanding of the data to be able to interpret it or of the technique to be able, given adequate time, to use the technique for an appropriate purpose. Still higher in level of achievement would be one which brought students to a fairly high degree of proficiency in understanding and use—a proficiency such that the students could utilize the data or the techniques almost unconsciously as part of a working kit of resources. In the case of attitudes a modest level would be simply making students aware of differences in attitudes pertinent to the course. A higher level would involve student understanding of some of the reasons for differences in values. Still higher in achievement would be a level in which the student developed new values or reinforced his old values through a conscious, rational process of thinking about the sources, implications, effects, and relationships of his values to those of others in society and to the relationships which he wishes to develop.

Achievement needs also to be thought of in terms of a class distribution. For some types of work it may be sufficient that the average member in class achieves a desired level of facility, even though a fairly wide dispersion about the central tendency exists. For other kinds of work it may be desirable to permit only a very narrow dispersion or at least that skewness be on the high side. For still other kinds of work it may be essential that a minimum level of achievement be reached by all students. Hence the character of the achievement distribution may become an important factor in the selection of teaching methods or in the determination of the amount of time required, or in the nature of evaluative methods used to determine outcomes.

Components

In a broad sense the first component really consists of the set of proposed goals. For these are essential to the purpose of the course and largely serve as criteria for the selection of other components. For example, the knowledge to be learned may be defined as a set of major topics within each of which more or fewer subtopics may be finally selected. Similarly, in planning experiences to develop skills to be acquired, one may give experience with a single skill in many different situations or one might develop proficiency in several types of a single class of skills. For example, if one wished a student to have proficiency in understanding the nature of standards, quality standards could be studied in many situations varying from control of sterile conditions in operating rooms to control of accuracy in filling prescriptions to control of cleanliness in restaurants to control of factory output quality of products. Standards could alternatively be studied as a class of measures in which students might have experience with quality standards, cost standards, output standards, time standards, rate-of-learning standards and the like. Similarly, the development of attitudes or values might involve exploration of a few specific values in many situations or of a wider variety of values.

Levels of achievement also become components because the level of the goal may lead to variation in the number or selection of subtopics to be considered or of skills to be acquired or of attitudes.

The second major component consists of methods and materials. These two are so interrelated it is difficult to separate them. Materials available may be in the form of books, motion picture films, slide films, programs, case materials, operating models and the like. Beyond the materials, which ordinarily determine method in part, there are methods independent of materials. Such methods include activities such as lecturing, discussing, role playing, interviewing, and the like. The variety of materials and methods available is substantial. A partial listing could include at least the following: lecturing, original source reading, textbook study, library research reports, motion picture film viewing, slide film viewing, record listening, tape listening, demonstration viewing, generalized discussion, use of a variety of case materials (such as illustrative cases, historical cases, diagnostic cases, decision cases, administrative action cases, incident cases, sequential cases, vertical case series, horizontal case series, springboard cases, hen-and-chicks cases), case demonstration method, incident discussion, laboratory work, field work, competitive field work projects, computerized administrative gaming simulation, labor negotiation simulation, programmed instruction, sensitivity training, role-playing, and an enormous variety of combinations of these and other methods.

Constraints

A significant constraint in most situations is the student mix. This is ordinarily a "given." How much education have the students had? Has it been formal or informal? What is their experience? How mature are they? What is their level of intellectual capacity? Achievement ability? Motivation? Peer relationship?

The determination of this constraint is important because it represents the beginning point from which changes are to be made and from which, insofar as possible, the success with which they are made should be measured. The mix, of course, consists of a set of distributions each relating to different aspects of the students, some of which represent previous development and some of which represent somewhat more capacity for development, although the two are certainly not independent.

Occasionally an instructor may have the opportunity to select his own students. If the group of students wishing to take his course, from which he makes his choices, is sufficiently varied, he may have an opportunity to create a student mix to fit his own purposes. In such a case student mix would become one of the components rather than a constraint.

The second significant constraint is the time available. Ordinarily instructors are told the number of sessions they may have for their courses, the length of the class period, the amount of preparation time to which they are entitled (within broad limits) from students and whether or not extra sessions may be held under unusual circumstances.

A third major constraint is the limitation in choice from among methods or materials available. Such limitations are sometimes made by administrative decision, as when instructors are told that they will give a lecture course or a discussion course, or that they may not use case materials or that they may not send students out into the field. Sometimes materials cannot be used because equipment necessary to their use are not available, such as an overhead projector, a motion picture projector, or a computer. Sometimes a limitation is placed on the amount of money a course may require students to spend for materials in connection with the course.

Still another constraint is the budget allocated to the course. Budget limitations may severely limit the acquisition of faculty, staff, facilities, equipment, or other aspects of the course that might otherwise be chosen.

Even the environment may constitute a severe constraint. Opposition, sometimes formal and autocratic, sometimes informal and attitudinal, may restrict or eliminate the opportunity for use of particular methods or materials. Such opposition may come from central administration, from departmental chairmen, from the senior faculty within a department, or from other faculty.

Selection of Components

Dealing initially with one component at a time, one must select from the variety of materials and methods available, one or several in combination that will produce in the allotted time the desired degree of achievement with regard to the particular knowledge, skill, or attitude sought. After thinking of the various ways of providing these experiences for each segment of the course, an instructor may start to think about how through a particular set of materials and methods he may achieve several components simultaneously.

For example, if one of the goals is that students should become interested in, indeed enthusiastic about, the central subject matter of the course, various methods may be available. If the instructor is a very stimulating lecturer, the lecture method may provide high success in motivating students. If the instructor is not of this quality as a lecturer, but is effective in leading discussions, the selection of materials particularly meaningful to the group of students concerned, dealing with difficult issues, and skillfully led by the discussion leader, may produce the desired enthusiasm. In some cases the interest may be produced by assigned reading of exciting research projects relating to the area of the course. Sometimes literature may produce the objective.

If a second goal of the course is to develop a substantial knowledge of what has been revealed by research, the use of exciting research papers for outside reading or the lecturing about the results of research by a stimulating lecturer may make available at least two methods, either of which would fulfill two of the course goals simultaneously.

If one of the goals is to develop within the students a perspective of time, mores, speed of change, and the like, a study of history might be particularly useful. Such a study might take place in the form of reading histories, of presenting interpretive monographs, of holding exploratory discussions.

For a goal of training in the skill of determining the questions to ask, Professor Pigors' Incident Method is an effective approach. Experience in interviewing or in questionnaire design may also be useful. Training in logic to help in the determination of pertinence may be helpful.

For developing an understanding of complex social problems, students may learn well from the study of individual case histories, of sociology, administrative cases, and the like.

For producing skill in the use of budgeting techniques, an instructor might utilize a combination of methods from texts, lectures, problem materials, programmed instruction, or case materials. Experience in administrative formulation and implementation of administrative policy within an organization may be gained by struggling with diagnostic case materials or simulated administrative gaming.

Central to the selection of materials and methods is the need to direct the focus to the learning experience rather than to a teaching transmission. In making choices, the instructor should keep clearly in mind the variety of constraints that may be pertinent in each case. Of particular importance among these are the constraints of funds, time, and facilities available. One must compare the values gained against the resource costs. Such costs include not only dollars but time of faculty, time of students and the occupation of space.

A good lecturer may be highly stimulating and may be able to convey through expression and intonation as well as language an understanding of nuances not available in the written word unless the writer happens to be exceptionally gifted. On the other hand, a student may not hear the lecturer. He may miss a point through no fault of the lecturer because of sneezing or other extraneous noisemaking about him; he may become interested in thinking about one point and in preoccupation miss a portion of the lecture. The lecture method is rather inflexible in terms of schedule, since a person must be present at the time of the lecture—sometimes an impossibility for him if he is sick or otherwise unable to fit the schedule. Furthermore, the lecture requires more time to hear than it would take to read its text.

If a lecture were available in printed form, the student could read it whenever he chose to; if he misses points, or wool-gathers temporarily, he may go back and reread; if he is sick at one time he could read it equally well later, and he can read more rapidly than he can listen. Hence, printed materials for reading often have many advantages over lectures, and many lectures would be more effectively presented in written form.

In programmed instruction, if the program is well conceived and presented, a student frequently will learn much more material more effectively and more rapidly than by either the lecture or by reading. He is able to move at his own pace with high concentration. Such a program may be preferable to either lecture or text.

If the subject is approached by a discussion method and if the subject is one in which the exploration of a variety of views of others is significant to understanding or to the development of values within each student, this method may be particularly effective despite greater time taken on the part of the students and if a larger lecture group needs to be broken down into smaller groups for discussion, despite the requirement for more faculty people and for more rooms.

If one is thinking of a situation in which a school with facilities already exists, what are the additional costs of the various methods on a per course per year basis?

If a student is asked to buy and read books on his own, the dollar cost to the institution is nothing and the student's per semester course cost is usually under $25. There are probably no additional costs to the institution in terms of numbers of people, space provided, or faculty time. For the student the time spent in reading is short relative to most other methods and therefore effective if he reads well.

If one is providing a lecture course, an institution is probably allocating to the course resources of the order of $5,000 to $15,000 for the lecturer and supporting help—a portion of faculty load and supporting services for the year and a lecture hall for the time needed.

Under programmed instruction a resource allocation running from $10,000 to several times that amount might be involved in the initial preparation of the program but considerably less involved in the revision and improvement of the program through experience with it, and thereafter there would be very little in the way of allocation required, other than the use of teaching machines and space or the effort in printing the program in the form of a "scrambled book."

Analyses of this sort may be made for the various methods and materials that could be used effectively.

Sequence of Components

Several criteria are involved in putting the various components together in a suitable sequence. The first of these is the need for certain specific knowledge of some topics before other topics may be discussed. The degree to which prerequisite understanding becomes a rigid determinant varies considerably with the level of achievement desired in the student. Furthermore, sometimes presenting students with a problem to which they do not have adequate tools for solution is worth while because of its effectiveness in stimulating their understanding of the need for and helpfulness from such tools.

Apart from understandings that must necessarily precede a segment of the course in order for that segment to be understood, there may be materials which may make the learning of a segment easier if they are presented before that segment arises even though they are not essential to understanding it. The broad orderly logic of the subject matter may often serve as a fairly useful base from which to work in the construction of a course. A systematic presentation in which both the faculty and student can see the sense of the broad structure and again see at each point in the course where they are in the learning of the subject may be helpful in keeping perspective and acceptance of progress.

On the other hand, the difficulty of the learning task may vary considerably from the subject matter logic. Should the variation in learning difficulty be great and should the learning of the easier materials help in later learning the more difficult materials, a sequence developed around the concept of moving from the easier tasks to the more difficult tasks may be better. Frequently a mixture of the two conceptual schemes is effective. Since the purpose of the course is the achievement by the student of the course goals, pedagogical logic or experience must ultimately carry a higher priority than subject matter logic. Fortunately the two are frequently not in conflict.

If one has not had experience in moving particular topics or experiential materials from one part of a course to another, he may be quite unaware of the great influence the sequence of materials has on the ease and speed of learning. The entire approach of students to a particular problem may differ significantly because of the material immediately preceding it.

Revised Goals

After arranging the various components in an appropriate sequence for the course, each component having its own number of classes determined, the instructor needs to add up the amount of time estimated to achieve his goals. With rare exceptions, when he then compares the figure of time required, as he had estimated, with the time available to him, he will find his estimated requirement greatly in excess of the time available. If he has chosen well the best materials and methods for achieving his purposes, he may have little opportunity for reducing the time while maintaining his original goals. He may find by further thought and ingenuity ways of accomplishing more goals through common materials. As a rule, however, he must revise his goals, giving up some of his earlier hopes for what he could achieve through the course.

Such revision of goals may involve the elimination of some of the knowledge, skills, or attitude development which he had hoped to achieve. It may involve a reduction in the achievement levels he had hoped to attain. One becomes involved in determining priorities and establishing trade-offs between the knowledge, skills, and attitudes on the one hand and achievement levels on the other. These secondary choices may be influenced by the availability of materials and methods that will bring students to a lower level of achievement with significantly less time, for if such materials and methods are not available and little time may be saved, the topic may have to be dropped.

This possibility points to a very important determination, one which I believe is all too frequently ignored. This determination is the question of whether at a lower level of understanding or achievement a particular aspect of the course should be included at all. There is great danger in "watering down" the learning experiences. If for later work a student needs a high level of proficiency in a particular skill, giving him some awareness or familiarity with it without that proficiency needed for later work, he may be led to take on advanced work in the belief he can handle it only to find himself in difficulty. Sometimes it is not worth doing "a little bit." The effort to cover everything without attention to the doubtful value of enabling a student to mouth "buzzwords" without real understanding of substance has produced many superficial "survey" courses.

Of particular significance today is the trend of education away from the light presentation of vast numbers of data toward depth presentation of a relatively few aspects of the subject area, through which the principal concepts may be learned. With the rate of advance in knowledge we know that a great deal of what we have as adequate data today will be inadequate within a relatively few years. Concepts tend to have a slower rate of obsolescence and afford much greater utility in understanding other parts of subject areas not directly studied. This trend may make easier the approach of dropping breadth of data in favor of depth of analysis of a portion of the subject.

It may also, however, lead an instructor toward thinking of his original goals insofar as knowledge is concerned, not in terms of specific pieces of information, but in terms of the concepts central to the purposes of the course. An extraordinary amount of double, triple, or quadruple value in terms of the development of student understanding may be achieved by eliminating the need for memorization of enormous quantities of data when the pertinent concepts may be developed through learning a relatively small portion of the total data.

The process of goal revision then becomes one largely of determining trade-offs and of establishing priorities with particular attention to the desirability of dropping material for which a sufficiently high achievement level cannot be attained in the time available.

Teaching Experience

Starting with the original course plan the instructor then presents the course. An instructor who is watching carefully for student learning may decide to vary from his original plan giving more time here and reducing or dropping time there as he finds that the student learning does not take place at the rate he anticipated. As he teaches the course he also notes the effectiveness of the materials for him, the degree to which the learning process is helped or hindered by the development of the informal class organization and its establishment of norms of behavior encouraging or inhibiting learning and its exercise of social pressure to enforce its attitudes. He will also need to be aware of the influence of external factors such as the draft, war conditions, campus events, or other significant forces at work. Out of this observation he may note the need for changes in materials, methods, allocated time, his role, and the like.

In addition to his own evaluation of the course he may wish to obtain either informally or rather fully through formal mechanisms student reactions and colleague reactions (insofar as the latter are in a position to have valid judgments). If an instructor is not aware of some of the methods and instruments used for evaluation purposes, he may wish to look them up in the literature.

Reevaluation and Evolution

Out of these evaluations develops an evolution of the course year by year. A constant reevaluation is necessary because student bodies change both in terms of knowledge brought to the course and in terms of capacity for learning. Environmental conditions change. The needed learning within subject areas changes as new knowledge and new techniques are developed. New conditions require new attitudes and values; new pedagogical materials and methods are becoming available. All these provide new opportunities for improved learning experiences.

There is, therefore, in the development of a course, a general direction with interplay at various points. Starting with proposed goals interacting with constraints, one determines the components available, makes selections of these components, and arranges them in a course sequence. Relating the course then to the time available one explores a three-way interaction among selection and sequencing of components and revision of goals. If a significant segment of the course is dropped because sufficient achievement may not be attained, one may move back to other components available in order to use the time effectively for some other aspect of the subject area. After the course has been tailored to fit the available, the process of teaching the course leads to a reevaluation of revised goals, completing a cycle.

Case Course Development

Because my own institution, the Harvard Business School, is ordinarily thought of as using "the case method" for its work, I am often asked about case course development. As the preceding discussion of course development would indicate quite clearly, the question is, in my opinion, the wrong question. One starts not with "case course development" but with "course development."

For the teaching of administration, however, the case method has a great deal of value. In my use of the terminology, using cases as illustrative materials, or assigning cases for students to use in applying principles previously taught, or lecturing about case situations would not fall within the definition of the "case method." By the "case method" I refer to the development of a subject by the students' study of a large number of cases in planned combination. Such study and attempted handling of many administrative problems develop within a student, often unconsciously, an understanding and facility for thinking in terms of the major problems faced by the administrator in the field together with the ability to analyze and evaluate the circumstances of the problems and to make decisions and construct programs of action for their execution appropriate for the particular situations. The process is inductive rather than deductive and the purpose is the development of proficiency in analyzing administrative problems, reaching decisions as to desirable action, and formulating programs for making the decisions effective. The purpose is not the development of generalizations or principles even though such development may be a useful pedagogical device to provide ideas for consideration in trying to handle a specific situation.

The curriculum at my school, despite its reputation as the most ardent user of cases in the field of administration, utilizes cases for only one half to two thirds of its instruction. Significant use is made of text material, research studies, pertinent literature of the field, library research reports, field research reports, computerized competitive gaming simulation, sensitivity training, written and oral reports, lecturing, and other methods.

If a body of factual information is needed in order to handle case materials, such data are ordinarily presented in the form of a printed technical note, such as information about an industry within which a company operates or information about a process utilized by a company, by a combination of descriptive and problem material or by assigning to the student the responsibility of learning the material independently on his own through library or field work. The case materials provide an excellent opportunity for analytical thinking in problems involving tangible and intangible data, concrete and abstract considerations, material and personal components. Since traditional practices, group norms, the technology of process, management goals, the power structure may all simultaneously be influencing particular management decisions, the nature of the analysis is complex and the decision-making and program-planning processes involve substantial subjective, analytic reasoning and imaginative, projective thinking. By using a number of cases involving a central type of problem under varied circumstances, a substantial "feel" for that kind of problem, for the considerations of importance in it, for the interrelationships among its parts, for alternative possible solutions, and for ways of carrying out a plan may be effectively developed. It is often little recognized also that in the course of presenting a number of cases, a very substantial body of factual material is almost unconsciously learned — and learned in a context of usefulness which not only improves retention but provides a greater understanding of the pertinence of the information to the problem.

In a course one might wish to develop perspective, to give training in question-asking and fact-gathering with regard to a kind of problem, to develop a capacity to discover the problem when it is not apparent in a situation, an ability to make wise decisions, and proficiency in planning to carry the decision into effect in an organization. In such a situation one might for perspective consider lecturing, reading historical material, or discussing historical cases. For question-asking one might draw on the incident method until the learning experience was sufficient to bring the student to the desired proficiency in that skill. For fact-gathering, library or field work could be used. One might then go on to analytic cases involving clarification of considerations pertinent to a stated central problem, following these with diagnostic cases in which the problem would be neither explicit nor apparent. Then one might move to action-oriented cases in which there was sufficient data to permit extensive planning of program action steps, sequences, timing, delegation, and follow-up for carrying out planned decisions. If the central problem is one in which certain specific analytic techniques such as ratio analysis, present value of future funds, linear programming, or the like are valuable, such techniques would be planned for presentation through methods that would provide the most effective learning experience in each for the students. There would be no presumption of using case materials for these purposes; in many instances the use of case materials for such learning would be inferior to other methods.

As is the case with musical instruments, the effectiveness of a teacher using case materials will vary greatly with his knowledge of and skill with the instrument. Some teachers may effectively use case materials for many purposes for which other teachers would find them wholly unsuitable. The case and the case method is essentially a vehicle through which learning may be promoted. Under the direction of one type of person it may be effective whereas under the direction of another it may not. One may not draw final conclusions about cases or the case method, since it is but one component of a situation in which one has a mix of goals, students, methods, and instructor, all with a set of constraints. If an instructor finds case materials or the case method useful for certain parts of his work, he may with intelligent care try its extension into other areas in which it appears to him it may have promise. Unless the method improves his ability to develop learning within his students, however, it does not seem desirable for him to draw upon this vehicle. An exception might exist where he was attempting to develop proficiency with it in the thought that the difficulty was in his lack of proficiency with the method. There is, of course, a learning period in working with case materials just as there is in the arts, the sciences, or other areas of learning.

One may say therefore that the case method provides an extraordinarily useful vehicle in the hands of an effective case teacher and under environmental situations favorable to it for learning about administrative situations. As any of the surrounding elements vary, the effectiveness of its use may also vary. The experience has been highly motivating and learning-oriented for students and unusually stimulating and satisfying for faculty members.

An Essay on Terminology: The Case Study, the Case Report, and Similar Terms

October 1966

Sagar C. Jain

The expression "case study" has a very floating meaning at present. Its concept seems to differ from field to field and even from person to person within the same field. This situation is further complicated by the fact that a variety of other expressions (such as case history, case problem, case report, case record, case, and case method), also in currency, are sometimes used as synonyms of "case study." Such a situation causes considerable communication barriers among scholars and teachers interested in and concerned with case studies in some way or another. To overcome such a barrier, it is necessary to identify the various meanings attributed to the term case study and to distinguish the meanings of case study from those of other similar sounding expressions.

Approaching the task in a reverse order, let us first pin down the meanings of the various terms and expressions which have "case" as a first element and which are often confused with one another. In the absence of standardized vocabulary, I have first indicated the customary usages of these terms. Then, to prevent confusion which results from the various usages of the terms, a simple meaning is ascribed to each of them. In ascribing these meanings care is taken to minimize the violence to the customary usages. This effort need not be considered as authoritative because it is not. The effort is only to suggest, to draw attention to a very confusing situation, and to invite further thoughts on the subject.

Ever since the case method of teaching was introduced by Christopher Langdell in the Harvard Law School in 1871, the "case" terms have been proliferating in the field of professional education and research. In this discussion we shall examine their usages in schools of Business, Education, Law, Medicine, Public Administration, Social Work, and Social Research. The information presented in this paper is derived primarily from the literature from the various fields. In addition many faculty members in these fields were interviewed.

Business

The term case and the expressions case history, case record, case report, case problem are in wide currency and are generally used interchangeably. Little effort has been made to delineate their exact meanings. In 1931, Malcolm McNair of the Harvard Business School suggested the following distinctions between case and case problems: "The term 'case' is used to denote a case where the decision is stated while 'problem' is used to denote a case which ends with a question rather than a statement of the company's decision." [1] However, such a distinction between the two terms is not always made.[2] Sometimes the expression case study is also used either as a synonym of any one of the expressions noted above or as a synonym of case writing.

The expression case method is used to denote both an approach to and a philosophy of education. In the context of the former it is argued that the theoretical contents of the business courses being imprecise, these courses are best taught through the inductive method, that is, through an examination of a variety of real life situations. In the latter context it is stated that the purpose of education is not to help students memorize information but to help them develop faculties of thinking, comprehension, analysis, integration, decision making, and action.[3] Often the term case method is used loosely. A teacher who uses cases to illustrate an otherwise theoretical or abstract point as well as the one who uses cases to help his students develop a general insight in the real life situations is also described as using the case method.

1. Malcolm P. McNair, "The Collection of Cases," in C. E. Fraser, *The Case Method of Instruction* (New York: McGraw-Hill, 1931), pp. 154–155.

2. During an informal discussion Professor Richard P. Calhoon of the School of Business, University of North Carolina at Chapel Hill, who is the author of *Cases in Personal Management and Supervision* (New York: Appleton-Century-Crofts, 1966), and a joint author of *Cases on Human Relations in Management* (New York: McGraw-Hill, 1958), made the following off-the-cuff distinction between "case" and "case problem": "A problem is a case in which one simple problem is indicated, but a case usually includes several problems."

3. See C. E. Fraser, *The Case Method of Instruction*, especially Arthur Stone Dewing, "An Introduction to the Use of Cases," and Melvin T. Copeland, "The Development of Principles by the Use of Cases." See also Malcolm P. McNair, ed., *The Case Method at the Harvard Business School* (New York: McGraw-Hill, 1954); Kenneth R. Andrews, ed., *The Case Method of Teaching Human Relations and Administration* (Cambridge: Harvard University Press, 1960); and John D. Glover and Ralph M. Hower, *The Administrator: Cases on Human Relations in Business* (Homewood, Ill.: Richard D. Irwin, 1963), pp. vii to xx.

Pigors and Pigors have evolved a variant of the case method and have termed it the "incident process."[4] This involves five steps:

1. The students are given a short description of an incident which is usually one short paragraph.

2. Since no background material is made available to the students, they interview the teacher to obtain background information (the teacher is briefed on the information beforehand). One student then summarizes the facts as they have been obtained.

3. The students must decide on what the central issues are.

4. Each student is asked to write a brief decision, which is discussed by the class.

5. Finally, the class discusses the broader meaning of the case in an effort to tie it in with similar situations or to suggest means of preventing such problems from arising in the future.

Although the expression case method is used primarily of a teaching method, it is also used in the context of research effort. The collected cases provide vivid details of organizational functioning and thus seem to offer a rich source of raw material for systematic, organized, and generally applicable conclusions. The series of *Harvard Business Reports* published between 1925 and 1932 was an effort in this direction. The cases were systematically classified and commented upon toward the end that "business wisdom" be developed inductively on the basis of empirical factors disclosed in these cases. Subsequent studies such as those of Culliton,[5] Tosdal,[6] and Butters *et al.*,[7] have used selected cases for inductive theorization on managerial problems.

Law

The most commonly used terms in law are case and case method. A case is a written statement which customarily includes: (1) a statement of the facts of a happening, occurrence or

4. See Paul and Faith Pigors, *Incident Process: Case Studies in Management Development* (Washington, D.C.: The Bureau of National Affairs, 1955), and their *Case Method in Human Relations: The Incident Process* (New York: McGraw-Hill, 1961).

5. James W. Culliton, *Make or Buy*, Business Research Studies No. 27 (Boston: Harvard Bureau of Business Research, 1942).

6. Harry R. Tosdal, *Salesmen's Compensation* (Boston: Harvard University, Graduate School of Business Administration, 1953).

7. Keith J. Butters *et al.*, *Effects of Taxation: Corporate Mergers* (Boston: Harvard University, Graduate School of Business Administration, 1951).

an event; (2) the limitation to an issue or legal problem; (3) the opinion of the court; and (4) the decision of the court.[8] The last two items are peculiar to legal cases in view of the fact that in law a case also serves as a legal precedent.

The case method is a method of instruction in which legal tenets are sought to be taught through the study of cases to the exclusion of the textbooks.[9] The teacher assigns a number of selected cases involving a definite class of interest, for example, "contracts made by minors," without the student being possessed with the pertinent principles of the law. In class, the student is to be ready with the salient facts, the issue, the decision and the reasons therefor. The student's presentation may appear erroneous to the teacher. Then his classmates and the teacher participate in a general criticism and the student is required to defend or amend his analysis of the case in question. This discussion is followed by a series of hypothetical corollaries presented by the teacher. Fact after fact is altered and at every point the student is required to weigh, for the purpose of decision, the importance of each difference and resemblance. Various similar cases are contrasted to determine whether they are logically analogous. Conflicting decisions are subjected to rigid scrutiny and the very point of difference is ascertained. After the individual cases have been thus analyzed, the various threads of thought are woven together. The correct decision having been established for each set of facts, the students attempt to formulate a principle which shall embrace them all. This is an optimum exposition of the case method in law. In actual practice it is executed in diverse ways and rarely in strict compliance with the above description.

A variant of the case method is the problem method advocated by Jacob Landman. The students are presented with a legal problem in a skeleton form. The facts in the problem are not stated in the same fashion as presented by the client. Neither the view of the court nor the decision is indicated. Instead, the students are supplied with a selected legal and extralegal bibliography. The students examine the problem in the light of their readings and then defend their views in the class.[10]

8. Wallace B. Donham, "Business Teaching by the Case System," in Fraser, pp. 14–15.

9. Jacob H. Landman, *The Case Method of Studying Law: A Critique* (New York: G. A. Jennings Co., 1930), p. 22.

10. Landman, especially pp. 78–101.

Medicine

In the field of medicine as in the field of law and business, the origin of the use of the case method has been traced to Harvard influence.[11] Apart from case method two other expressions, case and case history, are commonly used, but not interchangeably. The medical dictionaries include the last two expressions and define them fairly precisely.[12] A case is not a person, but an occurrence, a single instance or example of a disease. In medicine, as in business or any other field except law, the cases presented are observer's descriptions, whereas in law the cases are the courts' own record of their own doings and thus possess greater authority and at the same time less objectivity.[13]

A case history is the information gained from the patient or others regarding symptoms and the past history of the case.

Case method does not seem to have the same meaning in medicine as in business or law. It may refer to the use of case history as a working tool, which serves such very practical ends as ensuring continuity of treatment and facilitating diagnosis in the light of development rather than judgment from isolated symptoms. It may also refer to the system under which advanced medical students are asked to take care of certain selected patients under the guidance of a well qualified doctor. In medical education, cases (using the expression in the tradition of the Harvard Business School) primarily serve the purpose of providing illustrations and insights. However, a carefully studied and reported case or a series of cases that may lend themselves to statistical analysis serve useful research purposes. The expression case method or case-study method is also used in the context of research methodology.

Public Administration

The use of the case method in public administration is relatively recent. Probably the earliest efforts to produce cases in this field were made in 1940.[14] In the early writings the expression case

11. Abraham Flexner, *Medical Education in the United States and Canada*, Carnegie Foundation Bulletin No. 4, New York, 1910, pp. 98–99.

12. For instance see *Stedman's Medical Dictionary* and *Blakiston's Medical Dictionary*.

13. *The Encyclopaedia of the Social Sciences* (1930), Vol. 3, pp. 253–254.

14. In the early 1930's the Social Science Research Council set up the Committee on Public Administration. This committee in turn formed a sub-

report was used. These case reports were prepared not so much for teaching purposes as to serve the research interests. A case report was equated with the test-tube study in a laboratory.[15] However, in later years, especially after the organization of the Committee on Public Administration Cases in 1947, which later in 1951 led to the organization of the Inter-University Case Program, several other expressions have come into currency. Among them are case, case history, case study, and case problem. These terms, together with case report, which is no longer used in the test-tube sense, are often used interchangeably despite some effort to standardize their meaning. Professor Frank Sherwood of the University of Southern California using Ronald Bauer's writing[16] has suggested that there are essentially three types of case, which in general are graded according to length and depth of information included:

1. *The Case Problem,* which contains an identifiable problem and a brief statement of relevant facts. It does not contain the decision or its consequences.
2. *The Case Report,* which includes all that is contained in the case problem but adds more background, the administrator's decisions, and the consequences of the decision.
3. *The Case Study or Case History,* which follows the general pattern of the case report but is more detailed and more searching.[17]

Under the influence of the Inter-University Case Program (ICP) the term case method, which is used interchangeably with case-study method, has taken on the same kind of teaching and training orientation as is noted for the field of business administration. However, the ICP cases tend to be considerably longer than a typical business case, probably because the former are almost wholly given to the description of complex decision-mak-

---

committee called the Special Committee on Research Materials. It was this Special Committee which made concerted efforts to produce cases in public administration. As a result, beginning in 1940 and continuing through 1944, one hundred and twenty cases were published and were collected into three volumes under the title *Case Reports in Public Administration* (Chicago: Public Administration Service, 1940, 1941, 1944).

15. W. E. Mosher, "Case Studies in Public Administration," *American Political Science Review* 33:66–68 (February 1939).

16. Ronald C. Bauer, *Cases in College Administration* (New York: Bureau of Publications, Columbia University Teachers College, 1955), especially pp. 36, 192–194.

17. Frank P. Sherwood, "Some Aspects of Case Method Teaching," in Frank P. Sherwood, and William P. Storm, eds., *Teaching and Research in Public Administration: Essays on Case Approach* (Los Angeles: School of Public Administration, University of Southern California, 1960).

ing situations in which relatively higher level personnel are involved.

The Comparative Administration Group (CAG) of the American Society for Public Administration seems to view the terms case study and case-study method in the context of research methodology. To this group and many others in the field [18] a case study is a serious piece of research intended to enlarge knowledge and to test current hypotheses about a somewhat particularized aspect of public administration. The case-study method is a method of research through which an individual administrative unit or culture is probed and the data are analyzed by stressing developmental factors in relation to environment.

Social Work

Although the case method in business and public administration was imported from the law schools, it has grown organically in the field of social work in response to the professional needs. The expression case method is not commonly used in this field, and when used it implies a method of teaching based on case discussions in the class.[19] The expressions which have very wide currency are: case, case work, case approach, case record, case report, case history, case summary, and case study. A review of literature did not reveal any effort to standardize any of these terms except case work.[20] Even with regard to case work (often

18. For instance, see Frederick C. Mosher, "A Guide to Case Study Research" in Sherwood and Storm, pp. 32–33.

19. See Charlotte Towle, *The Case Method in Teaching Social Work* (New York: National Association of Social Workers, 1959).

20. Margaret Williamson, *Social Worker, Artist and Scientist in Human Relations* (New York: The Macmillan Co., 1964); Esther L. Brown, *Social Work as a Profession* (New York: Russell Sage Foundation, 1942); Werner W. Boehm, *Objectives of the Social Work Curriculum of the Future* (New York: Council on Social Work Education, 1959); Council on Social Work Education, *A Conceptual Framework for the Teaching of the Social Group Work Method in the Classroom* (New York: 1964); Frances T. Dover, *Field Instruction in Casework* (New York: New York School of Social Work, 1962); Ruth G. Wells, *Theory and Practice as a Single Reality: An Essay in Social Work Education* (Chapel Hill: University of North Carolina Press, 1963); Jean S. Heywood, *An Introduction to Teaching Casework Skills* (London: Routledge and Kegan Paul Ltd., 1964); Nathan E. Cohen, *Social Work in the American Tradition: Field Body of Knowledge, Process, Method and Point of View* (New York: Dryden Press, 1958); Norman A. Polansky, *Social Work Research* (Chicago: University of Chicago Press, 1960); Helen Perlman, *So You Want to Be a Social Worker* (New York: Harper, 1962).

described as social case work) there has been some controversy as to whether it is a specialized field, a method, or a focus of social work. Generally the expression social case work implies social work practice focused on individuals or family units unable to adjust to their socioeconomic environment. A detailed social study (with psychiatric overtones) of the history and environment of the "client" is made for diagnosis and treatment.

The term case approach is sometimes used to emphasize that some social problems cannot be dealt with *en masse* and that they require case by case treatment.

The term case frequently refers to a client, situation, or occurrence. It also refers to a specially prepared statement describing: (1) the problem situation, (2) the background facts, (3) the diagnosis, and (4) the treatment or action.

Case record is often used interchangeably with case in its latter sense. However, a case record is not a specially prepared statement; it is maintained routinely as a part of help-giving processes. A case record in a case work agency is likely to include information on: (1) the helping situation, (2) the client's perception of his problem, (3) the social study of the client, (4) the diagnosis, and (5) the treatment. In addition, it may also include all correspondence with the client and other concerned parties. All information is recorded chronologically.

A case summary is a digested version of a case record but the information may not be arranged chronologically. Often a case is nothing but a case summary.

Case history may be used interchangeably with case as well as with case record, but commonly it refers to the history of a client problem or malfunctioning.

Case study is not commonly used in the context of social case work practice. But in social group work and community organization fields the expression has a fair degree of currency. In social group work it may refer to social or behavioral studies of the individual members of the groups, or a study of the group as a whole. In community organization, it may refer to a community study or to a report describing or analyzing a community organization project.

Case report is used variously. It may refer to a specially prepared case, a social-behavioral study of an individual member of a group, a statement on the progress of a client, or a student's report evaluating an assigned case.

Education

The use of cases in the field of education seems to have been influenced by two different sources, social work and business administration. They were first employed by visiting teachers as an aid to pupil guidance in the early 1900's.[21] Since then cases have become an extremely important professional tool in student guidance work.[22] The use of cases in teacher education and in the training of school and college administrators is relatively recent.[23]

The guidance people and teacher educators hold different concepts of case or case study and use them in different traditions. Those in student guidance field seem to have been influenced by the tradition of social case work. However, there are some important conceptual and methodological differences between these two fields. These differences may be noted from the way the following expressions are used in the guidance field:

Case method — a method of guidance on the individualized basis.

Case approach — a synonym of case method.

Case — an individual pupil with a problem.

Case study — (1) a statement of problem; (2) information on physical, mental and social abilities of the pupil as well as on his academic, social, and economic background; (3) diagnosis; and (4) remedial plan. Some people in this field have started using the expression "pupil study" instead of "case study."

Case-study method pertains to the method of making a case

21. See Bauer, p. 34; and see D. Henryetta Sperle, *The Case Method Technique in Professional Training* (New York: Bureau of Publications, Columbia University Teachers College, 1933), pp. 16–20.

22. See Ruth Strange, *Counseling Techniques in College and Secondary Schools*, Chapter 8, "The Case Study" (New York: Harper and Brothers, 1949). James F. Adams, *Problems in Counseling: A Case Study Approach* (New York: The Macmillan Co., 1962).

23. See Elizabeth Hunter and Edmund Amidon, *Student Teaching: Case and Comment* (New York: Holt, Rinehart and Winston, 1964); Adam M. Drayer, *Problems and Methods in High School Teaching* (Boston: D. C. Heath and Co., 1963); Bauer, *Cases in College Administration;* Willard Olson, "General Methods: Case Study," *The Year Book of the National Society for the Study of Education,* 1939, Pt. II, pp. 329–332; R. E. Elder *et al.*, "Let Us Get Down to Cases," *Social Education* 12:160–162 (April 1948); Wallace B. Donham, "Why Experiment? The Case System in College Teaching of Social Science," *Journal of General Education* 3:145–156 (January 1949); A. S. Barr, "The Case Study Method in Education," *Journal of Educational Research* 21 (January 1930); and Stanley S. Marzolf, "Case Studies and Teacher-Training," *Educational Administration and Supervision* 27:383–388 (May 1941).

study. It refers to the use of case studies to sensitize students of guidance counselling to the needs of individual pupils and to help them gain the skills of giving guidance.

Case record or cumulative record is a highly structured summary statement that a school maintains on each of its pupils.

The use of the case method in the training of teachers and educators seems to have been influenced by the tradition of schools of business. The terms used in these two fields are fairly similar, although the meaning assigned to them is not exactly the same. The common terms are used as follows:

A case is a written statement of a problem or a description of a problematic situation. Information on the background of the problem as well as how the problem was handled is generally not included. However, the description of the problem or situation is generally followed by: (1) the case writer's comments in which he highlights the problems involved; and (2) a list of questions, some theoretical and some dealing with the practice.[24]

Case problem and case study are used interchangeably with case.

Case method refers to use of cases in teaching.

Case history, case record, and case report are not commonly used.

Social Research

In the field of social research, as in many other fields we have surveyed, there are a host of "case" expressions in use. Their meanings are not standardized, and two social researchers will only rarely use these terms in the same fashion. Therefore the meanings of the popular expressions listed below are conjectural in nature.[25]

24. Many case writers in business also include a list of questions at the end of the case. Such a practice is frowned upon by the Harvard Business School. See Andrews, pp. 122–123.

25. Observations in this section of the paper are based on a review of more than thirty writings. Several of these were concerned with methods of social research while others were "case studies." Among them were Claire Selltiz *et al.*, *Research Methods in Social Relations*, revised in one volume (New York: Holt, Rinehart and Winston, 1963); Pauline V. Young, *Scientific Social Surveys and Research* (Englewood Cliffs, N.J.: Prentice-Hall, 1956); Frederick C. Mosher, "A Guide to Case Study Research," in Sherwood and Storm, pp. 32–43; Nicholas Nicolaidis, "The Case Method as a Research Tool in Administrative Theory," in Sherwood and Storm, pp. 61–85; Paul B. Foreman, "The Theory of Case Studies," *Social Forces* 26:408–419

Case refers to an individual, an institution, a community, or any group considered as a unit for study.

Case study is a detailed study of a case to gain further insight into the conceptualization of a problem, to test a current theory,[26] to evoke hypotheses, or to open a field for research.

Case-study method refers to the research methodology of making the case studies. Although many well known case studies have been made through immersion strategy (primarily through direct observations, both participant and nonparticipant in nature), the use of personal documents and third person reports are not precluded.

Case method is used as a synonym of case-study method.

Case technique is another synonym of case-study method.

Case history is a case study in which the researcher gives his primary attention to the history and development of the case.

Case record refers to the descriptive portion of a case study.

In social research literature one comes across an expression "critical incident method" which must be distinguished from "incident process." As we have noted above the incident process is a variant of the case method of teaching and training. The critical incident method is a method of social research developed by psychologist John C. Flanagan.[27] Basically, it involves studying one or more exceptional behavior situations or occurrences to

---

(May 1948); Clifford R. Shaw, "Case Study Method," *Papers and Proceedings of American Sociological Society* 21:149–157 (1926); E. W. Burgess, "Research Methods in Sociology," in Georges Gurvitch and W. E. Moore, *Twentieth Century Sociology* (New York: The Philosophical Library, 1945); Herbert Blumer, *Critiques of Research in the Social Sciences: I. An Appraisal of Thomas and Znaniecki's* The Polish Peasant in Europe and America (New York: Social Science Research Council, 1939).

26. Claire Selltiz *et al.* believe that hypothesis testing is not an appropriate feature of case studies. According to them the attitude of the investigator should be of "seeking rather than testing." See their *Research Methods in Social Relations,* p. 60. I have rejected this view in the face of a number of well known case studies which were undertaken to test existing theories. For example, S. M. Lipset *et al.* in *Union Democracy* (Glencoe, Ill.: Free Press, 1956), set out to examine the two party political democracy of the International Typographical Union as an apparently deviant case for Michel's Iron Law of Oligarchy. Alvin Gouldner, *Patterns of Industrial Bureaucracy* (Glencoe, Ill.: Free Press, 1955), and Peter Blau, *The Dynamics of Bureaucracy* (Chicago: The University of Chicago Press, 1955), are efforts to examine the workings of the Weberian theory in real life situations.

27. See Ralph Wagner, "The Critical Incident Technique — Its Use in the Present Research and Its Place in Personnel Psychology," in *The Development of a Procedure for Evaluating Officers in the United States Air Force: Technical Appendices and Notes* (Pittsburgh: American Institute for Research, 1948), p. 1.

gain insight into the total personality of an individual, a larger social phenomenon, or a formulation.

The above survey is far from comprehensive. Even then it reaffirms my original observation regarding different meanings of terms like case study, case report, case method in different fields and at times within the same field. I need not overwork the argument that such a state breeds confusion and makes communication, particularly interdisciplinary communication, very difficult. Just imagine a situation where *A* hires *B* to do some case studies, and it turns out that these two persons have very different concepts of the term case study. To *A* a case study is a brief report describing a problematic situation in some detail. He needs such reports for his teaching and training programs. To *B* a case study is a serious piece of research with a view to evoking or testing hypotheses. The confusion and frustration that must result from these conflicting definitions of the term case study can easily be visualized.

To avoid confusion and to facilitate a meaningful exchange of ideas and skills between teachers and researchers in various fields, it is necessary that we develop a common language. In view of growing interdisciplinary curricula and researches, there is a pressing need for systematic efforts in this direction. The process of developing such a language may be more difficult than is usually realized. People tend to get attached to their speech usages. At times they acquire fanatical loyalty to them. Personally I have great faith in emotions and loyalty. But as people in the business of reason, we cannot afford to be irrational or unreasonable. To develop a common language we must rise above our preferences and proceed in the spirit of give and take. It is in this spirit that I suggest that some of the most popular "case" terms may be used in the following fashion in an effort to evolve a common interdisciplinary language.

Case — a single unit on which study is focused. This unit may be a person, group, community, a situation, an event, or an occurrence.

Case report — a complete written description of the case, which also provides information on the background and the ending of the case. However, it neither indicates the analysis of the facts reported nor any formulation based on these facts.

Case problem — a written report describing an observed problem. It may include information on the background of the case, but not on how it was resolved nor on the attempts to resolve it. It also does not contain anything on the analysis of the problem and possible solutions.

Case study — an intensive study of a case undertaken to generate new knowledge or to create opportunity for the generation of such knowledge. A typical case study will include the description of a case, an analysis of the case stressing developmental factors in relation to environment, and a conclusion shedding new light on the current theory or the concept.

Case method — a method of teaching in which instruction is based on discussions and analysis of case reports, case problems and similar other material. Case system and case technique may be used as synonyms of case method.

Case-study method — the method of making a case study.

Case record — an administrative tool for recording and maintaining information on a case.

Case history — a chronological description of the development of a case. It includes neither an analysis of the information reported nor does it record a conclusion based on this information.

Of all the terms described above, two, case report and case study, are of crucial conceptual significance. Therefore it may be useful to discuss and distinguish these two terms in further detail. This task is best accomplished by first identifying the major elements in the makeup of these two terms and then comparing these two in relation to each of these elements (see Table 1). Here it should be reemphasized that my description of these two terms does not necessarily conform to their common usages at present. Also it should be pointed out that in Table 1 I have taken a polar approach and have viewed these two terms as poles apart. This is done to emphasize the dichotomy. However, the differences between them are not always likely to be as absolute as are indicated. Ofter a case study will exhibit some of the elements which are attributed to a case report. The reverse may also be true. For instance a case study may be short, heavy on description, and written as much for teaching purposes as for research. On the other hand, a case report may run into hundreds of pages, the author as well as people and places involved in the situation may be identified, and its rich and accurate details may serve as a basis for conceptual refinement, hypothesis testing, and other similar research goals. However, such overlaps should be viewed as exceptions.

Table 1. A case report as contrasted to a case study.

Element	Case report	Case study
1. Purpose	Produced primarily for teaching and training purposes. Not intended to generate new theories, principles or formulations.[a] Instead it is to serve any one or more of the following purposes: (1) to illustrate an abstract argument; (2) to help students develop a general insight in the real life situations; and (3) to help students develop operational skills and mental faculties.	May be used as a teaching tool, but this is not its central purpose. The main purpose is to facilitate new insight in the current knowledge and theory in the field. May be undertaken to explore unknown research frontiers, to formulate or refine concepts in order to generate hypotheses or test a current theory.
2. Nature of the case	A. The cases are either typical (to help serve purposes number 1 and 2) or problematic (purpose number 3). Often a case will have both these characteristics.	A. There is no emphasis on typical and problematic cases. Often an atypical case or the one about which little is known better serves the research purpose than would a typical case. Generally the selection of a case is dictated by the intended purpose of the case study.
	B. Events in the near past are preferred.	B. Concurrent events are preferred.
	C. The case may be fictitious, although real life cases are preferred.	C. The case must be real.

[a] In the early phase of the evolution of the case method it was hoped that a systematic compilation of case reports (using the terms as I have described them) would lead to inductively derived "principles." This hope has not been realized despite the fact that thousands of case reports are now available. The Harvard Business School alone had produced over 20,000 case reports by 1954 (see McNair, p. 282). Lack of standardization and redundancy of data in the case reports are only partly responsible for the nonrealization of the original hope. A more important factor responsible for this situation is a gradual but a definite shift in the focus and the purpose of the case method. The inductively derived "principles" are no more aimed at, and instead the effort is to provide insight into real work situations and to help develop skills and abilities to cope with them.

Table 1. A case report as contrasted to a case study (*continued*).

Element	Case report	Case study
3. Method of data collection	The emphasis is on obtaining the whole "story" and not on "how." The method used is not reported. Useful guidelines for locating appropriate cases, for securing cooperation of people concerned, and for reporting have been developed.[b]	The methodology is a crucial consideration. A case study is only as good as its methodology of research. The description of the methodology is an important part of the report.
4. Content	A case is described to the end, and information is provided on (1) the event, (2) its background and (3) its conclusion. The author's analysis and conclusion are not included.	A case is described in full. In addition, analysis of the data together with author's conclusions is included.
5. Length	Length is an important consideration. A very lengthy case is cumbersome and often unmanageable for class use. A case which may run to fifty pages is often considered too lengthy.[c]	Length is not an important consideration. The important thing is to get all the data, analysis and discussion in. A case study reported in more than 1,000 pages is not too long.
6. Identity of the subjects studied	It is not important to identify the persons, places, organizations, and products by their real names. In fact the fictitious names are preferred to the real names[d] for two reasons: (1) to protect all concerned from any harm which might be caused to them if their real identities were made known; and (2) to permit a more objective and dispassionate discussion in the class.	Real identity of the subject is often crucial information without which verification possibilities are substantially reduced. The names may not be revealed only when this is justified on the grounds of research strategy or ethics.

[b] See McNair, *The Case Method at the Harvard Business School,* especially the last three essays; Andrews, *The Case Method of Teaching Human Relations and Administration,* especially Part III; Edwin A. Bock, ed., *Essays on the Case Method in Public Administration* (Brussels: International Institute of Administrative Science, 1962); and Sherwood and Storm, *Teaching and*

Table 1. A case report as contrasted to a case study (*continued*).

Element	Case report	Case study
7. Identity of the author	Identity of the author is not crucial. When an author is identified it is to reward him for the trouble taken in preparing the case report.	Author's identity is very important. The findings are often evaluated in the context of the author's standing as a researcher. In those cases in which the subjects studied cannot be identified by their real names, the author's identity serves as the primary basis for evaluating the integrity of the research effort.

Research in Public Administration: Essays on Case Approach. See also Bauer, pp. 181–204.

[c] The ICP case reports often run into such a length; and many people do not consider them too lengthy.

[d] The ICP case reports prefer to use the real names.

In the end let me reemphasize the need for a precise common language which could help the scholars from different fields communicate efficiently. Let me also underline that my attempt here is to draw attention to the problem and to provide a base for a meaningful exchange of views to solve it.

Appendix

A Note on the Use of the Case Method in the Teaching of Public Health Administration

Where does the field of Public Health Administration stand with regard to the case method? Several observations are relevant and need to be made. First, there are several "case" terms in currency. Some of them are case, case report, case study, case problem, case record, case history, case method, and case-study method. It is fair to say that there is a great deal of confusion in the use of these terms in this field. It is partly because these terms are not standardized, and it is partly because the field of public health administration draws people from a number of disciplines and people from different disciplines tend to speak with different idioms. There has been no systematic attempt to evolve common meanings for these terms.

Second, the case method of teaching is becoming increasingly popular and there is a growing realization of its utility and value. However, the understanding and thinking regarding the case method still are not precise. At times it is confused with other techniques like role playing, simulation, in-basket, and laboratory. At other times, the case method may be viewed as no more than supplementing class lectures with illustrative reading material. Indeed there are always some people in every field who view the case method as a mere fetish with which they will have nothing to do. A lot of this confusion and misunderstanding have resulted from a lack of exchange of ideas and discussion on this subject among people in the field of public health and between people in public health and those in other fields where the tradition of the case method is deep rooted.[1]

Third, there is a great paucity of teaching case material in the field of public health administration. There is not a single case book prepared specifically to meet the needs of teachers and students in this field. No university, professional body, commercial enterprise or any

1. The following writings can provide a useful base for a discussion of the concept, purpose and techniques of the case method: Kenneth R. Andrews, *The Case Method of Teaching Human Relations and Administration* (Cambridge: Harvard University Press, 1960); Malcolm P. McNair, *The Case Method at the Harvard Business School* (New York: McGraw-Hill, 1954); Paul and Faith Pigors, *Case Method in Human Relations: The Incident Process* (New York: McGraw-Hill, 1961); Edwin A. Bock, ed., *Essays on the Case Method in Public Administration* (Brussels: International Institute of Administrative Sciences, 1962, also available from the University of Alabama Press); Frank P. Sherwood and William B. Storm, *Teaching and Research in Public Administration: Essays on Case Approach* (Los Angeles: School of Public Administration, University of Southern California, 1960); Charlotte Towle, *The Case Method of Teaching Social Work* (New York: National Association of Social Workers, 1959); and Hugh Cabot and Joseph A. Kahl, *Human Relations: Concepts and Cases in Concrete Social Science* (Cambridge: Harvard University Press, 1953).

other kind of institution has taken any lead in this respect.[2] Individual teachers have put together some case reports for their own classes. Some of the ICP case reports,[3] community surveys and case studies[4] are also used. Sometimes case reports and case problems are also borrowed from the field of hospital administration.[5] But it is rarely that people in public health administration take advantage of the thousands of case reports in business administration. Why this gold mine of case reports in business administration has been almost totally neglected will make an interesting study. But in the meanwhile let me propose four somewhat interrelated explanations: (1) there is relatively little personal contacts between the faculties from these two fields; (2) the public health faculties have a negative stereotype of business schools; (3) the public health administrators are inclined to draw a very sharp line between their work and the work of a business administrator; and (4) the people in the public health administration field have not taken time out to identify precisely the knowledge, skills, abilities, faculties, and attitudes needed in the makeup of an effective administrator in their field. Without this knowledge they have been unable to shop selectively for the appropriate teaching and training material from other fields.

The last observation that needs to be made regards the nature of case reports and case studies used in the field of public health administration. By and large, the material used is focused on "outside" forces describing and analyzing how these forces bear on the effectiveness of the health agencies and the health personnel. Some of the ICP cases also describe the organizational pressures on decision making. On the whole, there is little case material dealing with intra-agency dynamics. Let me try to elaborate this point. Under the early influence of cultural anthropologists and sociologists, the people in the field of public health have rightly come to realize that community resistance caused by some social or cultural condition can frustrate even the most elementary public health scheme. This realization has

2. The Community Services Training Section of the Communicable Disease Center (CDC), U.S. Dept. of Health, Education and Welfare, Atlanta, Georgia, has shown some leadership and has published a community study called "Dixon Tiller County, U.S.A." It is a detailed and comprehensive survey of an allegedly fictitious county. In addition, the CDC has produced a few film strips which highlight selected problems faced by public health personnel.

3. Nos. 1, 9, 12, 14, 16, 21, 31, 32, 40, 47, 74, 82, and 89 have been used in one course.

4. The following collections are particularly popular: Benjamin D. Paul, ed., *Health, Culture and Community: Case Studies of Public Reactions to Health Programs* (New York: Russell Sage Foundation, 1955); and Dorrian Apple, ed., *Sociological Studies of Health and Sickness* (New York: McGraw-Hill, 1960). Gartly E. Jaco, ed., *Patients, Physicians and Illness* (Glencoe, Ill.: The Free Press, 1958) also has some case studies which could be adapted for class use.

5. For instance, see James A. Hamilton, *Decision Making in Hospital Administration and Medical Cases: A Casebook* (Minneapolis: University of Minnesota Press, 1960).

led the schools of public health to make special effort to sensitize their students to such hazards and to train them to avoid and overcome the difficulties which social and cultural conditions might cause. Unfortunately this emphasis on social and cultural factors seems to have led to a subconscious assumption that all of the problems faced by the public health agency administrators emanate from the community. Most people in the field of public health would agree that such an assumption is false. The effectiveness of an agency is also influenced by a number of other factors such as the structure of the agency, intra-agency relationships, quality of agency personnel, informal groups and cliques within the agency, patterns of decision-making, communication, control, appraisal system, rewards and punishment, and many others. Although intra-agency forces and behavior pattern are more easily controllable than the forces outside the agency, relatively little attention seems to be given to the former. The very fact that the intra-agency forces are more amenable may lead the public health people to ignore them. Here it should be pointed out that just because a thing is "easier" does not mean it is "easy." Proper management of the organizational life of an agency is a complex art which can be taught and should be taught systematically. Let me go a step further and state that it is more important for a public health administrator to be skilled in the art of organizational functioning than in the art of overcoming community resistance. The need for the latter category of skills comes into primary focus when new programs are to be initiated, which is not every day. The administrator needs organizational skills every day of his working life.

In the end, it needs to be said that I am not arguing that the case method is the only method or the best method of teaching and training administrators. What I have argued may be summarized in four points.

1. The case method is an important method of training administrators.

2. To utilize this method effectively, it is necessary that we understand it correctly and precisely.

3. A public health administrator needs multiple skills both in the area of community organization and organizational functioning. The university training programs have not been putting as much emphasis on the latter as on the former. The situation ought to be the other way around.

4. To be able to use the case method in training public health administrators in the art of organizational functioning, a large number of case reports dealing with subjects in this field need to be available. Many such case reports may be borrowed from other fields, particularly from business administration. At the same time efforts need to be made to produce new case reports from the field of public health itself.

Considerations on the Use and Nature of Case Studies in Teaching Medical Care Administration

March 1967

A. Gerald Renthal

It may seem superfluous to include in a collection of materials such as this, comments on their use in the classroom, since the decision to employ case studies is presumably based on a preconceived plan of instruction. However, it seems there is a large range of opinion as to what constitutes case studies and how cases should be used as a teaching device. Cases are not new to the teaching of administration or medical care and have been applied in a variety of useful ways, such as to illustrate the principles of good medical care, to present a historical perspective as a foundation for understanding current situations, to dramatize (and thus make more meaningful) a discussion of an effective or ineffective process, and so on. Although these are all legitimate uses of case studies they may fail to make optimal use of the ones collected here, which have been developed with a specific method in mind. It is important to emphasize this point, since the central consideration is not the case study but how it is used didactically. It is not the purpose of this discussion to present dogmatic assertions regarding the use and nature of case studies, but since we believe them to be a tool of the method, it seems necessary to dilate briefly on the advantages and technique of the case method.

A chronic problem in the teaching of medical care administration has been the difficulty of teaching administrative skills. The didactic techniques which serve to transmit the knowledge, concepts, and principles of medical care have not been adequate to develop in the student the personal and intellectual skills that are salient to effective administrative practice. Articulateness, perceptivity, discrimination, and analytic thinking cannot be taught by traditional methods. What is needed is a way to develop in the student an approach to analysis and problem-solving which involves broad understanding of the elements of the problem, the alternatives for solution, and the potential consequences of specific decisions.

It is in light of this assumption, that a major objective in teaching medical care administration is the development of a way of thinking and an interpersonal skill, that the merits of the case method should be judged.

The essence of the case method is the acceptance by the student of the responsibility for his own learning and his active participation in the learning experience. He learns by actively committing his intellectual resources to the analysis of the case and by being responsible for its discussion in the classroom. It is the student who performs the analysis, premise testing, sorting of alternatives, and decision-making. He is required to be alert to the thinking of his colleagues, to appreciate other points of view and assess their validity. Under these circumstances the teacher occupies a unique role. He remains the pivotal figure in the classroom, but his concern is with maintaining the flow of discussion along meaningful lines, stimulating the participation of the students, and challenging or correcting fallacious or incomplete reasoning and information. If he attempts to impose his own analysis and solutions on the students or if he assumes the role of "truth giver" he is defeating the objectives of his teaching. Indeed, in a case study there is usually no truth to give but a variety of alternative approaches to a problem. And the process of developing the alternatives is often more meaningful than finding the "right" one.

It is neither desirable nor possible here to write a manual of teaching technique, but there are a number of questions that anyone undertaking to teach by the case method should consider.

1. What preparation is necessary to teach a case?
2. How directive or nondirective should the teacher be in the classroom?
3. How can the process of classroom interaction be maximally used?
4. How can the teacher help the student articulate his thoughts most effectively?

1. *Preparation for teaching a case.* It need hardly be said that a mere cursory reading of the case to familiarize oneself with its elements is totally inadequate. The teacher should be thoroughly familiar with all aspects of the case. He should be in a position to challenge false assertions or interpretations based on incorrect or incomplete digestion of the case by the student. There may be a variety of interpretations or analyses possible, but it is important for the teacher to have isolated the major foci or issues and to have given considerable thought to the possible channels of interpretation and discussion that may develop from them. This is important not only because it enables him to focus and guide the discussion more effectively but anyone presuming to discipline the thinking of others should apply at least the same intellectual

rigor to himself. By anticipating possible directions in the students' discussion the teacher will be in a better position to expose and challenge logical inconsistencies as well as to recognize and nurture valuable but undeveloped elements in the students' thinking. It may also suggest additional information to have on hand. A particular line of reasoning may lead to a request for information that, although not included in the case, would open fruitful lines of discussion. Anticipating this in advance would allow for more effective case discussion.

A useful approach to preparing for discussion of a case involves analyzing it in terms of some general set of questions such as the following (which is not intended to be exhaustive):

A. Defining the problems and issues.

What are the manifest problems or issues defined by the case?

Are these real problems?

What is the priority of problems?

B. Assessing the pertinent factors bearing on the problems and issues.

What are the positions of the protagonists in the case?

What influences, positive and negative, manifest and latent, are acting on them?

C. Developing alternatives for resolution or solution of the problems and issues.

What are the possible alternatives?

What factors contribute to or inhibit the usefulness of each alternative?

D. Selecting among and implementing the alternatives.

What additional information is needed and how could it be obtained?

How can solutions be implemented?

2. One of the more difficult problems faced by the activist teacher is the adoption of *a more nondirective approach to teaching*. In order to develop a discussion that is meaningful as a learning experience for the student, it is often necessary to be quite permissive of interstudent verbal interactions.

He may have to tolerate some digression or deviation from his preferred sequence of discussion in order to obtain more active and meaningful student involvement. Modern learning theory agrees that a student learns what he is motivated to learn and one of the best indications of his motivation is his emotional involvement. Sensitivity to the emotional quality of students' responses will enable the teacher to recognize meaningful interactions in the classroom, which, although seemingly irrelevant to the main stream of discussion, may result in true learning if properly guided.

In the course of a discussion, it may often be more effective for the teacher to allow the necessary confrontation or challenge to come from another student rather than provide it himself. Indeed under ideal circumstances where students were capable of effective and purposeful analysis and problem solving the teacher would have a minimum of involvement in the classroom process.

Again, on the assumption that the most meaningful learning is that kind of insight that results from the student's self-discovery, it may be necessary to permit a certain amount of mental floundering on the part of individual students with the aim of allowing them to achieve this self-discovery. The temptation is often to interpose and give the student the benefit of the teacher's superior wisdom. But it is questionable whether this kind of wisdom is internalized, and the challenge to the student's thinking is lost.

3. At the heart of the case method is the teacher's awareness of *dynamics of the classroom experience.* An understanding of the issues of a case is obviously essential but more is required: sensitivity to the emotional content and the causal relationships in student-to-student and student-to-teacher interactions; ability to discriminate between the emotional and the intellectual aspects of a discussion; ability to stimulate a budding line of reasoning with the proper emotional climate as well as the proper mental rigor. These require that the teacher have a sensitivity to the quality of responses, which may be anywhere on a spectrum from overtly hostile to affectionate. It is often possible for the teacher, by exploiting the emotional content of the interactions, to create alignments or coalitions of thinking that more effectively expose the issues. But attention to the interpersonal dynamics has a much more basic importance. In terms of developing an administrative skill the ability to reason rationally, to communicate effectively, and to confront and resolve conflict are key considerations. To be able to assist the student's development the teacher should be aware of the interaction process.

Awareness of the dynamics of a class also involves some understanding of the phases through which a class may progress. The way the teacher opens the discussion sets the stage for a good portion of it. A general question such as "What do you think about this case?" has a significantly different effect than a specific one such as "What would you do if you were Dr. X?" A great deal depends on the nature of the case. Some cases may be quite general and require some exposition of the variety of issues involved before progressing to more specific considerations. Other cases may be very narrowly focused, and it may be possible to launch immediately into discussion of a decision. Again some of the issues in the case may be meaningfully discussed only after other considerations have been developed. For instance, it may be desirable to discuss implementation of a decision faced by an administrator, but the implementation cannot be adequately discussed until the adequacy of the decision has been assessed. At another time, analysis of a decision may hinge on defining the problem first, although it is sometimes a useful experience to discuss the decision and then discover that it concerned the wrong problem.

4. *The teacher's approach to the student* obviously may vary considerably depending on what he is trying to accomplish. He may be supportive — restating and clarifying what has been said, making positive responses, showing agreement or enhancing the student's statements with similar ones. It is often useful during the early part of a discussion to use this approach in order to develop a wide range of ideas and issues. The teacher may probe by testing the logicality of a statement, or by asking questions intended to develop an argument or pin down specific aspects of the student's discussion. Again, the teacher may be more challenging and engage in direct argument with the student, forcing him to defend or clarify his position.

Is it better to concentrate on interactions between the teacher and individual students or try to stimulate as much interaction between student as possible with the teacher assuming a more passive role? From what has already been said, a maximum of effective student participation is desirable, but how this is accomplished must depend a great deal on the "style" of the teacher and with what he is most comfortable. Whatever the approach or technique used it need hardly be said that it should not be overtly manipulative. Nevertheless, the important consideration is not the technique for its own sake but for the didactic purpose that it serves. Anyone who tries to teach is attempting to get something across to students. But it is sometimes forgotten that the student has to take it in.

Through all the concern with conducting individual cases some concept of the overall aims of a course of cases should be present. Hopefully by the end of the course the student will have developed a feel for and approach to effective problem solving that involves an orderly sequence of thinking, of defining the problem, asking the necessary questions, and evaluating the possible alternatives before making and trying to implement his decisions.

From the foregoing it follows that any consideration of the nature of a case study — its content, structure, and so on — should be in the context of how well it serves the teaching objectives. The focus should not be on the case per se but on the purpose it is intended to serve. Several points follow from this.

First, a case should have one or more dynamic foci to serve as the nucleus for the intellectual work of the student. This can be perhaps better considered as some sort of unresolved tension — an incompletely defined problem, a controversial issue, a pending decision, a conflict of interest, a plan to be designed or implemented, and so on.

Second, the case should be historically correct. Because we are attempting to develop in students an approach to the management of real life situations with which they will be faced, deviations from historical accuracy will compromise the value of the case. Real life situations usually include some degree of uncertainty, irrationality, and a variety of possible choices, and it is these same elements of reality which are so difficult to recreate in a fictionalized case. But it is worth noting here that the objective is not to expose the student to real situations as a substitute for administrative experiences. We could not hope to expose him to enough of the spectrum of real life situations to develop a comprehensive administrative experience. Rather the aim is to develop mental discipline and administrative skills that can be applied broadly because they are basic to all administrative practice.

Third, the case must be strictly objective. All indications of author bias or value judgment must be excluded if the student is to be allowed an independent approach to the analysis of the case. However, opinions of individuals in the case are not to be eliminated. In fact, it is important that they be included, since recognition of individual viewpoints and discrimination between fact and opinion are important attributes of an administrator.

In the real world, opinion is very relevant to people's actions, and one of the important things for the administrator to develop is the ability to perceive how the other fellow views the world. In this context opinion is a fact of life. Anyone who has seen the Japanese movie "Rashomon" will realize that truth is variously perceived but that these perceptions are all part of the truth.

The inclusion of opinions may also help the individual to uncover his own unrecognized bias. It is sometimes a valuable learning experience for the student to identify with the emotional position of a character in a case and discover its irrational element in the classroom.

Fourth, it is important that the foci or issues in the case be accessible for analysis. This does not mean that they should be explicitly stated. Quite the contrary, it is important for the student to discover them himself, but enough information should be included for him to identify them.

The whole issue of what should and should not be included is a subtle question of balance. It is desirable to have excess information so that there is an opportunity to separate the pertinent from the irrelevant. On the other hand, too much irrelevant material may make the case unwieldy and bury the important considerations.

Also, it is not always necessary to present all the material bearing on a particular analysis, issue, or decision, but it is important to provide knowledge of the setting sufficient to allow the student to determine what additional information would be necessary.

Fifth, significant characters should be presented in a way that their roles and both the internal and external forces acting upon them may be clearly identified. It may not be possible or necessary for the student to identify with the characters in the case, but he should be able to assess the factors which influence them.

Although the case method has a number of advantages, as we have hoped to show, it is also well to be aware of some of its potential disadvantages.

a. The content of a case may be unknowingly or unavoidably incomplete because of difficulties in the collection of material. It may happen that important information, issues, or considerations are suppressed or altered by informants because of their sensitivity or overlooked by the case writer because they are buried too deeply. Also, despite sincere attempts at objectivity, during the process of selecting material for inclusion the case writer may overlook or fail to appreciate the significance of material that he rejects. In such instances the validity of the case may be compromised. While such shortcomings in case preparation will diminish the value of the case as a reflection of the reality that the student will eventually encounter, its usefulness as an instrument for developing the students' analytical skills is not necessarily diminished.

b. Despite its attempt to reflect reality the case is, after all, not reality. The most important deviation from reality is probably the fact that the real administrator does not have a case writer who has collected the information and presented it to him for analysis. He has to be his own case collector.

It is possible to raise the criticism that a case cannot recreate in the classroom the realistic climate in which an administrator actually analyzes problems and makes decisions, although this argument is perhaps countered by the assumption that the less pressured and more controlled classroom atmosphere is a more effective locus for the student's development. The exigencies of an actual administrative situation may emphasize the immediacy of decisions and hinder the development in a student of an approach that is more capable of balancing the long-term and short-term considerations.

c. One of the major criticisms may be the lack of feedback for the student. Ideally, it is desirable to know the consequences of a decision, the correctness of an analysis, the adequacy of a proposed plan, but the case study may not provide these. Under such circumstances, the only assessment available may be the consensus of his colleagues or the wisdom of the teacher. It is important to recognize the sometimes tentative and uncertain nature of the results of a case analysis. Nevertheless this does not negate the value it affords in developing the analytic process.

In summary, a major consideration in the teaching of medical care administration is how best to develop certain basic, administrative skills. It is believed that the case method, as conceived of here, provides a unique and valuable contribution. Hopefully, partisan prejudices or commitment to other didactic approaches will inhibit neither its wider use nor the development of a more extensive body of case studies.

Cases Developed for the U.S. Public Health Service by Harvard University

Available from the Division of Medical Care Administration, U.S. Public Health Service

---

Medical Care Planning in a Small Urban Area I
A. Gerald Renthal

Medical Care Planning in a Small Urban Area II
A. Gerald Renthal

Concern for Long Term Care
- A. Nursing Homes in Massachusetts: A Historical Review
- B. Legislation Action and Rate Setting
- C. The Nursing Home Section of the State Health Department
- D. A Teaching Hospital and Extended Care
- E. Evaluation of a Nursing Home Consultation Program

Beryl M. Safford/Richard Elnicki

Southbrook Hospital
- A. The Hospital, Its Setting and Administration
- B. Medical Staff and Nursing Services
- C. Ambulatory Services
- D. Affiliation with a Medical School
- E. Comptroller

A. Gerald Renthal

Index

Bei Fragen zur Produktsicherheit wenden Sie sich bitte an:
If you have any questions regarding product safety,
please contact:

Walter de Gruyter GmbH
Genthiner Straße 13
10785 Berlin
productsafety@degruyterbrill.com